THE
TOYOTA
WAY
TO
SERVICE
EXCELLENCE

THE
TOYOTA
WAY
TO
SERVICE
EXCELLENCE

LEAN TRANSFORMATION
IN SERVICE ORGANIZATIONS

JEFFREY K. LIKER

KARYN ROSS

Mc
Graw
Hill
Education

New York   Chicago   San Francisco   Athens   London
Madrid   Mexico City   Milan   New Delhi
Singapore   Sydney   Toronto

1 2 3 4 5 6 7 8 9   QFR   21 20 19 18 17 16

ISBN   978-1-259-64110-7
MHID   1-259-64110-4

e-ISBN   978-1-259-64111-4
e-MHID   1-259-64111-2

McGraw-Hill Education books are available at special quantity discounts to use as premiums and sales promotions or for use in corporate training programs. To contact a representative, please visit the Contact Us pages at www.mhprofessional.com.

For our family, friends, and teachers.
We need you to inspire and teach us.

Jeff Liker
Karyn Ross

Contents

Chapter 9

Chapter 10

Acknowledgments

So many people have taught us and generously shared with us, it is difficult to know where to start—and end—in thanking you all. Karyn and Jeff chose to write separate acknowledgements.

From Jeff:

Unfortunately, I cannot acknowledge everyone who graciously agreed to lengthy interviews and reviewed parts of this book for accuracy. But several put an exceptional amount of time into sharing their stories, information, and then editing for accuracy. You will see there are many detailed case examples in this book. Thank you all for teaching me what the pursuit of service excellence means, not just in theory, but in the hearts of real people. Special thanks (in no particular order) to:

- Dr. Richard Zarbo, Senior Vice President and Chair, Pathology and Laboratory Medicine at Henry Ford Health System
- Betty Gratopp, Production General Manager, Zingerman's Mail Order
- Tom Root, Owner and Managing Partner, Zingerman's Mail Order
- Richard Sheridan, Chief Storyteller, Menlo Innovations, and author of *Joy, Inc.*
- John Taylor, General Manager and Vice President, Dunning Toyota and Dunning Subaru
- Einar Gudmundsson, CEO at Rejmes Bil (Volvo Dealer)
- Veli-Matti Mattila, CEO, Elisa
- Petri Selkäinaho, Development Director, Elisa
- Merja Ranta-aho, Executive VP, Human Resources, Elisa
- David Hanna, Partner, HPO Global Alliance, and author of *The Organizational Survival Code*
- Kai Laamanen, Management Consulting Professional at Innotiimi
- Jonathan Escobar Marin, Global Head of Lean Management, Hartmann Group
- Mariano Jimenez Torres, Organizational Development Manager, Inversiones La Paz
- Florencio Munoz, Senior Lean Consultant
- Brock Husby, PhD (my former doctoral student), lean healthcare consultant

- Eduardo Lander, PhD (my former doctoral student), lean services consultant
- Hiroshi Ozawa, Professor, Nagoya University (research collaborator)
- John Shook, CEO, Lean Enterprise Institute (one of my first and most influential teachers)
- Pierre Nadeau, Proprietor of SoulSmithing (was Swordsmith apprentice in Japan)
- Whitney Walters, Director, Lean for Clinical Redesign, University of Michigan
- Bill Costantino, Senior Partner, W3 Group
- Tyson Ortiz, Parent who saved his son Michael's life following improvement kata principles

I continue to learn and be inspired by every visit I make to Toyota, inside and outside of Japan. Mitsuru Kawai, a student of Ohno, was particularly inspiring in his unwavering dedication to developing people day by day through challenge and mentoring. I was also inspired by Latondra Newton, group vice president of Toyota North America, who took responsibility for turning On-the-Job Development as a concept in Toyota into a deliberate coaching and teaching approach.

In this book we define service excellence as a journey of scientific thinking toward a clear vision. By this we mean experimenting and reflecting to overcome obstacles toward a goal. We owe these key insights that run through the book to my former student Mike Rother who wrote *Toyota Kata*. A kata is a practice routine, breaking down a complex skill, in this case a scientific approach to improvement, to basic elements that can be practiced with a coach. Mike has developed a way of understanding this, drawing on brain science research, and a practical way to change our mindsets to think and act scientifically. We are very grateful to Mike for these deep insights and his personal coaching of Jeff in coffee shops around Ann Arbor.

Three times I have taught the ideas in this book in my graduate seminar at the University of Michigan. My students do lean projects in local organization using the framework of the improvement kata and coaching kata, mostly in service organizations. I have learned so much from their creativity and enthusiasm. The Dunning Toyota case in this book was based on a project by Xinhang Li, Mengyuan Sun, Ruqing Ye, and Zhenhuan Yu.

I asked Karyn Ross to partner with me because she is a skilled and experienced coach of service organizations dutifully (and joyfully) following the Toyota Way principles. To my delight I also got an artist and short story writer in the deal! The book is written in the first person from my perspective, but Karyn has been a true partner.

I am once again grateful to my family for their love and support throughout this very consuming writing process. I get much of my inspiration and ideas from Deb, Em, and Jesse. In this book Deb did detailed editing which all our readers will appreciate.

From Karyn:

I'd like to thank my husband, Brian Hoffert, and children Quinton Hoffert and Serena Ross for their support over many years as I've learned and practiced the Toyota Way. Whether through practice on home processes such as laundry, or outside, in countless conversations with service workers in restaurants, stores, hotels, etc., they've learned along with me and have become quite proficient practitioners themselves. My husband recently texted me from a line in an airport restaurant about flow problems and possible countermeasures.

As you will learn in this book, without teachers to coach and guide us, self-development and progress is nearly impossible.

Special thanks to my teachers and mentors. For the *real* Leslie Henckler, my first lean mentor and teacher, thank you for giving me an unbelievably strong foundation (go to gemba and see for yourself—stop making so many assumptions!), for teaching me that the only answer ever is "it depends" and most importantly for teaching me to "learn by doing" so that I could learn how to think and to teach others. Thank you to my friend and colleague, Dennis Gawlik, a real "kata geek," for constantly pushing, questioning and challenging me ("What's your hypothesis?") so that I don't stay comfortable for too long. I've become a better coach both by watching you coach others and being coached by you!

Thank you also to the many people I have had the joy and privilege of working with in service organizations large and small as they learn and grow and find ways to use the concepts and practices in this book to satisfy the real, live customers that they serve every day. In this regard, I owe a special thanks to the partners at National Taxi Limo. Your passion, commitment, and dedication to learning continues to inspire me and teach me. Thanks for your great story that became the centerpiece of our final chapter.

And for Jeff Liker, thank you for being the consummate teacher and mentor, willing to spend countless hours listening and responding to my questions, creating opportunities for me to learn (including this book), and for constantly challenging and pushing me out of my comfort zone. Thank you for being an unbelievable role model who constantly inspires me (and countless others) to continuously work to develop my thinking and practice, as you continuously work to develop yours. Unbelievable gifts for all of us!

Prologue

The Toyota Way as a General Management Philosophy

The thieves may be able to follow the design plans and produce a loom. But we are modifying and improving our looms every day.

—Kiichiro Toyoda, founder of Toyota Motor Company
(after design plans for a loom were stolen from his father's firm)

THE PROBLEM: MISUNDERSTANDING OF LEAN AND HOW IT APPLIES HERE

Lean (along with its variations, such as six sigma, theory of constraints, lean six sigma, and specialties in different industries like agile IT development, lean construction, lean healthcare, lean finance, and lean government) has become a global movement. As with any management movement, there are true believers, resisters, and those who get on the bandwagon but do not care a lot one way or the other. There are a plethora of service providers through universities, consulting firms, and not-for-profit organizations, and there is a book industry. For zealots like me (Jeffrey), this is, in a sense, a good thing—there are consumers of my message. But there is also a downside. As the message spreads and goes through many people, companies, and cultures, it changes from the original, like the game of telephone in which the message whispered to the first person bears little resemblance to the message the twentieth person hears.

In the meantime, well-meaning organizations that want to solve their problems are searching for answers. What is lean? How do we get started? How do these tools developed within Toyota for making cars apply to my organization, which has a completely different product or service? How do they apply in our culture, which is very different from Japanese culture? Do the tools have to be used exactly as they are used in Toyota, or can they be adapted to our circumstances? And how does Toyota reward people for using these tools to improve?

These are all seemingly reasonable questions, and unfortunately, there are many consultants and self-appointed "lean experts" ready to answer them, often in very different ways. But the starting point should be the questions themselves.

Are these the right questions? Though they may seem reasonable on the surface, I believe they are the wrong questions. The underlying assumption in each case is that lean is a mechanistic, tool-based process to be implemented in an organization in much the same way as you would install a new piece of software on your computer. Specifically, the assumptions can be summarized as:

1. There is one clear and simple approach to lean that is very different from alternative methodologies.
2. There is one clear and best way to get started.
3. Toyota is a simple organization that does one thing—assembles cars—and it uses a core set of the same tools in the same way every place.
4. The tools are the essence and therefore must be adapted to specific types of processes.
5. Because lean was developed in Japan, there may be something peculiar about it that needs to be modified to fit cultures outside Japan.
6. Toyota itself has a precise method of applying the tools in the same way in every place that others need to copy.
7. The formal reward system is the reason people in Toyota engage in continuous improvement and allocate effort to support the company.

In fact, none of these assumptions are true, and that is the problem. The gap between common views of lean and the reality of how this powerful thing Toyota has been pursuing *actually* works is preventing organizations from accomplishing their goals. The Toyota Way, by contrast, is a generic philosophy that can apply to any organization, and if applied diligently, it will virtually guarantee dramatic improvement.[1] It is a way of thinking, a philosophy, and a system of interconnected processes and people who are striving to continuously improve how they work and deliver value to each customer. At the heart is a passion to pursue perfection, by striving, step-by-step, toward clearly defined goals. The twin pillars of the Toyota Way are *continuous improvement* and *respect for people*.

As you read this book, our goal is to give you a clear understanding of "lean," or whatever you want to call it. Coauthor Karyn and I start by dismissing the common and simplistic notion that it is a program of using tools to take waste out of processes. If your organization views it this way, you are doomed to mediocre results, until the next management fad takes over to create mediocre results. We will demonstrate the real meaning of what Toyota discovered through discussions of the origin of the Toyota Way, the principles we have distilled, and actual examples of organizations that are pursuing service excellence.

The starting point will be the principles I described in *The Toyota Way* published in 2004. Those principles were developed as a way of organizing decades of observations of Toyota and direct experiences with many organizations that had struggled on their lean journey. Most of the examples in the original book came from Toyota and mostly from manufacturing, though there were some product development and service examples. The book continues to be widely read (over 900,000 copies sold) across many manufacturing and service sectors. People have been able to abstract the messages beyond manufacturing, but I repeatedly get questions like: "How do these principles apply to my organization in my culture? We are in services, which is not like manufacturing." While it is impossible to describe every situation you may face, we decided to write this book to bring lean closer to the world of services. We are focusing on service, although as you will see in Chapter 1, the distinction between manufacturing and service is messier than it seems at first glance.

Some of the best examples we have seen of lean in services were kicked off by visits to exceptional lean factories. One of the best in healthcare is ThedaCare in Appleton, Wisconsin. John Toussaint, CEO at the time, had an epiphany after he visited a manufacturer of snowblowers whose president was totally committed to lean. During the visit, Toussaint saw engaged people and a true flow of value through the factory. Certainly this factory was at least as complex as his healthcare systems! He could easily imagine healthcare systems where patients did not queue up and wait, but were flowing through the healthcare experience without interruption.[2] He also learned that he needed to lead the transformation personally. As his organizations learned and evolved, patient waiting time was dramatically reduced. Before the transformation, patients would have to make several visits to get required tests, test results, and a diagnosis, and then perhaps they'd have to return an additional time for treatment. The vision became to move from testing to treatment during the very first visit; if this was not possible, at least the patient should leave with a plan of treatment on the first visit. Bringing this vision to reality led to many changes in thinking and in processes including how and where blood samples were analyzed. In the past the lab work was centralized and could take days. Now most tests are completed in on-site clinics in minutes. In fact, after years of improvement, about 90 percent of the lab tests or imaging studies needed in primary care can be completed on-site, and 95 percent of the patients leave with a plan of care in a single visit.

There can be many barriers to learning, however. One may simply be getting the horse to water. Karyn has sometimes had to beg and plead to convince managers in the service organizations she has worked with to visit a manufacturing plant. She recalls one instance, after she succeeded in bringing a group of executives from an insurance company to Toyota, how delighted she was when one leader exclaimed: "The next time people say to us that 'we don't make widgets,' we're going to send them to Toyota. When they see how complex making a car is, they will run right back to work as quickly as possible, thankful that all they have to do is make some decisions, enter some information into the computer, and out comes an insurance policy!"

Having dismissed the common and simplistic notion that lean is a program centered on tools for taking waste out of manufacturing processes, in this Prologue we wish to convey the deeper meaning of the Toyota Way. We will briefly describe the origin of the Toyota Way within Toyota, how the concept of "lean thinking" fits with the Toyota Way, and what it looks like to pursue it in practice.

THE TOYODA FAMILY: GENERATIONS OF CONSISTENT LEADERSHIP

To understand a company's culture, we should begin with its roots—the core values of its founders—and Toyota is no exception. Many companies have drifted so far from their roots that the initial values are barely visible, but Toyota has maintained a remarkable degree of continuity of culture over most of a century, starting with its founder, Sakichi Toyoda.

Sakichi Toyoda: Creating Looms and Values

Sakichi Toyoda was born in 1867, the son of a poor carpenter in a rice farming village. He learned carpentry from the ground up, and he also learned the necessity of discipline and hard work. A natural inventor, he saw a problem in the community. Women were "working their fingers to the bone" using manual looms to make cloth for the family and for sale, after a full day of work on the farm. To ease the burden, he began to invent a new kind of loom. His first modification used gravity to allow weavers to send the shuttle of cotton thread back and forth through the weft by manipulating foot pedals instead of using their hands. Immediately, women worked half as hard and were more productive. Sakichi Toyoda continued to make improvement after improvement, some small, some big, and in 1926 he formed Toyota Automatic Loom Works.

He was a devout Buddhist and always lived strong values. One of his favorite books was called *Self-Help*,[3] by British philanthropist Samuel Smiles. Smiles dedicated much of his life to mentoring juvenile delinquents so they could become successful contributors to society. He wrote about the inspiration of great inventors, who, contrary to popular opinion, were not always privileged and gifted students but achieved great things through self-reliance, hard work, and a passion for learning. This fit well the story of Sakichi Toyoda, who raised himself from a poor background as a carpenter's son and did not appear particularly outstanding, but who through the passion of contributing to others, the hard work of learning the fundamental skills of carpentry, and a clear picture of the problems he wanted to solve, relentlessly made improvement after improvement, each to solve the next problem.

As Sakichi Toyoda grew, his ambitions and contributions also grew. He began to envision a fully automatic loom, and each innovation moved him toward that idea, continually improving toward his vision. He started by helping the women in his family and then the community; then he began helping to industrialize Japanese society, ultimately contributing to all society. He is considered by many to be the father of the Japanese industrial revolution and has been given the title "King of Inventors" in Japan. Along the way, he cultivated himself and his own values. These values eventually become the guiding principles of Toyota Motor Company and included:

- Contribute to society.
- Put the customer first and the company second.
- Show respect for all people.
- Know your business from the ground up.
- Get your hands dirty.
- Work hard and with discipline.
- Work as a team.
- Build in quality.
- Continually improve toward a vision.

Built-in quality was most evident in one of his most influential inventions—the loom that could stop itself when there was a problem. Every innovation by Sakichi Toyoda was problem driven. After the loom was reasonably automatic and could run at a relatively high speed, he noticed that when a single thread broke on the weft to make cloth, the cloth would be defective. A human had to stand and watch the loom and stop it when that happened, which he considered a tremendous waste of human capability. Yet another invention using gravity would solve this problem. This time, Sakichi added a metal weight on the end of a string to each thread in the weft. When a thread broke, this weight would jam the threads and stop the loom. He called this *jidoka*, a word that was formed by adding to the Japanese *kanji* for automation a symbol for a human. Thus he had put human intelligence into automation so the loom could stop itself when there was a problem. He later added a small metal flag that would pop up signaling, "I need help." Jidoka would become a pillar of the Toyota Production System (TPS), conveying the notion of stopping when there is a quality problem and immediately solving the problem.

Based on the teachings of Sakichi Toyoda, the Toyoda Precepts were created, which still guide the company today:

1. *Be contributive to the development and welfare of the country by working together, regardless of position, in faithfully fulfilling your duties.*

2. *Be ahead of the times through endless creativity, inquisitiveness, and pursuit of improvement.*

3. *Be practical and avoid frivolity.*

4. *Be kind and generous; strive to create a warm, homelike atmosphere.*

5. *Be reverent, and show gratitude for things great and small in thought and deed.*

Toyota Motor Company and the Toyota Production System

In 1937 Toyota Motors was formed by Kiichiro Toyoda as a division of Toyota Automatic Loom Works. Kiichiro's father, Sakichi, had asked him to do something to contribute to society, and Kiichiro chose automobiles, a highly risky major challenge. Automobile companies are very capital intensive, and it seemed Toyota was a lifetime behind Ford Motor Company, which at the time was pumping out over 1 million vehicles per year and getting all the attendant economies of scale. Why would a tiny start-up in an obscure part of Japan have any chance of competing, outside perhaps of the protected market in Japan? Like his dad, Kiichiro Toyoda saw a need, an opportunity, and believed in his team. Embodying one of the Toyota principles in starting up this company, Kiichiro, a mechanical engineer, and his team would learn about all the technologies from the ground up and get their hands dirty. This reflected the Toyota principle of self-reliance. Another core principle was announced in a speech Kiichiro gave in which he said: "I plan to cut down on the slack time in our work processes. . . . As the basic principle in realizing this, I will uphold the 'just in time' approach."

What was this "just-in-time" (JIT) approach? Operations management courses in MBA programs would not teach JIT for decades, and there were no books or articles about it. It seems he made it up! And he was not exactly sure what it was. Taiichi Ohno, a brilliant young manager in Toyota Automatic Loom Works, was given the assignment to develop the manufacturing system that would become the next great innovation in Toyota beyond automatic looms—the Toyota Production System. Turning just-in-time from a concept into a working system would be foundational for this new manufacturing system.

The methodology for Ohno's innovation was the same as Sakichi Toyoda's for the loom—relentless *kaizen*. Kaizen literally means "change for the better," but in Toyota's case it means systematically working toward a challenge, overcoming obstacle after obstacle one at a time. When Ohno started, he was running the machine shop for engine and transmission components and just began trying things—small experiments—to solve problem after problem. Nothing was worth talking about for Ohno until he actually tried it on the shop floor. The more problems he solved, the more problems were revealed.

For example, the factory was organized in the traditional way by type of process—lathes over here, drilling machines over there—and there were specialist workers for each machining department. Ohno's idea was to create a cell for a product family and have all the machines set up in sequence to make complete parts, which might mean a lathe, followed by a machining center, followed by a drilling machine and then an assembly process. He wanted the cells to build to *takt*—the rate of customer demand—with no inventory in the cell except one part here or there as a buffer between machines. This is what we now call one-piece flow. He also wanted the flexibility to adjust the number of people in the cells based on the rise and fall of customer demand without losing productivity. This meant that as demand went down, there would be fewer people, and some would have to operate more than one type of equipment, such as a lathe and a drill.

The concept of a cell building to takt was a magnificent idea but proved to be much harder to implement than Ohno expected. Lathe operators did not want to operate drilling machines and vice versa for the drill operators. His solution? Go to the *gemba* (where the work is done) every day and spend time with the workers convincing them, showing them, and getting them to try the new system. Over time, they found it was a better way to work, as it produced higher quality with less wasted effort, and it was even safer. Ohno learned a critical lesson—simply thinking of an idea is only the start, and the real work is the time-consuming process of training and developing people through repeated practice so the new system becomes "the way we work."

Much later, after the bugs had been mostly worked out, the system was put into writing and was represented as a house (see Figure P.1). The term "system" is not incidental, but very intentional as all the parts are interrelated. The two key pillars were Kiichiro Toyoda's just-in-time and Sakichi Toyoda's jidoka (built-in quality). If Toyota was going to work with very little inventory and build in quality at every step, the foundation had to be extremely stable. There had to be reliable parts delivery, equipment that worked as it was supposed to, well-trained team members, and essentially no deviations from the standard. Ideally, the foundation would provide the ability to build consistently to a leveled production schedule, without huge ups and downs, supporting the customer takt. Leveled production would provide a steady rhythm for the factory.

To maintain this high level of stability, quality, and just-in-time production would require intelligent team members who were vigilant in noticing the many problems that occurred every day and who took the time to think about and test countermeasures to address deviations from the standard. At the center of the house are highly developed and motivated people who are continually observing, analyzing, and improving the processes. The process gets closer to perfection through continuous improvement by thinking people; therefore, some in Toyota have described TPS as the *Thinking* Production System.

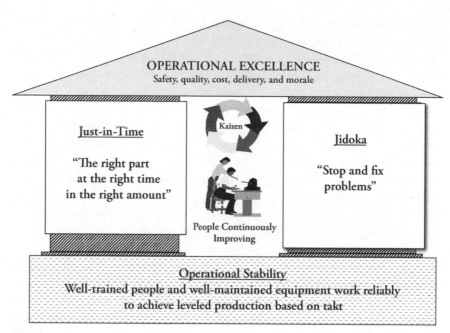

Figure P.1   The Toyota Production System house

The purpose of the system is represented by the roof—best quality, lowest cost, on-time delivery, in a safe work environment with high morale. As a system all the parts needed to work in harmony—weak pillars, a weak foundation, a leaky roof, and the house will come tumbling down. Perfect adherence to the TPS vision was never possible, but it provided a picture of perfection that could always be strived for—the purpose of kaizen.

WHAT IS LEAN?

The "lean movement" that has swept across manufacturing and services globally was originally inspired by the Toyota Production System. There are many definitions of "lean," but let's start with the term's origin as a descriptor of organizational excellence. It is not a term you will hear a lot around Toyota. It was first introduced in 1990 in the book *The Machine That Changed the World*,[4] which was the result of a five-year study at the Massachusetts Institute of Technology comparing the American, European, and Japanese auto industries. The researchers consistently found, regardless of the process or metric, that the Japanese auto companies were at that time far superior to the European and American companies in a wide range of areas, including manufacturing efficiency, product quality, logistics, supplier relationships, product development lead time and efficiency, distribution systems, and more.

The message was that the Japanese had developed an integrated enterprise based on a fundamentally different way of looking at the company, work processes, and people that can be best viewed as a new *paradigm* of management. The word "lean" was suggested by then graduate student John Krafcik, who argued that "lean" means doing more with less, like a superior athlete, and that the Japanese, especially Toyota, were doing more of everything they needed to do for the customer with less of almost everything. It was a holistic concept for the enterprise, not a tool kit for a specific type of process. It applied both to routine work, such as is done on the assembly line, and to very nonroutine work requiring specialized knowledge, like engineering design and sales.

The concept of "waste" in lean is central but often misunderstood. Waste is more than specific actions or objects that need to be eliminated. Waste is anything that causes a deviation from the perfect process. The perfect process gives the customers exactly what they want, in the amount they want, when they want it, and all steps that deliver value do so without interruption.

The concept of "one-piece flow" is the ideal. Each step in the value-adding process does what it is supposed to do perfectly, without the various forms of waste that cause processes to be disconnected by time, space, or inventory. Toyota often uses the metaphor of a free-flowing stream of water without stagnant pools. Of course, one-piece flow requires perfection in everything that is done by people or technology and is therefore an impossible dream. Toyota says this is its "true north" vision, which is not achievable and yet always the goal—striving for perfection while recognizing there is no perfect process.

This ideal, or some would say *idealistic*, vision arose in Toyota from some very special people, starting with Sakichi Toyoda. We would submit that any organization should desire this state of perfection, regardless of the specific product, service, or culture of the organization. The organization that can deliver pure value to its customers without waste, while continually innovating to improve the product, service, and process, will be successful.

Womack and Jones then built on *The Machine That Changed the World* with the book *Lean Thinking*.[5] Lean was even more than a highly effective system for delivering value to customers—it was a different way of thinking about the total enterprise. The book made clear that the lean model was not based on Japanese auto companies in general but on Toyota specifically. Toyota had the best performance at the time of any of the Japanese auto companies and was the best model for "lean thinking."

THE TOYOTA WAY: A PHILOSOPHY AND WAY OF THINKING

The Toyota Way begins with a passion for solving problems for customers and society. To do this requires deep respect for people and their ability to adapt and innovate. Building an enterprise that can withstand the tremendous pressures of the environment, decade after decade, requires a degree of adaptation that can only come from relentless kaizen from everybody. Since people are not born with the spirit of kaizen or the requisite skills, they must be taught. As with any other advanced skill, learning to improve processes requires some direction, relentless practice, and corrective feedback. And the practice cannot be limited to a specialized department of black belts.

If you believe findings by cognitive psychologists, such as Dr. K. Anders Ericcson,[6] mastering any complex skill requires "deliberate practice" for 10 years or 10,000 repetitions. Deliberate practice requires being self-aware of weaknesses and knowing the drills to correct them, one by one, and is helped by a teacher who can see the weaknesses and suggest the drills. Ohno had been doing this throughout his career. As he learned, he then taught, not through lecturing, but at the gemba (where the work is done) by challenging students, giving them (often harsh) feedback, and letting them struggle.

After the Toyota Production System was well established in Japan, Toyota had a dilemma. Could this finely tuned system work in a foreign country, without the Japanese workers and culture that seemed to fit so well with its principles? To find out, Toyota did what Toyota does—experimented. The company decided not to go it alone and partnered with General Motors in a 50-50 joint venture called New United Motor Manufacturing Inc. (NUMMI). NUMMI started up in 1984, hiring back over 80 percent of the workers from the GM plant in Fremont, California, that had been closed down in 1982. A reason for closing down the GM plant was horrible labor relations that led to low productivity and quality. With these seemingly discontented workers and the Toyota Way, NUMMI quickly became the best automotive assembly plant in North America in quality, productivity, low inventory, safety—in short, more like a high-performing Toyota plant than a low-performing GM plant. Toyota learned a lot about developing Americans and about creating a culture of trust, and then it decided to start up its own plant in Georgetown, Kentucky. The Toyota Motor Manufacturing Kentucky, or TMMK, plant began production in 1988.

Fujio Cho was selected as the first president of TMMK. If anything, it surpassed the performance of NUMMI, and all seemed well. But Fujio Cho saw a weakness. As the Japanese trainers left and Americans were increasingly taking over responsibility for the plant, they needed explicit training in the Toyota Way. He realized there was more to Toyota's company philosophy than is captured in the Toyota Production System, which is mainly a prescription for manufacturing. The broader philosophy was learned tacitly in Japan, by "living" in the company and repeatedly hearing the stories and being mentored. What he experienced in America was a lot of variation in the understanding of the core philosophy that Toyota expected all its leaders to embrace.

Fujio Cho put together a team who, over a period of about 10 years, worked to capture that philosophy in writing. After many versions, however, the document was still not approved. Toyota works toward consensus, and it could not get consensus. In 1999, when Fujio Cho became president of Toyota Motor Company globally, he revived the effort, this time for the company as a whole. He still struggled to get consensus because others said the philosophy was a living and breathing entity and could not be frozen in time as a document. He finally got agreement to call the document *The Toyota Way 2001*, with the understanding that it was the best they had developed by 2001 and could be modified in the future (it has not been so far).

It is represented as a house (see Figure P.2) supported by two pillars. One pillar is continuous improvement, and the other is respect for people. Continuous improvement means just what it says: people everywhere constantly challenging the way they are currently working and asking, "Is there a better way?"

"I urge every Toyota team member all over the world to take professional and personal responsibility for advancing the understanding and acceptance of the Toyota Way."
—Fujio Cho, former Toyota President, *The Toyota Way 2001*

Figure P.2   *The Toyota Way 2001* house

Respect for people goes far beyond treating people nicely. In Toyota, respect means challenging people to be their best, and that means they are also continually improving themselves as they improve the way they work to better satisfy the customer. Respect for people is intentionally generic. It goes beyond respect for people who are employed by Toyota. It starts with the purpose of the company, which is to add value to customers and society by providing the best means of mobility possible. Respect for society includes respect for the environment, respect for the communities in which Toyota does business, and respect for the local laws and customs of each community.

It is difficult to respect people who are treated as temporary, disposable labor. So Toyota makes a long-term commitment to its employees and to the communities where it sets up shop. Though it does happen, people rarely lose their jobs. Even in the Great Recession, Toyota carried tens of thousands of people globally whom they did not need to make vehicles at the low level of demand. During this period, the company worked on continuous improvement and focused on developing people through education and training, waiting out the bad economy and preparing for the inevitable pent-up demand when things got better. Toyota did not close factories, and this saved local communities from the devastating effects of massive job loss.

The right way to achieve continuous improvement and respect for people is represented by the core values in the foundation of the house. It begins with developing people who will gladly take on a challenge, even when they have no idea how they will achieve it. The process of improvement is kaizen, relentless experimentation, with learning from each experiment informing the next. From 2000 to 2015 Toyota engineering engaged in relentless kaizen to increase the number of vehicles on a common, lightweight platform and make manufacturing processes smaller and more flexible. Results include:

- 20 percent reduction in resources for new-model development
- 25 percent improvement in fuel economy with 15 percent more power
- 40 percent reduction in cost of a new plant
- 50 percent reduction in launching a new model, with almost zero production downtime

One hard-and-fast rule of kaizen is to practice it at the gemba, or what Toyota calls *genchi genbutsu*, meaning, "Go and see the actual place to observe directly and learn." Toyota leaders are obsessive about direct observation. In fact, they distinguish between data (abstractions of reality) and facts (direct observation of reality). Both are invaluable in understanding the current reality and determining what happens when you intervene in some way.

The final two values focus on people. People work to be the best contributors possible to the team. As stated in *The Toyota Way 2001*, "We stimulate personal and professional growth, share the opportunities of development, and maximize individual and team performance." The team is always given credit for accomplishments, while there is always an individual leader accountable for the results of the project.

Then we come right back to respect as the way in which improvement is carried out. This includes respect for stakeholders, mutual trust and responsibility, and sincere accountability. Accountability is described in the following way: "We accept responsibility for working independently, putting forth honest effort to the best of our abilities and always honoring our performance promises."

What happened to the Toyota Production System, you ask? What about JIT and built-in-quality and stable processes? In *The Toyota Way 2001*, these are part of the "lean systems and structure" that contribute to kaizen (see Figure P.3). These are the tools and concepts that we should consider when working to meet the challenging objectives.

At the start of this Prologue, I argued that lean management has lost perspective. It almost seems to be an end unto itself. Companies think, "Let's implement

Figure P.3   Lean systems are a contributor to kaizen in the foundation of the Toyota Way

JIT to reduce inventory" or "Let's install quality systems to build in quality" or "Let's put in standard work so that processes are stable." In the Toyota Way, however, these are powerful tools and concepts to *consider* when doing kaizen to strive toward excellence. The focus is on the goal and the right way to achieve the goal. Lean systems are side by side with innovative thinking and promoting organizational learning. Collectively, these contribute to kaizen. This is an entirely different mindset than the mechanistic view of implementing tools to get specific—and often short-term—results.

LEARNING THE THINKING OF THE TOYOTA WAY HAS NO RECIPE

As we reflect on the beginning of the Prologue, when we discussed the problem of companies and their many advisors viewing lean as a tool kit for waste reduction, perhaps it is now clearer just how far afield these mechanistic "lean programs" have diverged from the rich tradition developed within Toyota. We hope this book helps guide our readers back on track to the original purpose of the Toyota Way: to create a culture of people continuously improving to adapt and grow through the many challenges of the environment in order to satisfy each customer and contribute to society for the long term.

This is not to say that anyone you meet anyplace you go in Toyota follows all these principles to the letter. Think of *The Toyota Way 2001* as a holy document like the Bible or a government constitution. The fact that people deviate from the doctrine, or misapply it, is not an indictment of the doctrine. It is simply that we as humans are far from perfect, sometimes being misinformed, sometimes using bad judgment, rarely being perfectly disciplined, and often giving in to immediate needs and desires. In fact, if we were perfect, we would not need any written or spoken doctrine. We would just be.

The Toyota Way is often spoken about as "true north," a beacon that guides daily behavior and helps everyone detect whether they are on track or off track. The very basis of continuous improvement is to identify gaps between the actual and ideal and work relentlessly to reduce those gaps, including gaps in our own skills and behaviors.

If we think about trying to improve our bodies physically through exercise and healthy eating, we would all admit that we err from time to time—eating too much or skipping exercise. Our vision may be a great one, but the execution is often flawed. For those who have lost control of their bodies and are obese, it is extremely difficult to even get started. We have so far to go and need tremendous discipline and a great deal of social support. Those in relatively good shape may already have some of the skills and may have developed a degree of willpower. And the more we exercise that willpower to create positive habits, the easier it becomes to follow our daily regimen.

Being mediocre as an organization with few well-defined habits and poorly defined processes is like being obese. It is painful to even think of getting started on the path to true north. But as we try, sometimes fail, but also have some small wins, we get increasingly skilled in overcoming our weaknesses. Success breeds success, and diligent practice is the only true path to excellence.

Toyota is far from perfect, but it is comparatively healthy in many parts of the organization and in many different countries. The company has passionately developed leaders who endeavor to live the values—striving for true north. Middle managers have the social support of senior leaders consistent in their vision of true north—consistent over decades of development. Even for an organization very far from Toyota's maturity level, it is never too late to start the process of looking with brutal honesty at where you are and where you would like to get to—your true north. Then you need to take a first step, then a second step, and continuously improve your way to the vision.

As you think of how to get started in your organization, review the principles of the Toyota Way. Review the various methods discussed in this book for developing the individual habits and organizational routines that will lead to excellence, such as Toyota Business Practices and OJD. Where will you start? Identify a challenge that will bring your organization to a new level of customer service. Understand the current state. Define the ideal state. Then break down the problem into manageable pieces—step-by-step. For each step, identify a short-term target and begin to experiment toward each target through rapid learning cycles. Every step is worthwhile, successful or not, as long as you learn something. Additional guidance is provided by Mike Rother in his book *Toyota Kata*.[7] He has developed a clear model of the improvement process and practice routines to work your way toward the habit of daily improvement.

If you already have a lean program started, I encourage you to think about that program as part of the current state and compare it with the ideal state. What are the critical gaps in how the program is being executed? How are you doing at developing people in a respectful way? Where is a culture of continuous improvement starting to take root, and where is there stagnation? Investigate personally at the gemba. Learn from a coach. You will begin to understand the true condition of your organization and yourself as a leader.

In this book, Karyn and I will work to give you a clear picture of what lean transformation means in service organizations. As you read, remember, it starts with you.

Jeffrey K. Liker
Author, *The Toyota Way*

KEY POINTS

We will end each chapter with a summary of key points
we hope you will take away and use. These are shorthand
bullet points to help you recall what we are trying to teach
and also to help you think about how you might use these
ideas in your own work. In this chapter we learned:

1. The Toyota Way is a philosophy, way of thinking, and system of interconnected processes and people who are continuously striving to improve how
   they work and better deliver value to each customer.
2. The Toyota Way begins with a passion for solving problems for each customer and society. The underlying values of challenge, kaizen, genchi genbutsu (go study the actual conditions and learn), respect, and teamwork
   are the foundation of the system and support the twin pillars of continuous improvement and respect for people:
   ■ Continuous improvement means everybody, everywhere, constantly
     looking for new and better ways to satisfy each customer by experimenting toward challenging goals, striving to reach true north.
   ■ Respect for people means developing people both personally and professionally through challenging them to be the very best that they can
     be. Respect for people encompasses those who work for Toyota, as well
     as suppliers, the community, the environment, and the larger world.
3. There is no generic "recipe" or one "best-practice way" to mechanically
   "install" or "implement" lean in an organization. The Toyota Way principles, as described in this book, can, however, help you reflect on your
   organization, understand where gaps are to your true north, and begin the
   process of striving toward perfection: delivering the services that your customers want, exactly as they want them, now and for the long term.

Chapter 1

What Is Service Excellence?

We have to give people a reason to come to us and keep coming back. We are going to treat them like royalty. We are going to wow them and service the hell out of them and have the customers believe that the only reason we got up in the morning was on the chance that they would grace us with their patronage.

—Paul Saginaw, Zingerman's cofounder

DO WE NEED LEAN IN SERVICES?

Has anyone reading this book had a service horror story you would like to share? Put another way, is there anyone who has never had a terrible, frustrating experience? Recalling these abysmal experiences is easy. We wonder how many examples of excellent service our readers can come up with. Have you called your cable service provider, or your electric company, or the Internal Revenue Service, and quickly talked to a real person who graciously and efficiently solved your problem? The answer may be that service was excellent when you were dealing with a salesperson, but terrible once you made the purchase and then had a problem.

Do power outages get efficiently resolved? Is road repair efficient? When was the last time you remember passing a road repair operation and seeing people actually working? Anyone waited on the plane parked on the tarmac after the pilot explained there was a minor issue that would take minutes to fix only to find that nobody had arrived at the plane for 30 minutes or more? (I [Jeffrey] am doing that as I write this.) Read any interesting magazines in an office of a doctor, dentist, or your auto repair facility while you looked at your watch wondering when you would be served? Waited for a contractor or inspector on that exciting new construction project?

Accenture conducted an enlightening study of the life insurance industry—that bastion of service excellence. According to the study, about $470 billion of insurance business globally will be up for grabs because of unhappy customers. According to a survey of more then 13,000 customers in 33 countries, 16 percent (less than 1 in 7) said they would "definitely buy more products from their current insurer." Only 27 percent rated highly their insurance provider's "trustworthiness."

We have worked with many service providers that started the practice of surveying customers—rental cars, payroll contractors, information technology services, cell phone providers—and the story was the same in all cases. The companies were surprised to learn how unhappy their customers were. Customers were not only dissatisfied but angry and frustrated.

This book is about "service excellence," which for so many of us sounds like an oxymoron. Most service organizations are so far away from anything resembling adequate basic service that excellence becomes an empty slogan. Yet simply by measuring customer satisfaction, organizations repeatedly find ways to get better. Just focusing attention can make a difference. Excellence goes far beyond focusing attention. It requires disciplined practice and continuous improvement throughout the enterprise. Think of this as a long-term vision that might at the moment seem unattainable but provides the right direction.

In this chapter we will define service excellence, starting with two contrasting stories comparing a reputable appliance retail outlet that is pretty good with an automotive dealer network truly on the path to excellence. We will then begin to define service excellence, starting with these questions: What do we mean by service, and how is it different from manufacturing?

TWO CUSTOMER SERVICE STORIES

Gas Cooktop Purchase and Installation

It was almost Mother's Day, and I had a great idea. I would surprise my wife, Deb, with a gas cooktop as a Mother's Day gift. When our house was built, we'd selected a Jenn-Air electric cooktop, inset in a granite-topped island. Now Deb wished we had chosen a gas cooktop, as she preferred the consistency of the gas flame for cooking.

Wondering if Jenn-Air made a gas model that could replace the electric one and that would fit in the island, I measured the size of the opening of the insert, went online, and within minutes found the exact model number for the Jenn-Air gas cooktop that would fit. I then debated shopping around on the Internet to see where I could get the best deal, but decided instead to purchase the cooktop from the most reputable appliance store in town, as it specialized in Jenn-Air products. It wasn't the cheapest alternative, but I wanted to make sure I got the best installation and experience.

I drove to the store and waited at the front desk while a salesman fiddled around with the computer trying to locate the part with the model number I had provided. It seemed that the salesman, hunting and pecking on the computer keyboard, was typing a lengthy article, not selecting an item with a mouse click. I continued to wait patiently, and the salesman told some interesting stories as he continued searching the computer.

Finally, the salesman found what he was searching for and exclaimed, "You're in luck! We don't normally have that model as part of our regular stock, but it is available, and we have a truck coming from the warehouse in two days. If we order the cooktop now, we can get it on that truck!" The salesman showed me a similar model in the store, and I agreed to place the order. The salesman began hunting and pecking on the computer keyboard again. By now, about 15 minutes had passed, and tired of waiting, I started fiddling with my iPhone. After at least another five minutes, the salesman finally printed out an order. "The computer seems to be running very slowly today," he apologized.

The salesman then explained that an installer would need to visit the house prior to the installation to determine what parts would be needed for the new gas line and to estimate labor charges. I agreed that that would be fine, and the salesman then called up yet another computer program. Typing madly, he finally located the installer's schedule, and lo and behold there was an opening the next afternoon. I wouldn't be available at that time, and although it would spoil the surprise, I decided to let the cat out of the bag about the Mother's Day present and called Deb to see if she could stay at home to wait for the installer. Deb was available, so the salesman spent another few minutes working on the computer to schedule the visit. After I paid the 50 percent deposit, the salesman entered some final information and printed out the receipt. By this time, I had spent half an hour at the store. By the time I got home, the whole trip had taken me about one hour.

(Total lead time = 1 hour; "lead time" is the elapsed time
from the start to the end of a process.)

The next day, Deb stayed at home. After about one hour of waiting, two installers arrived and proceeded with the estimate, searching through the basement and taking many measurements. It took about 20 minutes for the installers to handwrite the type and quantity of the materials they would need (gas pipes, adapters, valves, etc.) and calculate the estimated labor hours. Total time for the installation estimate, including Deb's wait time, was an hour and a half.

(Total lead time = 1.5 hours)

I was a bit surprised to find out how much the installation would cost, but it was a Mother's Day present, so the next day I got back in the car and drove to the store to complete the order and pay the balance. The salesman I had previously spoken with wasn't in, so I explained the situation a second time to a different salesman. This salesman asked me for much of the same information that I had provided on the first visit—item name; model number; my name, address, and telephone number—and began typing furiously. This time, however, the computer screen was facing me, and it was immediately clear why this was such a lengthy process. The user interface looked as if it hadn't been updated since the 1980s, when computer programs were written in Basic. The salesman had to scroll down line by line, adjusting the cursor each time, and type in every bit of information, including part numbers, each of which seemed to be about 15 characters long. Every time the salesman finished typing a field, he had to press Enter and wait while the cursor blinked on and off. While this was fascinating to watch for a minute, I was soon back fiddling on my iPhone.

After about five minutes of typing, the salesman looked confused and said to me, "Seems like the cooktop is already here at the store. We can go ahead and schedule installation if you'd like." The salesman then called up a crude-looking schedule and found that there were openings on the following Tuesday and Wednesday. As I was going to be traveling, I again called Deb to check on her availability. Deb could stay at home the next Tuesday morning to meet the store's half-day time window, so the salesman scheduled the installation. After a few more minutes of typing, the salesman was ready to print the installation order and receipts. He tried to print out the documents but looked frustrated and said, "It appears we have printer problems. Let's move to the front desk." At the front desk he was able to print out the four documents. I paid and signed one document, and the salesman offered to staple the three new documents to the two that I already had. After spending 25 minutes in the store, I was again on my way home. Total time to schedule the installation and pay the balance was 55 minutes.

(Total lead time = 55 minutes)

On the day of the installation, Deb waited excitedly for the installers to arrive at 9 a.m. As was their policy, they called in advance to let the customer know that they would be there in 15 minutes, but since they called my cell and I was in Switzerland on a speaking engagement, Deb had no way of knowing that. Once the installers arrived, they efficiently completed the complex job of running gas pipes and wiring above the drywall ceiling of the finished basement. They expertly cut a hole in the shelf of the cabinet below the cooktop to install the gas-firing mechanism. Deb was impressed with the installers' expertise and professionalism. The experience wasn't totally perfect, however. The installation was noisy. Deb spent 3½ hours listening to loud banging and other noises. It was dusty, too. The installers made numerous trips back and forth between their truck and the house, leaving the garage door open the whole time. Deb had to clean the garage after they left. And the smell of gas spread from the utility room, through the finished basement, and up the stairs into the living room. But by 12:45 p.m. the installation was complete, and Deb was thrilled to have a gas cooktop that was properly installed, looked great, and worked! She tipped the installers, and they were on their way.

Later on that evening, however, Deb and I noticed that there seemed to be a continuous flow of air blowing through the new cooktop into the kitchen. Searching for the source of the problem, we found that an outside duct cover had been forced open by a nail, probably by painters the summer before to prevent the cover from getting stuck closed by paint. We removed the nail, and the problem was solved. My Mother's Day present was a rousing success!

To summarize our experience:

- Total installation time: 3.5 hours (see Figure 1.1).
- Total work time for the entire process (both value added and non-value added) including the installation: 6.9 hours.
- Total lead time from start to installation: 13 days.

After the installation was complete, neither Deb nor I received any follow-up calls or customer satisfaction surveys from the appliance store. We probably would have said everything was fine.

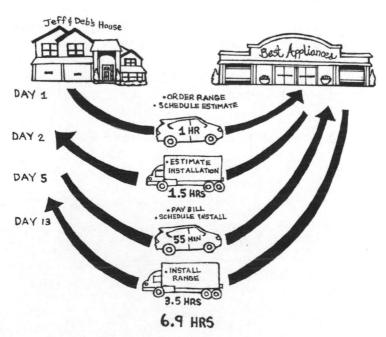

Figure 1.1 Appliance service lead times

Volvo Automotive Service & Repair

Like the appliance store, Volvo dealerships in Sweden had a solid reputation. But simply having a "solid reputation" was not satisfying to Einar Gudmundsson, vice president of Customer Service. A devout student of the Toyota Way, Einar brought many of its ideas to Volvo. He and his team crafted a bold vision to become the world leader in automotive dealer service (see Figure 1.2).

Einar started out by determining exactly what Volvo customers valued in automotive service. He had learned from a survey of 100,000 customers that the top three things they wanted were (1) positive relationships, (2) time reduced to the minimum, and (3) good problem solving to service and repair their cars.

One place Einar and his team focused on making a large difference in service was in the automotive repair bays. In the old system, a typical experience was similar to the appliance store case. A customer needing a repair would call the dealership. A receptionist would schedule a time for the customer to drop the car off to have the problem diagnosed. When the customer picked up the car, he would be told what the problem was and then have to schedule another appointment and bring the car back to be worked on. When the car was repaired, he would have to walk to the cashier's office and pay and then walk back to the service area to retrieve the car. Generally, the car would stay at the dealership for an entire day for each of these visits, and the customer would not have a car to use to get back and forth to work. There was a lot of queuing and waiting in the process as the customer was handed off from department to department, and often errors were made because of poor communication (see the original process flow in Figure 1.3).

One of the early steps taken by Volvo to improve this process was to develop a role called the personal service technician (PST). Under the PST there were, in

VOLVO SERVICE—LEADING IN THE WORLD

WHY	HOW	WHAT
• The Volvo brand promises world class personal service designed around timeliness, relationship and respect. Our global success will be driven by making life less complicated for people. Because satisfied customers will always come back.	• We fulfill that promise through a relentless construction of robust value chains designed around purpose and a determination to always put quality first.	• Lean leaders at all levels • High value added logistics • Personal and efficient service • Easy to buy attractive accessories • Connected Volvo customer • Tailor-made offers

Figure 1.2   Volvo service vision

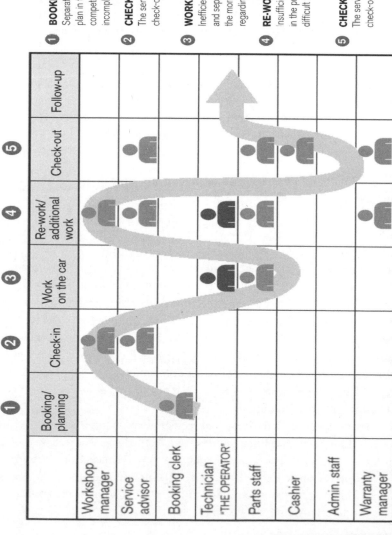

Figure 1.3 Customer value chain in traditional workshop

1 BOOKING/PLANNING
Separating booking and diagnosis makes it hard to plan in the most efficient way. Without the technician's competence there are risks of misunderstandings and incomplete planning.

2 CHECK-IN
The service advisor can be a bottleneck at check-in and check-out.

3 WORK ON THE CAR
Inefficiency and waiting times due to an uneven flow and separation of roles. Eg.: waiting for work orders in the morning, or for service advisor to contact customer regarding additional work

4 RE-WORK/ADDITIONAL WORK
Insufficient insight regarding what has happened earlier in the process results in quality problems and makes it difficult to solve all of the customer's problems.

5 CHECK-OUT
The service advisor can be a bottleneck at check-in and check-out.

	Booking/ planning	Check-in	Work on the car	Re-work/ additional work	Check-out	Follow-up
Workshop manager						🧍
Service advisor						
Team/Andon						🧍
Booking clerk						
Technician "THE OPERATOR"	🧍	🧍	🧍		🧍	🧍
Parts staff	🧍					
Cashier						
Admin. staff						
Warranty manager						

Figure 1.4   Customer value chain in one-hour stop workshop

theory, no handoffs, and the customer dealt with the same person, a technician, from initial call to payment, reducing errors and reducing the time that the customer spent waiting (see the improved process in Figure 1.4).

As VP of Customer Service at Volvo, Einar had taken this a step further to what he and his team called "one-hour stop." A core principle of lean is one-piece flow, and they asked, "What would it look like for the customer to flow from step to step without interruption?" The goal was to handle as many customers as possible within their own guaranteed one-hour time slot—starting from the first time the customer entered the dealer with the car until the customer left with a repaired car. They found that the PST system had limitations and that customers often did not reach the technician when they called in because the technicians were busy. They also found that the technicians often sent the customers to the cashier to pay at the end of the service, instead of taking the payment themselves. Customers didn't like either of these conditions.

Making one-hour stop a reality would require many changes beyond creating the PST role. One thing that Einar and his team learned was that to have a short and reliable lead time to repair a car, they needed two technicians in a repair bay working together. A single technician had to walk around and around the car to work on it, while having two technicians meant that each one could work on a side. They could then plan out the steps each would follow, which Toyota calls standard work. It was also important that they had the right parts and tools prepared for them in advance of the job, like a pit crew for race car drivers.

Einar's team had success in developing strong dealerships that could achieve one-hour stop, and customers began showing up without an appointment. Customer satisfaction rose. His team went from dealer to dealer making a proposal: "We will more than double your productivity of each repair bay based on teams of people working in each bay." Often a pair of Einar's technicians could do as much work as three or four of a dealer's technicians, and dealers, which were landlocked, could more than double capacity without investing in any new brick and mortar.

In 2013, recognized for his great progress transforming to lean in dealerships and the corporate offices, Einar was asked to personally run, on a full-time basis, an average-performing dealership. His goal quickly became to make it the most profitable dealership with the highest customer satisfaction ranking using what he had learned from the Toyota Way.

Here is how one-hour stop works now in Einar's dealership: fourteen technicians are organized into two teams of three pairs, with a lead service technician for each team. Each team has three service bays. When customers call in, they talk directly to a technician who does his best to diagnose the problem over the phone. The technician then calls the Volvo parts warehouse (which also was reorganized using Toyota-like principles) and orders (two days in advance) the parts needed. If the technician thinks it might be one of two problems, he orders two sets of parts. The parts come on a gray tray, arranged for that particular job. The pair then goes to work doing the repair. When the repair is complete, the technicians meet with the customer to explain what was done and collect payment. Customers can now spend the one hour waiting for their car to be repaired in a pleasant "living room" equipped with televisions, Wi-Fi, high-quality coffee, soft drinks, and snacks—all free—located beside the sales floor. While customers are waiting, the salespeople have a chance to interact with them, and this has led to increased sales.

The technician teams function mostly autonomously, though they have weekly coaching meetings with management. Each week they review key performance indicators on team target boards showing the performance of each pair. Measures include percentage of time the phone is answered the first time a customer calls, percentage of accurate diagnoses based on the phone call, time to invoice the customer, percentage of time the customer paid the PST versus had to go out to the cashier, and percentage of rush orders on parts versus parts delivered by schedule. The service performance measures are continually being updated with the team. It is a no-blame culture, and problems get solved. In fact, the technicians run the meetings, with management remaining quiet and then doing some coaching afterward. Managers even get graded by the technicians on the quality of their coaching.

Over time the teams have learned how to handle various common types of service issues, and within 1½ years they were up to completing 80 percent of the jobs in less than 1 hour—from the time the car first arrives until the customer drives away in the repaired car.

Also after only 1½ years, Einar's dealership moved from the middle of the pack to one of the top 10 dealerships in Sweden. Profits have increased significantly, and the company has doubled the use of each service bay. New construction was planned to actually reduce the number of service bays, cutting capital costs per repair.

Here is a summary of the results achieved using one-hour stop in Volvo dealerships in Belgium, Spain, and Taiwan:

- Only half the work bays needed for a given quantity of repairs
- Sold time per work bay up 114 percent to 193 percent
- Two to three times the productivity per repair worker
- Three to four times the profit as throughput increases and cost per repair drops
- Half the walking steps of technicians
- A rise in customers' ratings of service as very good or outstanding, increasing from 74 to 83 percent, with the main change occurring in the "outstanding rating" from 31 to 41 percent

One of the more interesting findings is the increase in customer satisfaction ratings. It is not surprising that it went up, but it is surprising that it was so high to begin with. In the traditional system 74 percent of customers rated the service as "very good" or "outstanding." Yet it was very inconvenient and time consuming for them compared with the new approach. This suggests that customers tend to adapt to mediocre service and will then appreciate a new level of service that in turn becomes their new expectation.

Was it difficult to create the change in culture necessary to institute one-hour stop in the dealerships? There was certainly some consternation about making these radical changes in each dealership, but after the fact the changes were greatly appreciated. For example, the customer service manager in Belgium said: "There is a much better use of the customer's time. There is also better communication, as technicians explain things directly to the customer. The customers react very positively." One service technician in Spain said: "For me, the opportunity to deal directly with customers is the main benefit. It builds trust and creates a stronger, more personal relationship."

And the results showed up in profits. While Einar was VP, the customer service business earned $2.3 billion with $800 million in profit.

Comparing the Two Cases

Overall, both organizations seem to be doing well. The appliance store has a long history as a stable local business and has survived ups and downs in the economy. At some points, Volvo has struggled and almost gone out of business. But at this point in its history, Volvo customer service is working tirelessly toward service excellence, whereas the appliance store appears to be stagnant.

Has stagnation hurt the appliance store's business? It seems that customers adapt and view a given level of service as normal. By most standards our appliance purchase and installation experience was "very good," and this particular store has done well for decades because of its reputation for great service. At every stage in the process, the salespeople and installers were friendly and professional and knew what they were doing, and the gas cooktop was properly installed. Overall, we were happy that we selected the store for the purchase and installation of our new cooktop, but can we really say that what we experienced was "service excellence"? When I calculated the time spent door to door on the first visit, at home waiting for the men to come to estimate on the second encounter, and door to door on the third visit, it had taken 6.9 hours between my time traveling to and from the store twice, my time waiting in the store, and Deb's time at home while installers were planning and later installing. A total of 13 days passed from the initial order to installation. All this time to get installed the exact item that I had identified on the Internet in a few minutes prior to starting this process—and for a product already in inventory. There were some hiccups, arguably minor, but there was no indication that anyone in the store realized this or cared. After the installation, we didn't receive any type of follow-up call from the store or a customer satisfaction survey. Since we did not complain about the service experience, perhaps the store assumed that all was excellent.

The Toyota Way encourages us to envision the ideal state and then compare it with the current condition. It is only if we think of an alternative that is much better than what we have that we become dissatisfied. What if I could have simply phoned the appliance store since I knew what I wanted, talked to a service technician, described the situation, and had the service technician come out with the new cooktop and install it? Now in many cases this could be difficult: for example, estimating the required length of the gas pipe and connectors and estimating the time and labor costs. But perhaps a service tech could have talked me through the measurements that were needed over the phone, and I could have sent some photos with my smartphone for the technician to look at. Then, like the Volvo dealer, perhaps it would have been possible to have the unit delivered and installed within one or two days.

And consider the installation experience. Although it was professionally done and the installers had obvious craft knowledge, was it really necessary for them to

Figure 1.5 Some weak points in Jeff and Deb's appliance service experience
Disclaimer: This is an exaggerated satirical view of a mostly positive experience.

make trip after trip back and forth to the truck over a number of hours, leaving the garage door open the entire time? Would it have been possible to have the adaptability to schedule installation when the installers could be let in to the house but family members did not have to be at home the entire time? Was it necessary for the installers to leave our house smelling of gas? Could they have checked the venting and noticed the vent was stuck open? (see Figure 1.5).

And what about the call to let us know that the installers were on their way? The call ended up going to me in Switzerland just before I was going onstage to speak, so I didn't answer. What if store policy had been not to go to the installation site if the customer didn't answer the call? Deb would have been waiting all morning without a way to know why the installers hadn't arrived. A major problem in service processes is having the best method of contacting clients and having an idea of whether they will be available for a call. Can this problem be fixed?

Karyn has experienced this while working in several service organizations. At a third-party payroll processor, this was a common problem that usually happened on a Friday. The person making the delivery was required to call the customer before leaving the payroll checks so employees could get paid. When the driver would call the number the customer provided but the customer didn't answer, the delivery service couldn't complete the delivery process, so the driver would call the customer service representative to check the number. The customer service rep would then frantically call every number on file and also send an e-mail. If the customer didn't respond, the delivery was not made, and employees didn't get the checks they expected. When the customer arrived back at work on Monday and found that the employees hadn't been paid, he or she would call the customer service representative and be extremely angry. Even if the rep could find a polite way to say that the number the customer provided did not work, there was never a happy ending. The customer didn't give the wrong information; conditions just changed that the service provider was not aware of, and there was not a clear understanding between the service provider and customer of when a call would be made and who would be available to receive it.

Karyn has also encountered a similar situation in insurance claims. The insured provides an address to send claim checks to and then moves. The insurance company doesn't know that and continues to send checks to the address on file. The insured is then upset when the checks are not received.

"Good" companies do the best they can. They believe that since they cannot anticipate everything that can possibly go wrong, they cannot be responsible for what their customers do. Excellent companies continue to work to find ways to improve in order to solve these problems, and they never blame the customer!

Volvo dealerships in Sweden had a fine reputation prior to lean. Customers needing car repairs brought their cars back to the dealership multiple times and thought it was "good service." But once they experienced one-hour stop, they would not want to go back to the old system of multiple phone calls and visits. In fact, our guess is that once customers experienced one-hour stop, they would be very unhappy if Volvo reverted to the old system.

It is well known in psychology that satisfaction depends as much on expectations as reality. You can lower satisfaction either by failing to live up to current expectations or by raising expectations and then not meeting them. This leads to a conundrum: the better we do, the more the customers expect and the more difficult they are to please. That has been the story of the auto industry triggered by the excellence of Japanese automakers, particularly Toyota. Customer expectations are through the roof, and high quality and safety are basic expectations just to be in the game.

In 2014 automakers recalled a record 63.95 million vehicles in the United States, reflecting 803 separate recall campaigns. This was more then double the previous record of 30.8 million in 2004. General Motors led the pack with 27 million recalls, most notably the highly publicized ignition switch debacle, but all automakers recalled large numbers. One would think that auto safety was abysmal and people were in serious accidents every day because of their defective vehicles, and yet this was not the case. In fact, it was just the opposite: automotive safety was about the best it had been since the first automobiles were riding alongside horses and buggies. There were a tiny number of serious accidents as a percentage of the vehicles recalled. Almost all the recalls were preventative—in case something might go wrong. This is not bad for the customers, but it does reflect their extremely high expectations for near perfection in a machine with tens of thousands of parts that are expected to last for 15 years or more under intense wear and tear while being operated in harsh conditions.

In some ways the people at the appliance store had an easier time meeting customers' service expectations than Volvo. They were good, and many customers like us kept coming back, even though they did not appear to have significantly improved customer service in decades. Their competitors are mostly national appliance stores with worse service, and as long as those competitors do not invest in a far better approach, the appliance store is in fine shape.

Coach John Wooden was a perfectionist in preparing his college basketball teams, who won at an astonishing rate. He said, "Success comes from knowing that you did your best to become the best that you are capable of becoming."

This leads to a number of interesting questions: How do we define service excellence? Can we rely on customer satisfaction as an indicator of whether we are excellent? How can we change the mindset of ordinary people working in services so that they are dissatisfied with the service provided even when customers appear happy? How can we develop a culture of people truly passionate to "become the best they are capable of becoming?"

WHAT IS A SERVICE ORGANIZATION, AND HOW DO WE DEFINE EXCELLENCE?

What Do We Mean by a Service Organization?

Let's first consider what we mean by a service. As defined by businessdictionary.com, a service is "a valuable action, deed, or effort performed to satisfy a need or to fulfill a demand." This seems straightforward enough, and points out that it is only a service if it fulfills a customer need.

An economic perspective on service provided by investorwords.com adds further definition: "A type of economic activity that is intangible, is not stored, and does not result in ownership. A service is consumed at the point of sale."

Now we have the notion of service as "intangible." Moreover, we consume it at the point of sale, so customers themselves are a part of the transformation process. If we can touch and feel it and store it for later use, it is not a service but rather a tangible good. If it is a process that directly changes us as customers in some way, it is intangible and a service. Services like hair styling, surgery, psychological counseling, and personal training clearly fit this definition of something intangible consumed at the point of sale. None of these services can happen if the customer is not present when it is happening.

Google's dictionary adds even more complexity to our definition of services:

1. "The action of helping or doing work for someone."
2. "A system supplying a public need such as transport, communications, or utilities such as electricity and water."

The first definition is similar to the two we have discussed, but the second adds the notion of a system that moves or transfers something that is at least somewhat tangible and storable. Electricity can be stored, and even though you do not want to hold it in your hand, it is a measurable physical entity. Bottled water is a physical product from a manufacturing plant, but a service provider transports it to a store that is a service provider. When we turn on the spigot in our home in many locations, we are getting a service provided by the water company that is pumping and treating water from a reservoir. Where does manufacturing end and service begin?

The world became more complicated with the advent of computer technology, and especially with the Internet. When I am using Amazon.com, am I using a service or a tangible product technology? Amazon itself is a system of people and technology that is supplying something tangible: software producing a user interface on our computer stored for use as we desire. We interact with the computer. Amazon data is stored in a complex infrastructure of over one million physical servers throughout the world. If we were to write our order on paper, we might say that the paper is a tangible good produced in a factory, but when we type our order into the computer interface, it is a service because it is virtual paper that was created in a software factory. Hmmm. This is getting more and more confusing.

To further complicate matters, the way services are measured by governments is as the complement of manufacturing. Services are everything that is *not* production of tangible goods as classified by national measurement systems. Encyclopedia Britannica online describes it in this way:

> *Service industry: an industry in that part of the economy that creates services rather than tangible objects. Economists divide all economic activity into two broad categories, goods and services. Goods-producing industries are agriculture, mining, manufacturing, and construction; each of them creates some kind of tangible object. Service industries include everything else: banking, communications, wholesale and retail trade, all professional services such as engineering, computer software development, and medicine, nonprofit economic activity, all consumer services, and all government services, including defense and administration of justice.*

This seems both sloppy and odd. A sloppy way to define something is as everything left over except something you define: service is everything that is not manufacturing. If we etch layers and layers of bits and bytes onto a circuit board at Intel, it is manufacturing, but a cable company that transforms bits and bytes into a movie we can consume on a computer is a service. These two cases seem to have more similarities than differences. If an engineer at Intel is designing the next new computer chip that will be smaller and faster, is she in manufacturing because Intel is a manufacturing company or in a service organization because she is doing knowledge work? If she does the same work in an engineering firm subcontracted by Intel, is she now performing a service?

How Are Manufacturing and Services Different?

When we try to teach lean to service organizations using Toyota as an example, a typical response is "We do not make cars. We provide an intangible service, which is very different. How can we learn anything from an automotive company?"

Is it true that service and manufacturing companies are so different that they cannot learn from each other? Year after year, Richard Daft's *Organization Theory and Design* is the bestselling textbook for organizational design courses, and he apparently thinks the differences between manufacturing and services are huge. Daft describes services as intangible and says that they cannot be saved for later use. He describes services as labor and knowledge intensive, with high customer interaction and a human element that is very important.

Some of the other distinctions seem to be based on outdated stereotypes of manufacturing. For example, Daft says the human element in manufacturing is less important than in services, but in lean, at least the Toyota Way version, team members working production are at the center of continuous improvement that drives the enterprise. Daft says longer response times are acceptable in manufacturing, but the just-in-time ideal is one-piece flow with no delays. It seems clear that from the perspective of lean, these kinds of dichotomies are oversimplifications.

Consider an electric and power company. It provides a tangible product that can be inventoried, it is capital intensive, there is little customer interaction with the power plants so the human element is less obvious to the customer, and quality is directly measurable. So in most regards it is more like manufacturing than a service.

Things become even more fuzzy when we consider an entire enterprise. Think about a hospital. Karyn made a highly simplified sketch in Figure 1.6. The areas shaded seem to better fit Daft's "Manufacturing" column than the "Service" column—areas like the pharmacy, the laundry, the pathology labs that test tissue samples, and the department that maintains all the complex equipment and facil-

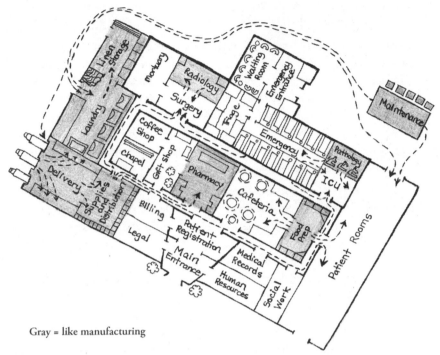

Gray = like manufacturing

Figure 1.6 Is lean in healthcare different than in manufacturing?

ities. Also if you consider orderlies who move people and things around the hospitals, they are very much like material handlers in manufacturing. In fact, there seems to be as much material moving about the hospital as we have seen in most manufacturing plants, and those materials need to be ordered, delivered, stored, moved to where they will be used, and disposed of. Sounding more like manufacturing all the time?

I (Jeff) had an interesting experience during a visit to the Toyota Memorial Hospital in Japan. I had heard they were applying Toyota principles in a service environment. I was accompanied on a tour by two senior Japanese managers who showed me the material flow system. All materials used by doctors or nurses were carefully laid out, for example, in well-labeled drawers, with addresses for their locations. Common small items like syringes were in a see-through bag and were easy to locate. Even more interesting in the bag was a small laminated card, which Toyota calls a *kanban*. The information on the card includes the part number and description of the part, its location for users and location in the warehouse, and the number of syringes in the bag (see Chapter 5). As we were going through the drawers a material delivery person came by with a cart on wheels and replenished what had been used and took the cards for items that were getting low so they could replenish those on the next trip. I asked the two managers what their background was and they explained:

> *Before coming here we worked for many years in Toyota factories as material flow managers. One week we got notification to start new jobs on the next Monday in the hospital. We thought this was a mistake. But once we were here we saw there were thousands of materials moving through the hospital, just like parts in Toyota factories. We could apply all the same principles to make the flow more efficient and get to our customers the right material in the right place at the right time. We were able to clear out about half the warehouse and improve customer service.*

In our experience, any service organization has elements that look like manufacturing, even though these may be invisible to the customers. Customers going to the supermarket see what is stored in inventory on the store shelves, usually attractively presented, and they may ask a question of a service representative, or they may directly deal with a cashier if that process has not been automated. The customers rarely see the pallets of materials in an internal warehouse that get unloaded from a truck, nor do they see the pallets broken down or the products brought out late in the evening to be restocked on the shelves and presented to the customer the next day. They do not see the routine physical processing of money. And somewhere in a back office is an accountant keeping track of all the numbers.

On the other hand, take a walk through a manufacturing plant, and you are likely to see large office areas where people are purchasing things, coordinating shipments, planning, answering customer calls, performing finance and accounting functions, coordinating insurance, and engaging in countless other "service functions." In some large facilities there are even doctors and nurses providing medical care to employees, and there may be a pharmacy.

In short, it is often more useful to consider differences across functional groups within manufacturing and healthcare systems, or even differences in individual jobs, than it is to treat manufacturing and service organizations as different animals.

We still might define an organization in terms of the core of what it does. If the core work is to create a tangible product for sale, then we could classify it as a manufacturing business. If the core work is to service customers by making it easier to access something they need, as in the case of Amazon, or by directly improving their health or well-being, we could classify it as a service. We often see in manufacturing organizations that services are support functions to manufacturing. Manufacturing is in the foreground, and service is in the background. In service organizations, we see the customer service process in the foreground and manufacturing as support functions in the background (see Figure 1.7).

Perhaps instead of thinking of service versus manufacturing, for the purposes of improving, it is more useful to think in terms of the complexity of the work:

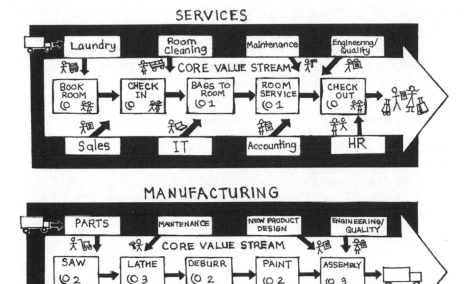

Figure 1.7   Services versus manufacturing value streams

- **Customization of work.** How routine (steps, sequence, time) is the operation (low) versus how specific is it to the unique situation (high)?
- **Intangibility of work.** How much can we physically see the transformation process (low) versus how much do we need abstract ways to describe it (high)?

Work complexity may vary by department, by project, by individual assignment, or even within the different jobs done by an individual. Consider a surgeon who, on the one hand, performs a routine checkup. Then think about open-heart surgery where the surgeon adjusts second by second based on the condition of the patient, the nurse is doing routine things like providing suction, and various orderlies are bringing tools and materials to the room as they are needed. We have a wide range of types of work occurring simultaneously even in the same room.

Work that is simple can be planned out in advance, and repeated cycles can be identified, timed, standardized, and rigorously taught using a clear recipe (see Liker and Meier[1]). This is characteristic of much of the assembly work in a Toyota plant, but we also find this work in any service organization. The Volvo dealership did most of its early lean work achieving one-hour stop and focused on standard procedures like oil changes and tire changes. On the other hand, when Einar and his team began to work on improving the sales process, they quickly noted that sales is a creative process, and they did not want to limit those skilled at this craft with long lists of standardized processes for selling. We will revisit this issue in the discussion of standard work in Chapter 6 on stable processes.

Four Types of Service Organizations

We've tried to sort services into four categories ranging from low to high complexity in the 2 × 2 table in Figure 1.8 based on two questions:

- How *customized* is the service? Standard (low) versus customized (high).
- How *intangible* is the service? Tangible product of service system (low) versus customer experience (high).

When we look at the various combinations of these, we get four types of services:

1. **Mass goods distribution.** This is a service system that produces something tangible and is most like manufacturing. We are distributing a product. We are defining a product broadly to include a burger from a fast-food restaurant, a movie on our computer from the Internet, a book delivered to our house from Amazon, a seasonal beer from a microbrewery, or electricity to a building. In many cases the service organization did not produce the product, though a fast-food restaurant does prepare and

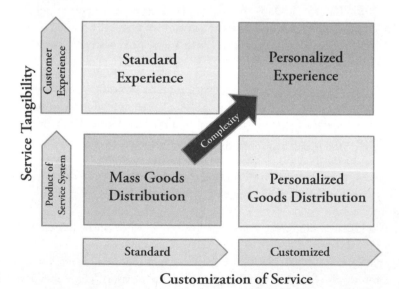

Figure 1.8   Classifying four types of services

assemble what it delivers, and a microbrewery is manufacturing the beer it serves us on the premises.

2. **Personalized goods distribution.** The system also produces something tangible that can be stored, but it is customized. Notice that these goods would typically be more luxurious and expensive versions of goods distribution such as a boutique clothing store that might make clothes to order. We would expect an actress buying a gown for the Oscars to go to a place like this. Later in the book we will talk about an exceptional software development firm that only creates customized software for a specific client. The firm spends a great deal of time and direct observation to understand how the customer currently works and how the software can function smoothly and easily to accomplish its objectives.

3. **Standard experience.** This better fits the definition of service as intangible, something that cannot be stored, consumed at the point of sale, with direct interaction between the service provider and customer. There is some variation in the service but it is pretty much standard across customers. We go to the bank to deposit a check and have direct contact with a teller. We go for a routine dental cleaning. Or heaven forbid, we have to call our cable company because we have a question about our bill. In these cases we are one of a long line of customers getting a very similar service. Sometimes, however, there is something special about our case, and it shifts from a routine transaction to personalized customer service. For example, the cable company representative cannot easily troubleshoot over the phone why our service is not working and must send someone out to investigate.

4. **Personalized experience.** This is also intangible, but it is customized and usually more expensive and luxurious. I have had a personal trainer come to my home, and each workout was customized to what the trainer thought I needed on that day. The trainer had a college degree in exercise science and a broad understanding of anatomy, muscle groups, and the impact of different types of exercises on the body. The cable repair person who comes out to our house to troubleshoot the problem is another example. The famed hair stylist that will study each client to create a unique hair style to fit that person is providing a personalized service.

As a general rule, as we move from mass goods distribution to personalized experience, the service becomes more complex. By complexity we mean there is a higher level of tacit knowledge involved—knowledge that is learned through repeated experience and cannot be easily documented as a standard recipe.

In Figure 1.9 we give examples that might fit in each cell. Any typology is an oversimplification, and this one is no exception. Any complex organization provides a variety of services that fit into more than one cell. There are call centers in

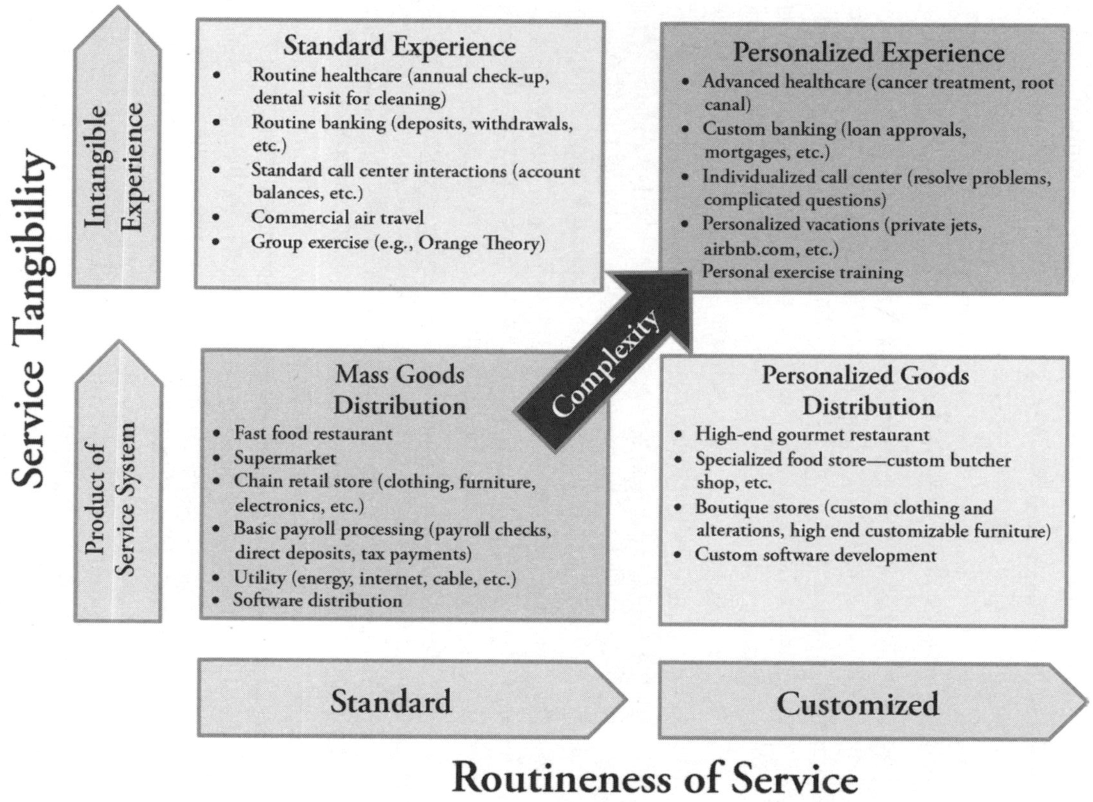

Routineness of Service

Figure 1.9 Examples of four types of services

Personalized Experience
- Advanced healthcare (cancer treatment, root canal)
- Custom banking (loan approvals, mortgages, etc.)
- Individualized call center (resolve problems, complicated questions)
- Personalized vacations (private jets, airbnb.com, etc.)
- Personal exercise training

Personalized Goods Distribution
- High-end gourmet restaurant
- Specialized food store—custom butcher shop, etc.
- Boutique stores (custom clothing and alterations, high end customizable furniture)
- Custom software development

Standard Experience
- Routine healthcare (annual check-up, dental visit for cleaning)
- Routine banking (deposits, withdrawals, etc.)
- Standard call center interactions (account balances, etc.)
- Commercial air travel
- Group exercise (e.g., Orange Theory)

Mass Goods Distribution
- Fast food restaurant
- Supermarket
- Chain retail store (clothing, furniture, electronics, etc.)
- Basic payroll processing (payroll checks, direct deposits, tax payments)
- Utility (energy, internet, cable, etc.)
- Software distribution

Complexity

Customized

Standard

Service Tangibility

Intangible Experience

Product of Service System

cable companies that handle standard inquiries (standard experience) and also solve complex customer problems (personalized experience).

The purpose of the model is to provide a starting point to think about the approach to improvement that will be needed. We will see in Chapter 6 on improving processes that the more conventional approaches to lean methods, like developing a documented standardized process and developing a timed rhythm to the work, can be more easily applied to "mass goods distribution" and needs more adjustment to apply to a "personalized experience."

So What Is Service Excellence?

We have dissected and bisected services to the point that the concept is barely recognizable as a distinct category. Yet we still need to define service excellence.

The starting point is the same for manufacturing and services—the customer. What does the customer experience? How satisfied is the customer? To what degree are we enhancing the life of each customer?

The process of understanding the customer and properly designing the service is similar to creating excellent product design. We must understand what customers expect and then go beyond that, giving them the unexpected. As Henry Ford quipped, "If I asked people what they wanted they would have said faster horses." We cannot expect the customers to know what would address their need. They are not the designers of the service and are generally limited by their own experiences.

Once the service is designed, we need to deliver on time, when the customer wants it, right the first time. In this sense customers' needs are the same for all four quadrants of our service typology. Yet there are some differences. Roughly speaking, beyond quality and timeliness, customers for each type want:

- **Mass goods distribution.** Major customer desires are functionality, reliability, cost, and convenience.
- **Standard experience.** Customer desires are similar to mass goods distribution with the addition of the human touch in interacting with the customer. We expect efficient service delivery that addresses our need at low cost, and we want to be treated respectfully.
- **Personalized goods distribution.** Customers want something special that they cannot get from the average company and that distinguishes them from the masses. It should solve their unique problem, not the problem of a generic set of customers.
- **Personalized experience.** This is perhaps the most challenging of the service types in that customers want to be wowed, pampered, and treated like VIPs. They want a memorable experience, and they are willing to pay extra for it. This is luxury service, and it is only the person's particular experience that matters, not the experience of anyone else.

DOES SERVICE EXCELLENCE MATTER?

Excellent firms don't believe in excellence—only in constant improvement and constant change.

—Tom Peters, author of *The Little Big Things: 163 Ways to Pursue EXCELLENCE*

According to the U.S. Bureau of Labor Statistics, the manufacturing sector is expected to lose 549,500 jobs between 2012 and 2022, an annual rate of decline of 0.5 percent. In the same time period, service-sector jobs are expected to increase from 116.1 million to 130. 2 million. This means that by 2022 the service sector will account for more than 90 percent of the jobs that will be added to the American economy.[2] As more jobs are added and the service sector grows, consumers will have an increasing range of options to choose from.

In the face of increased alternatives for customers, the question then becomes, How can service organizations keep the customers that they already have and attract—and keep—new customers? The answer is by continually improving their service. A 2013 Accenture research study found that in 2012, fifty-one percent of customers switched service providers because of poor customer service experiences, causing $1.3 trillion of revenue to be transferred between companies in the United States. Banks, cable and satellite providers, and retailers were among the most often switched services.[3] For service organizations in today's economy, customer service excellence is no longer a choice but a necessity.

Stories abound about remarkable service experiences in highly benchmarked companies like the Ritz-Carlton and Four Seasons.

- If you had stayed at any Ritz-Carlton in the past and had indicated a preference for certain things such as fresh fruit, feather pillows, black ink in the room's pens, or reading material, these would all be waiting for you in your room.
- A guest at the Ritz-Carlton in Boston mentioned to the doorman that he had been out fishing that day and caught a 200-pound yellow fin tuna. The guest said that the fish was in his cooler in the car and explained that he was going to have to clean it and cut it when he got home and it would help if he could have some ice for now. The assistant front desk manager took the cooler to the kitchen, where the cook supervisor cleaned the fish for the guest, breaking it down into smaller pieces. The cook supervisor went a step further by cleaning the guest's cooler and organizing the small pieces of fish in ice for him to take home.
- A guest at a Four Seasons hotel was walking toward his room when he saw that someone had his door open and was adjusting it. When he asked what

was going on, the engineer explained, "The housekeeper servicing the room next door noticed that when your door closes, it closes more with an indeterminate gentle closing sound, which is a little bit less definitive than the 'click' we prefer, so she called down to engineering to have us come up and zero in on the closing mechanism."[4]

The stories that seem to get the most press tend to be in what we call "personalized experience." These are direct customer experiences, usually with high-end luxury businesses that spare no expense and charge a premium for their fine facilities to make the customer experience memorable. Even for the luxury brands, the behind-the-scenes routine processes have to be fine-tuned, or the customer experience will be less than pleasant. Imagine an amazing Ritz-Carlton that has your hypoallergenic pillows waiting for you and the mangoes set out in Brazil that you once said you enjoyed in Hawaii—fantastic. Now imagine that you discover the carpet smells, the toilet does not flush properly, and your bill is incorrect. The Ritz also needs to make a similar investment in its people to ensure high-quality maintenance, high-quality room cleaning, high-quality laundry service, and on and on, to provide the reliable perfect experience customers have come to expect. While customers expect a customized special experience, there are also many elements of mass standard experience that have to be correctly done behind the scenes.

Grocery chains usually fit in our mass goods distribution cell—at the other end of the spectrum from the Ritz. This is also where Toyota would sit. Grocery stores have systems designed to bring you products that fit your needs, conveniently arranged for selection and attractively presented. However, even in the basic grocery store, there are organizations that are distinguishing themselves by their service. While Whole Foods emphasizes the healthfulness of its foods, Wegmans, the grocery chain that is the consistent leader in customer satisfaction, does not occupy a distinctive niche. It has huge stores that seem to have everything any shopper could possibly want. It also sells a variety of exotic items like rare cheeses, and produce is top quality and remarkably fresh. Throughout the store, associates go out of their way to be helpful, and customers find it an exceptional shopping and service experience.

Wegmans's exceptional customer service has much to do with how it invests in its team members. Cashiers are barred from interacting with customers until they have completed 40 hours of training. Hundreds of staffers are sent on trips around the United States and the world to become experts in their products. The company has no mandatory retirement age and has never laid off workers. All profits are reinvested in the company or shared with employees.[5]

Like Toyota, each of these exceptional service companies performs at a high level over long periods of time. These companies ride through downturns in the economy, they grow revenue, they steadily make profit, and they beat their industry in profitability. Unlike some of their competitors, they save cash to ride out downturns and reinvest a good deal of their profits into the business.

For more than a decade, Dr. André de Waal of the Maastricht School of Management in the Netherlands has studied many sectors to determine what makes a high-performance organization (HPO). He has learned that HPOs have a culture characterized by the following factors:[6]

- **Long-term orientation.** Continuity over short-term profit, collaboration with others, good long-term relationships with all stakeholders, focus on customers.
- **High-quality management.** Decisive, action oriented, strong trust relationships, coaching, holding others responsible.
- **Open and action-oriented management.** Communicating often with employees, open to change, performance oriented.
- **High-quality employees.** Recruiting those who want to assume responsibility and excel, from diverse backgrounds; those who are complementary, flexible, and resilient.
- **Continuous improvement and innovation.** A distinctive strategy; processes that are continuously improved, simplified, and coordinated; core competencies and products continuously improved; reporting important and correct information.

In Waal's study of more than 2,500 organizations throughout the world, large and small, public and private, manufacturing and services, the companies that met the five profile factors above also had financial advantages compared with other companies in the study that did not meet the profile. Specifically, compared with organizations weak on these dimensions, high-performance organizations were higher by the following percentages:

- Revenue growth + 10%
- Profitability + 29%
- Return on assets + 7%
- Return on equity + 17%
- Return on investment + 20%
- Return on sales + 11%
- Total shareholder return + 23%

The bottom line is that service excellence pays. And we can identify the types of leadership and organizational characteristics that lead to high performance and thus to long-term financial success. These are the characteristics of great companies like Toyota.

THE TOYOTA WAY TO SERVICE EXCELLENCE

As we consider the Toyota Way to Service Excellence, what we are thinking about is how whole systems can continuously improve the way they add value to customers. We are thinking about a management and business philosophy, not a simple tool kit. As you read this book, we will clarify and expand on what we mean by service excellence the Toyota Way. When we use the term "lean," it broadly speaks to service excellence including the following characteristcs:

- The ideal is always continuous flow of value to the customer without waste.
- Continuous improvement means both small steps and breakthroughs coming from innovative thinking.
- Organizations respect people enough to invest in developing them.

The application of lean concepts must be tailored to the individual organization:

- Specific countermeasures to problems will be different for different types of service processes and service organizations.
- Service organizations always include both routine processes that can be standardized and nonroutine processes that require different approaches to improvement.
- In the end there are no lean solutions, but rather ways of leading that engage everyonc in continuous improvement toward a vision of excellence.

KEY POINTS
WHAT IS SERVICE EXCELLENCE?

1. "Services" is a broad category of different types of organizations with different purposes:
   - Services may be intangible and consumed at the point of sale, such as hair styling, surgery, or personal training, or may supply more tangible public needs that are stored, such as electricity or water for your home.
   - Some services are knowledge intensive with a heavy human element, such as creating a piece of software, and others arc more repetitive and transactional, such as getting a mortgage or underwriting an insurance policy.
   - All manufacturing organizations include service portions, and virtually all service organizations handle physical goods in a way that is similar to manufacturing. We urge you to think about work in terms of complexity rather than whether it is manufacturing or services:

- **Customized work.** How routine (steps, sequence, time) is the service provided (low) versus how specific is it to the unique situation (high)?
- **Intangibility of work.** How much can we physically see the transformation process (low) versus how much do we need abstract ways to describe it (high)?

2. We introduced four different types of service organizations that become more complex as we move from mass goods distribution to personalized service experiences:
   - **Mass goods distribution (tangible—low customization).** Examples: fast-food restaurant, movie on our computer, a book delivered to our house from Amazon.
   - **Standard experience delivery (intangible—low customization).** Examples: routine medical checkup, routine bank transaction, group exercise class.
   - **Personalized goods distribution (tangible—higher customization).** Examples: boutique clothing store making clothes to order, meal in a gourmet restaurant, customized software.
   - **Personalized experience (intangible—higher customization).** Examples: personal training, luxury vacations.

3. What is service excellence?
   - **Mass goods distribution.** Functionality, reliability, low cost, and convenience.
   - **Standard experience.** Same as for mass goods distribution but with the addition of "a human touch" and respectful treatment.
   - **Personalized goods distribution.** Specialized products that solve customers' problems.
   - **Personalized experience.** Luxury: VIP treatment with over-the-top, wow service experiences.
   - **"Good" companies offer the best service they can.** Excellent companies work continuously and systematically to improve that service to satisfy customers.

Chapter 2

The Toyota Way Continues to Evolve

The Toyota Way 2001 is an ideal, a standard and a guiding beacon for the people of the global Toyota organization. It expresses the beliefs and values shared by all of us.

—Fujio Cho, former Toyota president

INTRODUCTION

In the last chapter we learned that the concept of a "service organization" is more complex than it might first appear, including both routine processes that seem similar to manufacturing and complex, customized processes that defy simple recipes. We learned that the most highly rated service organizations have some common features, including a heavy emphasis on developing leaders, teamwork, and continuous improvement. We defined excellence as a process of striving to better serve each customer. The best organizations do not see excellence as an accomplishment, like something you can get an award for achieving, but rather as a continual process of striving to get better.

Now let's return to Toyota to see how it builds the culture behind excellence. We will use as an example the Toyota Way in sales and marketing.

Toyota is the most valuable brand in the automotive industry and consistently leads the industry by almost any measure of quality, reputation, and financial performance. Perhaps because of its remarkable long-term success, the biggest fear of every Toyota president is complacency. As we saw in the Prologue, the Toyota Way philosophy driving the entire company is summarized in two pillars—respect for people and continuous improvement. Toyota leaders truly believe that if they focus intensively and continuously on these pillars, every other type of success will follow. And Toyota also knows that it is not enough to create this culture of improvement in the manufacturing portion of the company. Just as critical are those functions that would be viewed as service organizations if they were stand-alone companies: sales, marketing, purchasing, finance, accounting, strategic planning, information technology, service parts, research and development, and, of course, human resource management, for example. For Toyota, the challenge is how to drive the passion and skills to respect people and continuously improve in all areas of the business throughout an organization of over 340,000 people in sites around the world.

Over the last 40 years we have observed Toyota mature from a Japanese company with overseas branches to a global company with a common company culture that respects national differences. The Toyota Way mostly came naturally in Japan. Documenting the Toyota Way was primarily intended to develop overseas managers and team members.

In this chapter we will describe the long-term, intensive process that Toyota has used to develop a global culture of striving for excellence. It defies the quick-fix turnarounds that we all too often see associated with lean transformation, and we believe that it is a useful model that any service organization can learn from. We will then present an evolved model of the Toyota Way for services that builds on my original 4P model—philosophy, process, people, and problem solving.

DEVELOPING TOYOTA LEADERS AS COACHES: THREE WAVES

Developing people is the number one responsibility of every Toyota leader from the president to the team leader on the shop floor. *The Toyota Way to Lean Leadership* provides a detailed account about how Toyota leaders are developed to be coaches. By coaches we mean they are responsible for developing both the technical skills to do the work and the social and technical skills to lead improvement.

There are certainly many administrative tasks that managers must handle, such as meeting budgets, hiring, doing performance appraisals, and participating in business decisions, but for Toyota these form only the baseline of management. In fact, Volvo's Einar Gudmundsson, introduced in Chapter 1, quickly concluded that only time at the gemba reflecting and working on improvement was value added. When they measured the amount of time his management team spent at the gemba improving the flow of work, it barely registered—less than 1 percent of the time spent. He set an immediate target of 10 hours per manager per week, which required eliminating a lot of non-value-added administrative tasks. The long-term goal was 70 percent of a manager's time at the gemba acting as a coach to facilitate improvement.

Of course, sending people to the gemba to add value is a bit like sending novices into the wilderness to learn to fend for themselves. What will they do? How will they learn? There is a definite skill set that is needed to be productive at the gemba (the place where work is done) when you are not personally doing the core work. As Mike Rother concluded in *Toyota Kata*, there are three steps to the process of learning any complex skill, and this led to three waves of training within Toyota (Figure 2.1): (1) *aware of it*—learning the principles of the Toyota Way, (2) *able to do it*—learning Toyota Business Practices (TBP) as the

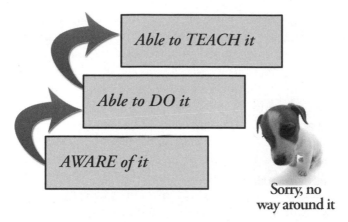

Figure 2.1 Developing a manager as a coach of continuous improvement at the gemba
Source: Mike Rother

concrete method for putting the Toyota Way principles into action, and (3) *able to teach it*—learning On-the-Job Development (OJD) as the means of coaching learners through Toyota Business Practices.

Wave 1: Teaching the Principles of the Toyota Way

By 2001, Toyota culture was fairly mature in most global regions. Still, unlike most companies that do not invest so deeply in developing people, every Toyota leader, even those with decades in the company, was required to go through Toyota Way training that lasted months, not days.

Like all of Toyota's major training efforts, *The Toyota Way 2001* training was developed and implemented using a similar sequence of steps:

1. The program went through intense development with pilot testing and kaizen until it was considered to be of sufficient quality to spread broadly (typically a one-year process).
2. Senior executives were trained first. Several days of classroom training were followed by a six- to eight-month period of practical application. During this period, the learners analyzed a case study requiring them to apply the principles of the Toyota Way outside the classroom. Several weeks later they reported back to discuss the case and agree on a project, which was then undertaken with a coach. At the executive level the training was intentionally cross-national to encourage global networking. Projects were undertaken locally.

3. After completing the period of practical application, the senior executives presented a report out of the project to an examining board composed of even more senior executives and subject-matter experts. Often some additional work on the project needed to be completed in order to pass.

4. After passing, the senior executives then took part in training their direct reports, including becoming part of the board of examiners as it was deployed within their organization.

5. As the training cascaded from level to level, every executive, and manager went through the same program, including classroom training, the completion of hands-on projects supervised by a coach, and the presentation of project report-outs to a board of examiners. At lower levels the scope of the projects was more limited and may only have taken three to four months to complete instead of the eight months taken by senior executives.

Deploying the Toyota Way training this way was a long-term undertaking. Working down through the organization level by level, with the people at each level becoming the mentors for those who reported to them, took about six years to complete. And as new locations are added globally and new executives are hired, there is still a need to continue the Toyota Way training.

Wave 2: Toyota Business Practices to Put the Theory into Action

Because the Toyota Way training was designed to teach principles rather than a specific methodology, the link to action was a bit tenuous, and Fujio Cho still saw a gap in the depth of understanding he expected. It became clear that even with the application of theory through case studies and projects, there was something missing—the skill development that only comes from action. This realization resulted in the development of a second wave of training—Toyota Business Practices. Fujio Cho explained this as the "concrete method for putting the Toyota Way into action." Many will recognize TBP as an eight-step problem-solving process (see Figure 2.2).

Notice that TBP follows the famous improvement process of Plan-Do-Check-Act, or PDCA. The development of PDCA is often attributed to Dr. Deming, who alternatively called it Plan-Do-Study-Act. The critical insight is that all "plans" are provisional and actually represent hypotheses being tested. From a scientific viewpoint the plans are theories until we test them by running experiments.[1] Unfortunately, in too many organizations we see lean "experts" who presume they know what the problem is and how to solve it. This disease of certainty discourages experimenting with alternative approaches, and it truncates the

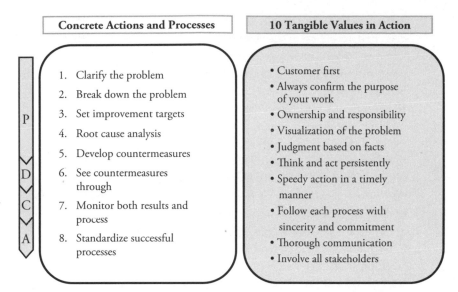

| Concrete Actions and Processes | 10 Tangible Values in Action |

P
D
C
A

1. Clarify the problem
2. Break down the problem
3. Set improvement targets
4. Root cause analysis
5. Develop countermeasures
6. See countermeasures through
7. Monitor both results and process
8. Standardize successful processes

- Customer first
- Always confirm the purpose of your work
- Ownership and responsibility
- Visualization of the problem
- Judgment based on facts
- Think and act persistently
- Speedy action in a timely manner
- Follow each process with sincerity and commitment
- Thorough communication
- Involve all stakeholders

Figure 2.2 In Toyota Business Practices, problem solving and people development go hand in hand

Source: Toyota Motor Corporation

opportunities for learning. The Do-Check-Act is running the experiment, checking the results, and reflecting on what has been learned.

In fact, the first five steps of TBP are all planning—establishing the hypothesis. We start with a broad definition of the problem based on identifying the ideal state and comparing it with the current state. We study the current state in detail through data and direct observation, going to and studying the gemba. We recognize that the ideal state is unachievable, so we break down the megaproblem into smaller, tractable problems that still represent major challenges, then set targets for improvement. We do our best to understand the root cause of the gap between the current state and our targets, recognizing that the root cause is our best-informed guess, and then develop a set of possible countermeasures that we believe may bring us closer to the target. The countermeasures are the hypotheses that we are directly testing by doing, then checking, and then taking further action such as standardizing what works. Let's consider each of the steps of TBP:

1. **Clarify the problem relative to the ideal (Plan).** Few problem-solving efforts start with defining the ideal state. By defining the ideal state first, TBP pulls the problem solver out of the present situation and its seemingly intractable problems and focuses her on envisioning what the process could be like if it were functioning to perfection. As well as envisioning a

perfect future state, in order to clarify the problem relative to the ideal, a deep understanding of the current state must be developed. And the only way to do this is by going to directly study the gemba, the place where the problems are occurring, so that the gaps between the ideal and reality become glaring.

2. **Break down the problem into manageable pieces (Plan).** In Step 2, the problem is broken down into challenging but achievable pieces. Although the ideal state is envisioned in Step 1, there is also an understanding that the ideal is probably unachievable. At first it may seem ridiculous to set blue-sky images of the ideal, but in reality that vision provides the direction, or true north. As the problem is broken down into smaller, attainable challenges, the path toward true north becomes clearer.

3. **Set targets (Plan).** In Step 3, specific targets are set. What do we expect to accomplish? These targets need to stretch beyond what seems achievable based on what is known today. Some would call these stretch targets.

4. **Root cause analysis (Plan).** In Step 4, the gaps that have been identified to work on are analyzed. "Why" is asked multiple times in order to get below the surface of the problem to unearth the underlying reason for the problem so that the root cause can be attacked.

5. **Develop countermeasures (Plan).** In Step 5, countermeasures to root causes are identified. These are not "solutions" since we do not know if they will work. They are our best guesses about what might reduce the gap between the target and the actual condition. A number of ideas are generated. Some of these ideas might come from benchmarking others who have solved similar problems, but they still remain only hypotheses until they are tested and refined in practice.

6. **See countermeasures through (Do).** In Step 6, the problem solver finally gets to do something. One at a time, some of the countermeasures that were generated in Step 5 are tried out in reality. This is "speedy action in a timely manner." Note, however, that the rigor of Steps 1 to 5 ensures that the countermeasures being tested are not just shots in the dark. Testing these countermeasures is an iterative process following rapid PDCA cycles trying each idea, checking what happens, and defining further action based on what is learned.

7. **Monitor both results and process (Check).** Step 7 goes beyond simply checking the final score to see if the end result is what was expected. In Step 7, the problem solver is checking constantly to see whether the experiments are moving the outcome toward the target results that were set in Step 3, and the problem solver is also checking the process being used to achieve those results. In Toyota it is commonly said that achieving results without a good process is simply luck.

8. **Standardize successful processes, adjust, and spread (Act).** Step 8 is sometimes called "learn," as it is the step in which the problem solver reflects and consolidates findings and determines what to do with what has been learned from the experiments. What actions will be taken next? What is working that should be standardized? What areas need further work? What should be shared with others so the organization can learn?

The training process for TBP was virtually identical to *Toyota Way 2001* training—a few days of classroom training followed by the completion of a project and a presentation to a board of examiners. Again, TBP training was cascaded down from the senior executive level and this time down to the group leaders on the floor. I visited the truck plant in Princeton, Indiana, during the Great Recession when about half the workforce was not building vehicles. This was viewed as a perfect opportunity to train in many areas, including Toyota Business Practices. It was also eight years after TBP was first introduced.

Some might think that Toyota is rather slow in taking eight years to roll out a program that many companies would complete within one year or less by running three- to five-day workshops and then sending people off to do an unsupervised project. The reality is that Toyota is not slow, but serious. Fujio Cho was serious that this was the concrete method for learning the Toyota Way— learning by doing, with a coach. Any complex skill requires practice with a coach to correct deviations from the proper method. And TBP continues to be central to the company today.

In Figure 2.2, to the right of the eight steps of TBP, we see 10 tangible values in action. As each of the eight steps is being pursued, the coach is reinforcing those values. For example, in order to clarify the problem, the needs of the customers, both internal and external, must be put first. What do they want? What do they need? How do you know that? Did you go and see firsthand to understand your customers? The coach will question the learners relentlessly until they have satisfactorily understood the customers and the broader purpose of the project and until what they have learned is reflected in the problem definition. The learners do not move on to Step 2 until there is a thorough understanding of Step 1. The learners continue to deepen their knowledge as they are coached day by day.

Take, for example, Steve St. Angelo, who had earned his way to become the second American president of Toyota's plant in Georgetown, Kentucky. As it turned out, he had a Latin American background and had run a plant in Latin America when he worked for General Motors. For his project, Steve elected to develop a long-term strategy for growing share in the Mexican market. With the help of his coach, he thoroughly explored the Mexican market to understand customers, the culture, Mexican politics, the economic environment present and forecasted, and more. He worked hard for eight months, over and above his president's role. Ultimately the strategy that he developed in his TBP project became the basis for Toyota's strategy for Mexico. And it seems fitting that he was selected to be the first CEO of Toyota of Latin America, allowing him to put into practice all that he had learned.

In some parts of Toyota, it is expected that immediately after every promotion, a new TPB project is completed. Not only does this continue to renew the depth of skill in improvement and the core values, but it also provides a powerful way to learn about the new job. For Toyota, problem solving is the way that the company improves to new levels of performance and develops as a learning organization.

Wave 3: On-the-Job Development to Learn How to Coach Leaders

Just as a master would teach an apprentice in the days of small craft shops, the natural way of learning in Toyota is through On-the-Job Development, or learning by being coached by a master teacher, usually your manager. However, in the past there was no handbook for the master teacher, and individual teachers developed their students in their own way. Toyota changed this by 2008.

North America was selected as the global pilot for developing OJD training. Outside of Japan, North America was the most advanced in learning the Toyota Way and could identify with others globally who were learning it for the first time. The Japanese coordinators had done remarkably well teaching the Toyota Way, but they had never had to learn about Toyota culture explicitly—all their learning was implicit as tacit knowledge passed on through daily living in the company. For this reason the United States and Canada had in some ways become better at formally teaching the Toyota Way.

The responsibility for developing the OJD training program went to Latondra Newton (now group vice president of Toyota North America), then general manager of the Team Member Development Center. The OJD program her team developed in 2007 required, as a prerequisite, TBP training. In TBP training the students learned to lead a major improvement project and had responsibility for developing team members through the process. Now OJD training would elevate this to another level, as the OJD students would be expected to coach a person leading a TBP project and the team.

Latondra's team developed a four-step model for OJD that followed the PDCA process:

1. **Pick a problem with your team (Plan).** The problem is selected with the leader's coach, the OJD student, in order to stretch the leader's under-

standing of how to develop suitable work to support the company plan (we will discuss this in Chapter 9 as "hoshin kanri").

2. **Appropriately divide the work among accountable team members and make the direction compelling (Plan).** The leader being coached by the OJD student then must both convey the purpose of each objective so that the work is meaningful to the team members and assign the right work to the right team members to stretch their capabilities. It is critical that the tasks and targets be carefully assigned based on each individual's capability so they are achievable but also stretch, grow, and develop each person.

3. **Execute within broad boundaries, monitor, and coach (Do and Check).** This is the phase in which the leader being coached by the OJD student is actually going through the steps of TBP. The leader must constantly observe how team members are carrying out the work, understanding what issues they are dealing with. If they are not meeting expectations, the leader must be able to identify why they are not performing up to the standard and take the right countermeasures to motivate them to complete the work to standard. According to Latondra:

   > Maybe what is unique to Toyota's way is there is a mindset of allowing the team members, if there is a direct line from point A to B, to waver toward the outer limits of what might be acceptable on the job such that you have coaching opportunities with them when they approach those outer limits. If they are going in the wrong direction, you allow them to go not too far off the beaten path and then use it as a teaching moment to get them back on the right track.

4. **Feedback, recognition, and reflection (Act).** The leader must provide a sense of achievement as the team is reaching the goal. How is each team member's work being evaluated? How are the team members being given feedback for improvement? How is recognition of achievement being provided when the goal is achieved? The leader being trained should also be reflecting regularly with feedback from the OJD coach on what she can do better next time, thus completing the PDCA process.

The training process itself was based on experiential learning with little classroom lecturing. The first step was a web-based simulation tool that leaders completed at their own computers prior to the class. The simulation was made with actual production team members using real problems in the plants. In order to familiarize the students with the four-step model, students were given a description of the problem and a series of multiple-choice questions. On the basis of their answers, they were then shown video scenarios, acted out by team members, of what happened as a result of their choices. They would be taken down successful or unsuccessful paths and could then backtrack and try again to see what would have happened if they selected a different choice.

Next came classroom training, also based on the four steps, in which students were engaged in role-playing different scenarios and then reflecting and getting feedback. With the high level of diversity in America, it was critical for the leaders to tailor the work assignments and their approach to coaching for each individual. The classroom training included a module on emotional intelligence and emphasized understanding the background and perspective of the person being coached.

The final assignment for the individual OJD students was a project to be completed in their home plant in which they deliberately coached one person in their group through leading an improvement project using TBP. Figure 2.3 shows an OJD student learning to coach the TBP project leader. The leader being developed in OJD had to use the four steps as taught and get feedback and coaching from the supervisor (who already completed the training) and from a member of Newton's team who was assigned to the region. The final evaluation was based on the student's reflection, feedback from the person she coached, and input from her supervisor.

Figure 2.3 On-the-Job Development student is learning to coach the leader of a Toyota Business Practices project

OJD training in North America started in 2008. Since there were a lot of layers to coach and a broad set of functions including manufacturing, sales, engineering, and all administration to train, it was a slow process taking years. As the top leadership passed the course, they were responsible for taking over the training of the course and continuing the coaching process internally. The training was highly successful. In fact, it was so successful that it quickly began to spread to other regions, including to Japan, The training was greatly appreciated and got comments like "For the first time I really understand the Toyota Way in practice."

THE TOYOTA WAY IN SALES AND MARKETING

For decades in Japan, Toyota Motor Sales, Inc., was a separate corporation from Toyota Motor Company, Inc. In response to antitrust regulations, these two parts of the company were separated in 1950 and the sales organization was not reunited with Toyota Motor Company, Inc., until 1982.

In the United States, prior to 2015, Toyota Motors Sales, U.S.A., Inc., continued to be a separate subsidiary with a separate location in Torrance, California. North American engineering and manufacturing team members saw the sales team members as living in an ivory tower in a pristine office complex that looked more like a university campus than a manufacturing site. Toyota executives had a vision of a unified Toyota Way culture and in 2015 began the move of both Toyota Engineering and Manufacturing and Toyota Motors Sales to a new campus in Plano, Texas.

While the Toyota Way model itself is generic, Toyota believed there was value for creating some specialized booklets and training for nonmanufacturing areas. *The Toyota Way in Sales and Marketing* was also introduced by Fujio Cho in 2001. Over time, other booklets were introduced for accounting, purchasing, human resource management, and other functions. Let's consider the sales and marketing document as an example of how the Toyota Way is applied to a pure service organization.

The Toyota Way in Sales and Marketing introduces a 5P model of *purpose, principles, people, process,* and *problem solving.* Although, on the surface, this may appear to be a somewhat different model, it is derived from the same general concepts of respect for people and continuous improvement (see Figure 2.4). As they are described in *The Toyota Way in Sales and Marketing* booklet, the 5Ps are:

1. **Purpose: Connecting to the fundamental idea of Toyota.** This includes the customer is number one and better car value through the "3Cs for harmonious growth"—communication, consideration, and cooperation.

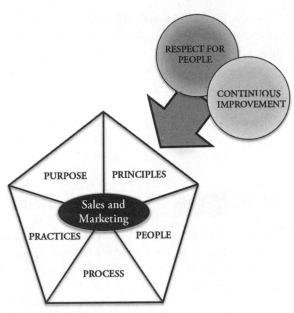

Figure 2.4 *The Toyota Way in Sales and Marketing* 5P model

2. **Principles: Connecting to the vision and mission.** The vision and mission are summarized in Figure 2.5. Note that sales and marketing contribute to developing lifetime customers and act as the radar for all of Toyota: "We need to convey appropriate information to *all of Toyota*, including suppliers, research and development, as well as the production side. In other words, our mission is to research and understand potential customer needs." One positive outcome of Toyota's recall crisis of 2009 was a resurgence of the role of Toyota Motor Sales, North America, in transmitting customer needs throughout Toyota. For example, the service call center had invaluable intelligence about the customer, information that had been mostly ignored but was now in great demand as engineering and manufacturing took up the challenge of being more responsive to customers.

3. **People: Connecting to and respecting our most important assets.** Former president Eiji Toyoda is quoted in the booklet: "People are the most important asset of Toyota and the determinant of the rise and fall of Toyota." The model for people is shown in Figure 2.6. Interestingly, the model also connects people to the Toyota Production System (TPS) concept of "just-in-time," describing a balance between "two opposing themes of providing *fast and flexible* response to customers and building sales mechanisms that are

Figure 2.5 *The Toyota Way in Sales and Marketing* principles connect to the Toyota Motor Sales vision and mission

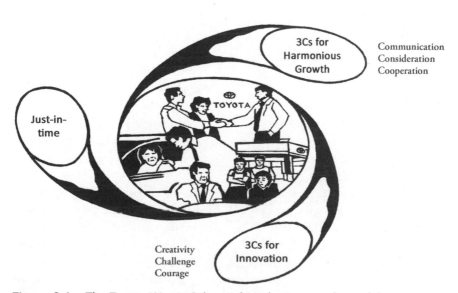

Figure 2.6 *The Toyota Way in Sales and Marketing* people model

efficient and waste free." As we will see in our chapter on processes, giving customers exactly what they want, when they want it, and having efficient, stable work patterns can sometimes require trade-offs. When he first became president, Shoichiro Toyoda introduced the earlier-mentioned 3Cs for harmonious growth (communication, consideration, and cooperation) and the 3Cs for innovation—creativity, challenge, and courage, which are central to *The Toyota Way 2001* values of challenge and kaizen. He gave a distinctively Toyota-like definition of the third C—courage:

> *It is most important to take the relevant factors in all situations into careful, close consideration, and to have the courage to make clear decisions and carry them out boldly. The more uncertain the future is, the more important it is to have this courage.*

4. **Process: Connecting to recommended strategies for satisfying customers.** All processes in Toyota should be customer-focused, whether on an internal customer (for example, R&D is a customer of sales during product development) or on an external customer who purchases a product or service. We see the general processes that sales and marketing are responsible for, such as "obtain necessary information quickly and easily" from the customer's viewpoint, in Figure 2.7. There is a good deal of detail below each of these steps in the booklet. For example, a way to

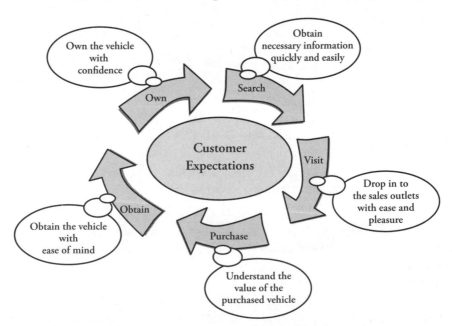

Figure 2.7 *The Toyota Way in Sales and Marketing* generic processes

deliver on a positive purchasing experience is through "Toyota Touch Customer Care," which symbolizes the special feeling customers should have in any dealings with Toyota, and is defined as "Customers will experience pressure-free and pleasant purchasing. By ensuring that every customer contact is of the highest quality, we can create a Toyota advocate."

Toyota Touch is very dependent on the dealers, and since these are independent businesses, Toyota takes responsibility for careful selection and development of dealers. This paid off during the recall crisis when these independent businesses throughout the United States went the extra mile to take care of customers, even when the problems had nothing to do with recalled components. And the company was rewarded with over 85 percent of Toyota owners reporting, during the worst months of the negative journalistic coverage of the crisis, that they trusted Toyota, believed in the safety of their vehicles, and would recommend a Toyota to their friends.[2] As well, we would expect sales and marketing processes to fit common perspectives of lean management, and this is emphasized in two regards:

- Supply Toyota value quickly and precisely with high quality (analogous to the TPS pillar of built-in quality).
- Exclude *muri* (overburden), *muda* (waste), and *mura* (unevenness).

5. **Practices: Connecting to actions and measures to ensure market success.** This is by far the most detailed section of the booklet, and there is a heavy emphasis on guidelines for partnership with dealers: "Set up dealer networks for pleasure, convenience, and high value and provide integrated 3S services (sales, spare parts, service), engaging in direct communication with customers to develop a long-term relationship." I once talked to the owner of a Toyota dealership who also owned an American automaker's dealership. The American automaker, he explained, "sent people to check on sales and push me to purchase undesirable vehicles that were not selling well. Toyota sent people to educate and inform me." He shared with me his shelves of Toyota training materials and a monthly document Toyota prepared that detailed the local automotive market conditions.

There are many models in the practices section describing guidelines for how Toyota and its dealers will work together to develop customers for life, but one comprehensive figure that ties together the intimate connections among Toyota, dealers, and customers is shown in Figure 2.8.

Of course, no Toyota document would be complete without an emphasis on the "continuous practice of kaizen" through the PDCA cycle (see Figure 2.9). This is communicated to the sales and marketing community in a powerful way

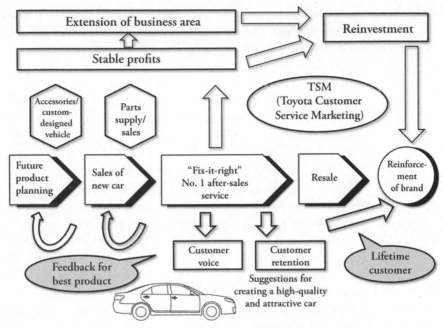

Figure 2.8 *The Toyota Way in Sales and Marketing* integrated practices

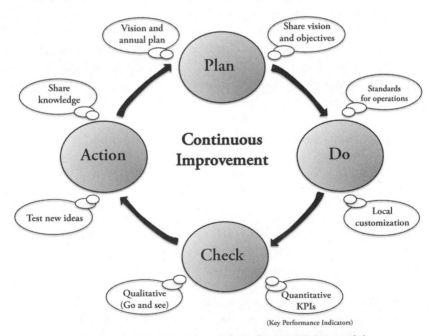

Figure 2.9 *The Toyota Way in Sales and Marketing* PDCA model

that emphasizes the desired way of thinking—shared objectives, customization rather than the blind copying of best practices, evaluation that is both quantitative and qualitative, and shared knowledge and know-how:

Plan. Share our objectives through our common format and process.

Do. Develop and customize the Toyota standard for local operations.

Check. Evaluate operations from qualitative (go and see) and quantitative (key performance indicators) points of view.

Act. Share the knowledge and the know-how throughout all of Toyota and further develop our methods.

Toyota trains its dealers (independent businesses) in technical and business skills and Toyota Way thinking. For example, a consultant contracted by Toyota's regional sales office comes to the Dunning Toyota dealership in Ann Arbor, Michigan, one day each month to help the dealership establish Toyota Express Maintenance—services like oil changes and tire rotation while you wait. The starting point was to improve the throughput and efficiency of routine maintenance through standard work, work groups, better presentation of parts and tools, visual management, and other methods. There are a series of phases to the training that can take several years for the dealer to complete. This is an intense process with strict checks by the consultant to be sure the improvements are made and sustained. The results of the transformation have been stunning, opening the eyes of the owners of the dealerships. The dealership pays for this intensive mentoring, but as long as the folks at the dealership do the work, the dealership gets reimbursed by Toyota.

LIKER'S TOYOTA WAY 4P MODEL ADAPTED FOR SERVICE ORGANIZATIONS

In the book *The Toyota Way*, after studying Toyota for 20 years and carefully studying *The Toyota Way 2001*, I developed my own model of the underlying thinking. Karyn drew it as a house shown in Figure 2.10. The 4Ps are:

1. **Philosophy.** What is the purpose of our organization? In excellent companies this always goes beyond enriching owners of the business. Customers do not pay to enrich owners. What will the organization contribute to customers better than anyone else? What are the organization's core values? What is important to the organization as a minisociety?

2. **Process.** The ideal process from the customer's point of view is always one-piece flow: the customer orders exactly what he wants or needs, and it comes immediately, as it is needed, in the amount it is needed. Customers pay for value added, not for extra activities that involve people or things

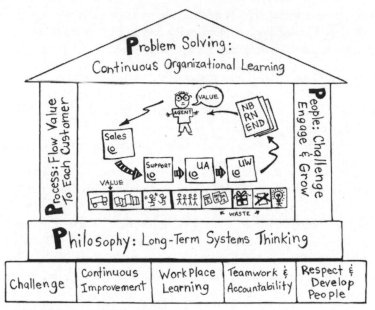

Figure 2.10   Liker's Toyota Way 4P model

Adapted from: Jeffrey Liker, *The Toyota Way*, McGraw Hill: NY, 2004.
Note: The example is from insurance underwriting. UW = Underwriter; UA = Underwriting Assistant;
NB = New Business; RN = Renewal

waiting, or work being done over because of defects, or extraneous material or information being generated. Internally, one-piece flow means continuous value-added work from step to step. There are some guidelines on the best way to accomplish this, such as working in a leveled way, without huge peaks and valleys in the workload. Technology can be important to the process, but it is not the process. The process needs to be carefully designed and then improved as conditions change and as we learn more.

3. **People.** Every mission statement I have ever read talks about how important people in the organization are, but the organization rarely treats people as the most valued resource. In most companies, people are "empowered" by giving them training and resources and "getting out of their way." In the Toyota Way that is considered downright disrespectful. People need to be simultaneously challenged to stretch to new levels of performance and coached so they can learn and be successful, the essence of OJD. At Toyota, it is actively developing people, not leaving them on their own, that shows how important people are in the organization and how much they are respected.

4. **Problem solving.** This is a term you hear constantly within Toyota, but our usual image of what it means to solve a problem is a shell of the intended meaning. We often think of problem solving as reactive. The dam is leaking, so plug the hole. As we saw with TBP, the team member in Toyota needs to start by asking, "What is the purpose of the dam?" Answer: "A regulated flow of water." "What would be the ideal state?" Answer: "Water flows without interruption only at the volume and speed we need." "How can I get closer to this ideal?" And so it continues. Problem solving then becomes aspirational rather than reactive and leads to innovation rather than quick fixes. Problem solving becomes a process of learning, which, when shared appropriately, builds a learning organization.

Many have found the 4P model valuable in thinking through how to structure lean transformations. My proudest moment was in a meeting with Eiji Toyoda, the family scion who grew the company from a small Japanese automaker for the home market to a global powerhouse. On his desk he had copies of *The Toyota Way* in both English and Japanese. He said: "You structured our thinking so well, and explained it better then we have, and I told all of our executives to read this book because we are not as good as what you describe. We still have a long way to go to live up to your explanations." I was glowing for months after that meeting.

Nonetheless, in the spirit of continuous improvement, we took a look at this decade-old model, and after thinking about how it applied to services, we improved upon it (see Figure 2.11). The original model, derived from manufacturing, was a bit overweight on process and underweight in the other areas. Here is a summary of the major changes discussed in detail in the chapters for each of the 4Ps:

1. **Philosophy.** In *The Toyota Way* I emphasized that living a philosophy requires long-term thinking, even at the expense of short-term financial considerations. We still believe this is the critical starting point. Organizations that focus on the short term expect any investment they make to have an immediate return on investment (ROI), even investments in people. In addition, they tend to think of discrete improvement of independent processes rather than improving the overall system of serving customers. The Toyota Way is based on systems thinking. How can we integrate processes, people, and problem solving to add ever increasing value to our customers? What will set us apart from the competition? This will change over time. To deliver on the strategy requires adaptable people who are continually improving the processes critical for the strategy. This is where culture and values come in. While strategies and business models can change, values are the bedrock of the company and rarely change. Investing in people, culture, and capability to deliver on a well-thought-out strategy

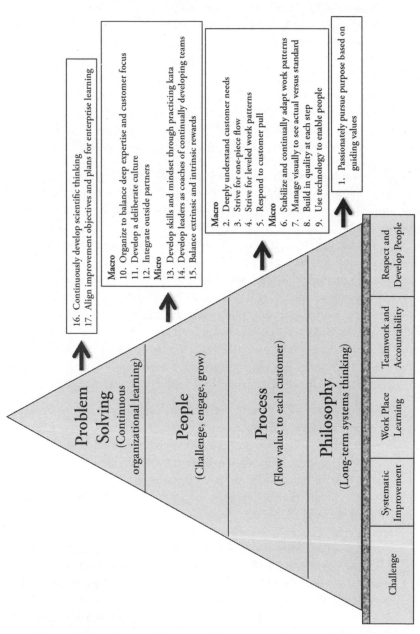

Figure 2.11 Toyota Way to service excellence 4P model

Problem Solving
(Continuous organizational learning)

16. Continuously develop scientific thinking
17. Align improvement objectives and plans for enterprise learning

People
(Challenge, engage, grow)

Macro
10. Organize to balance deep expertise and customer focus
11. Develop a deliberate culture
12. Integrate outside partners
Micro
13. Develop skills and mindset through practicing kata
14. Develop leaders as coaches of continually developing teams
15. Balance extrinsic and intrinsic rewards

Process
(Flow value to each customer)

Macro
2. Deeply understand customer needs
3. Strive for one-piece flow
4. Strive for leveled work patterns
5. Respond to customer pull
Micro
6. Stabilize and continually adapt work patterns
7. Manage visually to see actual versus standard
8. Build in quality at each step
9. Use technology to enable people

Philosophy
(Long-term systems thinking)

1. Passionately pursue purpose based on guiding values

Challenge	Systematic Improvement	Work Place Learning	Teamwork and Accountability	Respect and Develop People

is a long-term endeavor. Organizations that account for success quarterly do not stand a chance of building true capability for service excellence.

2. **Process.** We have found it useful to distinguish between process improvements at the macrolevel and microlevel. At the macrolevel, we are focusing on the enterprise, where improvements have to be led by senior management. The popular tool of value-stream mapping looks at how material and information flow at the macrolevel, beginning with the current state and then developing a vision of the desired future state. Value-stream mapping considers the architecture of the value stream—a 30,000-foot view—starting with the customers and understanding what they want, how much, and when and working backward to design how key processes need to function to achieve our value-stream objectives. This leads directly to what is needed from our suppliers to keep value flowing seamlessly from suppliers through our processes to our customers.

   The macroview is necessarily an abstraction—a theoretical image of what we would like to achieve. To put this vision into practice, it needs to be broken down to the microlevel. This is where detailed design is done and where we adapt as we experience daily obstacles and work to overcome them. The heavy lifting of continuous improvement happens at the microlevel by team members throughout the enterprise. They too are signing up for challenging objectives, understanding the current state, developing future state visions, and then, through daily PDCA, getting closer and closer to the vision.

3. **People.** We also find it useful to divide the way we manage and develop people into the macrolevel and microlevel. Too often we have found ourselves working with clients exclusively at the microlevel—focusing on small portions of value streams and individual processes. This is a more manageable way to learn the disciplined approach of daily PDCA, but we soon reach the limits of progress. In *Lean Thinking*, Womack and Jones[3] argued that we should organize around value streams with a role they called value-stream managers. There are many organizational design options, but we believe, over the long term, it is important to think about macrolevel design of the organization and human resource systems and make regular adjustments as we learn. An example is companies that find there is too much insulated focus within vertical functional chimneys—specialists talking to each other—and not enough customer-focus across the horizontal value stream. Matrix organization, or even organization around product families, may be necessary to generate the needed customer focus.

4. **Problem solving.** At the microlevel we have discussed TBP as the way individual leaders approach challenging stretch objectives. These objec-

tives need to be aligned to the company strategy. Hoshin kanri, aka policy deployment, is a system to provide that alignment. PDCA must take place at all levels and be aligned from the enterprise to organizational unit to work-group level. And the focus of improvement must be aligned with a clearly articulated business strategy.

THE TOYOTA WAY AS ONE VISION FOR PURSUING EXCELLENCE

The Toyota Way is not an enterprise model to be tuned to your organization and then rolled out. Principles are not recipes that can be installed in our organization as we would download standard software on our computer. Principles provide conceptual models but will not establish the patterns of thinking and acting needed for continuous improvement.

When Toyota executives in Japan realized they needed a standard way to develop their unique culture outside Japan, they began with the *Toyota Way 2001* principles, but they quickly concluded that teaching these was insufficient. When they analyzed the core competencies required of everyone in the company, it came down to the ability to continuously improve toward challenging objectives. This led to the development of Toyota Business Practices, the standard eight-step approach to improvement (described earlier in the chapter). They then realized that they needed coaches to teach TBP and that these coaches needed to be embedded in the very organizations they were teaching. Teaching needed to be on the job and continuous. The only logical choice was to create an expectation that all managers are coaches of continuous improvement, and the company developed OJD as the third phase of the program to train the managers to coach the leaders of teams striving to meet defined targets.

Underlying the Toyota Way is a mindset. It is not a mysterious mindset unique to Japanese culture. It is a universal mindset of scientific thinking. Teachers like Dr. Deming were taken seriously, and Toyota learned the benefit of the simple, yet elusive, scientific method of Plan-Do-Check-Act. The company learned the power of managing by fact. It learned that problem solving is superior to people blaming. And it learned that serving customers meant seeking to stay a step ahead of them, anticipating their needs, and then focusing on building work streams to deliver value unimpeded by stagnation of the product or service. Flowing value to each customer became a centerpiece of the company's vision of excellence. But vision is not reality. Presidents regularly lament the danger of complacency and promise to go back to the basics of the Toyota Way. They are painfully aware that Toyota is far from perfect and pursuing excellence requires continual dedication and perseverance. It is hard work!

Any service organization can learn from this universal wisdom. Learning is not the same as imitating. We cannot imitate the specific solutions that Toyota has evolved to deliver value to its customers. Toyota does not imitate its own solutions, but each part of the company continues to evolve new and better methods. We cannot imitate the culture that Toyota has evolved and continues to evolve. We cannot imitate the specific policies and procedures. Rather we can look below the surface and learn from Toyota's way of thinking:

1. The never-ending journey of striving for excellence must be embraced deeply by the top leadership of the company.
2. Every organization must evolve its own strategy, direction, and way.
3. Leaders at all levels must be trained to use the scientific method for improvement to support the direction.
4. Training must focus primarily on doing, repeatedly, with a coach to provide corrective feedback.
5. People occupying higher levels of leadership must learn first by doing themselves and then become coaches for the next level down.
6. A sustainable chain of coaching must be established, and the chain will be as strong as the weakest link.
7. When a chain of capable managers as coaches is developed, it is then possible to develop aligned targets for improvement and expect innovative approaches to meet these targets at all levels.
8. Managers must become role models for daily management that is focused on total customer satisfaction.
9. Deviations from standards of excellence must be treated as opportunities to learn and improve how we serve customers.

This is the only pathway we know to developing a culture focused on service excellence. It is a simple recipe in theory—and a very challenging daily struggle in practice. The struggle is not in identifying waste or coming up with solutions. The struggle is to continually challenge the organization to focus, question, and learn. Simple management practices, such as going to the gemba to deeply understand the daily reality, can become monumental challenges when managers have established patterns of going everyplace else but where the work is being done. In the remainder of the book we will work our way through the 4P service excellence model in greater detail. We will continually emphasize that conceptual understanding is not the same as acting, and it is only through repeated action that we truly learn.

KEY POINTS
THE TOYOTA WAY
CONTINUES TO EVOLVE

1. The Toyota Way philosophy of respect for people and continuous improvement applies just as well to services as it does to manufacturing.
2. Turning philosophy and theory into deep understanding requires practice through doing. Toyota spread the Toyota Way, starting with senior leaders, in three waves:
   - Teaching the theory of the Toyota Way
   - Putting the principles into action through Toyota Business Practices
   - Using On-the-Job Development training to develop managers as capable coaches who teach Toyota Business Practices
3. In order to connect all areas to the vision and mission of an organization, it is important to put principles into practice throughout the enterprise; Toyota did this by spreading the Toyota Way in nonmanufacturing areas such as sales, purchasing, and R&D.
4. We have updated Liker's original Toyota Way 4P model to address the specific needs of service organizations, balancing it more evenly across the 4 Ps:
   - **Philosophy.** Delivering service excellence is a long-term philosophy, not a strategy focusing only on short-term financial rewards:
     - What is your organization's purpose, and how will the company contribute to society through the service it delivers?
   - **Process.** Processes at all organizational levels must be designed and continually refined to deliver the services that customers want, striving toward single-piece flow:
     - **Macrolevel.** The architecture of the entire value stream must support service excellence.
     - **Microlevel.** All team members throughout the enterprise must be actively engaged in seeing gaps between the desired state and the actual state of services and then working toward closing them.
   - **People.** Respecting people in an organization means challenging them to stretch to new levels of service excellence through constant coaching, not "empowering" them through training and then "getting out of their way:"
     - **Macrolevel.** Overall organizational design must support customer-focused continuous improvement and respect for people.

- **Microlevel.** Process-level PDCA, with coaching, develops team member capabilities.
- **Problem solving.** Problem-solving efforts across the organization must be aligned to deliver service excellence:
    - **Macrolevel.** Objectives are aligned to company strategy through a clearly articulated, long-term business strategy (hoshin kanri).
    - **Microlevel.** All improvement efforts support the delivery of service excellence as defined at the macrolevel.

5. The Toyota Way principles provide conceptual models to use in thinking about our own organizations—they aren't recipes to be copied, rolled out, installed, or implemented.
6. The idea is to deliberately build your company's culture to focus on actively improving value for each customer.

Chapter 3

Principle 1: Philosophy of Long-Term Systems Thinking

We want organizations to be adaptive, flexible, self-renewing, resilient, learning, intelligent—attributes found only in living systems. The tension of our times is that we want our organizations to behave as living systems, but we only know how to treat them as machines.

—Margaret J. Wheatley, *Finding Our Way: Leadership for an Uncertain Time*

PHILOSOPHY IS THE MORAL COMPASS OF THE ORGANIZATION

In 1992 I was codirecting the Japan Technology Management Program at the University of Michigan to study and transfer knowledge from Japan to the United States. We were obligated to share what we were learning through our research, so I organized a one-day conference for our funded researchers to present their findings. Each academic compared U.S. practices to Japan's practices in his or her area of expertise, e.g., electronics industry, corporate strategy, supply chain management. Unbeknown to me, one of the leading TPS experts in Toyota was in the audience quietly taking everything in. At the end of the day, he introduced himself to me and said: "Interesting presentations, but you were missing the management philosophy. . . . In the future I recommend you add more discussion of philosophy." He then graciously excused himself. At the time I was mildly offended that he did not appreciate all the great data and observations presented. Later, on reflection, I realized we had presented a hodgepodge of loosely related academic presentations and he was absolutely right. I often reflect on that simple observation about philosophy. Why is a conservative nuts-and-bolts manufacturing company so obsessed with philosophy?

Philosophy has been defined as "a system of principles for guidance in practical affairs."[1] I think of it as the moral compass of the company. What do we stand for? Why do we exist? How is our existence making the world a better place?

How will we as an institution behave in the world? *The Toyota Way 2001* documents are one way of formalizing the underlying philosophy of the company.

The founder, chairman, and CEO of Four Seasons, Isadore Sharp, entitled his book *Four Seasons: The Story of a Business Philosophy.*[2] His goal was quite simply to "build the world's best hotel company." His conclusion was that the only path to accomplishing this was to stand out among global hotels for exceptional service through the customer's eyes. He further observed that he needed to "get it down to the front line: clerks, bell staff, bartenders, waiters, cooks, housekeepers, and dishwashers, the lowest-paid and in most companies least-motivated people, but the ones who would make or break a five-star service reputation." He pulled together his general managers and explained that none of them can directly affect the customer experience—they are completely dependent on their junior employees. He then gave them both the philosophy and the challenge in one statement:

> *That's going to be your managerial challenge: reaching our goal of being the best, down to the bottom of the pyramid—motivating our lowest-paid people to act on their own, to see themselves not as routine functionaries, but as company facilitators creating our customer base.*

As we saw in the last chapter, to put a philosophy into practice requires socializing all members until the principles become a way of thinking and acting. And it is a never-ending process. Every exceptional story that I have heard about the Four Seasons, the unbelievable service that shocks new customers, involves an encounter with frontline employees. I randomly selected a Four Seasons in London and found it rated five stars based on 614 customer reviews on TripAdvisor. Customer statements included:

- "Food, service, attention to detail throughout is fantastic. I must give a special mention to Veronica who served dinner with grace and enthusiasm . . . also James in concierge, top man, and to Annabell and Caroline you are stars!!!!!"
- "Everyone is very helpful but the best service is provided by the concierge staff—they are unbelievable."
- "The service was particularly excellent—a special mention goes to Nat, my waiter—he was brilliant!"
- "The staff were friendly and super-attentive to details and all had excellent name recall. It felt like I was coming home each day."
- "Hotel staff is amongst the best I have encountered anywhere in the world. The arrival experience is fantastically welcoming, and we never have to wait to check-in to our room, even when an overnight flight gets in early."

Of course, this wonderful service would mean little if the hotel did not include excellent amenities, a great location, terrific food, and things that work. The statements almost all commented on some aspect of the room, bedding, food, spa, or whatever the customer thought was important about the overall experience. Any critical comments were about something that went wrong, like food poorly prepared or the table not properly cleaned. One two-star rating cited "great environment, sad meal." An immediate response by management promised "to spare no effort to provide a perfect visit" next time and asked to speak personally to the dissatisfied patron. I am sure something exceptional was offered to the patron.

The service experience is one part treating customers like royalty and one part making everything work flawlessly or responding immediately to a flaw in a way that corrects the situation above and beyond customer expectations. Note that this all comes out of the philosophy of engaging every staff member to become an emissary of the company. It is easy to write a policy of greeting the customer with a smile on your face, but that does not automatically put genuine smiles on the faces of frontline staff.

This is not to say that the secret to service excellence for all organizations is wildly enthusiastic staff empowered to offer goodies to customers who have a special request or complaint. Four Seasons is in the personalized experience quadrant of our model and is a high-end luxury provider. The hotel's value proposition is to provide crazy levels of first-class service at a first-class price. Customers willing to pay for the luxury have a flawless experience—or get amply rewarded if they complain. This model would not work in the mass goods distribution quadrant, where value is often defined by a service that works flawlessly at an affordable price.

One company that lost its customer-driven philosophy and under a new CEO struggled to regain it is United Continental, a merger of United and Continental Airlines. The merger of the two companies seemed to follow the traditional route of cost reduction through "restructuring and synergies," without building a common culture and focus on customer service. The CEO at the time of the merger talked a great game about teamwork and set as a goal to have a new joint labor contract in place by the end of 2011. When he was ousted from his position in September of 2015, there was still no contract for flight attendants and mechanics, and coincidently the company had the lowest score in the annual airline quality report. The company is in the standard experience quadrant, but that does not mean that service excellence is irrelevant. Customers have a choice.

In September 2015 Oscar Munoz made his first public appearance as the new CEO of United Airlines. He started with an apology.[3] After anonymously experiencing a terrible flight on United, he said of the merged Continental and United

Airlines: "This integration has been rocky. Period." He continued: "We just have to do that public mea culpa. . . . The experience of our customers has not been what we want it to be."

Just before taking over as CEO, he experienced a flight from Chicago, one of the hubs of United. He watched as two people were denied boarding because the flight was oversold. He sat on the tarmac, in a cramped 50-seat regional jet, going nowhere for 30 minutes because of backups at the gate. He then waited five hours for his luggage. He struck up a conversation with other passengers, baiting them about the long delays. They agreed, but to his surprise they immediately followed with, "Wasn't that woman nice on that flight?" They were speaking of the flight attendant, Jenna. Oscar then had a revelation that Jenna was the highlight of an otherwise terrible flight. It was a watershed moment for him. "Everybody on that flight remembered that [Jenna]," Munoz said. "The process and systems and investments and all that stuff? Those are all wonderful . . . but what I've got to start with is people."

Companies merge to attain financial synergies, to get additional capabilities they otherwise lack, to acquire new technologies, and for many other reasons. Way down the list, if it is there at all, is the customer. As Oscar learned, merging two bad cultures does not magically produce a positive, purposeful culture. It did not help that the company had severe labor-management strife and that some unions were working without a contract.

Recently Karyn flew United out of her home base of Chicago. This is a main hub and one that United should try to get right. Her experience:

> *Truly awful. Not enough seating in the waiting area. Seats broken/ripped if you can find one. Nowhere to plug my phone in. Confused boarding process. Oversold by three seats, and people asked to give up their seats until tomorrow. They are paying $500 + hotel + all meals for the day so they are losing money . . . this flight cost only $250. All service people are trying to be nice, but there's no hope of overcoming this process mess.*

Clearly the new CEO has his work cut out for him, but he has the right perspective and passion. He quickly went to work on building trust with the unions including traveling around to understand worker concerns about relations with management. Unfortunately he had a heart attack, which put him out of commission for two months, but nonetheless he appointed an acting CEO who negotiated new contracts and began to work proactively with the unions. Munoz soon returned to work and is overseeing a slow and tenuous climb to becoming at least a decent airline.

Lean leadership too often brings to mind leaders who slash costs, cut fat, and streamline the organization so it is an efficiency machine. But a real lean leader starts with the customers and the people who serve the customers. Munoz was becoming a lean leader. In lean terms he went to the gemba, that is, where the core work of the organization is done and where the customers are served. He seems to have done it by chance. He wanted to visit his daughter and happened to experience what the rest of United and Continental customers experience all too often. That was the start of what he calls his "learning tour."

The passion for and focus on the customer is a great starting point, but there is more to lean leadership. How will United transform from a poorly operated airline with disengaged employees to one that gets everything right? A smiling face is nice, but most of us want to get to our destination without delays, in a comfortable seat, and have our luggage show up as it is supposed to.

Munoz is quoted as saying wishfully, "If I get maybe 5,000 Jennas working through this, I think I can make it work." But that is not going to happen. What he has to do is develop a lot more than 5,000 Jennas. He needs to build a culture of people in all parts of the airline who have Jenna's passion and commitment and the skills to improve every aspect of operations and customer service.

There is a distinctive way of thinking about the company purpose and how to build capability that separates the philosophy of excellent companies from the mediocre.

THE LIMITATIONS OF MACHINE THINKING

From an early age, we're taught to break apart problems in order to make complex tasks and subjects easier to deal with. But this creates a bigger problem . . . we lose the ability to see the consequences of our actions, and we lose a sense of connection to a larger whole.

—Peter Senge, *The Fifth Discipline*

Machine thinking is characteristic of early twentieth-century industry when the owner of capital had an insurmountable competitive advantage. If you owned the factory, the means of production, the workers came piling in and the money followed. The motivation of those workers was clear. They needed money. In fact, the most direct way to motivate them was paying by the piece—produce more pieces and you get more money.

In the early twentieth century, Frederick Taylor, the father of industrial engineering, turned this into a philosophy he called "scientific management." It had the following characteristics:

- **Scientific work design.** Engineers scientifically study the work and break it down into small pieces that are each precisely defined to be the one best way to do the job.
- **Scientific selection.** Workers are scientifically selected to have the capability to do the work, often meaning physical strength (men) or dexterity (women).
- **Scientific training.** Workers are trained in the one best way to do the job.
- **Scientific incentive pay.** The payment scheme financially rewards workers when they produce more units, and thus it provides more profit for the owner.

Frederick Taylor was genuine in his belief that scientific management was the key that would unlock shared prosperity for the worker and for society. The triggers for that shared prosperity were, on the one hand, brilliant engineers who did all the thinking for the enterprise and, on the other hand, self-interest that provided the most efficient route to the only thing that mattered to workers or owners—money.

Fast-forward to 1986, and Eli Goldratt seemed to make this even more explicit in his wildly successful business novel, *The Goal,* in which Jonah, a kind of guru, teaches a business owner how to build a successful business. Jonah repeatedly asks what the goal of the business is. The only acceptable answer—to make money. The "theory of constraints" provided the only solution needed to meet the goal. Find and break any constraints to making money. Goldratt created a business based on training "Jonahs" who were to run a computer simulation to find the constraints and become the engineers who did the thinking for the enterprise. They were carrying on the tradition of Taylor's scientific management.

These methods and others led to what system thinkers call "reductionist thinking." A system can most simply be defined as a set of interconnected parts. When we focus on fixing one part or one connection, to the exclusion of working on the system, we are reducing the problem to that part only. This leads to sub-optimization of the system, which leads to all sorts of other ailments.

Take, for example, an organization that Karyn worked with in which a problem in one department was "solved" by eliminating the seemingly time-consuming production of a weekly report. The people in the department felt that they had done their due diligence and involved everyone who used the report in determining the solution, and so imagine their surprise when they started receiving angry phone calls and e-mails from other departments in far areas of the company asking, "What happened to my weekly report? I can't do my work without it." The decision makers in the department doing the problem solving didn't set out to disrupt the work of other departments. They simply had no idea that the information contained in the report was used in so many different ways by so many different departments. They were too disconnected to even imagine who their customers were for that report.

Machine thinkers view even complex human organizations as big machines. Humans are parts of the machines—interchangeable parts. We even hear organizations described this way: "We function like a well-oiled machine." This type of organization is the ultimate bureaucracy—each person specializing in his part performing the job the one best way as determined by experts on work design. Process improvement is also handled by experts trained in the one best methodology for improving processes, and the experts in industrial engineering or lean six sigma see their job as control, including preventing others from tampering with their perfect process designs.

It is now a well-known story that this was efficient, and even effective, in an age of little competition and relatively slow changes in technology and the market. Companies like Ford and General Motors could be the kings of the industry by owning the biggest, most modern equipment and depending on economies of scale. People could be ushered in and out of job positions with very little training, and as long as they did not mess up too badly, customers would get a car that was good enough for their relatively low expectations.

The model worked until the "Japanese invasion" in the 1970s that brought much higher quality, fuel-efficient cars from companies like Mazda and Honda and Toyota. Then it all broke loose: the auto industry began to study the Japanese management system, and the quality revolution was born. Gurus like Dr. W. Edwards Deming preached a focus on serving customers and developing the capability to design and build in quality.

Unfortunately for the Western auto companies, it did not compute. What Deming was talking about was systems thinking, which did not register to die-hard machine thinkers. I recall a friend who was sent by GM to NUMMI, a joint venture of GM and Toyota, in 1984 to learn and teach the Toyota Production System and help transform GM. He came back to GM to try to teach what he had learned, and said it was like "trying to explain what Technicolor is to people who had only ever seen in black and white." In fact, it is the black-and-white perspective that puts blinders on machine thinkers and makes it so difficult to understand the complexity of systems.

Unfortunately, what we see in modern twenty-first-century organizations is a lot of machine thinking. Bureaucracy reigns supreme. Karyn has been battling for a decade to teach Toyota Way thinking in different service organizations, but the progress is slow and there are huge obstacles to overcome. These obstacles have everything to do with machine thinking. Karyn explains:

> Most of the organizations I have worked with don't actually refer to customers in terms of living beings at all. In payroll we just called them "account 1234," and in human resources services, the service reps would refer to them as "service requests" or "tickets." These are inanimate, nonhuman things. In

insurance, we tend to simply refer to them by the type of transactions they are: new business, renewals, or endorsements or claims. And if we don't process the work that customers need on time, we refer to them as "out-of-service items." If we don't speak about—and think about—our customers as people, but simply inanimate objects, parts of the "machine," how can we have a hope of treating them like people?

When I am coaching and I hear managers referring to something like "out-of-service items," I will go up to them and ask, "What is the name of the customer that the work was not completed on time for?" The manager is then usually quite surprised, because it hasn't even occurred to them that there is a real, live person involved.

In most of my experience, in service organizations, we don't actually see the customer as part of the system, somehow, even though they are usually tied to creating the service with us. This leads to a very internal focus on improving things that are "personal preference" or that service providers find irritating, with no thought of the customer at all.

THE NEW AGE OF ORGANIZATIONS AS LIVING SYSTEMS

It was an academic specialist in social cognition who helped me understand "East versus West" differences in machine thinking compared with systems thinking. Richard Nisbett's *The Geography of Thought* summarizes many experiments that compare the world views of Asians and Westerners.[4] The upshot was that a variety of cognitive experiments indicated that Asians from a variety of countries were much more likely to see the connections between parts and the Westerners were more likely to see only the parts.

For example, one of Nisbett's doctoral students wanted to test the thesis that Asians see the world as through a wide-angle lens and Americans have something more like tunnel vision. He developed a simple black-and-white graphic of fish in a sea.[5] Each scene had a "focal fish" that was larger, brighter, and faster than the others. There were also rapidly moving animals and plants, rocks, and bubbles. He asked students at Kyoto University and University of Michigan what they saw. Japanese participants tended to begin by describing the environment, such as whether it looked like a pond or the ocean. The Americans were three times as likely to begin detailing the focal fish. Other studies tested recall. Japanese, compared with Americans, were much more likely to remember specific objects if they were presented in the same context in which they originally saw them. The consistent finding: Asians saw relationships and context, and Americans saw isolated items, suggesting Asians were more natural systems thinkers.

Nisbett speculated on the historical origins of these different ways of thinking. Plato and Aristotle were key actors in developing the Western world view. Aristotle, a student of Plato, emphasized defining the world in fixed categories and looking for defined relationships between those categories. In the modern vocabulary of statistics, as taught in six sigma programs, $Y = f(X)$. That is, some dependent variable (Y), like number of defects, can be explained as some function of one or more independent variables (X), like how well employees are trained. The reasoning is that if we properly measure the variables and find the right statistical relationship, then we can accurately predict what we need to change to get the desired level on the dependent variable. Of course, it takes specially trained process improvement specialists to work this mathematical magic and find the one best way—sound familiar?

Nisbett argued that the deterministic, machine-like world view in the West can be traced back at least as far as the Greek philosophers:

> *Greeks were independent and engaged in verbal contention and debate in an effort to discover what people took to be the truth. They thought of themselves as individuals with distinctive properties, as units separate from others within the society, and in control of their own destinies. Similarly, Greek philosophy started from the individual object—the person, the atom, the house—as the unit of analysis and it dealt with the properties of the object. The world was in principle simple and knowable: All one had to do was to understand what an object's distinctive attributes were so as to identify its relevant categories and then apply the pertinent rule to the categories.*

The Asians, on the other hand, were influenced by a different set of philosophers such as Confucius and Buddha, along with a different set of experiences as farmers in complex growing conditions. Nisbett summarizes the contrasting world view that resulted from the different cultural influences in the Asian environment:

> *Chinese social life was interdependent and it was not liberty but harmony that was the watchword. . . . Similarly, the Way, and not the discovery of truth, was the goal of philosophy. Thought that gave no guidance to action was fruitless. The world was complicated, events were interrelated, and objects (and people) were connected.*

Nisbett attributes the Asian proclivity toward the collective, and their views on how the world operates, to the ecology of rural living, particularly rice farming that is so central in China and Japan. He explains: "Agricultural peoples need to get along with one another—not necessarily to like one another—but to live together in a reasonably harmonious fashion. This is particularly true of rice farming . . . which requires people to cultivate land in concert with one another." He also notes that irrigation systems require centralized control and that the Chinese and Japanese peasants lived in a complex world of social constraints.

The largest-ever cross-national survey, by Dutch social psychologist Geert Hofstede, supports the observations of Nisbett.[6] Asian countries tend to rate highly on both collectivism and long-term thinking. Western countries, and particularly the United States, rate highly on individualism and short-term thinking. In fact, the United States is the only country in the world in which individualism is the most dominant cultural characteristic. This is not surprising in a country that celebrates its independence every July Fourth. Liberty and individual freedom are among the most fundamental and inalienable rights, as defined in the U.S. Constitution.

Historically, in Japan, men put the needs of the collective above their own personal interests. The company as a collective became primary, even sometimes eclipsing time with family. I recall that the Japanese who were sent over by Toyota to teach the Americans were at wit's end trying to understand the "American idea of work-life balance." Why would Americans want to race home to their families when there was still important work to do?

According to Confucian philosophy, as we grow and "become human," we identify with larger collectivities from selves to family to friends in the community to the workplace to society at large. Toyota leaders were intensively committed to helping Japan become an economically strong industrial society. In fact, founder Sakichi Toyoda is considered the father of the modern Japanese industrial revolution. From the 1970s, Toyota turned its attention to a larger purpose—becoming a global company, which it has been working on ever since. The purpose of Toyota is always stated first as contributing to society, not Japanese society but global society. And all employees are considered team members contributing to this lofty ideal.

In sum, the short-term bottom-line focus of Western companies, that for decades has been world dominant, seems a better fit for the simpler world of the twentieth century but increasingly outdated in the twenty-first century. The thinking needed to thrive in the future seems more characteristic of Eastern views of holistic systems, teamwork, adaptation, and learning. A short-term focus on results actually seems to impede our ability to get the results we desire. A longer-term focus on building the capacity for innovating in the way we serve customers actually gets better results. The difference is a matter of the philosophy reflected in the organization's culture.

SYSTEMS THINKING FOR HIGH-PERFORMANCE ORGANIZATIONS

The high-performance organization movement evolved separately from lean management. It began with the concept of sociotechnical systems. The term "sociotechnical systems" was coined by Eric Trist, Ken Bamforth, and Fred Emery at the Tavistock Institute of Human Relations in London. One of the early works to come out of this tradition, published in 1951, looked at technological changes that came with long-wall coal mining in England and how the changes altered the structure of work.[7] In the long-wall method of getting coal, the work was spread over three shifts. The researchers observed that workers were isolated along this wall of coal working in a very regimented way, as if on an assembly line. The workers did a very narrow, defined task that was only a part of the job, and they could not see how it connected to a larger whole or to the customer. The researchers document the dysfunctional consequences of this form of work organization including the psychological stress and alienation that led to intentionally withholding productivity. The authors compare this method with the earlier, traditional method of going into the mine in small teams who work collaboratively, which they argued was actually a superior system from a social-psychological perspective and that modern technologies should be designed to facilitate the benefits of teamwork and self-direction:

> *A primary work organization of this type has the advantage of placing responsibility for the complete coal-getting task squarely on the shoulders of a single, small, face-to-face group which experiences the entire cycle of operations within the compass of its membership. For each participant the task has total significance and dynamic closure.*

Sociotechnical systems theory continued to evolve with the study of actual work environments. Increasingly sophisticated steps were taken to create the social and technical conditions to support accountable teams who took responsibility for an intact unit of work. One of the early pioneers in this arena was Procter & Gamble, when in the 1970s the company began introducing the "technician system" of work. P&G made a variety of consumer products such as diapers and cosmetics that required highly automated processes. The major challenge for humans in this system was not the repetitive manual work, but rather the ability to control all the disturbances that interrupted the work flow, such as machine breakdowns. In the technician system, teams of workers were responsible for a complete automated line.

David Hanna[8] was one of the P&G internal change agents introducing this new way of working based on systems thinking. By introducing this system he, and his colleagues, were repeatedly able to transform the lowest-performing plants in P&G into the highest-performing plants on measures of cost, quality, morale, and on-time delivery. David noted that there was a natural organizational life cycle for mechanistic companies. They may have started with a clear purpose and some product or service that the market demanded, but over time as they became increasingly complex and bureaucratic, they lost their purpose and began to turn inward, leading to win-lose scenarios, copying the competition, and eventually either going out of business or restructuring as a new business. He describes the process of shifting thinking from mechanistic to living systems as a way for the organization to self-renew, continuing to pursue, and even redefine, its purpose through organizational learning.

The starting point is getting the leadership team to understand the current system and its limitations and then envision a future system that would perform at a much higher level. A model used to facilitate these discussions is shown in Figure 3.1. It always begins with stakeholder analysis. Whom do we serve, and what value do we provide to each stakeholder? This leads to defining the strategy of the company to fulfill its mission and identifying the capabilities required to achieve the strategy. The internal capability includes the organizational systems and culture as defined by structure, processes, people, and rewards. Results get defined as aspirational—what is the level we need to achieve in the near term to move us closer to satisfying stakeholder needs. David's conclusion: "You must adhere to the natural laws of living systems if you would continuously extend your organization's life cycle."

PURPOSE-DRIVEN ORGANIZATIONS

What Is Your Purpose?

Those who have been mentored by Toyota *sensei* (teachers) quickly get tired of the question, "What is your purpose?" It is easy to get bogged down in the details of your work, or the details of an improvement process, and lose the bigger picture. Why are you working on this project? What do you hope to accomplish and why? This is why defining the ideal state was included in Toyota Business Practices—it forces you to define the future-state direction, often called "true north" at Toyota.

Machine thinkers routinely lose sight of the bigger picture. Cause and effect are assumed to be simple and linear: "I do this because I want this outcome on that metric," and the metric is usually financial. This myopic mindset is actually the root cause of many failed improvement programs. Tom Johnson, an accounting professor, systems thinker, and student of the Toyota Way, calls mechanistic thinking the "lean dilemma":[9]

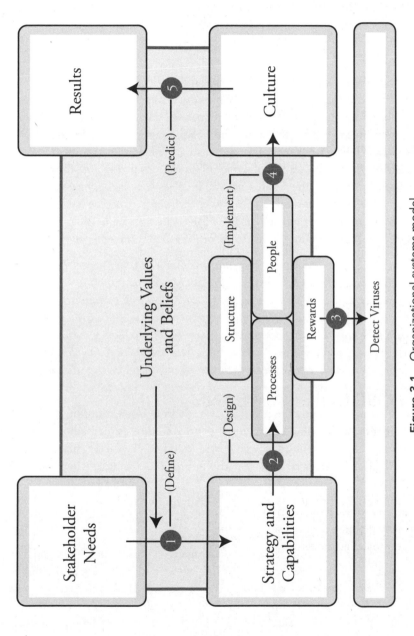

Figure 3.1 Organizational systems model

Source: David Hanna, The Organizational Survival Code, Hanaoka Pub., 2013

*In (the mechanistic) view, financial results are a linear, additive sum of inde-
pendent contributions from different parts of the business. In other words,
managers believe that reducing an operation's annual cost by $1 million sim-
ply requires them to manipulate parts of the business that generate spending
in the amount of $1 million each year, say by reducing employee compensa-
tion or payments to suppliers.*

Reducing spending does not improve anything. Try improving the quality of
your life by reducing spending. You may reduce some stress of meeting your
budget, but nothing in your life will change for the better. And cutting out something important to your health, say annual health exams, may significantly harm
your life in the long term. To improve something, we have to make it better. And
particularly in the complex world of service organizations that require direct interaction with customers, this almost always involves generating new ideas and
changing the way people think and act to put the new processes into practice.
Thus, Johnson argues that viewing organizations as living systems provides a completely different sense of purpose and is the only path to sustainable improvement:

*Were managers to assume, however, that the financial performance of busi-
ness operations results from a pattern of relationships among a community of
interrelated parts, . . . their approach to reducing cost could be entirely different. In that case, managers might attempt to reduce costs by improving the
system of relationships that determines how the business consumes resources to
meet customer requirements. . . . Viewing current operations through the lens
of this vision would enable everyone in the organization to see the direction
that change must take to move operations closer to that vision.*

As one might expect from a rogue, systems-thinking accounting professor,
Johnson identifies prevailing management control systems as the leading cause of
the common narrow-minded, mechanistic mindset. It causes managers to
"mechanically chase financial targets" without nurturing the underlying system of
relationships.

Karyn and I experience this routinely in trying to advise our clients. Even
after we lead them through exercises in which they conclude that their processes
are broken and their people disengaged, they still ask, "What is the return on
investment of lean? Can you take me to benchmark an organization like mine that
has gone lean and where I can see the results?" We want to grab them by the shoul-
ders, stare them in the eyes, and shout, "You just mapped your value stream, you
led the exercise, you saw 10 times as much waste as value added, your customers
are screaming for better quality and more timely service, we identified a great
future vision, and you are asking about ROI?" Clearly, shouting at somebody
would be counterproductive and more likely to lead to a harassment lawsuit than

a change in thinking. However, we do need to find a way to shift thinking from short-term cost reduction and immediate ROI to investing to achieve a longer-term purpose.

A purpose is more than making money. In fact, advanced lean-thinking companies like Toyota see profits as an outcome of providing superior value to customers and society, and these companies are more profitable than their competitors. Every decade Toyota gets an executive team together to develop a global vision. This is discussed intensively and refined to build consensus. Toyota Global Vision 2020 states:[10]

> *Toyota will lead the way to the future of mobility enriching lives around the world with the safest and most responsible ways of moving people. Through our commitment to quality, constant innovation and respect for the planet, we aim to exceed expectations and be rewarded with a smile. We will meet our challenging goals by engaging the talent and passion of people who believe there is always a better way.*

Toyota has extended its vision beyond automobiles to "mobility." This paves the way for the evolution of the company into new markets. For example, Toyota has done a great deal of work in advanced robotics and wishes over the long term to become a major player in the use of robots in homes and public institutions. It has robots that help move incapacitated patients in hospitals in and out of bed and robots that patients can operate by remote control to fetch things in the room. We learn that Toyota is committed to fostering innovation and respecting the planet. And the reward from customers is that they are happy with the product, as indicated by a smile. Akio Toyoda has hammered away on his company known for precision and reliability to appeal to the raw emotions of customers. The vision also tells us that Toyota will accomplish this through its people pursuing challenging goals and always searching for a better way—the spirit of the Toyota Way.

Mission Statements That Don't Suck

In a humorous video called *How to Write a Mission Statement That Doesn't Suck,*[11] Dan Heath illustrates how a reasonable-sounding mission statement can become obfuscated by a well-intentioned team. In the video, team members challenge each other by wordsmithing the mission statement to broaden it and consider all possible situations. It becomes so vague and meaningless that almost anything could be done and the mission still would be fulfilled. Heath goes on to provide two useful tips for a well-written mission statement. First, use concrete language so that the purpose is so clear that anyone could identify with it. Second, talk about the "why" so it is unmistakable about what would make you care about the mission. To illustrate a well-crafted statement, Heath cites Johnson & Johnson's famous credo: "Our first responsibility is to the doctors, nurses, and patients, mothers and fathers and all others who use our products and services."

Contrast this to the mission statement of General Electric: "We have a relentless drive to invent things that matter: innovations that build, power, move and help cure the world. We make things that very few in the world can, but that everyone needs. This is a source of pride. To our employees and customers, it defines GE." What did that say? What speaks to you that tells you what makes GE special?

The company Strategic Management Insight created a way to grade mission statements, and it gave the GE mission a 55 percent—a failing grade in most schools.[12] Here's why: On the plus side, the statement gives at least a vague idea of GE's products and services and mentions employees and customers. It emphasizes innovations and the reason—"to help cure the world." On the negative side, it is unclear what it means to "cure the world." The company is proud, and supposedly so are the customers, of the great innovations of the company, but innovations for what purpose? What are the values of the company, and how do they serve customers?

David Hanna views a clear articulation of purpose as the starting point for developing an integrated, aligned human system.[13] He points to a common gap between what the written mission statement says and what customers and employees experience on a daily basis. We all have experienced going to a restaurant or hotel or hospital and waiting endlessly, getting treated rudely, learning in frustration that there was a mistake in our order or in the information recorded in the computer, and then noticing the prominent mission statement on the wall: "Our commitment starts and ends with completely satisfying you, our customers. . . . " What a joke!

SOUTHWEST AIRLINES' COMPELLING MISSION: WHAT SOUTHWEST WILL AND WILL NOT DO

Imagine a company that knows what its customers expect and chooses to do the opposite. Ludicrous, you say! Well that is exactly what has made Southwest Airlines a stunning success in the up-and-down airline industry. Customers expected assigned seating, but at Southwest it is first-come, first-served. Customers expected free meals but got only a selection of for-purchase snacks. Customers expected their luggage to be transferred from one airline to another, but Southwest refused to participate in that process. Why would a company do such absurd things? The answer is that it defined a clear purpose that was operationalized as a strategy.

Michael Porter, the guru of corporate strategy, defined strategy as "performing activities differently than rivals do." This requires "defining a company's position, making trade-offs, and forging fit among activities." He goes further in arguing that companies that focus on operational efficiency to the exclusion of strategy are playing a losing game.[14] They are benchmarking and copying the activities of their competitors and simply cannibalizing each other's profit margins.

Southwest is an example of a business in our standard experience quadrant that gets it right. The airline is, by design, not the high-priced, luxury business that we saw in Four Seasons. The company provides efficient, reliable service with a smile. Southwest has been a benchmark for its success, experiencing its first quarterly loss in 17 years in 2008, while its major competitors experienced huge swings in the business cycle including actual or near bankruptcy. Like Toyota, it immediately returned to profitability in 2009. It has dominated the limited point-to-point markets where it does business and has typically traded at about twice the price-earnings ratio of its competitors. And its safety record is at the top of the U.S. airline industry.

Southwest Airlines states as its purpose, in a simple yet eloquent way: "To connect people to what's important in their lives through friendly, reliable, and low-cost air travel" (see the broader mission and employee commitment statement in the boxed insert). It invests heavily in its culture of friendly associates who are

---

SOUTHWEST AIRLINES MISSION AND EMPLOYEE COMMITMENT

The Mission of Southwest Airlines

The mission of Southwest Airlines is dedication to the highest quality of Customer Service delivered with a sense of warmth, friendliness, individual pride, and Company Spirit.

To Our Employees

We are committed to provide our Employees a stable work environment with equal opportunity for learning and personal growth. Creativity and innovation are encouraged for improving the effectiveness of Southwest Airlines. Above all, Employees will be provided the same concern, respect, and caring attitude within the organization that they are expected to share externally with every Southwest Customer.

January 1988

NOTE: This was penned in 1988 but still remains as the credo today.

known to do extreme things to entertain and please customers like engaging all the customers on the plane in a singalong. In fact, Southwest is able to achieve low-price ticketing while paying among the highest wages in the industry.

To do this requires a network of interconnected and innovative activities. These include focusing only on short-haul, point-to-point routes, limited passenger service, high utilization of aircraft, and lean, productive ground and gate crews. For example, lean productive gate crews that can rapidly turn around the planes enable high aircraft utilization, and these together support low ticket prices. Lean productive gate crews also support frequent, reliable departures, and the combination of reliability and low prices is very attractive to customers.

Strategy requires trade-offs, and in fact Michael Porter says that you cannot have an effective strategy without defining what you will *not* do. Many companies define what they want to accomplish, but the subtext is to do anything that will earn a profit. A summary of what Southwest Airlines chooses to do and not to do is provided in Figure 3.2. Southwest will not use travel agents, serve full meals, assign seats in advance, or transfer bags to other airlines. The company uses only one model of aircraft for all of its routes, which makes it quick to turn around, and plenty of spare parts are available in case of a maintenance issue.

The activities that support Southwest's strategic choices in turn depend on engaged, committed employees who feel more like part of a team than cheap labor. For example, it takes dedication and teamwork to rapidly turn around a

DO	DON'T
Fixed, low cost	Higher prices with variety
20-minute plane turnarounds	Delay turnarounds
Longer air-time hours	Long delays
Focus on Internet sales	High use of travel agents
Quality snacks for sale	Meals
First-come, first-served seats by zone	Assign seats in advance
Schedule for connections to other Southwest flights	Focus on connections with other airlines
Transfer baggage to other flights	Baggage transfers to other airlines
737 aircraft	Variety of aircraft

Figure 3.2 Southwest Airlines trade-offs to achieve its purpose

plane and then become a friendly, smiling face for all your customers. Southwest employees came to view challenges as inspiring.

In its formative years, the company had only four planes. To afford staying in business, it had to sell one of them, so Southwest challenged its highly motivated ground crew to turn around a plane in 10 minutes when previously it was taking 45 minutes to an hour. The crew members had no idea how they were going to do it, but through a series of experiments they were able to reliably achieve a 22-minute turnaround, enough to keep the flight schedule with 25 percent fewer planes.[15] In effect Southwest is living the core Toyota Way principles of respect for people and continuous improvement.

Southwest Airlines could have followed the lead of its giant competitors and simply tried to beat them on cost. It could have benchmarked best practices and imitated them. Instead Southwest chose to develop its own strategy, which made clear its distinctive purpose and positioning in the market. That included deciding what it would not do. Realizing that strategy was an evolutionary process, it engaged the entire workforce to meet challenges to its very existence. By hiring well, paying well, and developing a culture of fun and engagement, Southwest created advocates in every employee who represent the company philosophy and rally to meet each challenge.

Karyn had a recent experience with Southwest that illustrates its innovative and lean approach to customer service. We are all used to waiting in long lines in airports, and many airlines would say it is the fault of the airport that they cannot control. But Southwest does not accept that and refuses to simply copy its competitors.

I arrived at Midway airport and it was crazy—the Monday after the long July 4th weekend. I wanted to try out Southwest's service so decided to check my bag. A Southwest employee affirmed that I had my boarding pass and then directed me to a huge line marked "Express Bag Check." I joined the line and noticed that there was a position number above each customer service station. I prepared myself for a long wait. However, it didn't happen. The line never stopped moving and I got to the front in about five minutes. I was shocked. At the front of the line there was a monitor that pointed to the station I should go to. I scanned my boarding pass on my phone, pressed "Check 1 bag" on the monitor, and then the friendly Southwest agent took my bag and said, "Hi Karyn! I'm sure you will enjoy your flight to Atlanta today. Your gate is B7 and your flight is on time. Anything else I can help you with, Miss Karyn?" Then off I went! I was all done in seven minutes maximum. As it turned out, our plane was 15 minutes late in arriving, but they turned the plane around so quickly that we left on time and got to our destination early.

A SUMMARY OF MACHINE VERSUS SYSTEMS PHILOSOPHY

Writing down a mission statement is one thing. Making it a living reality in a stable culture is something entirely different. It involves socializing people to think and act according to core values, one person at a time. Let's review the living systems philosophy and how it is different from the more typical machine thinking (see Figure 3.3).

The differences start with the perceived purpose of the enterprise. In the mechanistic view we want each investment, each part of the machine, to work and give us a predetermined ROI—now. Otherwise there is no point in investing.

One of the most innovative companies in the world, 3M, was nearly destroyed by a mechanistic CEO who decided to eliminate most of the new ideas in this new-product incubator, attempting to predict with statistics the most likely products to succeed. The predictions turned out to be wrong much of the time, new products declined, and the company was on a death spiral. Fortunately a systems thinker who had been with the company much of his career gained control. As a systems thinker he realized the world is full of uncertainty and it takes many promising ideas to find the one that actually works. The company eventually regained its competitive edge.

The mechanistic view sees an organization as a set of divisible parts and leads to simplistic notions of how to adapt—eliminate this, acquire that, change job descriptions, and so on. This is why organizations spend millions on computer software that will "streamline the organization" only to find the technology has little impact or even fails. This is why organizations spend millions on consultants

	Machine (Mechanistic) Thinking	Living Systems (Organic) Thinking
Purpose	Short-term results	Long-term adaptation to prosper
World view	Divisible parts	Interconnected network
Cause-effect	Simple, linear	Complex interactions
Processes	Static thing to improve	Dynamic, evolving
Process improvement	Technical change by experts	Sociotechnical changes by all
People	Specialized machines	Creative learners
Problem-solving	Experts find right solution	Learn through experimenting (PDCA)
Lean deployment	Experts implement methodology	Leaders evolve the culture

Figure 3.3   Organizations as machines versus living systems

to streamline processes only to find that once the consultants leave, the shiny, new processes implode on themselves.

Seeing the organization as a network of human and technological elements that are interrelated leads to a more complex and complete view of where we are and what needs to happen to improve the actual system. Viewing the organization this way allows us to see that "how we get there"—the means through which we fulfill our purpose and mission—is more important than simply getting to where we are going—short-term quarterly results in the mechanistic view of the organization.

With mechanistic thinking, cause and effect are direct and linear. The mechanistic manager demands to know, "Why did that happen?" The subordinate replies sheepishly, "We are not sure, sir. There are many possible causes." The manager, getting frustrated, now issues his orders: "I do not pay you to give me excuses. I pay you for answers. There was a defect in the processing of that transaction. It happened for a reason. Find out what or who is to blame and report back to me by the end of the day what you intend to do about it."

Let's consider a similar situation under the leadership of a Toyota-trained teacher. Ritsuo Shingo is the son of the famous Shigeo Shingo who contributed to the creation of the Toyota Production System. Ritsuo worked his way up to the executive level in Toyota manufacturing over 40 years and retired to begin teaching and consulting. During one of his workshops, while leading delegates through a factory in Mexico, he noticed a defect in assembly as it was occurring. He immediately began observing and questioning the worker and discovered the assembly was difficult because one of the parts was out of specification. He asked where the process was that created the defect and immediately led the team back to that machine, again observing and questioning the operator. It turned out that the material purchased was out of spec. He charged off with the team in tow to the purchasing department and found out which supplier had shipped that material and asked the people in the department how they responded to a defect like this. He was set to get into a car and drive to the supplier when the workshop organizer suggested that there was not enough time in the workshop to go and the task could be left as a management assignment.

This is called the "5 why" method in Toyota's vocabulary. Shingo kept asking why, and it drove him to understand the underlying system causes. Were he like the mechanistic-thinking manager, he would have insisted the assembler or assembly process was to blame, and the root cause would never be addressed. In fact, there may have been reason to contain the problem in assembly with a short-term countermeasure, but then the managers needed to spend time finding and addressing the root cause. A systems thinker is never satisfied with a localized bandage when the real problem has not been addressed.

Unfortunately, we see many examples of mechanistic, linear cause-and-effect thinking in complex service organization processes. Although these organizations often use multiple computer systems, have multiple people performing similar job functions (for example call centers), and create the service experience while interacting with the customer, people are in a rush to proclaim that they "know" exactly why problems happen and what can be done about them.

One organization that Karyn worked with spent quite a bit of time trying to figure out why some customers did not have health insurance benefits on the first day of employment even though they had completed the paperwork well in advance. Although the problem did not occur frequently, it certainly was a big problem for the person waiting at the doctor's office, or even worse, needing care in the emergency room. To "solve" the problem, a "standard operating procedure" was put in place, and all customer service representatives were trained on what to do to work with the healthcare provider if they received that type of call.

Karyn later worked with a team in the organization to investigate the deeper system causes of the problem. The team found that there had been a change in timing of when information was transferred from one computer system to another. Depending on when the customer's information was input into the first system, there was a small chance that the information would not be transferred on schedule to the second system. Once the timing of information transfer was synchronized properly, the problem was solved, and all customers had health insurance coverage on the day that they expected it.

The underlying philosophy of Plan-Do-Check-Act embraces uncertainty. We view our Plan as a hypothesis, the Do as running an experiment, the Check as an opportunity to learn, and the Act as deciding what to do next with what we have just learned. Thus we are learning through experimenting instead of predicting and controlling. We might think that the systems thinker wants to change the entire system at once, to preserve its integrity. Ironically, a lean systems thinker sees the world as too complex at the systems level to model and change in one fell swoop. She prefers to chip away at understanding through small experiments. In later chapters we will learn how this is done. At this point we are emphasizing the underlying assumptions that lead mechanistic thinkers to see processes as real things that can be molded and shaped through expert adjustment, while lean system thinkers see processes as theoretical constructs that can help guide the way people actually improve how work is done through iterative learning.

THE CHALLENGE OF CHANGING PHILOSOPHY

Philosophy is the foundation of our 4P model. It influences everything else that happens in an organization, including how to learn and improve. When senior leaders are mechanistic thinkers and are focused principally on short-term results, they will expect the implementation of measurable tools with a clear financial return on investment. Unfortunately this all too often leads to a "leaning out the enterprise mindset" of chasing easy-to-find, obvious cost-reduction opportunities—the low-hanging fruit. Hire a consultant to do this, and companies can usually save three to five times the cost of the program. Some will be one-time savings and others so-called recurring benefits year to year. The recurring benefits are suspect, as they normally depend on people following the procedures the consultants have defined—and also depend on the world remaining stagnant so the highly developed standard operating procedures do not need to change. Neither is a good assumption.

In contrast, the organic approach requires considerable up-front investment in developing people. In fact, that is the main focus in the early stages. A systems thinker might explain lean as a journey that starts with developing people:

> *We are beginning by investing in people doing localized projects so they can develop the skills to take on broader projects and coach more people, and we are confident we will get a multiplier effect over time in satisfying customers, increasing revenue, and decreasing cost. We cannot precisely calculate exactly what the ROI will be, or how long it will take to get it, but we are confident it will have a large and sustainable impact over time on sales and cost reduction.*

In order to accomplish this, senior leaders must understand that improvement is not a "program" but a philosophy that connects their people, processes, systems, and customers together in an organic, living system.

We would like to say there is a magic elixir that will change mechanistic thinkers to systems thinkers. There is none. Moreover, we cannot change people through facts, logic, motivational speeches, or intensive classroom training programs. We cannot change the core—the heart—through trying to logically manipulate the brain. Our brains have too many defense mechanisms that attempt to justify our current way of thinking. Fundamental change in thinking is possible, but it is hard to do and takes time and repeated practice, along with repeated corrective feedback from a skilled coach. It is exactly the opposite of what a short-term-oriented mechanistic thinker wants to hear. You cannot order, buy, or quickly achieve changes in philosophy. Does that mean it is hopeless?

When I travel the world speaking about the virtues of high performance, lean organizations, and the philosophy needed to get there, most participants have mixed reactions. On the one hand, it is clear they yearn to work for an organization like I am describing, and they see a large gap between where they are and where they desire to be. On the other hand, they feel some frustration at what seems like an insurmountable barrier. They ask questions like:

- **How do we document return on investment?** "I have been trying to do what you are talking about in my department. We have gotten great results in lead-time reduction and improved customer satisfaction, but we cannot document a clear financial return. How does Toyota prove the ROI of the Toyota Way?"
- **How can we change senior management?** "I personally believe in what you are saying, but the senior management of my company clearly does not. How can I get them to change the way they run the business?"
- **How do we change senior people set in their ways?** "What would you advise to a young professional like me who is working every day to improve how we work and the results we get, but I am going against the grain and managers have been here for decades and seem to be satisfied with the way things are."
- **How can we find the right benchmark to visit?** "We have a lean six sigma program and, just as you say, senior management does not understand it and is only looking for the financial results. So we cannot afford to invest in developing people, but are forced to chase the money. Is there a place I can bring my senior managers to see a real high-performance, lean organization in practice? We specialize in employer liability insurance—it is not like making cars—so ideally it would be a service organization like ours and not a manufacturing company."

Let's consider each of these in turn.

Proving ROI the Toyota Way

It should be clear by now that the people at Toyota do not attempt to prove that the Toyota Way is worth investing in. They believe it. It seems rather obvious to them that doing the right thing for the customer and society and developing people at all levels of the organization to continually innovate is the true path to sustainable competitiveness. They see the world as dynamic, competitive, and challenging. If the recall crisis of 2008 did anything, it reinforced this world view. Akio Toyoda's reaction was that the company needed to strengthen the Toyota Way, not reconsider it. He preached that Toyota would redouble efforts to strengthen the basics so that it could never again be accused of endangering customers or failing to listen closely to customer concerns. One major change he has led is the movement toward regional autonomy, appointing a local CEO of major regions of the world. For example, Jim Lentz, who spent decades as a manager and then executive of Toyota Motor Sales, USA, was put in charge of Toyota of North America. Akio Toyoda took established local executives, who he believed had the Toyota Way in their DNA, and charged them with strengthening the local culture so there is one Toyota with appropriate regional flavors. Not only did Toyota go on to recover from the crisis, and then recover from the worst earthquake in the history of Japan, and then recover from the worst flooding in Thailand where many of Toyota component parts are made, but then it went on to run off a string of three years of record sales and profits—not records for Toyota but records for the entire auto industry.

Changing Senior Management Thinking

How to go about changing senior management thinking is the most difficult question I get. The question is difficult because I do not have a ready-made answer that I believe in. I have dealt with enough mechanistic-thinking C-suite executives to know that they got to where they are because they have verbal and political skills and are confident, passionate, and convincing and believe they are right. In my experience, because of the self-confidence that has gotten them to where they are and the way their success is usually judged—the bottom line—it is difficult for them to see the benefit of changing. They have been focused on the bottom line for so long—profits that can be easily calculated as revenue minus costs—that anything that will grow the business is good and anything that reduces costs is good. Remember that a mechanistic thinker looks for direct cause and effect. Acquiring a business, adding a new product line, or simply selling more will directly influence revenue. Cutting out something or someone will directly reduce cost. If you can "lean out" the business and reduce cost, you are speaking the language of most CEOs. Abstract concepts like investing in people to improve customer service simply do not compute.

The problem is that sincere professionals in the middle of the company who want to change, who want to be excited about the purpose of the company, and who are willing to work hard to remake themselves and develop their teams are stifled by the lack of support for any improvements that do not have a direct and linear relationship to ROI. They feel blocked rather than supported, and it all starts at the top with the short-term, bottom-line, mechanistic philosophy of the CEO. For the midlevel professional who is caught in this situation and wants to know what to do, I offer only one answer:

> *Do your best to learn and grow and make your team the best in the business. The worst that will happen is that lower performers will resent you. But in the long term you will win because you are learning and developing your*

*team, and you will be rewarded at your current or next employer. Taking on
the kingdom and attempting to transform the culture of a multinational corporation is self-defeating. Do what you can with what you've got. Start by
changing yourself and then find ways to positively influence others, one person
at a time.*

The long-term possibility is that enough of the organization improves performance in measurable ways that it attracts the interest of the CEO, or at least
someone in the C-suite. Even if this does not happen, the C-suite turns over, and
when the new executives come in, they will have an opportunity to learn from
what has been accomplished. Is there any certainty this will work? No, but it is
certain that giving up will fail to change the organization.

Changing Thinking of Senior People

There is a concept called "neuroplasticity" that we will talk about in Chapter 8
on developing people. It is a fancy way of saying that we can change our brains
even as we grow old. It has even been demonstrated scientifically with brain
scans. Those little neurons and the pathways that connect them are actually not
set in concrete. They can be strengthened, they can be weakened, and new ones
can be created throughout our lives. Habits are hard to break, but they are regularly broken and replaced with new habits. As people age, it does become more
difficult to develop new skills and habits, but through deliberate practice we can
and do change.

If the mechanistic-thinking CEO can be difficult to change, why would we
suggest that any other tenured worker is easier to change? People removed from
the intense pressures of those at the very top, in our experience, are often more
open to change, especially if you can convince them there is a better way that will
make their jobs more pleasurable and help them to achieve their objectives. Since
they are responsible for a smaller, more defined part of the organization, they can
often see the direct benefits of operational excellence. Older people may have to
work a bit harder at change, but when the new systems perspective is combined
with the wisdom and knowledge that comes with years of experience, the result is
powerful. Once older people experience working in the new way and see the positive outcomes created for their colleagues and customers, they generally enthusiastically embrace the new way of thinking and working.

Benchmarking Best-Practice Sites

I get a request like this at least every month. My reaction is generally to sigh—a
combination of frustration and futility. We all enjoy being tourists and seeing
interesting places. It rarely changes our life, but it can be fun and gives us some-

thing to talk about. The rationale behind visiting a lean six sigma benchmark that is similar to our place, but more advanced, is to get ideas and inspiration. We can see what we might look like if we pursue this journey. We can get specific ideas for practices that we might choose to implement. We can hear firsthand from those who have gone down this path what obstacles we might expect.

My concern is that the visits will inspire copying and reinforce mechanistic thinking. These field trips reflect a desire for certainty in what in reality is a transformation process fraught with uncertainty. We want to know. What does operational excellence look like? How did the people do it? What will we have to do? What bottom-line results should we expect? What "lean solutions" can we implement right away? The truth of complex systems is that there is no one best way and no single best practice good for all circumstances. In fact, what we need to learn is how to find our own way—how to become thinking, learning organizations.

Short-Term Mechanistic Thinking Is Self-Reinforcing

In sum, it is very challenging to change those who have come to think of organizations as if they were machines to understanding organizations as living systems. Yet doing so is essential if we truly want service excellence. We must think long term. We must be willing to invest in our people and in creating an infrastructure that will indirectly lead to the passionate pursuit of satisfying customer needs. We must understand that the place where we see a problem occurring is not necessarily the place where it originated. We must understand that causation is complex and can be circular, not necessarily unidimensional and linear.

In fact, circular processes are a major barrier to changing philosophy. Vicious circles run rampant, reinforcing mechanistic thinking in the way organizations choose to improve. Mechanistic thinkers will only invest in projects with a clear financial return. This leads to experts doing all the thinking to implement their solutions. Since they cannot understand all the details of the work and since they fail to get the people who work in the process to learn and buy in, the results are not sustainable. This leads mechanistic managers to want to tighten controls even further through audits to ensure compliance, which starts the self-reinforcing loop all over again (see Figure 3.4).

Contrast this to the virtuous cycle of an organic approach to improvement. The starting point is satisfying customers and developing our people so they will provide excellent service. This is a purpose that people can rally around. The core job of the leader is to coach and develop people who become engaged in achieving challenging objectives as a team. Suddenly the creativity of people is unleashed, and they have a personal stake in the improvements. Over the long term we continually grow our capabilities and improve our service, which leads to better sales

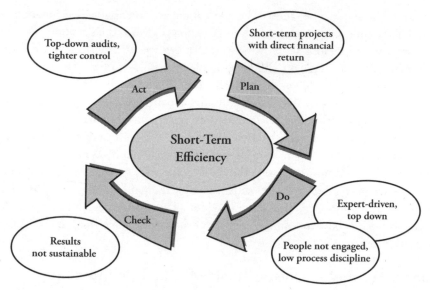

Figure 3.4   Vicious cycle of mechanistic improvement

and financial results for the business. Learning from improvements in one part of the enterprise is shared with other parts, and we become a learning enterprise (see Figure 3.5). Success reinforces the philosophy that we are building a living system, not deploying tools.

PHILOSOPHY IS THE FOUNDATION

Philosophy is the foundation of service excellence—and the remaining 3Ps: process, people, and problem solving, We shift next to exploring lean processes, first through examining a fictional but realistic case study in Chapter 4 and then by exploring processes at the macrolevel and microlevel in Chapters 5 and 6. An underlying message will be to think of processes as changing and adapting, not as static and fixed. Above all else we will insist that copying "best-practice lean processes" from another organization is a bad idea. Service organizations are in fact different, and each service organization is unique and needs to follow its own path and develop and adapt its own processes guided by thinking people who work in the processes they are improving.

It is only when we aim for greatness, for the long term, that we will be willing to make deliberate investments in the long and arduous process of building a culture of service excellence. The organization's way of thinking about the vision for success, and how the organization will get there, is philosophy. Thinking of organ-

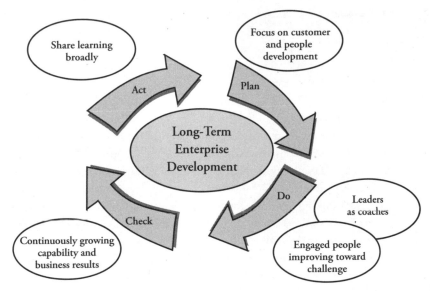

Figure 3.5 Virtuous cycle of organic improvement

izations as machines to be tinkered with is necessarily limiting. All machines eventually break down and become obsolete. It is not only more successful, but even liberating to think of organizations as living systems that can self-adjust in response to feedback from the environment in order to learn, adapt, and grow.

KEY POINTS
PHILOSOPHY OF LONG-TERM SYSTEMS THINKING

1. Although philosophy is abstract, it is absolutely fundamental and the foundation for service excellence in our 4P model:
   - Philosophy gives purpose and direction to all of an organization's efforts.
2. "Mechanistic" thinking views human organizations as big machines in which people are interchangeable parts and in which cause and effect are direct and linear:
   - This leads to suboptimizing, reductionist thinking, in which fixing one part of the organization is focused on to the exclusion and detriment of working on the whole.

- Companies with mechanistic thinking tend to have a short-term, results-only view (ends).
3. "Organic" thinking views human organizations as living systems in which all parts are interdependent and interrelated in a network of human and technological elements:
  - A system is a set of interconnected parts with a goal of survival of the whole organism.
  - Companies with an organic philosophy are focused on finding ways to fulfill their purpose over the long term by adapting to changing customer and environmental needs by creating new products, services, and processes (means).
4. Systems thinking supports long-term survival and supports high-performance organizations by building the capacity for innovating in the way we serve customers throughout the organization and over time.
5. Purpose-driven organizations have strong, underlying philosophies that focus on providing superior value to customers and society and look beyond making money; making money is an outcome of fulfilling purpose.
  - A strong, well-known, and understood purpose reduces myopia and allows everyone in the organization to keep sight of the big picture.
6. Changing your company's philosophy is challenging but not impossible.
  - A fundamental change in philosophy is hard to accomplish and takes time and repeated practice, along with repeated corrective feedback; it cannot be accomplished by copying other companies, including Toyota!
  - Changing from short-term mechanistic to long-term purpose-driven, organic ways of thinking and working is essential to creating a culture of service excellence.

Chapter 4

Developing Lean Processes: A Short Story

Conventional project management attempts to define what to do and when by defining a detailed plan and trying to stick to it. . . . This almost never works. Lean companies create a web of small, constantly operating, rapid, cadenced cycles.

—Allen Ward and Durward Sobek,
Lean Product and Process Development

HOW DO WE CREATE LEAN PROCESSES?

Efficiently flow high value to customers and get it right every time. Can anything be more simple? Do this, and you have lean processes, your customers will love you, and your competitors will be quaking in their boots. Of course, it is anything but simple. It seems simple when we tour a Toyota assembly plant and vehicles are flowing down the line, one by one, and exiting at one a minute. One-minute jobs seem simple. However, zoom out, and we see tens of thousands of parts flowing through a complex network of suppliers and departments with tens of thousands of opportunities for something to go wrong. Making everything work perfectly on time every time seems overwhelming, but what most people miss is that Toyota is not trying to optimize a complex value stream. What it is doing is working to ensure that all production team members can accomplish their 60-second tasks with perfection, and when anything goes awry, group leaders and team leaders react instantly, stopping production if there is any real threat to safety or quality. Thousands of small loops of PDCA are locally managed every hour of every day throughout the value chain.

This is not the case in most companies, in which the mechanistic mindset we talked about in Chapter 3 pervades process improvement efforts. Senior leaders want their processes fixed to reduce cost and stop customer complaints. To accomplish this, processes are reengineered, constraints found and protected, and variation statistically analyzed, in efforts to optimize processes so "everybody does it the same way." Mostly these efforts start with one appealing, but terribly flawed, assumption: processes are seen as real things that can be bent, twisted, leaned out, and shaped to streamline the flow of value to customers, like cutting and bending pipes to flow water.

In reality processes are theoretical constructs—metaphors. Consider the work of many engineers producing the design of a product or piece of software in most companies. Like any work undertaken with a traditional project plan, it looks like distinct stages with certain deliverables at gates in between. The engineers develop a concept that they test with the customer, do detailed design, verify the product, and work with manufacturing to launch into production. But it is not nearly this orderly if we watch what happens. A lot of people are meeting, thinking at various times, writing things down, and using computers, and at key points management checks in on progress. It is messy and nonlinear. There are rework cycles, target dates slip, and somehow at the end the product or software is produced, to be tested in the market. Shaping the patterns of work to ensure a semblance of flow, regular checking in short cycles, ongoing customer feedback, deliberate improvement, clear deliverables, and accountability has more to do with shaping how people think and work than the unrealistic image of "optimizing a process."

When we work with companies on improvement, we never walk in with a prepackaged set of solutions or a 10-step model for leaning out the organization. We do, however, have at a high level a generic approach to process improvement, and simultaneously to people development, that consists of the following steps:

1. **Be sure that senior leadership is serious about need for change.** The starting point, of course, is the need for change. Someone in a position of authority must believe there is a reason to change. We often say you need a burning platform, and that seems true more often than not. But from time to time we are pleased to find a senior leader with a positive vision to get better even when all seems to be going well.
2. **Understand senior leadership vision.** What is the senior leaders' strategy to achieve business objectives? What do they value as an organization? What is their vision for lean, and how does it fit into their objectives and values? This often involves some work with senior leaders to get them thinking about their vision for the company, its processes, and its people.
3. **Grasp the situation.** What is going on in the company, its culture, and its business priorities? How is the company performing? Are senior leaders' values actually visible in action? On what major business challenge should our initial attention on improvement be focused? How can we get senior management on board to learn from the experiments that will be conducted? Where should we begin to focus and with what team(s)?

4. **Understand the current state.** In relation to the main business challenge, what is the current state of the work processes? Where is the leverage to make an immediate impact to move in the direction of the key business challenge? Who are the key people who need to get on board?

5. **Identify gaps and prioritize.** How can the big gap between the current state and desired future state be broken into smaller, manageable chunks of work to assign to people so that they can get started working toward improvement right away?

6. **Strive for the future state through small cycles of learning.** This is where PDCA is practiced, step by step, to work toward the future state—that is, planning an improvement (Plan), testing it (Do), checking what happened (Check), and reflecting on what was learned and what further actions should be taken (Act). This iterative process both moves the work toward the future state and develops in people positive habits for improvement.

We have organized the process layer of the Toyota Way as a set of three chapters that may seem to be in reverse order. We often think about learning principles—or a model of the right way to do something—and then illustrating the principles with examples and how-to tips. Instead, in this chapter we will start with how to approach process improvement, illustrated by a composite case, and then in Chapters 5 and 6 build on the case to define principles of macro-lean and micro-lean processes in service organizations. By macroprocesses we mean the big picture as one would depict in a value-stream map. Microprocesses are the daily work at the level of a department or work group, as is illustrated in this chapter. The composite case was developed by Karyn based on her 10 years of experience in large service organizations. It is an artificial company, but she can relate all the details of what happens to actual experiences. Let's dive into the case of NL (Not Lean) Services, Inc.

In this story a credit transaction company is in deep trouble. It is not growing, and in fact unhappy customers are leaving. The crisis is enough to push a vice president, Sam McQuinn, to seek help from a trusted friend who points him toward her lean consultant, Leslie. Fortunately for Sam, Leslie is a rare consultant who knows how to engage people and push and prod in just the right ways. As you read the story, notice the tight integration of process, people, and problem solving. This is a key point and a far cry from the common view that processes are like mechanical entities that can be improved by simply applying the right lean tool. Let's look in on NL Services.

THE NEED FOR CHANGE AT NL SERVICES, INC.

A Day in the Life of NL Services

It was a typical Monday morning at NL Services, Inc., an American company with 13,000 employees in 95 offices that processed credit transactions for companies that accepted credit payments. John Edwards, manager of Credit Transaction Processing for the Southern Region, presided over his weekly staff meeting. His six managers oversaw teams that handled credit transactions. As per the standard agenda, John went slide by slide through a PowerPoint of the previous week's data sent by the company's corporate office.

"Doesn't look any better this week," John said sternly, using his laser pointer to highlight a plethora of graphs and charts. Not a single team in the Southern Region was even close to the targets that corporate had given for new business growth, client retention, customer satisfaction, or profit. "Corporate really doesn't like any of these numbers. I had a very unpleasant conversation with our VP this morning. His perspective is that 'the number is the number' and that he doesn't care how we, or our people, make those numbers, but he better see some marked improvement in the next couple of weeks, or else. By the end of the business day I need a plan from each of you for how you will make your numbers."

The six CTPMs (credit transaction processing managers) stared alternately at the PowerPoint, at John, and around the room at each other. Some crossed their arms tensely, leaning forward in their chairs. Others just looked bored and resigned. They'd all been through this before. Every few months, when the numbers dipped down for a few weeks in a row, they heard the same speech. And every few months, after they offered the credit transaction processors some incentives, like pizza parties or jeans days, and also threatened possible layoffs and other dire consequences, the numbers came back up. They knew they would make it through this time too.

Meanwhile, back in operations, Kathy, one of a team of 12 credit transaction processors had just hung up the phone. It was only 9 a.m., and her ears already hurt from listening to an angry customer complaining about how his bill was wrong . . . again. After spending 20 minutes on the phone going through all the records with the customer, Kathy was able to correct the error, but now she needed her manager's signature on the Billing Correction form to credit the customer's account and give him the discount that she had promised him for his trouble. It seemed to Kathy that she was always giving customers discounts. The credit processors had to fix so many errors that it seemed to be the only way to keep customers happy and to stop them from changing to another credit processing service.

As Kathy looked around for Joe, her manager, she remembered that it was Monday morning and that he would be, like he always was on Monday mornings at 9 a.m., in the weekly staff meeting. "Customers are just going to have to wait," Kathy thought to herself. "Mondays are always like this. And it doesn't look like the week's going to get any better. I already have a backlog of 25 credit transactions that just seem to have popped into the system over the weekend, and one of the credit transaction processing systems is down, so anything that needs to be input into that system is going to have to wait. You wouldn't think that credit transaction processing would be this hard. But with having credit transactions come in by e-mail, fax, and phone calls, needing to use four different credit transaction processing systems that don't talk to each other, and having to wait for answers about transactions from so many different departments, it's not as easy as it looks. And stopping to fix billing problems for angry customers doesn't make it any easier, that's for sure."

Looking around one more time to see if Joe might be on his way back from the staff meeting, Kathy dropped the Billing Correction form on Joe's desk and headed back to her cubicle. As Kathy sat down, Linda, the credit transaction processor who sat beside her, looked up from the pile of paper transactions that she had printed and was going to input and asked, "Everything okay? Smile, it's Monday! The fun's just beginning!"

"Right!" said Kathy. "Another week, but the same old problems. Customers already unhappy, and I'm sure this isn't the only billing correction I'll be processing this week. Every time we enter transactions involving more than 10 line items, this problem seems to happen. I've told Joe about it a number of times, but he tells me I'm just imagining it, so I've given up trying to talk to him about it, and I guess we'll just fix the problems when they happen. Anyhow, I'm already way behind, so I'd love to chat more, but I better get back to work."

Finally, around 10:30 a.m., John's weekly staff meeting wrapped up. The CTPMs headed back to their teams, armed with an incentive plan offering a free dinner and jeans days for a month to all credit transaction processors who would be willing to work overtime for the next two weeks to catch up on backlogs and make extra calls to customers. The program was "voluntary," but the credit transaction processors understood that those who didn't participate might be the first to go if there was another round of layoffs. The CTPMs were confident that in a couple of weeks, with all the extra focus and work, their numbers would be fine and that John, and corporate, would be off their backs . . . until the next time.

After announcing the program to his team, Joe headed back to his desk, signed the Billing Correction form, and gave it back to Kathy. Kathy called the customer back and gave him an extra discount for having to wait so long for her response.

All fires out for now.

Reflection: The Troubling State of NL Services

Obviously all fires are not out. John just can't see them festering throughout his organization. In *The Toyota Way Fieldbook* we talked about the concept of "clearing the clouds." When the normal state is chaos, it is difficult to even see the processes. They seem hidden by clouds. There are in fact existing work patterns, but you need to clear the clouds to see them. We see that some standard practices are responding to problems by giving little bribes to customers for their troubles. We see that Kathy is spending much of her time reacting to customer complaints, which prevents her from getting the work right the first time. Lingering problems, like transactions that come in with more than 10 lines, are avoided, not solved. Kathy does not feel any support from her boss, but she regularly works around her boss's busy schedule of doing who knows what.

The culture is one of going for results at all costs and fighting daily problems. Figure 4.1 compares the problem-solving culture of traditional versus lean organizations. In traditional organizations management specifies solutions and results and does not particularly care how frontline managers put the solutions into practice as long as they get results. This is a target-rich environment for lean intervention, but the people in the organization seem unable to see how they can get out of the vicious cycles that entrap them. The Toyota system is more concerned with team member development to learn a good process for improvement. The specific solution is less important than following a good process.

Reaching Out for Help

Sam McQuinn, one of NL Services' vice presidents of Credit Transaction Processing, checked his watch again. "Already 6:30 p.m. . . . how can that be?" he thought to himself. "Don't know where this Monday has gone, but I certainly can't say it's flown by because I'm having fun."

Management System	Solution	How to Develop Solution
Toyota's	Leaves open	Specified, guided, and coached
Traditional	Given/directed	Leaves open

Toyota teaches a common pattern for developing solutions

Figure 4.1   Process improvement approach for lean versus traditional management system

Source: Mike Rother

Truth is, Sam wasn't having fun. Between conversations with corporate office people on the East Coast and the four regional managers that reported to him, Sam hadn't gotten off the phone since he arrived in the office at seven that morning. And none of the conversations had been pleasant. For the third week in a row, none of the regions that he was responsible for had hit their numbers—the third time this year—and corporate was breathing down his neck hard.

"Don't know what's wrong with those regional managers," Sam muttered. "I keep telling them that this isn't acceptable, but they just don't seem to get it. No matter how many times I make it clear that they need to get their acts together, things only improve for a little while, and then I'm back on the phone, threatening and cajoling again. We can't keep going on like this; something's got to give."

Shutting down his computer, Sam checked his watch again. If he left right now and there wasn't too much traffic, he should be right on time for dinner and drinks with his friend and former colleague, Sarah Stevens. Sam and Sarah had worked together at NL Services for more years than Sam cared to count before Sarah had moved over to take a higher position at a smaller company that was just starting out. Sam was looking forward to both commiserating with Sarah and asking for her advice. She'd know just how he felt—and she had a knack for solving problems in unusual ways too.

When Sam arrived at the restaurant, Sarah was already seated, poring over the menu. As Sam sat down, Sarah looked up and said, "Must have been a typical Monday at NL Services. You look totally beat up!"

Slipping his cell phone into his pocket so that he could avoid the inevitable phone calls and e-mails from corporate that he knew would keep coming, Sam answered, "Yeh. Regional numbers are down again—for the third time this year. Between dealing with corporate and the regional managers, I haven't had a break all day. Just when I think the regional managers have things under control and are making their numbers, everything falls apart again. No matter how much I threaten or promise, they just can't seem to get their people in line and hit their targets. I just don't know why it's so hard . . . it's not like we haven't known what the numbers are since the beginning of the year. I'm at the end of my rope."

Frowning slightly, Sarah shook her head and sighed. She knew what Sam was going through. It was one of the reasons that she had left NL Services. She was tired of feeling beat up every time her region's numbers weren't where they were supposed to be. "I know how you feel, Sam," Sarah said. "One of the things that I'm enjoying most about my new job is getting off that roller-coaster ride. Although I was skeptical at first, the consultant that we hired to help us is really making a difference. Her name is Leslie, and she is a lean management advisor. You've heard of lean management made famous by Toyota, right? Well, I thought that all that lean stuff was just for manufacturing organizations . . . after all, neither my company nor NL Services makes widgets, but it's been about a year now, and for the most part, I've stopped having the kind of Mondays that I was used to at NL Services—and that you're having today. If you'd like, I can give you her card and let her know you might call. I will warn you that Leslie really is an advisor and facilitator, but you and your people have to do the hard work—she will not do it for you. Her philosophy is that you need to develop the capability to improve your own people and processes."

Reflection: Reaching Out for Help

There is an old Buddhist expression, "When the student is ready, the teacher will appear." Sam did not realize he was ready for a teacher, but he sought support from a trusted peer. Sarah had walked in his shoes in his current company and left because of the very types of daily crises that Sam was still living. She had learned a better way at her new job. She listened empathetically and made a suggestion, with no pressure and no self-interest. As we will see, Sam was willing to take Sarah's advice because it was the right time and he trusted Sarah.

UNDERSTANDING AND ENCOURAGING LEADERSHIP VISION

Leslie Meets Sam and Asks for His Vision

Two weeks later, Leslie Harris, the lean consultant that Sarah had recommended, was sitting in Sam McQuinn's office waiting for Sam to finish up a call. As she looked around the room, she noticed the picture hanging on the wall behind Sam's desk: a sculling boat with all the oars in the water. "Interesting," she thought to herself.

After the introductions and required pleasantries, Sam got straight to the point: "I'm not usually one to ask for help, and I'm not totally convinced that this lean stuff can work here at NL Services since we do not manufacture any physical products, but Sarah Stevens said that you really helped her company. To be honest, I am desperate and willing to listen to what you think you can do for us here. The problem is actually quite simple. The credit transaction processors aren't doing what they're supposed to be doing, so we're not meeting the numbers that our corporate office has set for us on a regular basis. We need to find a way to get the credit transaction processors and their managers and the regional managers all under control so that we can get those numbers back to where they should be once and for all. If Sarah thinks that you're the person that can get that done for us, I'm willing to give you a chance."

Leslie thought for a moment before she replied. "Sam," she said, "I'm happy that Sarah thinks so highly of the outcomes at her company that she would recommend me. Her company thought the problems were simple in the beginning too, and that it would be a quick and easy fix, but it has been a lot of hard work to get where we are today. Before we start 'fixing' problems and putting solutions into place here at NL Services, we're going to have to spend some time really understanding what's going on in credit transaction processing and what your vision is for the organization. This may sound strange given your immediate problems, but it is important that your direction is clear before we start randomly fixing things. Sam, I know you have heard this before, but it all starts with the customers. What can we do to make their lives better, and how are we doing against that vision?"

Leslie paused a minute to give Sam time to think about what she had just said. Then she went on, "It's like that picture of the boat with the oars in the water that you have hanging behind your desk. When all your processors, managers, and regional managers are working together toward the vision that you have of how to deliver value to your customers, the boat is going to be going in a straight line in the water! Instead of thinking about 'making our numbers,' we need to understand how NL Services' credit transaction processing is going to deliver that value. So Sam, what is it that your customers value, and what is your vision for delivering that value?" Folding her hands in her lap, Leslie sat back in her chair and waited quietly for Sam's response.

Sam didn't say anything for a couple of minutes. Each time he started to speak, he paused again. Leslie seemed different from other consultants he had hired. They all wanted to make a good first impression by providing their brilliant solutions right away, not by asking a set of questions . . . questions that he had to admit to himself he was not sure how to answer. Reflecting, Sam realized that he hadn't really thought about NL Services' customers in years—or what they might value. He was focused on "making the numbers" and getting corporate off his back. And a vision of how to deliver that value? Sam was pretty sure he'd need some help figuring that one out. But Leslie came highly recommended by Sarah, and Sarah's company was doing better than most of the competition, even though the company was pretty new. Sam turned and looked at the picture behind his desk and then turned to Leslie. "Leslie," he said, "I'm not sure that I know how to answer your questions, but if you're willing to work with me to figure this out, I would like to invite you to help us at NL Services, Inc."

Understanding Leadership Vision

Despite his friend Sarah's warning, Sam immediately looked to Leslie for solutions. She would not allow herself to be baited by Sam into jumping into his idea of what the problems were and offering solutions. If she did that, she would be violating the very principles she was trying to teach her clients. Instead she deflected the conversation by asking Sam what his vision was for his organization. This caught Sam off guard and made him think. He was not used to consultants making him think. He was used to consultants giving him what they thought he wanted to hear so that they could win his business.

In this case, Sam is acting like the ideal learner and quickly concludes he has not spent enough time establishing a vision for customer service. This short interaction convinces him he wants to work with Leslie. Obviously life is not always so easy, and many managers in his situation would push back at Leslie, looking for answers. "If I wanted questions, I would not need a consultant." In such cases it may be that the student really is not ready for the teacher. As it is, Sam will begin to develop a vision. It will not be an elaborate vision, and Leslie is not using a structured process to develop a strong vision. At this point that would be too much for Sam. She has to meet him where he is, which is just starting the process of reconsidering his basic assumptions of how to lead.

Notice that Sam did not immediately establish a committee to find the right consultant based on competitive bids. Often large corporations have a standard practice of competitive bidding, and a committee issues a request for bid. The usual suspect consulting firms write elaborate proposals promising the world, often without knowing much about the company and its situation. They propose generic solutions to generic problems. As we get to know Leslie, we can safely bet she would not have been willing to play the competitive bidding game. By engaging Leslie from the start, based on his gut feeling, Sam is giving Leslie an opportunity to follow an organic process of coaching him, drawing out of him his vision, and grasping the situation to learn how to proceed rather than walking in with a detailed proposal and off-the-shelf solutions.

GRASPING THE SITUATION

Getting to Know the Organization, Culture, and Issues

It was a beautiful sunny morning, clear skies with just a few clouds drifting by, as Leslie Harris pulled into the parking lot of the NL Services' Southern Region building. As she walked across the parking lot, Leslie thought about how much she was looking forward to this, her first visit to see NL Services' operations. Although it had taken quite a few lengthy discussions, she and Sam McQuinn had finally determined that what NL Services' customers valued was credit transactions processed accurately within each state's regulations for timing. Because the acceptance, processing and reporting on these types of payments was heavily regulated, this prevented the customers from having to pay the fines the states imposed for late payments and reporting and stopped them from having to deal with the resulting stress.

After signing in, Leslie made her way to the third floor, where she found John Edwards, the Southern Region's manager of Credit Transaction Processing, sitting in his office, memo in hand, waiting for her.

"Leslie, nice to meet you," John said, extending his hand. "You seem to have made quite an impression on Sam. He's sent out a number of memos—just like this one—talking about things like focusing on what our customers value and the vision that he has for our region's credit transaction processing: 'Every customer's credit transaction right and on time, every time.' Sam said that you're going to spend some time with us today taking a look at our operation. I'm sure that you'll find everything is in order."

Leslie smiled. She shook John's hand and said, "John, I know you're going to find this hard to believe, but I'm not here to review your operation to report on whether things are 'in or out of order.' I'm simply here to spend time with the people who process the credit transactions for your customers to learn about how they do their work each day. And the best way for me to learn about how they do their work is to spend time with them as they do that work. I'm really looking forward to that—it's one of my favorite parts of what I do!"

John and Leslie walked downstairs to the first floor, where three teams of credit transaction processers sat. John explained to Leslie that the credit transaction processors primarily answered phone calls from business customers who accept credit cards. The customers accumulate a set of transactions and then either call them in by phone, send them electronically through the Internet, or mail in credit card receipts. Most of these businesses call in to report the transactions or send e-mails. If the credit card was read electronically, as at a gas station, then a report is generated via e-mail to the credit card agency. Unfortunately the computer systems do not communicate well with each other and even in the electronic case have to be manually reentered into NL Services' computers. In most cases there are fewer than 10 transactions at a time from one customer. Less often, the processors enter credit information with more than 10 transactions, which customers send by Excel spreadsheet attached to an e-mail or fax. The processors spend a small percentage of time fixing errors on completed transactions and handling billing questions.

As John and Leslie looked across the rows of cubicles, John asked, "Where would you like to start?"

Leslie answered, "If you could introduce me to a manager of one of the teams, that would be great."

John led Leslie around the corner, where they found Joe, one of the CTPMs, reviewing an Excel spreadsheet on his laptop's screen. "Joe, I would like you to meet Leslie Harris," John said. "I know you've seen some of the memos that Sam has been sending from the regional office. Leslie's going to spend the day reviewing how we process our credit transactions, so please do whatever you can to help her out."

"Nice to meet you, Leslie," said Joe. "Would you like to pull up a chair? I'm just going over the 'daily report'—tells us how we're doing on our credit transaction processing. What's on time, what's not. How many calls we took yesterday. How we're doing making our numbers . . . all that good stuff . . . it'll give you a really good look at what we do and how we do it."

Leslie pulled up a chair and sat down next to Joe. "Thanks for offering to walk me through your report. I'm sure it has a lot of data, but what I'd really like to do first is . . ." But before Leslie had a chance to finish her sentence, there was a tap on the cubicle wall.

She and Joe looked up to see one of Joe's team members, Kathy, looking agitated and holding out a piece of paper. Before Joe could say anything, Kathy said, "Look, another Billing Correction form for you to sign. And it's for the same customer that I had to give that big discount to last month. He's so angry he wants to leave NL Services and switch to our competitor. Every time there are 10 or more credit transactions on the spreadsheet in his e-mail, there's always an error. I know you think it's just my imagination, but this keeps happening, and now we might lose a big customer."

Joe, looking a little sheepish, said, "Kathy, let me sign the Billing Correction form, and then I'll give the customer a call and see what I can do. And by the way, this is Leslie; she's here to learn about NL Services' credit transaction processing process."

Leslie reached out and shook Kathy's hand. "Nice to meet you, Kathy," she said. "Seems like you've identified a problem in the credit transaction processing process. I'd love to hear all about it. If you have a few minutes, Joe and I can come over to your desk and take a look and see what happens when you process transactions with 10 or more credits."

Leslie and Joe spent the next two hours together watching how his team of credit transaction processors worked. As they sat together watching and listening, they saw how hard it was for his team members to process transactions with more than 10 credits. And they heard how unhappy the errors on those transactions made customers. Even worse than billing problems, quite a number of them had fines from the states to deal with as well.

Just before lunch, Joe and Leslie headed back to Joe's cubicle. "Joe, do you have any idea approximately how many errors are occurring because of the problem of processing 10 or more credit transactions at one time?"

Looking a little worried, Joe replied, "Actually, Leslie, it's a lot more than you might think. I know it's not good for our customers and it's hard on my people, but there's just nothing we can do about it. And if I bring it up in the management meeting, all I hear is 'no excuses, just make those numbers.' I wish I knew what else I could do . . ."

"Joe," said Leslie, "don't worry. I have an idea—an idea that I think will be able to help Kathy, you, and NL Services' customers too."

Reflection: Getting to Know the Organization, Culture, and Issues

Sam's direct reports are getting the news that Sam is excited about the new consultant and is on board. Sam has even developed a simple but powerful vision statement, and it is focused on service quality from the customer's perspective. Now we have the beginning of a direction for improvement.

Leslie did not have a fixed agenda on her first day at the gemba. She was watching and waiting for the right opportunities to understand what was really going on. On cue as John was explaining things, Kathy walked in, and Leslie saw a golden opportunity for a quick win solving the 10-line problem. It was clear that simply sitting with John and listening to him go over reports and expound on what he thought the key issues were was not going to give her a picture of the current condition. They needed to go to the gemba. And encouraging Joe to go to the gemba with her was an opportunity to do some coaching.

Narrowing the Problem Space and Establishing the Team

Sam McQuinn was pacing back and forth in his office. It was Wednesday afternoon just after lunch: 12:45 to be exact, and he had a one o'clock meeting with Leslie. "What could possibly be taking her so long?" Sam wondered. He'd spent his whole morning on the telephone again. He'd had to field calls from angry executive VPs, calls from the corporate quality department, and, worst of all, calls from corporate audit. Next there was the required round of calls to all the regional managers. "What could be so hard about getting to those numbers? Especially the client retention numbers. What could they possibly be doing down there in operations that was causing so many customers to leave?" Sam fumed. "And where is Leslie?" he thought to himself again. "Leslie should know how to get to the bottom of this. She's certainly spent enough time with the credit transaction processors to have figured out what the problem is—and what can be done about it—not next year, but right now." Just as Sam was about to pick up the phone again, Leslie, calm and cheerful as always, rounded the corner into his office.

"Sam, how are you today? Good to see you again," said Leslie. "I've really learned a lot about your business since the last time we met, and I'm looking forward to sharing that with you today."

"Leslie," said Sam, "that's exactly what I was hoping to hear. I've spent the whole morning on the phone with corporate, and it seems that the credit transaction problems have gotten so bad that we've just lost our biggest customer. That's a huge hit to the Southern Region's retention numbers, and it's going to have a huge impact on our revenue. And if that isn't enough, the fines the customer got from the state are so huge that now I've got corporate quality and audit threatening to come down here to go through my operation with a fine-toothed comb. You've spent the last two weeks taking a look at what they're doing in operations. I expect that by now you've pinpointed the problems and know what to do about them. I'm ready to hear what solutions you have for us, and I'm ready to hear them right now."

Leslie took a deep breath and leaned slightly forward in her chair. This was always one of the hardest parts of her job: helping clients understand that she wasn't going to provide them with immediate solutions but, instead, would help them learn to see what and where the obstacles were that were causing the problems their customers were experiencing. "Sam, I understand how upsetting it is to lose one of your biggest customers. And you're right, I have been spending time getting an understanding of what's going on in your credit transaction processing operations, and I've been able to see some of the problems firsthand. What I've learned from watching how the credit transaction processors do their work is that a number of the processes that they use don't support your vision of processing 'every customer's credit transaction right and on time, every time'—especially when processing more than 10 credit transactions at a time for your larger customers. I know that you really wish that I could offer you a 'quick fix' that would make all the problems go away, but in my experience, there isn't any.

"I know that this may seem counterintuitive, but I believe that what we really need to do is put together a team of the people who do the work—the people who really understand how the work is done and know the problems from the customer's point of view—to study the problem in depth, identify the obstacles that are causing problems for your customers, and come up with what we call 'countermeasures'—possible solutions—to those problems. We'll then test the countermeasures to see if they solve the problems."

Leslie paused a moment to let Sam absorb what she had just said. "Think about it, Sam. When you just put 'Band-Aids' in place to try to 'fix' the problems in the past so that you could make your numbers, what happened? The problems seemed to go away for a little while and then they just came back. If we want a different result, we're going to have to try something different."

Sam looked at Leslie thoughtfully. This wasn't what he expected, but he had to admit that what she was saying was correct. No matter what they seemed to try, the problems kept coming back, and now they seemed to be getting worse.

"Leslie," Sam said, "this isn't what I expected, but at the moment, things are so bad that I'm willing to give anything a try."

Leslie smiled and said, "Thanks, Sam. The first thing we'll need to do is put a team together. We'll need credit transaction processors, people from their supporting departments, and some managers. And we'll need a 'lead' for this 'pilot' project. When I was visiting operations, I spent a good deal of time with Joe, one of the CTPMs. He's really thoughtful, and I think he might be a great lead. He was willing to spend time with his credit processors watching how they do their work so he could see where the problems are coming from. He seems very open to learning, and that's exactly what we need. I'll need your support to get the ball rolling and get John, your regional manager, to approve the time and the resources."

Sam didn't say anything for a minute. Then he got up from the table where he and Leslie had been sitting and moved to his desk. "Leslie, I'll send John a note now. I know he's not going to like giving up the resources and the time—especially since we're under such close scrutiny at the moment. But we'll give your way a try." Sam typed for a couple of minutes. Shutting his laptop, he moved back to the table where Leslie was still sitting, looking calm and collected as ever.

"Thanks, Sam," Leslie said. "This is going to be a new way of thinking and working for NL Services, so your support is going to be unbelievably important. We need to solve the problems your customers are having. Right now, you hear about the problems from corporate, when your numbers are low or customers leave. But I have to ask you, when was the last time that you went over to operations to see what was happening for yourself?"

"Go to operations and see what's happening?" Sam thought about it for a moment, realizing he couldn't actually remember the last time he'd gone over to operations. "Leslie, to be honest, I haven't been over to operations in a very long time. Too long. Can't seem to find the time between phone calls from corporate, I guess," he laughed. "But if you think that's what I need to do, I'll do it. Since nothing else has worked, I'm willing to give your way a try."

Reflection: Narrowing Problem Space and Establishing the Team

In this meeting Leslie is energized by her time at the gemba and she sees Sam in his usual state of panic seeking solutions to today's problems. Again, Leslie will not bite. Instead she points out the large gap between the vision he crafted and the current reality. She has selected John's region for the first pilot program; she knows that it is important to win over John, and she also knows she needs strong support from Sam to move forward. There is a clear direction. She needs to pull together a team that will work through customer issues—as an outsider, Leslie cannot solve the problems of NL Services in a sustainable way. She is also continuing to coach Sam to change his way of thinking and managing—a shift from fighting fires to make the numbers by remote control, to going to the gemba to understand the actual concerns of customers and how they are handled by his organization. In so doing she is teaching him to put into practice one of Dr. W. Edwards Deming's 14 Points:

> Point 2. *"Adopt the new philosophy. We are in a new economic age. Western management must awaken to the challenge, must learn their responsibilities, and take on leadership for change."*

UNDERSTANDING THE CURRENT STATE

Leslie had arrived early. The parking lot of the operations building had almost been empty. But she wanted to give herself enough time to set up and review and make sure everything was ready. She taped the long piece of butcher paper that would later become a diagram of the process steps used by credit transaction processors to the wall. She then reflected on her meeting with Sam and thought, "I'm definitely lucky on this one." Sam was much more open to listening than most of the senior leaders she encountered. And not only was Sam willing to listen, but he actually had made good on his promise of going to see for himself.

True to his word, two weeks ago Sam had cleared his calendar, and they had spent the morning in operations, watching and listening as the credit transaction processors answered calls and entered transactions into the system. Sam had obviously been surprised. "Not at all like I remember it," he had said to Leslie. "Why do the credit transaction processors have so many papers on their desks? And why do they have to keep getting up and going over to look for their CTPMs? Every time they leave their desk, the phone rings, and they miss a call from one of our customers. And even more importantly, where are the CTPMs? They don't ever seem to be in their cubicles."

Leslie was pleased that Sam had been paying attention and was asking so many questions. "Not sure, Sam," said Leslie. "Only way to find out is to ask."

Sam had spent another hour or so talking with the credit transaction processors and the one CTPM that could finally be found. Leslie could see that Sam was listening carefully. As the credit transaction processors headed off for lunch, Sam and Leslie found a small conference room to sit in. "Leslie," said Sam. "I have to admit that I am really surprised by what I'm seeing and hearing. I know that the numbers I get from corporate haven't been good, but every time I ask the regional managers about it, they send me spreadsheets and PowerPoint decks showing that everything is getting better. Just from spending the morning here, though, I can see that things are really a mess. The CTPMs are never around, the phones are ringing off the hook, its obvious that the credit transaction processors can't keep up and aren't happy, and if I were a customer, I wouldn't be happy either. And I wouldn't have believed it unless I'd seen it for myself. We've got to do something, and we've got to do it fast."

And so this morning, Leslie was preparing to work with a team of three credit transaction processors and three CTPMs that Sam and John, the regional manager, had helped her put together. The six team members headed for the small conference room to meet Leslie (see Figure 4.2).

Although the team members had been a little bit skeptical at first—"After all, we've been telling our CTPMs about the problems for years, and no one's listened to us before," Kathy, the credit transaction processor that Leslie had spent time with on her first visit to operations, had said—things were different now that they saw how serious Sam looked.

"When have we ever had three days off the phones to do something like this?" Tabitha, one of the other credit transaction processors on the team, asked. For a change they were getting excited that something positive might happen. Rounding out the team were Joe, Kathy's CTPM; Jorge, Tabitha's CTPM; and Laura, a CTPM, along with one of Laura's credit transaction processors, Jimmy.

"I trust Leslie," Joe had assured them. "She came and watched Kathy and me work, and after she saw what was going on—especially the problems with trans-

NL Services, Inc. Organizational Chart

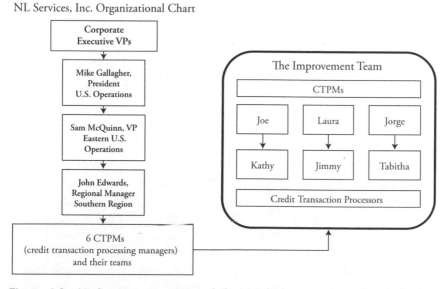

Figure 4.2 NL Services organizational chart and improvement team, which was made up of representatives from three of the credit transaction processing teams

actions with more than 10 lines—she really got Sam all fired up and got the ball rolling. I really believe she is going to be able to help us figure things out so we can make things better for us—and our customers."

At 8 a.m., just as Leslie finished taping up the flowchart paper, the members of the team arrived. Settling into their seats, sipping their morning coffees, they looked expectantly at Leslie.

"Good morning everyone," Leslie said cheerfully. "I'm so excited to be working with all of you. We've got a lot of work to do over the next few days, but I believe that we're going to all learn a lot that we'll be able to use to help us and our customers. Thank you so much for agreeing to be on this team. I know that this is a new way of working at NL Services, so I appreciate your willingness to give it a try." Leslie paused for a moment as she handed out a template that she had created for the team to use.

"Before I explain what this template is for, I have a quick question for the team," Leslie continued. "How many of you think that all the credit transaction processors do their work in the same way?"

Tabitha answered first. "Absolutely," she said. "We all receive the same training, and we have SOPs for each type of credit transaction. And we all want to do what is best for our customers."

Jimmy and Kathy nodded their heads vigorously in agreement with Tabitha. "And we all sit so close to each other," said Jimmy. "I can hear what the other credit transaction processors on my team are saying to customers, and I can pretty much guarantee, we're all doing our work the same way."

"CTPMs," asked Leslie, "what do you think?"

The three CTPMs looked back and forth uncomfortably from Leslie to each other. Finally, Jorge, in a low voice, said, "Leslie, I'm going to be honest here. I have no idea. I assume they do—my team members are all good people and do their best to make our customers happy every day—but between going to meetings, reading reports, and answering e-mails, I really don't have any time to spend figuring out how the credit transaction processors do their work. Truthfully, when I really think about it, I have no idea how any work gets done on my team."

Leslie walked over to stand beside Jorge. Looking at him kindly, she said, "Jorge, thank you so much for your honesty. It takes a lot of courage to admit that you don't know. When we go to work, we aren't paid for uncertainty—to 'not know'—but to be certain and know things, especially as a supervisor or manager. In my experience, though, oftentimes the assumptions that we have about how we work and how things get done for our customers are just that— assumptions. And as we all know, assumptions are, more often than not, wrong. So this morning, what we're going to do is go on a 'fact-finding mission.' We're going to go to the gemba—that's the word that we lean folk use for the place where the actual work that our customers want and need us to do for them gets done. And we're going to record what we see and hear so we can find out what the facts are."

Leslie then spent a few minutes explaining how to use the templates that she had distributed. They would use two different forms in two stages of observation. In the first stage, each CTPM and credit transaction processor pair would spend one hour listening to another credit transaction processor answering calls and then one hour watching that credit transaction processor enter e-mails. For this first stage they would simply time cycles of work. How long did it take for each case from start to finish? There was also a place on the form for general notes about the transaction. They would also note what type of call it was in case this made a difference in the times (see Figure 4.3). They would use this information to plot a run chart of how long it took for each call (on one chart) and e-mail (on a second chart) and get a picture of the variation in cycle times by type of work and credit transaction processor doing the work.

In the second stage they would then spend half as much time observing using a more detailed form showing steps followed. There would be one sheet to fill out for each call or e-mail. The CTPM would write down the steps used by the credit transaction processor in the first column on the left-hand side and add any comments or notes about interruptions or problems in that step in the column beside it. The credit transaction processor would time each step and record the time for each step in the right-hand column. They'd use one sheet per call or e-mail. They would

Process Being Observed: Calls Team Member Being Observed: Gabby		CYCLE TIME OBSERVATION FORM	Observer: Joe/Kathy Date: 9/27
Type of Call (For example: Transactions, Billing)	# of Transactions	Problems Observed or Reported	Total Time for Call
Transaction	3		6 min 15s
Transaction	7	Customer didn't have all info ready	10 min 35s
Billing	—	Mistake on bill – customer charged too much	8 min
Transaction	2		5 min
Transaction	1		3 min 10s
Transaction	3	Hard to hear customer on cell phone	8 min
Transaction	5		7 min
Correction	2	2 miskeyed transactions	4 min 45s
Transaction	1		2 min
Transaction	8	3 miskeyed transactions – had to re-key	11 min

Figure 4.3 Cycle Time Observation Form

Process Being Observed: Phone Transactions	PROCESS STEP TIME OBSERVATION FORM		Observer: Joe/Kathy
Team Member Being Observed: Gabby			Date: 9/27
	Transaction Calls		

Step #	Description of Step	Problems Observed/Reported	Time for Step
1	Answer phone		00:00:15 / 15s
2	Greet customer		00:00:30 / 30s
3	Access customer's acct in system	Hard to see which screen to open	00:01:00 / 25s
4	Verify transaction process date		00:01:25 / 15s
5	Key Transactions (3 total)	Hard to hear customer Miskeyed/re-keyed 2 transactions	00:01:40 / 3min 15s
6	Repeat Transactions back	Had to go back to the beginning to start with first transaction	00:04:55 / 1min 50s
7	Verify total # transactions		00:06:45 / 30s
8	Tell customer next process date	Customer will be on vacation Adjusted date	00:07:15 / 15s
9	Thank customer		00:07:30 / 10s
10	Hang up phone		00:7:40
	Page 1 of 1	Total Time for Steps:	7min 25s

Figure 4.4   Process Step Time Observation Form

also record the call so they could confirm times (see the form in Figure 4.4). This second stage would lead to a detailed picture of the steps followed, the sequence, and the time per step for different tasks and different credit transaction processors.

As Leslie explained the process, she could feel a combination of nervousness and excitement in the room. They'd never done anything like this observation before, but finally, after years of frustration, something was happening. After she finished, the CTPMs and credit transaction processors spent a few minutes discussing among themselves whom they would sit with to observe. Once they were organized and Leslie was comfortable that everyone knew how to use the forms, she sent them off. "I'll be around to check on you," she reassured everyone. "I know that you'll all do a great job."

"Leslie," said Laura, "this is so exciting! I feel just like a detective. I can't wait to see what we find out!"

Two hours later, the team members reconvened around the conference room table. After a few minutes organizing themselves and posting on one section of the board the run charts and on another the activity timing sheets, they looked expectantly at Leslie. "Well," said Leslie, "what did you think?" Everyone started to talk at once.

"I didn't realize that customers made so many changes in the credit transactions that they were calling in," said Laura.

"And that Kelly, my teammate, doesn't follow the same steps to enter the credit transactions as I do," chimed in Jimmy.

Kathy broke in, "And you know that 'more than 10-line' problem I've been having? Well, Erica said that she was having it too!"

"Now that we have all this information, what are we going to do with it?" asked Tabitha.

Leslie laughed and said, "Now you know why I was so excited this morning. Going to see what's really going on gives us a very different view of what is happening. I'm glad that everyone saw and heard so much. The next step is for us to take the information that we've gathered and put it together in a way that we can all 'see' what story it's telling us." Leslie pointed to the wall where she had hung up a number of pieces of flip-chart paper. On one page she had printed the heading "Process Timing Run Chart—Less Than 10 Transactions"; on another, she had written "Process Timing Run Chart—10 Transactions or More." On the third page she had printed "Problems Observed." For the next half an hour or so, Leslie worked with the members of the team to help them create graphs to analyze the data and observations that they had collected on the flip-chart pages. They posted a run chart for each of the transaction processors they observed. When they were finished, what they produced looked like the run charts in Figure 4.5.

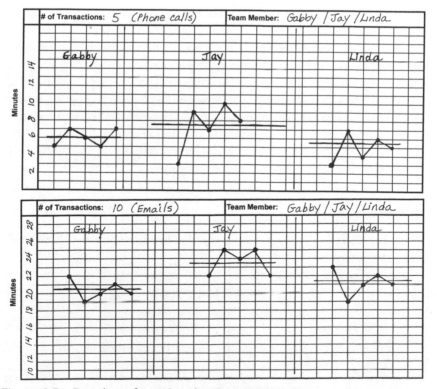

Figure 4.5   Run charts for <10 and >10 transactions

Sitting back in their seats, the team members focused on Leslie as she instructed them to take a few minutes to think about what they saw. Looking around, she could see that they were quite surprised.

Joe spoke first: "Leslie, look at the difference in the time that it takes to process the credit transactions. Some take such a short amount of time, and others take so long."

"And look how long the transactions with more than 10 lines actually took!" exclaimed Jorge. "My team has so many large customers. I didn't realize it took so long to enter those transactions."

Kathy, who had been excitedly waiting her turn to speak, interjected, "And look at the chart of the problems . . . transactions with 10 lines or more are definitely the biggest problem, just as I suspected!"

Leslie congratulated the members of the group on their excellent observations. Then she taped up another piece of flip-chart paper that she labeled "Questions" (see Figure 4.6). She then described the next step: "We need to look at this great data and analyze it. First, what problems did you see in the processes?" The group called out problems and Leslie separated them by problems with calls and problems with e-mails. Then, for the next 15 minutes, she helped the team brainstorm a list of questions that seeing the information on the charts made them think of.

After everyone had a short break, Leslie said, "Team, we have one more thing to do before lunch. I think you are really going to enjoy this." Turning to the long piece of butcher paper that she had labeled "Process Steps," Leslie said, "Remember when I asked whether you thought all the credit transaction processors used the same steps to do their work? And everyone 'assumed' that they did?

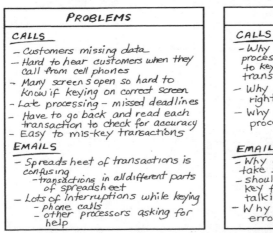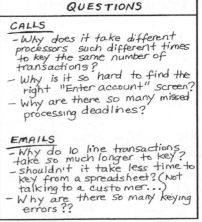

Figure 4.6 Flip-chart notes of problems and questions

Well, now we're going to find out whether our assumptions were correct. What we're going to do next is create a diagram that shows the steps, in sequence, for each credit transaction processer, and then we can compare them."

As Leslie handed out a pad of colored Post-it notes to each person, she continued, "Using your timing sheets, write out the steps that the credit transaction processor you observed used to complete the transaction. When you've finished writing out the steps, one per Post-it note, come up here to the butcher paper and stick the Post-its up in order." To make things clearer, Leslie put a Post-it note with each transaction processor's name on it up on the butcher paper so that people could see where to start their row of notes. "Once all of you have put up your Post-its, we'll be able to see if the steps are the same or not." Twenty minutes later, the butcher paper, filled with colored Post-its, looked like the one in Figure 4.7.

Leslie was not surprised at what the team had created, but she knew that the team would be. Looking at the process steps diagram, it was obvious that no credit transaction processors did the work in the same way. Standing back, Leslie waited for the team's reaction. After a few moments, Joe spoke first. Laughing he said, "I would not have believed it if I had not seen it laid out clearly like this. Leslie, we thought that everyone was doing the work in exactly the same way. But it's obvious that no two people are doing the work the same way! No wonder we have so many problems. No wonder it takes some people longer to do the same work than others. Everyone we sat with was very confident that they were working exactly the way that they had been trained to! Our assumptions this morning were definitely wrong!"

"Definitely," agreed Tabitha. "How could we have been so sure of ourselves? And now that we can see that everyone is doing the work differently, and that processing the transactions takes different people such different amounts of time, and that we have so many problems, especially with transactions that have more than 10 lines, what are we going to do about it?"

"That," answered Leslie, "is exactly what we're going to discuss . . . right after lunch!"

Reflection: Understanding the Current State

The current state is starting to reveal itself, and the team is getting excited. People are getting excited because they are accountable for the process of discovery. Many things were clear to Leslie from the beginning, but she was not going to reveal her own observations. First, she was not certain of her own observations and wanted real data and facts. Second, she needed to teach the members of the team how to see the state of their own processes. It is interesting that they lived in this organization and yet had strong misperceptions, for example, assuming all the credit transaction processors do the work in the same way, following the SOPs. Through

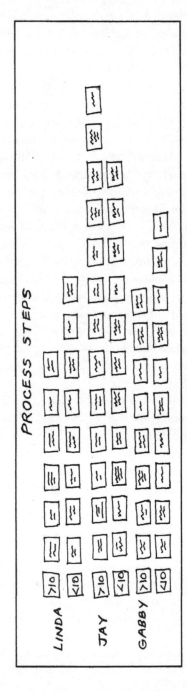

Figure 4.7 Process steps diagram by processor

108

structured observation it immediately became clear they were wrong. Leslie asked the question because she wanted public predictions. This was not to make fools of them, but so they could learn about the dangers of assumptions and about the gap between what they assumed and reality. People learn more by becoming aware of gaps between what they think they know and what they actually know than by being consistently right.

IDENTIFY GAPS AND PRIORITIZE

Prioritizing What to Strive For

When they returned from lunch, Leslie was pleased to see how obviously excited the team members were to continue their work. For the first few moments, they gathered around, chatting among themselves and pointing things out on the charts. After they all had finally settled back into their seats, Leslie said, "Team, I'm really proud of the work you did this morning. Looking at the process steps diagram and the other charts on the wall, we can see how much we've learned already about the wide variation in the way credit transactions are being processed and what some of the problems are. Now, as a team, we need to decide what we want to tackle to make the process better for everyone—especially our customers."

"Yes," said Tabitha, a little nervously, "I agree. But as I was saying before lunch, we seem to have so many problems, how do we know where to start? We can't work on everything all at once . . . can we?"

Leslie smiled and shook her head. "Tabitha," she said, "you're right. Sometimes when we have problems, we try to tackle a lot of different things and try a lot of different solutions, all at the same time. Has anyone here ever experienced that?"

Jorge said, "Leslie, are you sure you don't actually work at NL Services? Every time our numbers dip down, corporate yells and screams so much that we CTPMs make a list of every possible problem and every possible solution, and we just start trying to do all of them as quickly as we can. We just throw things at the wall and hope something will stick!"

Laughing, Leslie nodded her head and said, "Jorge, I promise you that I haven't worked at NL Services before, but I've certainly seen exactly what you're describing in many different places. And in my experience, it doesn't work very well: when we try to tackle too many things at once, we can't focus, and we don't end up doing anything well. And we can't understand why something worked or why it didn't."

Looking around the room, Leslie could see that the team was in agreement. "I'm going to suggest we try something different this time," Leslie said. "Let's decide together on one or two problems to work on and go from there." She continued: "I know we've identified a lot of problems. Can anyone think of a way that we could choose which we should start with?"

Kathy, who had been staring at the process steps diagram and run charts the whole time that Leslie had been speaking, suddenly turned to Leslie and the team. "Leslie," she said, "when I look at the run charts, what jumps out is that 'Transactions with more than 10 lines' take a lot more time to process. And we know that when there are problems with those transactions, our customers get fines from the state, and sometimes they're so angry that they change credit transaction processing companies. That's what happened three weeks ago with my biggest customer, E-Z Credit. Errors on transactions with 10 lines or more is a problem that's really bad for our customers—and it's really bad for us." Looking around the room, Leslie could see the team nodding in agreement.

Getting up from his seat and going over to the process steps diagram, Jimmy zeroed in, "Just look at this. You can see that none of the credit transaction processors do their work in the same way. It's no wonder that the run charts show that there is so much difference in the amount of time it takes to process the credit transactions. And I can't tell you how often my customers call and complain that their transactions aren't processed on time. Maybe if everybody worked in the same way, it would take less time and we could get the credit transactions processed when our customers want them."

Looking around excitedly, Tabitha said, "Maybe that's it—our charts and graphs are showing us that the two problems we should start with are fixing the problem with transactions that have 10 or more lines and figuring out how all the credit transaction processors can do their work in a way that all the credit transactions get consistently processed on time! If we can fix those two problems, our customers will be happier, and we'll be happier too!" Jorge, Laura, and Joe agreed with the credit transaction processors. If they could make a dent in those two problems, they'd certainly get fewer angry phone calls from their customers—and from corporate.

"Great job, team!" exclaimed Leslie. "Looking at the work that you did this morning, I agree that fixing those problems will be of great benefit to your customers—and your colleagues. I find it useful to think in terms of what we are trying to strive for rather than what problems we are trying to fix. For each of these two problems, what would success look like?"

Kathy looked thoughtful. "I guess if I stated the 10-line problem as something to strive for, I would say that we need accuracy and low processing times regardless of the number of lines."

Jimmy joined in, "And for the other problem, we would like a consistent, quality process regardless of which credit transaction processor does the work.

Now that I think about it, in both cases we want consistency and quality, and these are two different obstacles to those goals."

"I like it!" said Leslie. "Looking at the data that we have now, though, I'm not sure that we know enough about what's really going on in the transactions with 10 lines or more. My suggestion is that we spend the next couple of hours learning as much as we can about how those transactions are processed. Anyone have an idea of how we could do that?"

"Let's go back to the gemba and look and listen more," Kathy suggested. "I know how we can look up which credit transaction processors have transactions with 10 or more lines to process this afternoon. We could ask them if we could sit with them while they process the transactions so that we could see how they do it and what problems they are having."

"And," said Jimmy, "we could look really carefully to see how each of them is doing the process—record the steps again and then map them out to see if anyone has found a way to do the process more efficiently and with fewer errors."

"Plus," Tabitha said, "one of my best customers, Credit A2Z, always sends in transactions with 10 or more lines. I bet if we called the people there, they wouldn't mind telling us about how they feel about our processing. That might help us figure things out too."

Twenty minutes later, Kathy had distributed a list of all the transactions with 10 or more lines that were going to be processed that afternoon, and Jimmy and Tabitha had talked with all the credit transaction processors who were going to process those transactions to let them know about what the team was doing. Timing sheets in hand, the members of the team set off to learn as much as they could. Leslie promised that she would come and get them two hours later.

Reflection: Identifying Gaps and Prioritizing

Organizations often either experience a lot of angst over what problems to start with or else develop a laundry list of problems, quickly identify solutions, and then create an action list of who will do what and by when. Both are mistakes.

In the first instance, it actually is not critical that the team identify the optimal problem to work on at the outset. If the teams follow an approach of rapid experimentation they can quickly test their assumptions about the impact of solving various problems. There are a number of ways to quickly prioritize problems. Teams often use a simple 2 × 2 effort-impact matrix to classify problems by the likely cost of solving them and the potential impact on the customer and business. Obviously it is desirable to start with low cost and big impact problems. But we are still making subjective assumptions, and it's not until we run the experiments that we will learn if we are correct.

Developing long action lists is usually ill advised, as Leslie points out, because if many "solutions" are developed and many things implemented simultaneously and we see a change in the outcome, it is impossible to know what is having the impact, positive or negative. Single-factor experiments—in other words, trying one thing at a time—are ideal for learning what works and what doesn't.

STRIVE FOR FUTURE STATE THROUGH SMALL CYCLES OF LEARNING

PDCA Cycle 1: Deeper Dive at the Gemba

That afternoon, they all did their gemba study as agreed. At exactly 3 p.m., true to her word, Leslie gathered the team together, and they headed back to the conference room. As soon as they arrived, before Leslie had a chance to settle the team, Joe took a piece of flip-chart paper, stuck it to the wall beside the run charts they had made in the morning, and wrote ">10-line transaction problems." As the members of the team began to call out more of the problems that they had uncovered while sitting with the credit transaction processors, it soon became obvious that the majority of problems happened when the credit transaction processors entered the transactions from e-mails that customers sent in. When the team added up the number of 10-line-or-more transactions with which the credit processor had had a problem, there were three times as many that were submitted by e-mail.

"Interesting," Laura said. "I wonder why that would make a difference?"

"I have some ideas about that," Kathy answered. "When we enter credit transactions that have more than 10 lines, the information usually comes in an Excel template attached to the e-mail. When we open up the spreadsheet, there are 20 to 30 columns that have all kinds of information in them. We don't need to use most of it—just the transaction numbers and the dates. But in order to find those, we have to scroll back and forth across the columns and then up and down the different rows. It's like being a detective looking for what you need. Sometimes the spreadsheet is so big that we print it out so that we can highlight the transaction numbers and dates before we try to key them into the system. Whether you do it on the screen or from the paper, if you're not really careful, it's easy to make a mistake and pick up the wrong number in the wrong column."

"And all that hunting and pecking for the right number in the right column takes a long time, too," Tabitha noted.

"I've had that problem lots of times myself," Jimmy added. "And it's even worse when you're scrolling back and forth on the Excel template trying to get all the right transaction numbers, and the phone rings. Then you have to stop, open another window, process the credit transactions for the customer on the phone, and then go back and try to figure out where you were on the 10-line-or-more transaction spreadsheet. I'm always worried I've made a mistake when that happens, no matter how many times I check the transaction before I send it out."

"You know what, Jimmy?" Jorge said. "Lexi, the credit transaction processor I was sitting with, said exactly the same thing. She said that e-mail transactions with 10 or more lines were the worst because she knew she was going to be interrupted and probably make a mistake. She said she got a stomachache every time she had to process one."

Kathy finished the conversation by adding, "Think about it. When we process credit transactions by phone, the customer reads us the transaction number, and we repeat it back after we enter it. If it's wrong, we just fix it right away. And if we're on the phone already, no one can interrupt us!"

As the team continued to add to the list of problems, Leslie tore off another piece of flip-chart paper and stuck it on the wall beside Joe's. Under the heading "Obstacles," she listed six points, as shown in Figure 4.8.

After she finished writing the list of obstacles, Leslie checked her watch and said to the team: "Wow! It's almost 4:30. Time certainly has flown by. I think we're at a really good stopping point for today, but before we go, let's make a plan for tomorrow. Now that we have more information about the 10-line credit transaction problem, I'd like to suggest that we break up into two teams. One team will work on figuring out how to create a process that all the credit trans-

PROBLEMS	OBSTACLES
- Spreadsheets difficult to read - Need to print spreadsheets to key from - Hard to find the right transaction on the spreadsheet - Easy to make keying mistake - Lots of interruptions while trying to key accurately	1. Spreadsheets have many columns 2. Transactions not located in standard columns 3. Looking up and down from printed spreadsheet to computer screen 4. Moving back and forth between customer screens when interrupted by a customer calling in their transactions 5. Many customer screens open at once 6. Many papers on desks

Figure 4.8 Flip-chart pages of Joe's list of problems and Leslie's list of obstacles

action processors can follow so that it takes a similar amount of time to enter similar kinds of credit transactions, and one team can work on figuring out how to overcome some of the obstacles in the 10-line transaction process. How would everyone feel about that?"

Kathy and Joe looked quickly at each other and the team. Kathy said, "If everyone else is okay with it, I'd love it if Joe and I could work on the 10-line problem. I've complained to him about it so long and so often, I'm sure he thinks I'm like a broken record. But I'm only complaining because the problem is so important to me. And if I can do something to stop customers like E-Z Credit from leaving, it would make me really happy."

"Absolutely," said Laura. "Absolutely."

"Great!" said Leslie. "We're all set for tomorrow. Kathy and Joe will work on the 10-line problem, and Tabitha, Laura, Jimmy, and Jorge will work on figuring out how to create a process that will allow all the credit transaction processors to do a quality job on time for each customer."

Chatting among themselves, the team started packing up. As Jorge headed out the door, he almost collided with Lexi, the credit transaction processor he had sat with in the afternoon. "Jorge," Lexi said, "when you asked to sit with me today, I was a little nervous at first. But then when I saw you taking detailed notes and realized how interested you were, I began to get excited about it. I just wanted to come by and tell you that." Then seeing the charts and flip-chart pages on the wall, Lexi said, "Looks like you guys did a lot of work today!"

"We sure did," said Jorge. "And we couldn't have done it without your help—and the help of all the other credit transaction processors. Let me show you what we learned."

As Leslie watched Jorge explain the run charts and process steps diagram to Lexi, she smiled to herself. "Always best to go to the gemba and see for yourself. Works every time." It had been a great day today, and Leslie was sure that the next two days would be even better.

Reflection: Deeper Dive at the Gemba

We often think of PDCA at a macrolevel where we develop a plan for the entire problem, then implement it, then check what happened, and then define further actions. In any effort to improve complex processes, there are many embedded PDCA loops. And PDCA does not necessarily mean we "implement" something. It can mean we check our assumptions through further study. In this case the plan is determining what to study, for example, the 10-line problem, and how it will be checked. Then the doing is going to the gemba to do the study. Then we discuss what we saw and learned and define next steps.

PDCA Cycles for the 10-Line Problem

Over the next two days, both teams would be surprised at the amount of progress that they could make with Leslie's help.

Reviewing the data that they had gathered on the transactions with 10 or more lines and the list of obstacles that they had created, Kathy and Joe decided to concentrate on two things: finding ways to reduce the amount of interruptions that the credit transaction processors were having when entering e-mail transactions and seeing if there was a way to change the Excel template that contained the transaction numbers they needed to enter. They put up two flip-chart pages on the wall and brainstormed ideas. After about 20 minutes, they had generated two robust lists (see Figure 4.9). Sitting down at the conference room table, Kathy pondered, "Joe, now that we have all these ideas, I'm just not sure how to choose which one—or ones—to try first . . ."

Joe agreed: "I'm not sure either. Maybe we should see what Leslie thinks."

Leslie reviewed both lists of ideas with the team. "Excellent work," she said, standing back and looking at the lists. "I can see how you are having trouble deciding—and also why you are tempted to try everything at once. So many good ideas that might help. However, remember when we talked yesterday about trying too many things at once? When we do that, we don't have a way of knowing what, if any, of the things we tried moved us toward the target. In my experience, choosing one thing to change, trying it out, and seeing what happens is a better way to learn about what works and what doesn't."

Reducing Interruptions	Improve the Spreadsheet!
1. Turn off "pop-ups" for email notifications	1. Reduce number of columns so it's not so wide...
2. Turn off phone ringer	2. Review columns and see if all are still needed
3. Cover voicemail notification light on the phone	3. Hide columns without needed transactions
4. Set up a new "Aux" code on the phone to use when keying email transactions	4. Find a way to sort so that the transactions are in the same column
5. Key email transactions first thing in the morning when there are fewer calls	5. Don't print the spreadsheet
6. Make a "DO NOT DISTURB" sign for processors to use	6. Copy/paste from the spreadsheet to the system How?? Find a way!!
7. Create "no interruption" times during the day	

Figure 4.9 Flip-chart pages with ideas to improve the 10-line-or-greater transaction process

Figure 4.10   Plan-Do-Check-Act cycle

Leslie then went on to explain PDCA, the Plan-Do-Check-Act cycle to them (see Figure 4.10). "Trying things out with PDCA doesn't have to take long," Leslie explained. "It's like doing an experiment when you were in a lab in high school. You choose something to try that you think will make the problem better—you make a *prediction* about what is going to happen—then you try it out in a quick 'learning experiment.' We call that testing a countermeasure. Once you've tried your countermeasure, you can see if your prediction was actually correct . . . Did what you think was going to happen actually happen? Or did something else occur? Working like this helps stop us from making all those 'assumptions' that we all love to make."

Leslie smiled and looked at Joe and Kathy. Kathy looked at Leslie and then at Joe. "So," said Kathy, "if I understand correctly, we need to choose one of our ideas, figure out how to try it out quickly, and then do what we did yesterday! Go to the gemba with our timing sheets and see what happens when we try it out!"

"Absolutely correct," said Leslie.

With a thoughtful look on his face, Joe said, "It sounds like we don't need to get too hung up on trying to figure out which one to try first. We don't know what is going to happen with any of them. They're just ideas now. Until we try them out, we won't know which one is better. We can only guess. And our guess could be right or wrong. The important thing is to pick one, try it, and see what happens. Then we can move on."

"Absolutely correct, once again," said Leslie. "How many times do we get stuck trying to figure out what would be the *best* thing to try? Since everybody has an opinion based on his or her own personal preference, often nothing actually gets done."

Joe started to laugh. "Leslie," he said, "I know you keep saying that you haven't worked at NL Services before, but I am not sure that I really believe you."

Joe and Kathy decided to work on reducing interruptions first. Jorge asked Lexi, the credit transaction processor that he had spent time with the day before, if she would be willing to help Joe and Kathy try some things out. Lexi enthusiastically agreed to help. For each "countermeasure" they tried, Joe and Kathy used their timing sheets to see how long it took to enter the transactions with 10 or more lines. They also kept a record of how many errors were made.

By lunchtime, with Lexi's help, Kathy and Joe ran three experiments to test what happened if the credit transaction processors turned off the pop-up alerts on their e-mail, put their phones on "do not disturb mode," and taped a small red stop sign with the number 10 on it to the side of their cubicle wall to let other credit processors know that they were processing a transaction with 10 or more lines.

When they got the results of these three experiments, they discovered that the amount of time to process a 10-line transaction was cut in half and the number of errors was reduced by about one-quarter. Joe and Kathy were excited to share the results of their "learning experiments" with Leslie. "Great work, team!" Leslie exclaimed. "Looks like you've found some good countermeasures."

"Yes," agreed Joe. "This afternoon, we're going to work on some changes to the Excel spreadsheet. You can see that the amount of time it takes to enter the 10-line transactions has gone down a lot. But there are still too many errors."

"And no customer wants to have errors in their transactions," reminded Kathy. "It's not really going to help our customers if we process their work on time, but there are mistakes. Then they'll still get penalties from the state. We need to process their transactions on time and error-free! When we were sitting with Lexi, we could see how many problems using the printed spreadsheet caused her. She had a lot of great ideas about how to fix them that we added to our list, and we're going to work on those this afternoon."

Joe and Kathy spent the afternoon trying out their ideas and the ideas that Lexi had given them. By the end of the day, working together they had found a way to easily sort the columns on the Excel spreadsheet so that all the credit transaction numbers were lined up on the right-hand side of the page, one right under the other. They also found that since they didn't need to scroll back and forth through the spreadsheet anymore, they could make the spreadsheet much smaller on the screen, so that it fit right beside the credit transaction system window (see Figure 4.11). By doing that, Lexi could simply easily cut and paste the credit transactions from the spreadsheet into the system . . . and she didn't have to waste time walking back and forth to the printer. "Wow," said Lexi. "It's also a relief not to have all those papers on my desk. I don't have to worry that I'm keying from the wrong credit report spreadsheet anymore."

At four o'clock, Joe and Kathy headed back to the conference room. Having finished entering all her credit transactions, Lexi went with them. Reviewing the

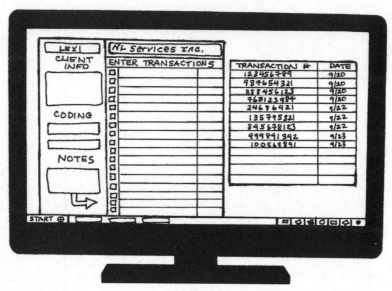

Figure 4.11 Lexi's computer screen with credit processing window and spreadsheet side by side

charts and graphs that they had created to record the results of the afternoon's "learning experiments," they found that they had been able to reduce the number of errors by three-quarters and that they had further reduced the time it took to enter the transactions by another half (see Figure 4.12).

Lexi, Kathy, and Joe were thrilled. Seeing their excitement, Leslie came over. "Team," she said, a big smile on her face, "looks like you've made some really great progress. I can't wait to hear all about it."

"Leslie," said Kathy, "you were right. By trying small changes, one at a time, we were able to see what worked!"

"And," interjected Joe, "look at the results! Errors and time to process both reduced by 75 percent! Our customers are going to love us!"

"Yes," agreed Lexi gleefully. "And think how much better it is going to be for us, too. I won't have to start each day dreading all the phone calls from customers angry about errors on 10 or more credit transactions—or fill out as many Billing Correction forms. That will certainly make my day easier and give me more time to process other customers' credit transactions. And I bet that not having to rush so much will also help with processing accuracy."

"Great work," said Leslie. "Look how much you have learned that will help your customers and everyone who does the work. Lexi, thank you for helping the team try all these things out."

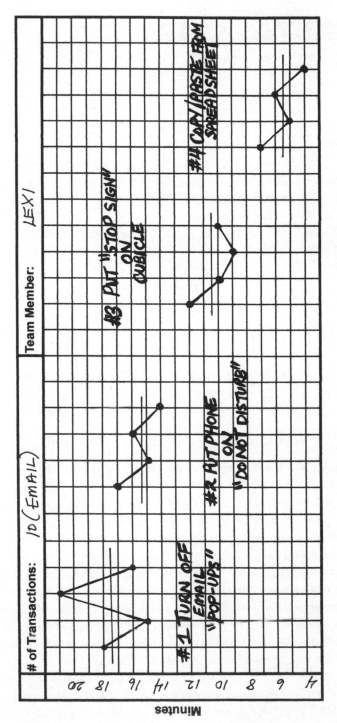

Figure 4.12 Run chart of times for each countermeasure

119

"No problem," said Lexi. "I was happy to help. This has been a big problem for a long time, and all of us wanted to solve it. We just didn't know how. I have a question though. This really worked for me today, but how do we know that it will work for the other credit transaction processors?"

"Great question," said Leslie. "We don't know yet. But I think we might have a way to find that out. Team, what do you think?"

Joe, Kathy, and Lexi looked at each other and then started to laugh. "Leslie," said Joe, "we need to try it out and see what happens. What if we asked one credit transaction processor from each team to try out the new process tomorrow."

"Yes," agreed Lexi. "In the morning, I could tell those credit transaction processors about my experience today. I bet that once they hear how much it has helped me, they'll be willing to give it a try."

"And," added Joe, "I could show the CTPMs from the other teams how to use the timing sheet. When the credit transaction processor on the team who is helping us has a 10-line transaction to process, the CTPM could do the timing for us."

Kathy jumped in, "Here's an idea! What if we put up a piece of flip-chart paper for each team. Then both the credit transaction processor who is helping us and the CTPM can record the results for everyone to see—time and accuracy! At the end of the day, we can pick up all the flip-chart papers and see if we were correct in our predictions of what would happen if other credit transaction processors used these countermeasures!"

"Sounds like a great plan to me," said Leslie. "A really great plan."

Reflection: PDCA Cycles for the 10-Line Problem

In a sense this is the easiest part for motivating people—actually doing something. In PDCA people love the doing, especially when they can see results. Planning takes more self-control. It can get tedious discussing, thinking, observing, charting, analyzing, prioritizing. One of the benefits of teamwork is that people help motivate each other even through the tedious work of planning, checking, and thinking about what actions should follow.

The biggest challenge in the Do stage is holding people back from wanting to try all their ideas at once. We cannot wait—we're like kids finishing the main course and having to wait for dessert. We want to see what happens—now! But as people experience the benefit of one-by-one experimentation, they come to appreciate what they are learning. They also start to appreciate that many of their assumptions about what will work are simply wrong. And they learn the all-important lesson that experiments do not need to be expensive and elaborate—simple ways of testing our ideas can be very powerful. We will go into much more detail about this in the people and problem-solving chapters when we talk about Toyota Kata—a method developed by Mike Rother for developing in people sound scientific patterns for achieving their goals.

PDCA Cycles for Common Process

By the end of the day, Laura, Tabitha, Jimmy, and Jorge had also made quite a bit of progress on the work that they had been doing to create a process to enter similar types of credit transactions. Since most of the credit transactions that were under 10 lines came in by phone, they decided to focus on those first.

They started out by carefully reviewing the process steps diagram that the team had created the day before. "Interesting, isn't it," said Tabitha. "It looks like it takes Linda and Gabby the shortest amount of time to process the transactions and that they use the fewest number of steps. I wonder if the steps are the same or different and why?"

"Yes, I wondered that as well," said Jimmy.

"If we line Linda and Gabby's Post-its up, one under the other, it should be easier to see," suggested Laura. After Jorge had rearranged the Post-its, the team spent an hour carefully going through the steps for both credit transaction processors.

"They're almost the same, but not exactly," said Tabitha. "It's interesting to me, though, that both Linda and Gabby ask the customer if there are any changes to the account that need to be made as one of the first steps."

"And both Linda and Gabby verify the number and total amount of the credit transactions at the end of the call," said Jorge. "I don't see those steps in the processes that a lot of the other credit transaction processors use."

"I wonder," said Tabitha, "if it takes Linda and Gabby less time to process the credit transactions because they don't repeat each credit transaction back verbally to the customer."

"I wondered that too," said Jimmy, "but when I was trained, I was told that I had to do that to ensure that the transactions would be accurate. I've always done it that way myself, as I don't want to make any mistakes. And looking at the process steps, I can see that most of the other credit transaction processors also do that. Maybe it takes Gabby and Linda less time because they use fewer steps, but how do we know if their work is really accurate?"

Jorge suggested that the team review yesterday's timing sheets to see how accurate Gabby's and Linda's entries were. Laura said, "Here's another idea of how we can check. I can generate a report to look back at accuracy over the past three months. It will only take a few minutes for me to pull it."

By the time Laura returned with the report, Tabitha, Jimmy, and Jorge had finished reviewing yesterday's timing sheets. They found that transactions processed by both Linda and Gabby were, indeed, highly accurate. Laura's report confirmed that over the last three months, Linda and Gabby had the best accuracy rates on both of their teams.

As the team members were finishing their discussion, Leslie came over to see how they were doing. "Leslie," said Tabitha, "we're doing great. We've found something that we think is really interesting, but we're all pretty surprised by it. The two credit transaction processors who take the shortest amount of time to process the transactions and who have the fewest steps in their process are also the most accurate. We were also surprised to find that, although their processes are similar, they're not exactly the same. All this is great information, but we're not sure what to do next."

Looking very pleased, Leslie said, "Great observations, team. It looks like you've learned something really important. Just because a process has a lot of steps, with a lot of checking, doesn't always mean it's the most accurate. And just because the process has fewer steps doesn't mean it's less accurate! That's a great thing to learn. How do you think you could find out why Linda and Gabby follow the process steps that they do?"

Jimmy answered almost instantly, "We could simply ask them!"

"Wonderful," said Leslie.

Jorge said, "I'll go ask their CTPMs if Linda and Gabby can spend some time looking at the process steps diagram with us. It will be really interesting to hear what they have to say."

Half an hour later, after reviewing the process steps with Linda and Gabby, the team found that the differences in the way they processed were just personal preference. "The way I do it just feels easier to me," Gabby said. "I've always done the steps this way. But Linda's way makes sense too."

"I feel the same way," said Linda. "I've always done it my way, but Gabby's way looks like it's also good."

Listening carefully to the discussion, Leslie said, "Team, I have a suggestion. Since we now know that the differences between Gabby's and Linda's processing steps are very minor, what if we created one set of steps that kind of combine Gabby's and Linda's, but at a higher level that does not lock in a specific script? And if Gabby and Linda and their CTPMs don't mind, perhaps both Gabby and Linda could try using those steps to see what happens this afternoon. Gabby and Linda, would that work for you?"

Working together, Gabby, Linda, and the team drew out the generic process steps that they would try on an 8.5 × 11 piece of paper (see Figure 4.13). At Leslie's request, Laura made copies and gave one to each team member. "Team," said Leslie, "this afternoon, Gabby and Linda are going to follow the process steps that each of you has a copy of. Laura and Jimmy will sit with Gabby while she processes transactions, and Tabitha and Jorge will sit the

Credit Transaction Process Steps—Telephone Calls

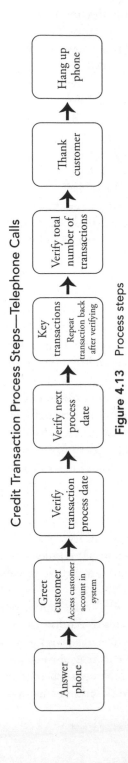

Figure 4.13 Process steps

Linda. Laura and Jorge will use the timing sheets to time each transaction, and Tabitha and Jimmy will note on the process step sheets any problems in the process that Gabby and Linda are trying out. At the end of the day, we'll all get back together to see what happened."

Just before four o'clock, Leslie gathered the team back in the conference room. Linda and Gabby came too. Looking at the timing sheets, the team could see that with the new combined process it had taken Linda and Gabby almost the same amount of time to process similar transactions. Their accuracy was also about the same and consistently high. There were a couple of notes and questions about possible problems on the process steps sheets, but they were very minor. "Team," asked Leslie, "how did that feel?"

"At first it felt a little bit strange to do things differently than I have always done them," said Linda, "But by the end of the day, I was already used to the new way."

"Me too," agreed Gabby. "I never would have thought that. One part of the new way was actually easier. I'd never have thought of it myself, so I'm happy I got a chance to work on this."

"And the times and accuracy were all very good," said Laura.

"Gabby, Linda, thank you so much for giving this a try," said Leslie. "I know how hard it is for people to change the way they do things. Now that we've found that this process seems to work for both of you, and that the timing and accuracy are good, how do you think we can help other people to try processing their work this way too?"

The team thought about it for a few minutes. Then Gabby said, "I have an idea. What if we made copies of the process steps sheets and gave them to the credit transaction processors on my team to try out tomorrow? I could tell them about my experience and how strange it felt at first to try a different process. But then it started to feel natural. I don't usually like to try new things, so if they hear my story, maybe they would be willing to try it too."

"I could do that on my team too," said Linda.

"And Jorge and Tabitha could sit with one of the teams to record the times and any problems in the process, and Jimmy and I could sit with the other team," suggested Laura. "That way we would be able to learn a lot more, and we could see what problems there are and how people would feel about processing in this new way."

"All great ideas," said Leslie. "Looks like we've got a plan."

The next day, each of the teams put its plans into place. Leslie spent the day in the gemba, checking on each team's progress, answering questions, and giving suggestions and guidance and encouragement when needed.

By the end of the day, looking at the data gathered on each team's flip charts, Kathy and Joe were confident that the countermeasures for the 10-line transaction problem that they had put in place worked as they had found in their small tests on the second day. Time to process was reduced by 75 percent, and errors were also reduced by 75 percent. With Leslie's help, they created a plan to work with the CTPMs to begin testing the countermeasures on all the teams. Each team now had a flip chart to record the data for timing and accuracy, and the CTPMs would check the results at the end of every day. Kathy and Joe would continue to work with the credit transaction processors to test new ideas that came up.

Gabby and Linda had each spent the first 15 minutes of the morning explaining the new process steps to each of their teams. Supported by Tabitha, Jorge, Jimmy, and Laura, both of their teams had spent the day trying out the new process and noting questions and problems on the process steps sheets. By the end of the day, the team members had collected a lot of good suggestions for improving the process steps even further. They decided that they would update the process steps sheet and try the changes with the two teams for the next two weeks. After that, if everyone agreed, they would expand their test, one team at a time, to the rest of the credit transaction processors. Tabitha, Jorge, Jimmy, and Laura would continue to work on process steps.

At the end of the day, the team gathered back together to pack up and reflect. Just as Leslie was about to thank everyone, she and the team were surprised by the sound of Sam's voice at the conference room door. "All right if we come in?" asked Sam.

"Of course," said Leslie, a huge smile on her face. As Sam and John, the regional credit manager, entered the conference room, the team members looked worriedly at each other. John only came down from his office on the third floor if something was really wrong, and Sam . . . well, other than the time that he had spent with them a few weeks ago . . . Sam never came to operations at all.

As the team looked nervously around, Sam started to speak. "Team," he said, "I know that you all must be very surprised to see John and me here. But with all the commotion and with my phone ringing off the hook for the past two days, I just had to come and see what was going on for myself. Normally corporate is calling me with bad news, but for the past two days, John and the CTPMs have been ringing my phone off the hook about how excited everyone has been. And walking around here for the past 15 minutes, I've heard and seen the excitement myself. The credit transaction processors have told me about all the hard work you've done over the past few days. They said the changes you're helping them make are really going to make a huge difference for our customers and for us. John and I both want to thank you personally and tell you how proud of you we are."

Smiling, Leslie said, "Sam, I can't agree with you more."

Reflection: PDCA Cycles for Common Process

To lean proponents, "common process" means standard work that is the best we know today but should be improved as we learn more. To most people, common process can mean we are all forced to do it the same way: "Our creativity and individuality are being subjugated to the corporate process, and now we have to act like robots." We will discuss standard work in Chapter 6 and argue that, if managed properly, it can actually be liberating instead of confining. We have some clues here when we see how the team became energized by doing what industrial engineers have done for the last century, often in conflict with workers.

Laura, Tabitha, Jimmy, and Jorge are part of the team, and they, not outside engineers, collected the observational data, posted it, analyzed it, and began to ask important questions. They did not hastily draw conclusions, but were thoughtful and tentative. They also did not immediately create their own process that they wanted everyone else to follow. Instead they observed that Gabby and Linda were the best performers and used a simpler process, one that even contradicted some of what the central office had taught as "best practice." They engaged Gabby and Linda by walking through the process and getting their perspective. Then they did something brilliant. They enlisted Gabby and Linda as advocates to help engage the other CTPs peer to peer. What could have been a sensitive, confrontational process became a collaborative process that further enhanced engagement and a sense of we as a team. And it immediately showed in the results—less time per call and more satisfied customers.

WHAT HAPPENS AFTER THE EARLY EXPERIMENTS?

The Next Challenge: Building on the Initial Excitement

As Leslie was heading out to her car with the last load of supplies, she ran into Sam. He and John had just finished meeting, and he was heading home too. "Leslie," he said. "Sarah was right. She knew that you'd be able to save the day over here at NL Services. I can't thank you enough." Leslie paused a moment.

Reaching out to shake Sam's hand, she said, "Sam. I appreciate the kind words. But the real thanks goes to the people that you just talked to down in the conference room. The credit transaction processors and CTPMs who worked on the team and who do the work every day. They know what the problems are and have great ideas about how to fix them. I just helped them get started putting those ideas in place. You've got great people working here, Sam. They really care about your customers. And they care about making NL Services successful. They're off to a great start, but they can't continue working this way without your help. My question for you, Sam, is what are you going to do to help keep this going?"

Sam smiled, "Leslie, you've always got the right questions. I'll be looking forward to having you help me and my team figure that out."

Next Steps: Two Possible Paths

Hanging up the phone, Sam thought to himself, "Who'd have believed it? I certainly wouldn't if I hadn't experienced it myself." It was a Monday morning—almost exactly six months to the day that his former colleague Sarah Stevens had suggested that he reach out to Leslie Harris—and the call he had just received from corporate wasn't an angry one, but a congratulatory one. Mike Gallagher, president of North American Operations, didn't usually call personally unless there was really bad news. But today, to Sam's surprise, Mike hadn't called to complain, but to congratulate Sam on the vast improvement the Southern Region was showing.

"Sam," Mike had said, "I was reviewing the numbers today, and for the third month in a row, your Southern Region is out in front on new business, client retention, customer satisfaction, and profitability. You're hitting on all cylinders. Just wanted to call and congratulate you personally. And find out what you're doing down there. The last time we talked, six months ago, it was quite a different story. People here are starting to say that you must be some kind of miracle worker. Want to find out what the 'special sauce' is and how we can share it with the other regions so they can get those results too."

After explaining the work that Leslie and the credit transaction processors and CTPMs had been doing, Sam had wrapped up by saying, "Mike, in the beginning, I didn't believe that lean management stuff could work for a service organization like ours either. But we've been working at it slowly but surely over the past six months, and you can see the results. But even better is what you don't see: how excited and engaged the folks are here who are doing the work, credit transaction processors and CTPMs alike. They've really taken our vision of 'Every customer's credit transaction right and on time, every time' to heart and are constantly striving to find better ways to work to make sure our customers' credit transactions are processed accurately and on time, which is exactly what our customers want. I'm really proud of the work that they've been doing. Leslie Harris, the consultant we hired to help us, has really opened my eyes to a new way of working."

"Well, Sam," Mike said, "sounds like you've got a good thing going down there. Why don't you put a PowerPoint together and send it up to me. I'll review it with the executive team, and we'll see what we can do. End of day Wednesday sound good to you? And by the way, pass my congratulations on to the team, too."

From here, our story could take one of two paths. NL Services could revert back to a mechanistic approach, or it could continue on an organic lean path.

Path 1: From Organic to Mechanistic

Three months later, sitting in his new office at Sarah Stevens's company, chatting with Leslie, Sam reflected on all that had happened since his call with Mike Gallagher that day. "Funny," he said, "even putting that PowerPoint together made me feel uneasy somehow. Maybe I should have been able to see what was coming, but my mind-reading skills aren't that good, I guess. Anyway, hindsight is 20-20."

After sending the PowerPoint to corporate, Sam had had quite a few meetings with the executive team. The team loved the results—think how thrilled the shareholders would be if management could replicate that throughout the company and document the improvements and results. But what the executive team didn't like was the amount of time it would take to get the rest of the organization up to speed. Think how long it would take for people in the rest of the regions to learn by identifying and solving problems themselves . . .

Meeting with the big-box corporate consultants that they'd used on other projects, the executive team had come up with a plan to implement an "out-of-the-box" lean management system: four months at the most, and the system would be deployed to all regions, and all regions would be up to speed. Once the consultants came in, figured out what the problems were, and came up with the solutions to address them, the lean management system would take care of the rest, and they'd be making money hand over fist. Mike had even asked Sam to lead the effort. It would be a promotion: executive vice president of Corporate Lean Strategy. Sam would be responsible for making sure that the regions were all on board and that the consultants were implementing all the right solutions so that everyone, in every part of the company, made the required numbers . . .

Sam agonized over this opportunity: more money, and a promotion . . . what he had been working for all this time. Funny, though, now that he had the offer, something just didn't feel right. So, he turned again to his good friend Sarah for advice. Sarah suggested that getting joy from his work might be more important than the money. To his surprise, she then found an executive position for him at her company. It did not pay as much, but well enough, and with stock options in this fast-growing company it might make him more money in the long run. Sam accepted. And he found that Sarah was right. Joy mattered to him more then he had realized. Then he met with Leslie to share the news.

"In my experience, that's the way it often turns out," said Leslie. "Can't tell you how many contracts I've lost to those big-box consultants that promise cookie-cutter solutions and quick fixes. It always seems much easier to focus on the bottom line and short-term results than focus on satisfying the customer and teaching people how to identify problems and strive for constant improvement. But I'm glad that we still get to work together, Sam."

"Yes," said Sam, "I am too. I'm glad there was an opening at Sarah's company. I've certainly still got a lot to learn. And on that note, let's go to the gemba and see how our teams are doing today!"

Path 2: The Road Less Traveled . . .

Six months later, sitting at the table in his office, chatting with Leslie, Sam reflected on all that had happened since his call with Mike Gallagher that day. "Funny," he said, "even putting that PowerPoint together made me feel uneasy. Looking back on it, I can see that I had already learned that PowerPoint 'data' couldn't tell the story of what we were working to accomplish in the Southern Region—that Mike Gallagher and the executive team would only be able to understand by going to the gemba to see for themselves."

"Yes," said Leslie. "And it's a good thing that you understood that. Not many people in your position really do. Most would have just sent the PowerPoint as their boss had requested. And even more importantly, most certainly wouldn't have spent as much time and effort as you did convincing Mike to come down here and see what was happening for himself."

Laughing out loud, Sam agreed with Leslie. "Yes," he said, "even I was surprised at myself! But it was definitely worth it. Things couldn't have turned out like they have if I hadn't been able to convince Mike to come see." It had taken many phone calls and meetings and a lot of begging, pleading, and refusing to send PowerPoints or any other kind of reports, but finally Mike Gallagher had agreed to stop by Southern operations. He had already had a trip to that area planned, and Sam had never been so insistent about anything before. After his initial frustration about Sam's refusal to send the PowerPoint had worn off, Mike had to admit to himself that he was actually intrigued.

After Sam, Mike, and Leslie had spent the morning touring the Southern operations and talking to the credit transaction processors, CTPMs, and John Edwards, the regional credit manager, Mike had been so impressed with what he had seen that he asked the members of the executive team to come down for a visit themselves. There was no other way for them to understand how different the operation was from any of their others: visual boards tracking problems and countermeasures that teams were working on were displayed for every team. CTPMs weren't in meetings the majority of the day, and they spent at least 25 percent of their time out on the floor gathering data or helping the credit transaction processors make improvements in the way they were working. The credit transaction processors' desks were neat and tidy, and there was no evidence of the frantic, chaotic atmosphere that Mike had seen in the company's other operations units.

Mike Gallagher had visited a few other companies implementing lean management systems that the big-box consultants that they normally used had suggested, but none of them had looked—or felt—like this. After the executive team members had visited the Southern Region, they all agreed that even though it would take longer than the plan the big-box consultants were trying to sell them, they couldn't deny what they had seen for themselves in Sam's region: that working to engage people in the way that Leslie was teaching and Sam was supporting was what would be best for their customers and their teams. And the results continued to show that.

"In my experience, that's not the way it usually turns out," said Leslie. "Can't tell you how many contracts I've lost to those big-box consultants that promise cookie-cutter solutions and quick fixes. It always seems much easier to focus on the bottom line and short-term results rather than focusing on satisfying the customer and teaching people how to identify problems and strive for constant improvement. I'm glad it worked out this way, Sam."

"Yes," said Sam, " I am, too, because I've certainly still got a lot to learn. And on that note, let's go to the gemba and see how our teams are doing today!"

REFLECTION ON DEVELOPING LEAN PROCESSES

The NL Services story is one we have lived through more times than we care to remember. Unfortunately it most often morphs from a vital organic pilot to a big-box consulting firm deploying tools mechanistically across the organization (as is illustrated in Chapter 6). Senior leaders often lack the mindset to understand the remarkable thing that happened in their own organization and what it takes to replicate it. What must be replicated is the experience and learning, not the tools and solutions.

NL Services just got started on its lean journey. Leslie's primary goals in the early pilot stage were:

1. **Develop Sam as an executive champion.** Without Sam on board, the game would be over. We saw that in the second ending of the story he was critical in persuading President Mike Gallagher to continue building on the organic approach instead of shifting to what would have been a deadly mechanistic approach. Does that mean that Sam was the ideal champion with the ideal training by Leslie? The answer is decidedly no! In an ideal world Sam would have been at the gemba regularly, daily if possible, learning along with the team. Sam would have gotten his hands dirty and participated in the observation, measurement, and analysis. Leslie quickly concluded this was not likely and the way to win over Sam was to demonstrate what lean can do, in results, in a better process, and in engaging peo-

ple. Notice that what got Sam so turned on was the people engagement he saw when he finally did visit the gemba. Since Leslie won, there would be plenty of time to continue to educate Sam. In the later chapters on developing people and implementation strategies, we will talk more about how to win over the right people. The main point is that it is critical to develop an executive champion, and the most effective approach will depend on the individual.

2. **Create a successful demonstration (pilot) project.** Leslie needed to prove that lean applies in not just a service operation but in NL Services' operations. In our experience almost all people think their organization is unique. This applies to NL Services and unfortunately even to individual departments within NL Services. "We are different. We do not build cars. We do not have repetitive operations. We have to behave differently with every customer, and we cannot estimate times or forecast demand. We can only rely on our own experience to get through each day and don't need advice from consultants who do not understand our business."

The only way to begin to sell people on a new vision is to give them an opportunity to directly experience what it can be like—they need to experience success. Success in this case goes beyond results. Recall in Figure 4.1 that in a real lean management system, it matters more how to develop a solution than the specific solution developed. Mechanistic deployment of lean means specifying solutions and auditing whether people have all the boxes checked. In organic deployment we want people to experiment and learn through experience, both successes and failures. But the search process itself is specified: present a clear challenge, gather data and facts, go to the gemba, work as a team, experiment in rapid PDCA cycles, and treat people with respect. None of these are optional. A successful demonstration project means engaging people in a good process that leads to desired results.

3. **Begin to educate.** Education in lean happens primarily at the gemba. Well-run classroom training programs can be effective in raising awareness. They can even teach certain technical skills. But to truly understand lean transformation, one must experience it firsthand at the gemba. That is why Taiichi Ohno did all his training at the gemba on real problems. Through the demonstration project Leslie educated people about what, how, and why. She developed advocates who could help persuade others to develop a good process yielding successful results so they could become further advocates, and so on. The demonstration project can also serve as a go-and-see classroom. By touring people

through the project area, with the people working there as guides, we can raise awareness and generate a degree of enthusiasm for lean. "If they can do it, why can't we?"

Where does NL Services need to go from here? It would be very clear if it had hired a big-box consulting firm. NL Services would have spread lean broadly and quickly according to a prescribed recipe. What NL needs is to find the right balance between breadth and depth, and this balance will be constantly shifting as the company progresses. The reason for a vision is to provide a general direction for a long-term journey. The journey is a process of discovery, not a process of implementing known solutions.

With Leslie's guidance, NL Services took a step off the ledge into a zone of uncertainty. It has to accept that the prevailing assumption about the one best way to organize a process is limiting progress. The company needs to learn to adapt and learn, not specify and expect obedience. The transformation process itself is filled with uncertainty. Instead of a prescribed recipe, we want thinking leaders who are learning through PDCA cycles. They are constantly trying things, reflecting, and making informed best guesses about the next step—driven by a true north vision.

Does this mean that there are no guidelines and there is no body of knowledge that can help NL Services on its journey? Not at all. There is plenty that is known. Leslie in fact was quite knowledgeable about the tools and principles of lean. When she suggested that the team use a certain method for observing and recording data, it was based on standard tools applied in the right way to the right problem. As the demonstration area advanced, the team members were beginning to apply tools like visual management, metric boards, and standard work. Leslie realized that teaching them small bits of information about tools and methods as they needed them to address problems was more effective than running a "lean basics" training class.

In this book we will not be teaching the technical tools of lean, though these are very powerful. They are covered in depth in a variety of books, including *The Toyota Way Fieldbook*. At the end of this book we have a recommended reading list. What we will provide in the next chapters are some generic principles for lean processes. These are intended as guidelines to answer what a lean process looks like and why. As we will see, NL Services, Inc. had only scratched the surface of what is possible.

KEY POINTS
DEVELOPING LEAN PROCESSES

1. Processes are theoretical concepts that involve the interdependence of many people and the way their work is completed, not concrete things waiting to be "leaned out" using a generic, prepackaged solution.

2. We suggest following these six steps as a general, high-level approach to improving processes and simultaneously developing people in any organization:

   - Be sure that senior leadership is serious about a need for change.
   - Understand senior leadership's vision and strategy to achieve business objectives and fulfill the organization's purpose.
   - Grasp the situation about how the company is currently performing in relation to senior leadership's vision.
   - Understand the current state of work processes in relation to challenges the business is facing.
   - Identify gaps and prioritize so that big gaps can be divided into smaller, more manageable chunks of work to be improved on right away.
   - Strive for the future state through small cycles of learning using the iterative process of Plan-Do-Check-Act.

3. Traditional management systems specify solutions and leave the development of those solutions to team members, whereas Toyota's management system specifies *how* to develop solutions using PDCA and leaves creating the solution to team members.

4. Instead of mechanically sorting problems and trying to predict what the internal impact of solving them might be, test quick countermeasures to learn whether solving the problem will make a significant impact for the customer and organization.

5. Use PDCA to check whether assumptions are correct or not through quick learning experiments.

6. Creating a successful demonstration project allows people to learn lean practices and tools through doing and is a powerful way to engage senior leaders as they see business results and positive effects for customers and employees right away.

Chapter 5

Macroprocess Principles: Create a Cadence of High Value Flowing to Customers

The supposition is prevalent the world over that there would be no problems in production or service if only our production workers would do their jobs in the way that they were taught. Pleasant dreams. The workers are handicapped by the system, and the system belongs to the management.

—Dr. W. Edwards Deming, quality guru

WHAT IS THE VALUE OF LEAN PROCESS PRINCIPLES?

Principles Are Not Solutions

Principles can help us think about what we want to accomplish; they do not solve problems. Mechanistic thinking seeks "best practices" to imitate. We see an excellent organization do it, we start to do it, and we are convinced we will achieve the same outcomes as the benchmark organization. As Dr. Deming warns, "Pleasant dreams." We know little about what the benchmark organization went through to achieve the results, and it was almost certainly more than copying someone else's solutions.

Systems thinking strives for new levels of performance by learning our way beyond our current knowledge threshold. We cannot be sure how to achieve our goals, so we must learn, scientifically, how to do so. In the scientific process of PDCA, the principles primarily help us in defining our future state, developing intermediate target conditions, and thinking through possible countermeasures to test in the Do stage. After that we should leave it to experimentation, deep thought, and the learning that comes from the experiments.

We repeatedly see organizations with a mechanistic orientation adopt lean or six sigma or some combination as a program. They copy the most obvious features of Toyota. Toyota has the TPS house, so they develop their own (company name) operating system, and it often looks like a house. Usually it includes a flow pillar, a built-in quality pillar, and a foundation of stable processes and a management

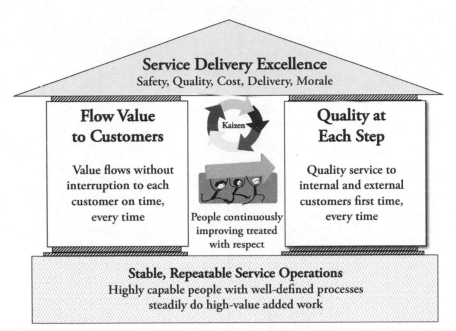

Figure 5.1   The Service Company X operating system

philosophy. We have adapted the TPS house for services, and as an image it seems to be a useful starting point (see Figure 5.1). The basic concepts of one-piece flow to customers, built-in quality, continuous improvement, and stable, repeatable processes are powerful indeed for both manufacturing and services and form the basis of the process principles in this chapter and Chapter 6.

Positive images are a starting point and, as such, can be powerful, but we know that culture runs much deeper than visible artifacts. It makes no difference what the picture shows. What matters is what people do and how they think on a day-to-day basis. Mechanistic organizations do something with those pictures that Toyota actively avoids: they turn them into corporate standards to be implemented and enforced through audits. The elements of the house are broken down into a list of things that thou shalt do . . . or else.

I consulted to a massive Russian company that sought out help to learn TPS directly from Toyota. The CEO used political connections, and Toyota sent its top TPS expert as a consultant for one year. The company president took the advice of the Toyota expert very seriously, treating him as his most trusted advisor and doing virtually anything he asked.

I had a long meeting with the vice president of Continuous Improvement who was perplexed by the TPS expert. He explained that the Toyota guy wanted the company to dismantle almost everything that had already been set up in the name of lean. The company had installed an elaborate auditing system to ensure all plant managers implemented all the lean tools, or it would hurt their annual bonus. The Toyota sensei looked at the auditing system and said: "Please stop doing this. Plant managers will obey, but they will not understand." The sensei was also not pleased with a macro value-stream map that showed the entire process from getting raw materials from the ground to delivering the finished product to the customer. The sensei bemoaned, "Problems, problems, where will you start?" He seemed to dismiss the macro map. The company executives had begun to bring lean to the office and wanted to spread it enterprisewide, but the sensei discouraged them from enterprisewide transformation and instead focused on one value stream of one factory.

The VP and I had a long talk, and I explained my best guess about the reasoning of the Toyota sensei. Simply implementing tools is not the same as having a living system that continually improves. I also explained that the purpose of the model area in the one plant was to teach everyone, including him, what real TPS is. As it was, there was not a single example anywhere in the company of real lean as a living system. Until the people at the company experienced it firsthand, they would not understand. The VP was very grateful for my explanation, which was much more detailed than anything the Toyota sensei had given, and then the VP confided in me that the company had secretly kept the audit system for grading plant managers.

As we go through our distillation of lean process principles, please do not think of them as a checklist of things to do. Think of them as guidelines or as positive visions to strive for. We have intentionally kept them very general so they apply to any type of work process. The important thing is that each step of your transformation process should be purpose driven, not tool driven.

Value-Stream Mapping to Develop a Macrovision

Value-stream mapping is probably the most popular of the lean tools. It originated within a group of specialists at Toyota called the Operations Management Consulting Division. The purpose was to understand the current flow, or lack of flow, of material and information. From a 30,000-foot perspective, how does material flow through the factory or supply chain, and how is information used to influence the flow? Then the more important question: How *should* it flow to achieve our desired results? It was originally used as a tool for the TPS master trainers to quickly get a picture of the current state and generate a challenge for the students, for example, suppliers who were learning about TPS. The trainers intentionally did not share the maps, as they believed the students would not understand. Rather the sensei would use mapping to generate challenges that the trainers would

present to the students one at a time so that the students unknowingly were building toward the future state. Later, when value-stream mapping became popularized
by Mike Rother and John Shook in *Learning to See*,[1] Toyota gave it the name of
the material and information flow diagram (MIFD). Since then, value-stream
mapping has taken on a life of its own, not always in positive ways.

We use value-stream mapping regularly in technical and nontechnical service
work, and it is powerful. The team members learn to map their current process
from the customer's perspective. Often a benefit of value-stream mapping is
understanding how to reduce lead time from the customer order/request to when
the customer receives the service. Figure 5.2 gives an example of the process steps
in an accounts payable process. There are multiple steps being done by multiple
people, so the cases are batched before being moved and then worked on. The
obvious result—customers wait a long time to get paid. The less obvious problem
is that any defects are apt to be hidden for quite some time before the customer
discovers them—feedback loops are very long. Seeing this, there is a temptation
to immediately implement a variety of "solutions" to eliminate waste. Don't do it!
It will limit your learning and progress. With value-stream mapping a visual image
of the current process is developed, but then we go further to develop a future state
that flows value more quickly to the customer with better quality.

Among the well-informed, value-stream mapping has become a popular
approach in lean services to understand the waste and to develop a future state
vision.[2] It is a common sight in conference rooms for multifunctional teams to
place sticky notes on the wall working to represent the current process. This is
often done in a workshop format of a few days. Our best experiences include a
gemba walk, even if that means talking to personnel sitting at their desks who
explain what they do. Rother and Shook warn us not to stop at identifying and

- Analyze process lead time
- Calculate value-added ratio = VA/total lead time

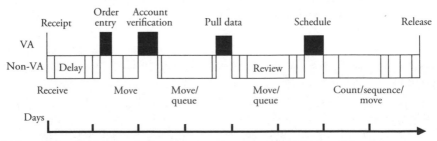

Figure 5.2   A picture of the current state of an accounts payable process

fixing wastes in the current state. The real power of the tool is getting the team to jointly envision a preferred future state. Simply fixing problems in the current state will rarely get you to a desirable future state.

When my associates and I use the tool, we do not get deeply involved with technical details, especially when dealing with highly variable service work. The 80-20 rule works well for value-stream mapping—get 80 percent of the benefit with 20 percent of the effort. Mostly what they put on the wall are steps, rough times for a step (sometimes ranges of times), arrows connecting the steps, and some sort of icon for queues of work in process. It is big picture and rough. We have seen lean specialists in companies agonize over detailed data to get precise estimates of value-added time and non-value-added time, and mostly we see this as waste. Many service processes are simply too variable and complex to get so precise, and it is not really the purpose of the tool. The purpose is to get people to see flow and waste and envision what is possible within their value streams. When they get into implementation to achieve the challenge of the future state, they will delve into a more detailed understanding of the current condition and learn far more as they begin to actually experiment with new ideas for improvement.

We often start the current-state analysis by asking several team members to put together a rough process map before the workshop. The team members generally start by mapping the formal system—how they think the process should work. When a cross-functional team comes together for the workshop they dig deeper into the current state, adding a lot more Post-it notes to the wall, and more complex feedback loops are added for rework. In the final analysis it is almost comical how obtuse the process is—so full of waste. And we want the team members to see the contrast between the theoretical formal system and what is actually happening. Most experienced lean manufacturing consultants I know see much more waste in services than in manufacturing.

In Figure 5.3 we show the cleaned-up results of a mapping workshop we led on the process of creating a purchase order. This form of mapping divides tasks by swim lanes. Along the left-hand side are different roles or departments. Across the top is a time scale. The Post-it notes are lined up in rows showing who does what and when. Notice that depending on the type of purchase order, there were three different approaches. Even though you cannot read all the steps on the Post-its, it is clear at a glance that this is an overly complicated process for what would seem to be a straightforward task.

The group considered lean process principles and worked to develop a streamlined approach that also improved accuracy and had less documentation. The results are shown in Figure 5.4. In the course of the discussion, one member almost naively asked if it was really necessary to have three different approaches.

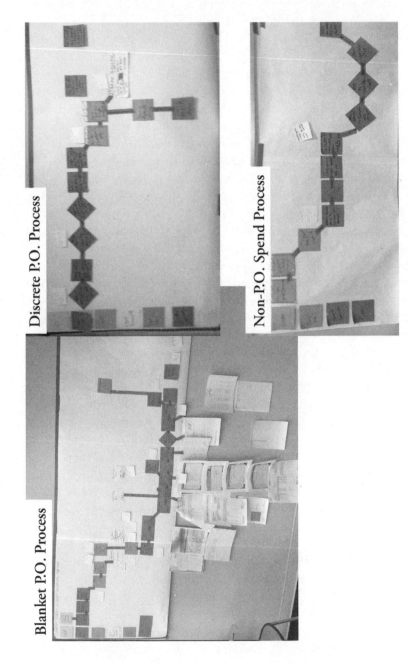

Discrete P.O. Process

Non-P.O. Spend Process

Blanket P.O. Process

Many Opportunities for Lead-Time Improvement

Figure 5.3   Three current-state maps for three types of purchase order processing

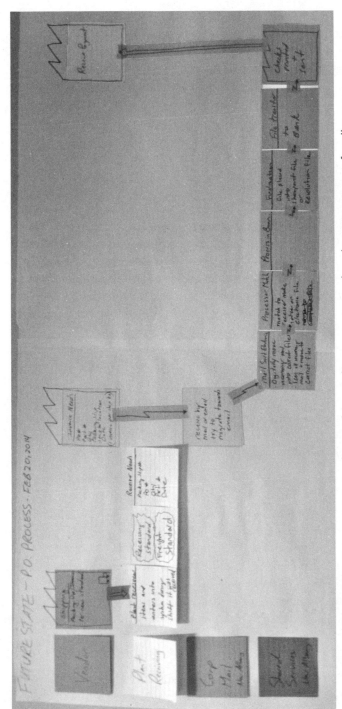

Figure 5.4 Future-state map for purchase order processing reduced to one process for all cases

The initial reaction was "Of course, they are different types of POs with different requirements." As they dug in, the team came up with one standard process for all three types of POs. The result was a much improved process including the following highlights:

- Documents are digitized upon receipt.
- Documents move through the entire process in electronic form.
- Only necessary documents are retained in electronic form.
- The check-printing and mailing processes might be outsourced to a bank (subject to a cost-benefit analysis).
- The process is clearly defined.
- Clearly defined performance metrics are visually posted for daily meetings.

Through a lot of work after the mapping exercise, the team achieved a 50 percent reduction in lead time, reduced the number of steps and reports, and eliminated the waste of 120,000 pieces of paper (minimum) per year, and the group for the first time had clear performance metrics for quality and productivity.

The purchase order maps are by no means complex or elaborate. In fact, compared to most manufacturing value-stream maps they are missing a great deal of information. The rate of customer demand (takt) was not calculated. There is no data at all, nor even times required for each step. Few of the icons that are common in value-stream mapping are used, such as inventory buffers. In this case the process was so variable that it did not seem worth getting to that level of detail. In other cases we have included more data, particularly when the service process is more routine and repetitive. For this team, and all others we have worked with, value-stream mapping has a number of benefits beyond the technical details of the maps:

- Teams communicate across functions to understand the perspectives of others.
- Team members are shocked at the amount of waste, and that shock therapy ends questions about whether lean was needed or whether it applied to them.
- Team members increase their appreciation for the customer perspective and begin to identify the causes of customer complaints.
- Team members begin to think about their processes intentionally and scientifically, including how to measure performance and continue to improve.

Lean Principles Inform Target Conditions to Strive For

In *Toyota Kata*, Mike had a moment of clarity when he realized that tools like pull and standard work were neither process improvements to be implemented nor ends unto themselves. Instead he called them possible "target conditions." A target condition is a work pattern that we hypothesize will move us a step closer to our desired goals. Consider a sports example. A desired outcome in basketball is to get the ball into the basket a high percentage of the time when we get to the free throw line. We might set as a target to accomplish this 80 percent of the time, and currently we are at 60 percent. Simply telling a shooter that the goal is 80 percent can perhaps lead to more practice, but if the posture, motion, and release of the shooter are poor, there is probably a limit to how well the person will be able to shoot.

A good coach will observe the shooter and notice obstacles to successful outcomes. Perhaps the coach will video the shooter in action and go through the tape in slow motion with the shooter so they both can see what happens. The coach is trying to understand the current process of shooting that leads to the outcome of hitting or missing the basket. A good coach will avoid inundating the shooter with a long list of things to improve. The shooter will simply be overwhelmed in thinking about so many things at once—how to set the feet, how to position the arms, how to hold the ball, how to move the arms and body in the shooting motion.

It is more effective to suggest one thing to practice at a time. Perhaps it is a change in the initial stance of the shooter. The desired stance can be considered a target condition that the coach, through experience, believes will lead to a higher success rate in getting baskets. And perhaps that alone might be expected to increase baskets by 2 percent. Both the way of shooting and the expected result would constitute the next target condition. After practicing that one thing sufficiently to achieve that target condition, the coach will again observe and suggest a next target condition, and so on. In other words, the coach is breaking down the complex task into specific desired patterns, which are learned through practice one by one, and a target for results. After each target condition the coach will decide what is next based on what was learned from the last experiment. The best coach will follow a somewhat different process for each student based on the student's unique circumstances, even though the coach has a general set of principles and a sense of an approach that works. Through this iterative learning process, the student will get better, though perhaps with setbacks here or there. The setbacks are some of the best opportunities for the coach to teach the student—and for the coach to learn.

Deming taught us to focus on the process as well as the results. Identifying target conditions brings into focus process patterns we are trying to achieve. We often think of a tool such as value-stream mapping or a one-piece flow cell as a generic solution to a problem. We think that we aren't getting the improvement results we expected from our lean management system because we didn't create value-stream maps of all our processes, or we may think that if we have a cell, we will automatically get better flow, better productivity, more consistent production, and better quality.

When Mike Rother reflected on value-stream mapping, he realized that the future state map is actually providing a set of challenges and target conditions. Each piece of the map, such as setting up a cell, is actually a bundle of target conditions.[3]

If we think of establishing a one-piece flow cell as a target condition, it provides a totally different image than the usual one of implementing a tool. First we must answer the question of why. What is the challenge, and why do we believe a cell will get us closer to our particular challenge? A good understanding of the current condition relative to the challenge will help us identify whether this target condition, or some others, makes sense to test. If our analysis and time at the gemba suggests a one-piece flow cell is worth pursuing, then we would view this as a target condition. On a certain date in the future, our goal would be to have the cell operational. The concept of a target condition as something to strive for is well illustrated in Rother's diagram (Figure 5.5).

The Role of Process Principles

In short, please do not confuse principles with solutions. A better approach is to view them as guidelines to stimulate thinking. As we show in Figure 5.6, the principles are mostly useful in the Plan stage of PDCA.

Establishing a Target Condition Is Like Time Travel

If we fast-forward to the achieve-by date and look at the focus process, the Target Condition is a description of what we would see

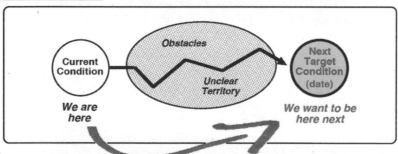

A Target Condition answers questions like:
 • *What do we want this process's operating pattern to be by (date)?*
 • *How do we want this process to be functioning by (date)?*
 • *What functionality do we want to have by (date)?*
 • *Where do we want to be next? What is the target pattern?*

Figure 5.5   A target condition is a work pattern to strive for

Source: Mike Rother

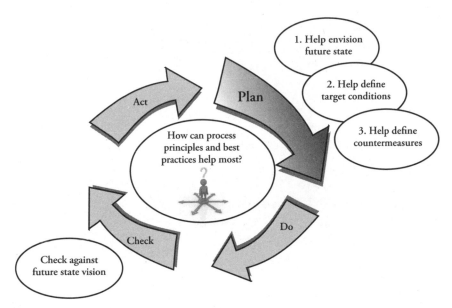

Figure 5.6 Process principles and best practices help most in identifying challenges, target conditions, and ideas for experimentation in the Plan portion of PDCA

They can help us to visualize our future state. They help us define our target conditions. This does not mean we fill in the blank in a statement like "Our target condition will be (*principle*)." A good target condition should be be far more specific and measurable and appropriate for our situation.

Process principles can also help us to identify possible countermeasures. Again the principles do not provide countermeasures. But they might trigger thoughts about possible countermeasures.

Beyond this we could refer to the principles in the Check stage to help us evaluate how well we did in implementation, but again there are dangers in this. We do not want generic lean audits, but rather we want specific checks that are appropriate for the specific target condition and countermeasure we are testing.

We have identified four macroprocess principles (see Figure 5.7), and we will explain each with examples. The principles were first introduced in Figure 2.11, where all 17 principles arc listed.

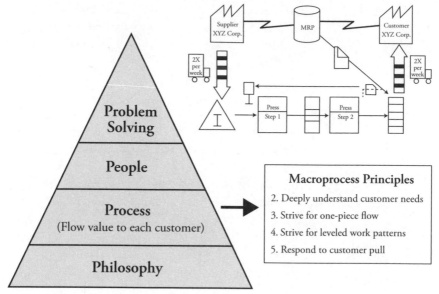

Figure 5.7   Macroprocess principles

PRINCIPLE 2: DEEPLY UNDERSTAND CUSTOMER NEEDS

Menlo Innovations: Creating Joy for Customers

When I think of a customer-centered organization, Menlo Innovations immediately comes to mind. I have visited hundreds of service organizations with some type of lean program, but Menlo is as close to a service organization that practices Toyota Way principles as I have seen, and the company knew almost nothing about Toyota when it formed its system. In fact, one of the founders, Richard Sheridan, learned about me when he was presenting about Menlo at a conference in California and an associate told him about *The Toyota Way*. Richard became excited and wanted to meet me only to learn we both live in Ann Arbor, Michigan. We became fast friends.

Menlo Innovations, LLC, is a custom software design and development firm for hire, located in Ann Arbor. If you go to the company website, you will see its funky, and very personal mission:

> *Our mission as an organization is to end human suffering in the world as it relates to technology. For our clients, we do this by creating software that is widely adopted and enjoyably used by their intended end users. We do this*

through a unique set of practices that include High-Tech Anthropology, paired programming, and working in an open and collaborative environment. Within our organization, we achieve this mission by intentionally choosing to create a culture founded on the Business Value of Joy.

Richard explains that Menlo focuses on three key stakeholders, who are often poorly treated in the software business:

1. Software project sponsors who traditionally have had little hope of steering projects to a successful conclusion before money and executive patience are exhausted
2. End users of the software who, far too often, have no voice at all in the design and yet must ultimately live every day with decisions of people who know little about them
3. The software teams themselves, who typically labor under years of overtime, missed vacations and family celebrations, and broken relationships and unrealistic expectations only to have many of the projects they work on never see the light of day

Menlo, a small but growing firm that by 2016 was up to 70 people, has cast a long shadow on the software development industry. On a typical day one might see tour groups from five different countries, a Fortune 100 company that has sent a team to go through a several-day workshop on the Menlo system, and customers lingering in the offices working with Menlonians (as they call themselves). There are remarkable aspects to Menlo's culture that we will discuss in Chapter 7. For a detailed description of its systems for customer engagement, software development, and the development of a deliberate culture built on collaboration and learning, read Richard Sheridan's *Joy, Inc.*

At Menlo, the customer experience starts with a discussion with the customer about the possibility of working together. The initial discussion can be pretty straightforward if the customers are already familiar with Menlo's different approach to software development, or rather odd for the customers if they are not. As Michael Porter says, a real strategy includes what you will *not* do. There are certain givens that the customers must accept, or they are not suitable partners:

1. They must pay for a pair of High-Tech Anthropologists.
2. They must pay for pairs of software programmers who will be rotated every week.
3. They must be active participants in a collaborative learning process, including weekly meetings to review the work completed in the prior five days.
4. They must pay for an up-front stage of developing their requirements before they get a price estimate.

A customer who says no to any of these four conditions will not be a customer, and Menlo will even recommend competitors as service providers. Secretly the Menlonians will be thinking, "You will be back." They specify those conditions, not to be stubborn or belligerent, but because it is the only way they know to achieve their mission of a joyful experience for all.

The actual development process begins with a pair of High-Tech Anthropologists who live with users to understand their beliefs, values, and work patterns and ensure the software meets actual needs, not simply professed needs. Interestingly Menlo has found the best at this role rarely have anthropology degrees or technology backgrounds. They have a certain combination of empathy, creativity, observational skills, listening skills, and a practical skill of turning what they learn into a vision for the software.

Though it is creative work, the High-Tech Anthropologists have a somewhat standard process that in lean terms starts with going to the gemba to see, without preconceptions, how the users do their work and use any existing software for the task.

An early challenge for the customer is to identify a primary user, and this is visually represented using a persona map (see Figure 5.8). The High-Tech Anthropologists, through their investigations, develop an image of each persona and write a story, a fictional account of a typical user role. The task of the customer is to identify one type of user as the primary persona who will be the focal point when developing the software. Menlo has learned that focusing on an average user, or too many users with different needs, muddies the process and leads to software that misses the mark for everyone. Customers struggle to pick one as they are at first convinced that all types of users are equally important, but eventually the customers settle on one primary user and a few secondary and tertiary users, with all others outside the target area.

Menlo developed a sample persona map based on a fictional company called Wedding.com that helps customers plan their wedding. One could imagine that the bride or groom would be the obvious primary persona, but the anthropologist and customer decided differently. They found the mother of the bride was most often the planner and also had less experience with web user interfaces than the couple getting married. Menlo created a composite profile of the "mother" called Kathleen Tiber. Among other characteristics she "hates having to call her kids for simple tasks on the computer." Her goals are to "plan the wedding of the century" and "avoid situations where people use terms she does not understand." Undoubtedly a simple and clear user interface is critical. The wedding couple are in the secondary circle, and the groom's parents are tertiary users. Their needs will also be considered, but the features they use that are not of value to Kathleen will be a few clicks away from the home screen.

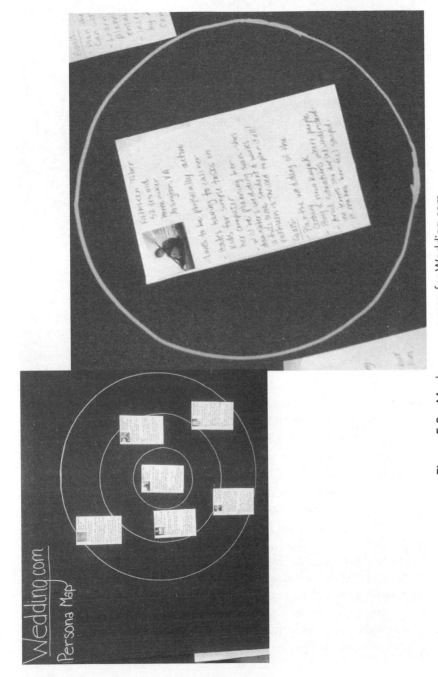

Figure 5.8 Menlo persona map for Wedding.com

Figure 5.9 Mind maps to see the whole

The anthropologists have intense discussions at whiteboards and develop mind maps of characteristics of the users and the software (see Figure 5.9). They spend a good deal of time crafting the purpose and desired features of the software. They consider many alternatives with the customer, often comparing pros and cons.

As the anthropologists get a clearer picture of the users and software features, they write very specific "story cards," one for each feature. For example, creating a button to call up possible floral arrangements is a feature that gets its own story card. Making a schedule is another feature that would get a story card.

These story cards become the basis for selecting what to include in the software to deliver value determined by the customer, and the cards also become the method for organizing the work of the programmers. In fact, a complete project plan will be built from these cards. The time to develop the actual code for each card is first estimated by several pairs of programmers. Then the cards are laid out on standard sheets to add up to 32 hours of work in a week (the other 8 hours are for various meetings like the customer review). This leads directly to a cost estimate based on a standard cost per sheet for a pair of programmers. The customer works with the team to decide on the actual project scope, "playing cards" and seeing what it adds up to in cost. If the cost is over budget, the customer must either drop some features, by eliminating story cards, or perhaps push them into a later budget cycle.

Every week, the customer meets with the Menlonians working on the project. These in-person meetings are usually at Menlo, or if necessary, at the customer's office if it is located too far from Menlo. Virtual meetings are a last resort and at least one monthly meeting must be face-to-face. When the software is being developed, the customer tries the results of one week's work on the computer while the anthropologists and programmers are watching. The customers have the story cards so they know what the feature should do. With no user manual they should be able to make the feature work—and be delighted by what they see. Otherwise it is back to the drawing board. At the end of the customer review, the customer decides what cards to play the next week. This is PDCA at its best, in short cycles with rapid feedback!

Notice that this process makes the standard practice of competitive bidding almost impossible. Typically the customer puts out a request for bid and then compares the proposals of different firms. The assumption is that the customer knows what he wants, or with a little research the contractor will figure out the scope of work, a project plan, and the cost. Menlo needs the customer to pay for a collaborative process to learn what the customer actually needs, which precedes any competitive bidding. If the customer were to shop these requirements to competitors, the competitors would not have the in-depth knowledge to create the software that will bring joy to the users. Menlo simply will not participate in conventional bidding games.

The result of this, and other parts of Menlo's system we will cover later in the book, is 100 percent customer satisfaction. Often in companies using a traditional software development process, at the end of a major software project that takes one year or more to complete, there are long lists of change orders to correct buggy software that does not meet expectations. At Menlo the software is developed with the customer, and week by week it is either working to the customer's satisfaction or not. In the last week of the project, all that needs to be reviewed is the last week of work. Menlo has a hotline for any customer complaints, which actually will ring over an intercom for all to hear, only it never rings. The people at Menlo cannot recall the last time they had a customer call to complain. Any issues with the software are uncovered week by week as it is developed and reviewed.

Zingerman's Five Stupid Ways to Lose a Customer

In our experience a minimum condition for an excellent company is that customers come first. This does not mean that customers are always delightful, but service providers still need to be delightful. Another of the most customer-focused companies we know is the Zingerman's group of small companies in Ann Arbor, Michigan. Zingerman's has a number of food-related businesses including the original delicatessen, a restaurant called Zingerman's Roadhouse, a creamery, a coffee roaster, a bake house, a working farm, as well as a mail order business, which we will discuss throughout the book.

Zingerman's mission statement is as emotional as that of Menlo and equally reflects the reality of values practiced daily: "Enrich as many lives as we possibly can, make you happy, make you smile, showing love and care in all of our actions."

Zingerman's employees in all of its businesses are continually trained and educated through Zingtrain, the training portion of the business. It starts with the "Zingerman's Guide to Good Service." It is of, course, in the form of recipes. A three-step recipe card says:

1.   *Find out what the customer wants*
2.   *Get it for them accurately and enthusiastically*
3.   *Go the extra mile*

Zingtrain dramatizes what not to do when dealing with customers by teaching "five stupid ways to lose customers." For each way there is a Zingerman's countermeasure or recipe:[4]

- **Ignore them.** Zingtrain notes that there are many ways to ignore your customers, but among the most popular are not greeting them when they come in the door and avoiding all eye contact with customers in your physical presence.
  - **Recipe: The 10/4 rule.** "When a customer comes within 10 feet of any staff person, we make eye contact and smile. Within 4 feet, we greet the customer."
- **Make excuses.** Explaining to a complaining customer how he or she caused the problem by failing to follow the rules.
  - **Recipe: Five-steps to handling customer complaints.** Step 1 is "acknowledge the complaint" and step 2 is "sincerely apologize."
- **Don't let them into your business.** This is my favorite. Keep customers out and they cannot disturb you! For example, don't answer the phone and your customer will be effectively "locked out."
  - **Recipe: Immediately answer all calls.** Answer any phone after no more than three rings. If a call goes to voice mail during business hours, return it the same day. After hours return the call the next business day.
- **Read them the rules.** When you tell your customers what they have to do to place an order or pick it up, you are setting up the rules by which customers have to do business with you.
  - **Recipe: Avoid the words "should" and "have to."** Staff are authorized to "do whatever it takes to make things right" and to "break the rules to give a customer a great Zingerman's experience."
- **Make it hard for them to give you money.** Businesses say they are in business to make money, yet they make it hard for the customer to pay.

- **Recipe: "Work to eliminate any systems or policies that make it hard for the customers to give us money."** One example is an honor system for customers in the deli who want coffee: they can put money directly into a box with prices and instructions for payment written clearly on it.

Another policy is that whomever a Zingerman's associate serves, the associate should communicate through actions that "you are the best part of my day." This policy goes beyond treating paying customers this way to treating in the same way anyone the staff comes into contact with.

Do We Know Anything About Our Customers' Needs?

Working with many different types of service organizations, Karyn is often surprised by the lack of knowledge that they have about their customers, even in call centers in which customer service representatives talk directly to customers on a daily basis! Karyn often finds that organizations do not have any information at all about what their own customers want or need, but instead the organizations simply use industry benchmarks to set standards for customer requirements such as accuracy of the service or time to deliver the service. When organizations meet or exceed these industry benchmarks, such as 80 percent customer satisfaction or five days to process a financial transaction, they conclude that they are doing well and that their customers are satisfied. But arc they really? What about the 20 percent of customers who are not satisfied?

Disatisfied service customers may not complain—or even fill out a customer satisfaction survey—they just simply won't use the service again. As the Internet makes it easier for dissatisfied service customers to find and switch to different service providers, it is critical for service organizations to find out what their customers want and value and feed that information back to the processes that create those services and service experiences.

An organization that Karyn worked with had a problem with one particular part of its human resources process and did just that. The customers were the employees of the company. When Karyn first began working with the organization, customer complaints about the leave-of-absence process outweighed all other types of complaints. No matter where you went in the organization, or whom you talked with, that particular process was called out as problematic. As Karyn worked with the people on the team who were responsible for leave-of-absence processing, she found that they didn't have direct access to information about the types or volume of complaints about the leave policy. Although the team members who processed the leave-of-absence transactions worked as hard as they could to improve their process, without information about what the errors were, all they could do was attempt to guess at what to try to change to fix the problems that they happened to hear about.

In order to solve this problem, Karyn and the processing team began to work with the customer service center that was responsible for receiving all customer complaints by call or e-mail. Every time there was a complaint related to a leave of absence, that information was electronically transmitted to the manager of the team who processed the leave-of-absence transactions. In addition, the manager of that team personally contacted each person who had been on leave of absence recently so that the members of the team could understand what their customers' specific needs and requirements were of the process. A clear picture began to emerge: there was a policy on how customers (employees) got paid what was still owed them when taking a leave of absence. Customers wanted timely and accurate payments.

As the team members more clearly understood what their customers valued, they started to look for obstacles in their process that prevented them from creating leaves in a timely manner and processing payments accurately. And the way that they looked for those obstacles was to use the information about customer complaints that they received from the customer service center. Each time the manager received a service ticket about a complaint, he and the team member who had created that leave-of-absence transaction reviewed the process by which the leave had been created to look for the underlying cause. Once the causes were found, countermeasures were created and tested by the team. After a few months, the team was so proficient at using the information it received from the customer service center that the number of customer complaints was reduced to almost zero.

In services, our customers want us to solve problems for them—and they may not even know what those problems are—so we need to find out so that we can add value. Unless we know that, we are not ready to focus on other process principles, such as flow. There is a clear benefit from direct contact with customers. We saw in Chapter 3 what happened when the new CEO of United took a flight and learned firsthand what ordinary customers experience. Insulating airline executives from normal customer experiences also insulates them from understanding the customer. It is not always so easy to put yourself in the customer's shoes, but it is always a powerful and sobering experience.

PRINCIPLE 3: STRIVE FOR ONE-PIECE FLOW WITHOUT STAGNATION

Value-Added Versus Stagnation

Have you found any of the following discouraging? Piles of stuff lying around your home or office, a lengthy list of e-mails in your inbox, customers waiting to be served, junk accumulating in your garage, a freezer full of old food? Then one-piece flow is for you.

Dr. Travis Bradberry, coauthor of *Emotional Intelligence 2.0*, provides what may be the best single white-collar productivity tip you will ever learn.[5] He says, "Never touch things twice." Never put anything in a holding pattern, because touching things twice is a huge time-waster. Don't save an e-mail or a phone call to deal with later. As soon as something gets your attention, you should act on it, delegate it, or delete it.

Further insight comes from work by a group of academics. They studied what happens when people switch tasks frequently and found it has a devastating effect on productivity. In fact, it can take an average 25 percent longer when we switch between tasks A and B repeatedly instead of completing A before we start B. As the leader of the study, David Meyer, explains: "Multitasking is going to slow you down, increasing the chances of mistakes . . . Disruptions and interruptions are a bad deal from the standpoint of our ability to process information."[6]

Karyn experienced this problem firsthand when her husband, Brian, an Asian studies professor, came to her feeling overwhelmed by grading papers. He was teaching three courses and did not have a student assistant to help him grade. He had multiplied the amount of time it took him to grade one paper by the amount of papers he had to grade each week and found he could not possibly complete the task in the amount of time he had. Karyn asked if he would like help to solve his problem, but of course, at first he said, "No. Academia is too different. There is no possible way what you do with lean could work for me." Karyn waited.

Two weeks later, totally exhausted from very little sleep, Brian decided that he was ready for Karyn to help him take a look at his current grading process. So Karyn went to the gemba, Brian's home office, to grasp the current situation. What she found was that Brian's students e-mailed their papers as attachments. As soon as Brian received the e-mail, he would open the attachment to check to see if it had arrived in proper and readable format. Brian would then respond to the e-mail to let the student know that he had received the paper. Then he would go on to the next e-mail. After Brian had let all the students know that he had received their papers, he then went back to each e-mail, opened it and the attachment again, and printed out the paper to grade by hand (an undertaking not so value added for the student, as even Brian has a hard time reading his own hand-writing). In order to maintain consistency in grading, Brian would begin by reading a paper, then read another for comparison, and then go back to the first, switching repeatedly between papers before applying a grade to each. After grading all the papers, Brian would then go into each e-mail a third time and respond to the student that the paper was graded and could be picked up at his office. Opening and closing each e-mail three times took a lot of time—none of it really value added to the student.

Karyn explained to Brian what he was doing, and together they generated some alternative methods. After a number of iterations of trying different things to reduce the number of touches *and* increase readability of comments to students, here is how the process works now: Students submit papers online on a Blackboard application the school uses. This ensures that they are in a correct and readable format, so Brian doesn't have to check that; nor does he have to e-mail students that he received their papers, as the students can see online that their papers were posted. He types his comments directly onto the electronic copy of the paper, which is much better for readability. In the syllabus, he has given the students dates the papers will be graded by, so when they are ready, the students can just go into Blackboard and "pull" their graded paper. Brian scans through a sample of the papers online to understand some of the variation in approach and then grades the papers one by one, completing one before going on to the next. This has significantly reduced the amount of grading time to a manageable amount. And Brian even gets to sleep once in a while!

What Dr. Bradberry is suggesting, and what Brian began practicing, is striving for one-piece flow. If you watch an assembly cell in manufacturing, you want to see a smooth flow of work from station to station. The product is constantly in motion—going forward—with value-added work being done to it. An interruption in flow is waste. That includes rework because of defects, so automatically this requires zero defects. It requires equipment to function flawlessly all the time, so that preventative maintenance becomes essential. This image is often likened in Toyota to the smooth flow of water. Stagnant pools are the enemy of flow. I have been with Toyota sensei while they are walking through a manufacturing plant pointing and harshly saying, "Stagnation, stagnation, stagnation!!!"

Stagnation is another word for waste. The Japanese word *muda* (waste) has gotten into the lean lexicon, and unfortunately, sometimes lean is defined as a war on waste—eliminate *muda*. As we will discuss in later chapters, lean is much more then eliminating wastes one by one, but understanding the wastes in your system is useful nonetheless. The Toyota Production System identifies seven deadly wastes. We use healthcare examples to illustrate each waste:

- **Overproduction.** Duplicate charting, printing of clinical reports in batches to distribute whether they are needed or not.
- **Inventory.** Retaining unnecessary forms or obsolete items, overstocking medications in closets, accumulating blood samples waiting for tests.
- **Transportation.** Patients walking or being transported from place to place or materials moving around the hospital.
- **Defects.** Medication or surgical errors, incorrect charges and billing, or mislabeled blood samples.

- **Overprocessing.** Taking down unnecessary information from patients on admission, multiple forms with redundant information, requiring lengthy paperwork on release of patients.
- **Waiting.** Patients sitting in waiting rooms, waiting for people to phone back, and waiting for equipment from supply departments.
- **Motion.** Keeping materials and tools in a location far from work, looking for information, moving or searching for patients, equipment, medication, or charts.

What customers are actually paying for is value-added work. Value added is any concrete thought or action that advances the work toward satisfying customer needs. For a patient that goes into the hospital because of chest pain, the only value added would be when relevant tests are conducted, doctors conduct the exam, the nurse or doctor explains the problem and its treatment, and the treatment is provided. Track a patient from when she arrives at the hospital to when she is back in her car, and it is likely she will spend three or more hours on a visit like this, even if it was a false alarm, while the value-added work probably takes 15 minutes or less.

If we were to discuss this with a hospital administrator, he might get agitated and explain that it is impossible to beam the customer from her car to the various places where she has to sign in and get examined. There is legally mandated data the hospital must collect on each patient, or it could be sued or shut down. What the administrator is describing is called "necessary non-value-added work." By adding "work" to the term "non-value added," we recognize that even someone checking a patient's identification for the hundredth time is doing work and that it may be necessary in today's context, but it is still not value added to the patient. It does nothing to address the chest pain. Even necessary non-value-added work can be sped up. What if we could take a thumbprint in a fraction of a second and have all the personal data we need called up and verified? We can do it using our smartphone, so why not in a hospital?

The Concept of Cells in Service Organizations

Cellular manufacturing is manufacturing's way of making smaller versions of moving assembly lines. While the Toyota automotive assembly line is very long with hundreds of workstations snaking through the plant, a cell is generally small (5 to 10 processes) and may be shaped like a U or L or configured with two parallel banks of machines. The goal is to attain one-piece flow and also to be flexible enough to add or subtract people based on customer demand. Customer demand is represented as takt—the average rate at which customers are buying the product and different variants of the product (see Figure 5.10). When demand is stable or the schedule is effectively leveled by a scheduling group (as discussed in the section

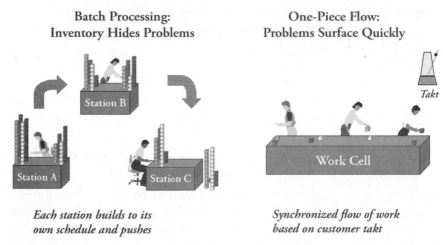

Figure 5.10   From hiding problems in batch processing to making problems visible through one-piece flow

on leveling in this chapter), it is possible to accurately calculate the number of people, machine capacity, and work-in-process inventory.

This is all well and good if you have a relatively small number of products that physically flow and it is feasible to calculate a takt. How do we calculate takt and get so precise in highly variable service processes? In many cases the answer is simply that we cannot get so precise and it is a waste of time to try. Sacrilegious! For those who deeply understand lean, there is no religion—just practical realities. For many services one-piece flow is more of a metaphor to help envision a future direction than a precise model to imitate.

As an example we helped an auto rental company with a lean transformation focused on rental sites and all office functions. Behind the scenes of the rental sites that the customers see, there is a fleet office that manages the purchase of cars from auto companies and the allocation of those cars to different rental sites. Frankly, when we began working with the company, it was a mess, and sites never seemed to have the right cars at the right time based on customer needs. Part of the current-state analysis looked at communication patterns and waste of walking in the fleet office's layout. On a typical workday, each employee walked almost 16,000 feet. They were grouped by specialty, and communication was poor (see Figure 5.11).

A complete redesign of the work area layout to eliminate walls and create work cells composed of people in different functions working side by side cut walk time in half, improved communication, and improved getting the right cars to the right sites (see Figure 5.12).

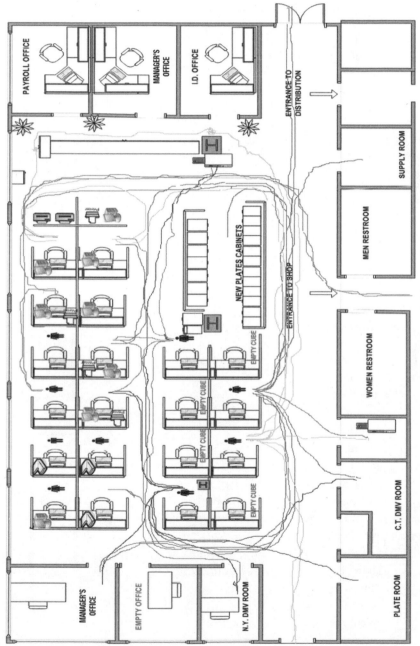

Figure 5.11 Auto fleet office functional layout before—spaghetti chart

159

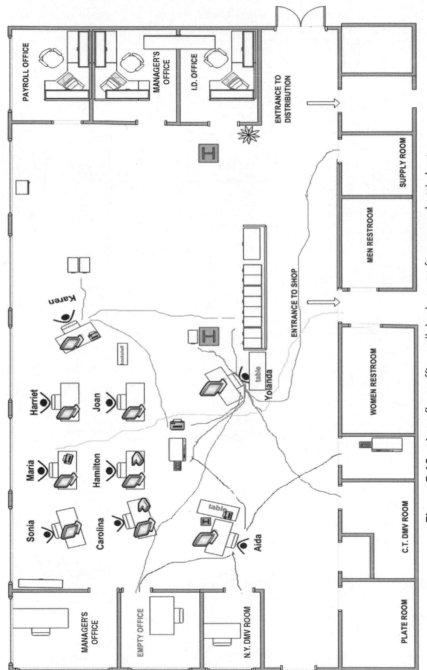

Figure 5.12 Auto fleet office cellular layout after—spaghetti chart

We worked on a similar issue for a Navy repair and overhaul facility where employees put together work packages. These work packages were documents that needed to be filled out and placed in a folder to authorize a particular job done to repair or overhaul a submarine. Part of the task included researching the repairs needed and creating engineering drawings. Mapping of the current state and a spaghetti chart (Figure 5.13) of the work package process revealed a large number of handoffs (58), often from one department to another, and the documents were very well traveled (almost 31,000 feet).

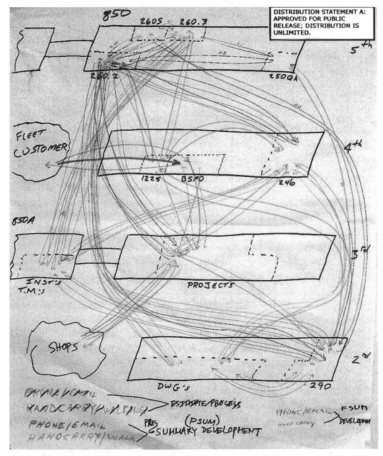

- 30,744 feet documents traveled
- 58 Handoffs
- Redundant communications

Figure 5.13   Spaghetti chart of moving of paper for work package in Navy shipyard

After changing the work area from people scattered across three floors of a building organized by functional departments to work cells for specific categories of work packages, there was a 55 to 92 percent reduction in travel distance (depending on the nature of the work package), a 67 percent reduction in process steps, and an 80 percent reduction in handoffs (Figure 5.14). Total lead time of creating a work package so that actual repair work could begin was reduced by 73 percent. As the new system was refined within the new layout, quality and productivity also improved dramatically. It is remarkable what can come of people with different expertise sitting side by side and working collaboratively.

This is not to say that creating cells by changing the layout of the office is an ideal lean solution. Once again we emphasize that each organization must understand its own desired future state and find creative ways to achieve the right goals. We only want to emphasize that striving for one-piece flow, which has been so effective in manufacturing, can also be effective for office work to streamline communication and reduce lead time.

Zingerman's Mail Order and One-Piece Flow

One type of service organization that learned this lesson is Zingerman's Mail Order. Launched in 1996, ZMO receives and ships high-quality "artisan foods" throughout the United States. The core crew includes about 70 employees, but the workforce can grow to more than 400 during the holiday season, Thanksgiving through Christmas, when the company sells 50 percent of its yearly volume. Fortunately for ZMO, it grew rapidly, but unfortunately that meant even more chaos each year, as it needed to store more stuff and quickly outgrew whatever facility it was in. Every few years ZMO went through the painful process of moving to a larger warehouse where it could store more stuff. It was costly, but the company was profitable, so it thought the situation was one it had to live with.

In 2004 ZMO decided to try its hand at lean and sought help from one of my doctoral students, Eduardo Lander, who was studying lean in high-variety, low-volume organizations. Eduardo immediately noticed stagnation everyplace he looked. Boxes of stuff were piled high, raw materials were scattered everywhere—including in aisles—and there was no discernible flow. ZMO was doing a lot of batching. For example, it prepared all the orders for cheese on trays at the beginning of the day, and then the trays were piled meters high and stuck someplace. Team members seemed to spend as much time walking around finding stuff as preparing customer orders. As Eduardo explained:[7]

> *At the beginning of the day each support process would work to prepare the product indicated in the end of day sheets. The line would only start running when all support processes were done with their prep work and all products*

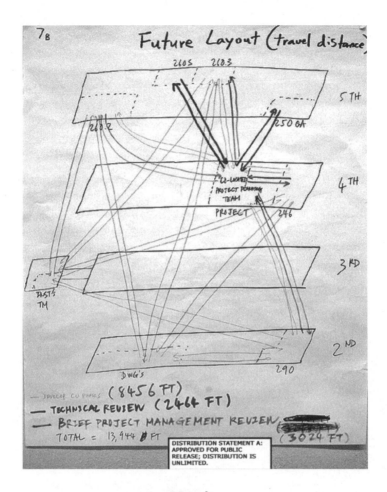

Results

Document Travel Distance:
30,744 feet down to
2,464–13,944 feet
Lead Time:
97 days to 26 days
Process Steps:
70 to 23
Handoffs:
58 to 10

Figure 5.14 Spaghetti chart of moving paper for work packages in Navy shipyard after new layout

were available for picking. At this time, the order starter would place pick sheets in tubs and put them on the conveyor as fast as the line would take them. If she saw that a station had little work, she would sort through the orders and release some that increased the load for that person. Alternatively, she would also move people from low to high load areas to try to speed up the line. Unless done very carefully, the combination of these two practices created waves of orders that exacerbated the imbalances and further amplified precisely the problem the order starter was trying to solve.

As a first step, Eduardo recommended creating some semblance of flow using a conveyor system. At the start of the line, employees select the items customers order (see Figure 5.15) and put them in bins. Flowing on conveyors, they go through a variety of checking and boxing steps, and then the packaged orders

Figure 5.15 Flow through Zingerman's Mail Order
A. Picking product on a flow line
B. Packaging orders and moving boxes directly onto a UPS truck

flow directly to the truck they are loading for shipping. To their credit the senior leaders worked with Eduardo and took the risk of developing and using the flow line just in time for the busy Christmas season. It worked a bit crudely but was a marked improvement. Next, Eduardo said the company needed to stop batching and instead cut the bread and cheese and prepare the dairy products, one customer order at a time. It was rough, but there was an immediate positive impact. Order was being introduced into what once had been chaos. Customers' orders were being assembled faster, in sequence, and the error rate was reduced. Aisles were cleared, and space was freed up.

ZMO has continued on this path for almost a decade, and now flow is clean and smooth. A daily takt (the minutes in a day divided by expected customer demand for a given day) is calculated showing the number of seconds available to pick an order and put it into a container. This paces the operation. What is interesting is that the number and size of orders varies every day and throughout the day. Under such conditions it is easy to throw up your hands and say takt cannot be calculated. Instead ZMO has developed five standard takt levels measured in seconds, all of which are multiples of 8 (8 seconds, 16 seconds, 32 seconds, etc.). Standard staffing has been established for each takt. Each day, based on actual orders and forecasted orders, the takt is set. At the beginning of the line, in the pick zone, a computer system schedules customer orders based on the takt and prints out the picking list for each customer at the rate of takt. The takt is not precise, as orders are being added as people call in during the day. If there are fewer orders than expected, employees leave early, and if there are more orders, employees will work late. Throughout the day, floor leaders have some latitude to change the takt if they see a need.

Notice on the takt board in Figure 5.16 that there are places to write in the planned takt, the forecasted takt, and the actual takt, along with a column for why. Forecasted takt is what is forecasted based on general trends. Planned takt is what is set for the day based on what is entered into the computer system about actual orders and backlog by that morning. Actual takt is the adjustments made by managers as the day proceeds. Making these differences visible is an important part of the continuous learning system. Differences between what is expected and what actually occurs have many possible causes, and as those deviations from expectations are addressed, the system becomes increasingly stable.

One of the most dramatic benefits for ZMO is that it has been able to stay in the same facility for almost a decade. It has also seen large increases in customer satisfaction and profitability. In the short term when the changes were first introduced, labor cost as a percentage of sales was reduced by 38 percent, boxes per labor hour increased by 47 percent, defective shipments were reduced by 18 percent, and the cost of mistakes was reduced by 29 percent. Needless to say, the owners are deeply committed to lean over a decade later.

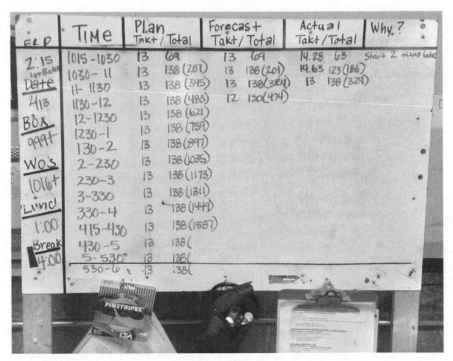

Figure 5.16 Actual versus planned and forecasted takt at ZMO

Striving for One-Piece Flow in Payroll Processing

What about service organizations that don't have a "product" that they can see moving down the line like ZMO does? What if your organization processes bank transactions or answers customer inquiries? In working with these types of service organizations, Karyn often experiences conversations in which people can explain the concept of flow in theory, but they cannot answer the question, "Please tell me what flow would actually look like in one of your processes?" Even if you can't easily see your "product" moving, it is still possible to create flow. The key is to find the places where batching and stagnation are occurring.

One such organization, a third-party human resources and payroll processing company that Karyn worked with, had a problem that surfaced as customers called to complain about seemingly incorrect delivery charges on their bills. The customers' bills seemed to show charges for extra payrolls that had not been requested. When the customer service representatives who answered the phone researched these situations, they found that the extra processing and delivery that the customers had ordered had taken place two or three months in the past but had never appeared as a charge on their bill for that time period.

As you can imagine, having extra charges on their bill that they couldn't account for caused customers to be very unhappy, and the customer service representatives who handled those calls had to spend a lengthy amount of time researching and correcting bills and refunding those charges. The company was also unhappy, as it did not get revenue for extra processing and delivery that customers had requested months earlier. In order to solve the problem, a team of customer service representatives, accounts receivable clerks, and delivery personnel was created. The first thing that the team did was go to the gemba to study the process and deeply understand the current state.

Here is what the team found:

1. When a customer called to order an extra payroll during a billing cycle, the customer service representative would create a paper billing form for the extra processing and delivery fee.
2. The customer service rep would then leave her workstation and walk downstairs to the basement processing area, where she would give the paper billing form to the delivery coordinator. The delivery coordinator would then arrange for the extra payroll to be processed and delivered.
3. After the delivery coordinator had arranged for processing and delivery, he would put the billing form into a pile to enter into an Excel spreadsheet "when he had time."
4. Since the delivery coordinator was very busy arranging for deliveries, he only had time to enter the billing forms onto the spreadsheet about once a month.
5. After the delivery coordinator entered all the charges from the batch of billing forms that had built up during the month, he would print a copy of the Excel spreadsheet and bring it back upstairs to the accounts receivable department.
6. The accounts receivable clerks would then enter the charges from the Excel report onto each customer's bill; unfortunately, however, this was sometimes two months after the customer had requested the extra payroll processing and delivery.

   The team also found out that there was no way to put a note in the system that would print the original date of the transaction on the bill so that the customer would know when the extra payroll was processed. All extra payroll and delivery charges appeared to be from the current billing month, whether or not they were processed in that month. Since there was no way for customers to tell that the charges were from previous months, and at that point, most didn't even remember these transactions, they would call their customer service representative to complain.

As the team members examined the process and understood the current state deeply, they realized that what had first appeared to be a billing problem was really a flow problem: batches of billing forms were backed up and waiting to be entered into a spreadsheet; then those same batches of billing adjustments had to be entered onto clients' bills—stagnation, stagnation, stagnation.

After coming to the realization that the problem was not a billing issue but a flow problem, the team worked together to create countermeasures that would eliminate batching and waiting. With some help from the IT department, the team came up with the following process to use when customers ordered extra payroll processing and delivery:

1. The customer service representative who answered a customer's call to process an extra payroll and delivery entered the information onto a SharePoint form (created with the help of the IT department) while on the phone with the customer. The form calculated the processing and delivery charges automatically, and on that same phone call the customer service rep would give the customer the total charge that would appear on the next bill.

2. After the customer approved the processing and delivery charges, the customer service rep would immediately submit the form, which was routed automatically to the processing department so that the extra payroll could be created. At the same time, an e-mail, with a standard subject line, was generated to the delivery coordinator so that he could arrange for the delivery. Also, as soon as the form was submitted, the information about processing and delivery charges automatically went into an Access database.

3. Each day, at the end of the day, an accounts receivable clerk would call up the Access database and pull the information for that day's extra processing and delivery charges and enter the information onto each customer's bill— the same day the extra processing and delivery took place.

No more batching. No more waiting. Information flowed directly from the customer service representative to all parties who needed it. Charges were entered on the same day that they occurred, and since the customers were already aware of and had approved the charges, they recognized them when they saw them on their bill. No more angry calls to customer service representatives. Also, since the customer service representatives no longer had to leave their desks to walk paper billing forms to the basement, they no longer missed processing other customers' payroll and HR transactions. Once they hung up from processing the extra payroll a customer needed, they were immediately available to help another caller.

Does the principle of flow apply in nonmanufacturing environments? Of course! No matter what type of service organization we work in, we should aim for a smooth flow of work without stagnation, completing one task before moving on to the next. Whether it is an academic process such as grading papers, a transactional office environment, or a highly variable operation like assembling food orders, it is possible to use the process principle of flow as the catalyst to finding unique solutions to address the unique problems each organization has.

PRINCIPLE 4: STRIVE FOR LEVELED WORK PATTERNS OR BE LIKE A TORTOISE

We have discussed the misconception that lean is only about eliminating waste. In a broader sense, we are striving for flowing value to customers, and as a result of that striving, we will identify obstacles that are wastes and find ways to overcome them; however, the desired future state should include more than what we are doing today, with less waste. We also need to work to achieve a more leveled state. In Figure 5.17 we show the need to overcome obstacles of *muda* (waste), *mura* (unevenness), and *muri* (overburden)—the three Ms. In other words, smooth flow means low variability. We would like to achieve a steady, stable process like the tortoise, not a fast and uneven process like the hare in the famous fable. This will

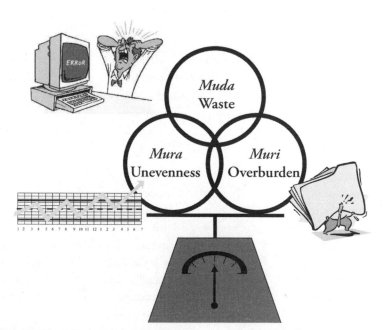

Figure 5.17   Eliminate waste, unevenness, and overburden
Source: Jeffrey Liker, *The Toyota Way.*

be good for customers and our team members who are no longer overburdened.

The three Ms are interrelated. Unevenness, or starting and stopping, leads to waste as we restart. Unevenness also means that we will have a light workload sometimes and be overburdened other times. Wastes like defects and overproduction will lead to unevenness and overburden.

Leveling Production at Toyota

Toyota works very hard to achieve a leveled flow. In manufacturing this translates to a leveled production schedule. Customers order vehicles in a somewhat random sequence and timing. We cannot ask customers to order one vehicle each minute in a sequence convenient to build. But if average demand is for one Camry each minute, it would be ideal if orders came in at one Camry per minute. Toyota makes multiple models on the same production line, such as a Camry with a gas power train on the same line as a Camry with a hybrid power train. The hybrid power train requires extra parts and takes longer to build. Building exactly to order would create unevenness, which could mean many hybrids are scheduled in a row, overburdening the assembly line. So Toyota does not build in the sequence of actual customer demand. Production control takes in orders and smooths out production, so that manufacturing and assembly departments build orders in equal intervals and in a leveled mix: for example, three gas Camrys followed by one hybrid, and so on, at a rate of one car per minute (see Figure 5.18).

Of course, production control can only level within the limits of actual customer orders, which may be overwhelmingly one type of vehicle one day followed by a different type the next day. How production control handles this problem depends on the purchasing patterns of each country. In Japan, cus-

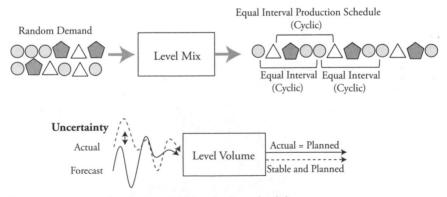

Figure 5.18   Production control levels the schedule
Source: Hiroshi Ozawa and Jeffrey Liker, "Balancing sales needs with supply chain needs: Production control as the arbiter," *Int. J. Lean Enterprise Research*, Vol. 1, No. 4, 2015.

tomers usually know well in advance when they must sell their cars to avoid large taxes on older vehicles. Since they must plan ahead they order new vehicles months in advance of needing them allowing Toyota to level the schedule. Production control can then schedule production over those months to fit the way manufacturing want to build them.

To achieve a leveled schedule, production control balances sales, operations, and demands on the supply chain (see Figure 5.19). In the United States, production control has divided the country into regions with regional sales offices. The regional offices provide their requests based on requests from dealers and forecasts, and production control allocates the number and mix of vehicles to each region. The regional Toyota offices then allocate the vehicles to dealers. This allows production control to allocate based on the constraints of production and supply chain and balance the interests of these three parties. Since the dealers hold inventory on the lots, this provides a buffer so the factories do not need to produce exactly what the customers want in the order of demand. By leveling the schedule at the final production stop in the Toyota assembly plant, the company also is smoothing production to suppliers, which has an even bigger positive impact.

The result is that an individual dealer may not have the ideal vehicle for a customer. When this happens, the dealer has several options. (1) Negotiate with the customer on price for a vehicle that is almost what the customer wants, (2) go online and look into the inventory of other dealers and negotiate a swap of the vehicle that is close with a vehicle that has exactly the options the customer wants, and (3) order the exact vehicle desired from Toyota. Toyota has the ability to

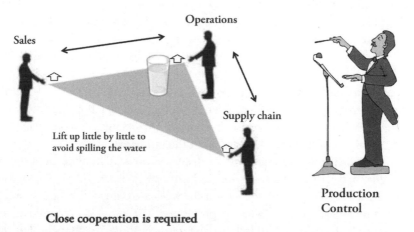

Figure 5.19 Production control balances sales, operations, and supply chain
Adapted from Hiroshi Ozawa and Jeffrey Liker, "Balancing sales needs with supply chain needs: Production control as the arbiter," *Int. J. Lean Enterprise Research*, Vol. 1, No. 4, 2015.

change the schedule in the factory within days before production. The trade-off is that the customer can either get something similar on the spot, get a swap within one to three days, or order a car to exact specifications that would be delivered within weeks. In the United States, the majority of vehicles are purchased off the lot, about 25 to 30 percent are swapped, and about 5 to 10 percent are built based on a specific customer order. The large majority of customers simply do not want to wait for their special order vehicle to arrive.

Now you may be thinking that you do not have the power of Toyota to manipulate the timing or specific service your customer requests. "We only supply based on actual customer orders, which are uncertain." This is the case with ZMO, and as we saw, it adjusts the takt every day and even within the day. So at least within a day the work is quite level. The leveling point is when the customer items are picked and placed in bins. A computer system takes in actual orders and levels them as best as possible so the pickers are not walking all over the place to select items. They pick from one zone and then move to another zone in a stable sequence. Depending on the actual orders, this is not always possible, but the computer system still works to level as much as possible, which greatly reduces wasted walk time and improves productivity. Before ZMO learned about lean, it did not even try to level the schedule and incurred the penalty of extra waste and overburden.

Leveling Software Development Work at Menlo

The people at Menlo Innovations also do what they can to level the workload, even though they are doing knowledge work and it is uncertain how long it will take to create computer code for a certain feature. As we discussed, the technical anthropologists create a story card for each feature. Then several pairs of programmers discuss each feature and estimate how long it will take to code in intervals of 1, 2, 4, 8, and 16 hours. They do not attempt to be accurate to the minute. They combine their estimates into one that is then written on the story card. The cards are put onto schedule sheets in full days of work, and the cost estimates are determined by the number of estimated hours. The customer then decides which "cards to play" week by week. The customer is only charged for the actual time taken, which could be higher or lower than the estimates.

The cards for the week are visually displayed on work authorization boards (see Figure 5.20). The names of various pairs of programmers are written on cards across the top, and cards with the days of the week are pinned down the side. The programmers select a card to work on, program it, test it for quality purposes, and then use colored sticky dots to indicate the status of the card; yellow means they are working on it, orange means they have completed the programming but are waiting for a quality advocate to check it, green means it has passed the check, and

Innovation Does Not Have to Be Chaotic

Work authorization board: the daily visual work schedule—
simplicity and clarity!

Time actual completion of each card versus planned
Yellow, orange, green, and red dots

Program to a story card to pace knowledge work

Figure 5.20

red means they are behind and having trouble. The program manager can easily see how all the teams are doing against the plan, and the cards show that the teams are working steadily toward the goals. Lateness is not punished. It is expected that the time estimates are rough and often wrong, but on average they are quite close to the actual time. And everyone learns from the differences between planned and actual, so estimates tend to improve with experience.

Menlo also has a more level workflow because the programmers get rapid feedback and can design in quality as they work. The quality advocates approve each story card when it is programmed. Customers review the software every week. The paired programming allows each teammate to check their partner's work as they code. In traditional software development, those checks are at milestones that are months apart, so programmers will work at a certain comfortable pace for months, perhaps being distracted by other demands, and suddenly have to hit the gas pedal and go like crazy to finish in time for the milestone review. We all have heard of programmers who work through the night to finish their software. The quality of their work suffers, and they suffer personally from all that stress. The Menlo programmers have a certain level of stress all the time, but it is good stress, the stress of working slowly and steadily, knowing other people care about their work enough to continually review it.

Menlo employees work slow and steady each day like a tortoise and are remarkably productive. Customers are often concerned when they learn that they will need to pay for a pair of programmers working on each task. Most software programmers work alone on their own computers. Comparisons have suggested that even though Menlo insists on people working in pairs, the company is several times more productive than its nonlean competitors. The stimulation of working with another person keeps each programmer focused, and they can work slowly and steadily where the individual programmer often has a burst of energy and then takes breaks. And Menlo employees go home after eight hours and do not work weekends keeping fresh. Menlo speaks of the joy of completing tasks one by one and the joy of going home on time.

Leveling Call Center Work at ZMO

Karyn has found that service centers in direct contact with customers find it hard to imagine how they could possibly level their workloads. Calls, e-mails, and faxes come when they come and have to be dealt with immediately. Service providers lament, "There is absolutely no way for us to predict how many customers are going to call us today." Yet Karyn will also hear, "Once the West Coast goes online, we see a spike in calls every day between 11 a.m. and 1 p.m." She has heard operations complain, "It is impossible to know when and how many orders sales is going to be able to sell this month, so there is no way to plan," while the same groups will then complain, "Since sales has monthly quotas and a deadline during the last week of the month, we're always light on orders at the beginning of the month and swamped at the end." As a starting point it is important to study the actual state to see where there are patterns. It is quite common one will find at least some self-inflicted peaks and valleys.

There are two ways to deal with the wild swings in demand: reduce the variability in customer orders or find a way to adjust staffing to the highly variable workload. Reducing variability may require changing sales incentives plans. For example, a cost-benefit analysis might show that, like Toyota, the disruptions caused by end-of-month sales bonuses are not worth the gains. Or it may be necessary to change the way resources are scheduled to deal with uneven demand. In the case of the big jump in calls between 11 a.m. and 1 p.m. each day, further study showed that customer service representatives' lunch hours all took place between 11 a.m. and 1 p.m. After experimenting with alternative lunch schedules, wait times decreased, customer satisfaction increased, and customer service representatives felt much less burdened.

Zingerman's Mail Order call center found a creative way to flex resources to deal with highly variable sales calls. The staff members witnessed the remarkable lean transformation of the warehouse while they were on the sidelines and decided to try their own lean concepts.

Throughout the year there are peaks and valleys in calls day to day and within a day, and Zingerman's policy is each caller is the "best part of my day." This means that the employees will never discourage callers or try to cut calls short. And when the company studied demand, it found there were some clear busy periods during a day, but not in such a way that ZMO could have staff come to the office for busy periods and then go home. The company decided the answer was to flex resources based on call volume.

Typically, staff members would sit at a computer and wait for calls. Some were busy, while others were waiting, and it was almost random who would answer the phone. The staff had seen the systematic and standard processes in the warehouse and decided to experiment with a "hot seat." When call center representatives are in the "hot seat," the only thing that they will do is answer phone calls from customers. They are totally dedicated to taking care of customer calls, and their attention is not diverted, nor is their flow broken, by trying to do other work at the same time. When more calls come in than the person in the hot seat can handle, a second hot seat will be opened up, and so on. Customer service reps rotate through hot-seat assignments, each of which lasts two hours.

While some reps are dedicated full time to the hot seat, other reps are freed to leave their stations to do ancillary tasks in the room, such as deal with web orders, check voice mail, issue refunds and credits, and even water plants and

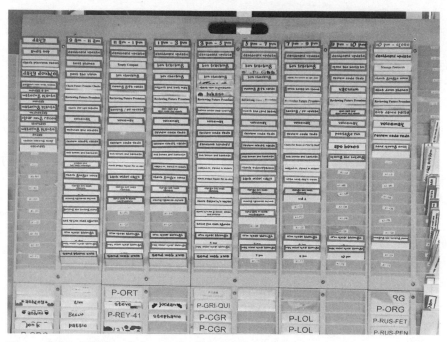

Figure 5.21   ZMO call center ancillary work board

empty compost. In order to ensure that all tasks are completed, each day the call center representatives make the ancillary work "visible" by using a board for all these ancillary tasks (see Figure 5.21) organized by time of day.

Each card in a slot on the board represents one task and is red on one side and green on the other. Tasks that are not yet completed are red. When reps are freed of the hot seat, they select the next red card and go to work. When they complete the task, they turn the card over to the green side and place it back into the slot; this allows all the call center representatives to see if the tasks are being completed during the planned time frames. If the time slot has passed and a card is still red, the team members can easily see it and make that a priority. They can also study why their planning process failed and improve how they plan.

It was particularly important to work out the system in the quiet part of the year so they could deal with all the chaos of the busy holiday season. By the time the holidays hit, the system was fine-tuned and could be taught as standard work to the temporary workforce. Also, with the huge increase in volume, the hot seat becomes a "hot cell" of a group of service representatives.

Although service organizations often believe that leveling is impossible for them because they cannot simply copy what Toyota does, as we can see from the above examples, with some creative thought it is possible to become *more* level.

Leveling is not something to implement with one solution, but rather a challenge to work to achieve step by step over time. There will always be variability, but there are many ways to reduce variability—making better plans, using standard processes, influencing customer orders, building in buffers, doing the job right the first time, finding ways to assign people to the customer-facing work with ancillary tasks for those available at the moment, and so on. Each organization must experiment over time to get as close as possible to stable, leveled flow to customers. Each service organization, with its own set of customers and circumstances, will have to deeply understand its particular causes of variability and, over time, work to reduce them.

PRINCIPLE 5: RESPOND TO CUSTOMER PULL

Of course, fabulous flow is not useful if too much of the wrong product is produced. Think of a smooth-flowing river that overflows its boundaries and floods the town. Then we need a dam to protect the town. Dams are buffers, which is often part of a pull system.

There are many simple examples of pull in daily life. We go to a coffee shop and order exactly what we want, and the barista makes it to order. In other cases we keep some inventory and then replenish that inventory based on usage. For example, we look in our refrigerator and see how much milk we have and decide whether to purchase more. We may have a general, or even specific, policy—when we are down to one quart of milk, we purchase up to two more depending on our plans for the next three days. In lean terms we are using our refrigerator as a marketplace.

Toyota's concept of a marketplace in which we store inventory and replenish it based on usage was inspired by supermarkets. No good supermarket will continually bring product out to the shelves regardless of usage. A stock clerk looks at a defined space for a product and sees how much the customer takes away. The clerk replenishes up to the space allotted on the shelf.

Let's consider the basic concepts for using our refrigerator as a marketplace:

1. A customer (family) and supplier (store)
2. Defined location to store the inventory (specific shelf space)
3. Trigger point for replenishment (e.g., one quart remaining)
4. The batch size to be picked up (e.g., two quarts of milk)

As we can see from this example, if we misjudge usage or fail to replenish according to our plan, we might end up with too much milk and have to dispose of some when it gets old; or we might end up with too little milk and are stuck without milk for breakfast. In other words even a well-designed pull system does not automatically solve all our problems and is dependent on human judgment and discipline.

An even simpler example is the way I use pull for the salt for my water softener. The salt comes in 40-pound bags that I periodically lug home. I pour the salt into the water softener and close the top, and the only way to know how much salt is left is to remove the top and look. Periodically I forget to check, and my wife notices the water is funny. I check, and there is no salt. I do not want it to be empty until I get some more, so I keep one bag in a designated spot and only use it when the water softener is near or at empty. This is my safety stock. The space on a floor with the last bag of salt is a kanban, a signal, telling me when I use the last bag to go to the store and lug some more home.

At ZMO there are small inventory buffers throughout the building. Before lean there were mountains of inventory, and they were stored wherever there was space. Now everything is deliberately controlled by kanban. Pickers use printed-out pick lists to fill customer orders from items on flow racks. When the pickers first pick a product from a new bin, they take out the kanban, a ticket that describes the food and specifies the size tote, the quantity that is kept in the tote, the address in the warehouse, and the address on the flow racks. The addresses are like postal codes. This is an order for the material handler to refill a small tote on her next material handling route to the warehouse—like a shopping list made by the customer. The dry goods inventory is stored in a warehouse in designated locations. Material handlers bring bins of goods to the picking line and load gravity-fed racks from the back that slide to the pickers, and the cycle continues. The process is diagrammed in Figure 5.22. Photos of the labeled racks and kanban are shown in Figure 5.23.

Following processes withdraw what they need when they need it.
Preceding processes replenish what is taken away.

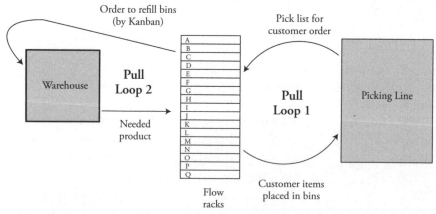

Figure 5.22   Pull system to ZMO line to pick customer orders

Kanban for
1 Bin

From: 65GG –__
Quantity: 28
In Small Tote
Width toward front

A – BRO

HS 3 of 3
To: V5 – B4

Figure 5.23 ZMO flow racks for pick line and kanban (replenish from back)

A type of pull system can also be used to control the flow of knowledge work. One example is from a company's engineering analysis department we worked with. In this department, analysts used a sophisticated computer system to determine stresses and strains on automotive exhaust system parts. Customers made requests, and the engineers determined who would do the analysis. In the past it was a push system. As customers pushed work, the tendency of the engineers was to get started on the analysis as soon as possible. There were typically 20 or more active projects in various stages of analysis for three engineers. When a customer called in to complain that his request was taking too long, the status of his project was not even clear. The engineers then tried to expedite the work, pushing back other work. There was concern because the workload was expected to increase, but there was no money budgeted to hire more engineers. The target of the lean project was to eliminate enough waste so the existing engineers could handle 25 percent more work.

The solution was to make the status of projects visible and put a cap on the number of projects that the engineers would have in process at one time. It was determined that 12 active projects was the maximum the group could handle. A work status board showed the active projects assigned to each engineer and the expected start and completion dates (see Figure 5.24). A new project would not be started until 1 of the 12 active projects was complete. Think of the 12 projects as the number of slots in the supermarket. When one slot is empty, it

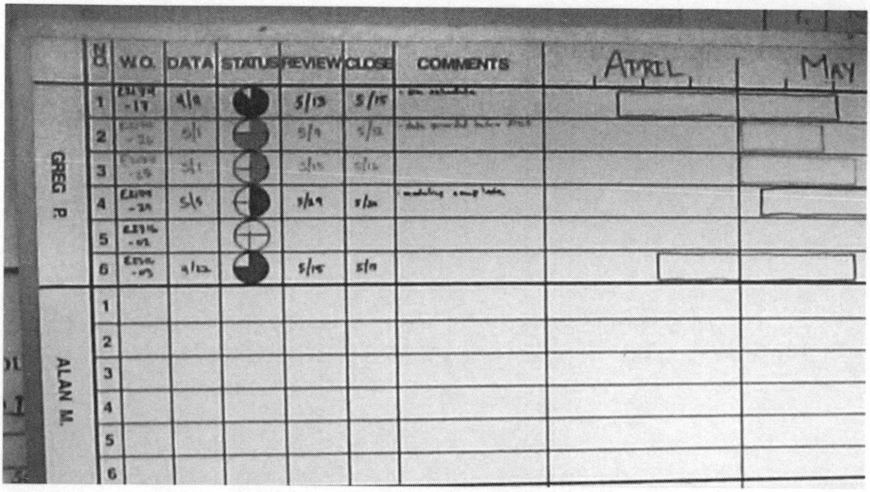

Figure 5.24 Work status board for engineering analysis

is a pull signal to begin one more project. The engineers also recorded on the board the percent complete on a pie graph. There were a few other changes to support this, such as developing standard work for performing the analysis to make the time to completion more predictable. The result was that the engineers were able to perform the 25 percent additional work, the company didn't have to hire an additional engineer, and on-time completion went from an average of 80 percent to near 100 percent. Ironically they were starting some projects later but completing them earlier.

USE PDCA TO IMPROVE PROCESSES TO ACHIEVE DESIRED OUTCOMES

Dr. Deming warned, "We should work on our process, not the outcome of our process." We suspect, as the opening quote at the beginning of the chapter suggests, he was frustrated by regularly observing people struggling to meet management targets while trying to overcome poorly developed processes—or no formal process at all. If your manager asks you to be 10 percent more productive and you do not have the knowledge or tools to improve how you work, the only alternative is to work faster and harder. Rushing work may produce more defects. If your manager then tells you to reduce defects by 10 percent and you lack the capability to create a quality process, you will be more careful, perhaps slowing down or adding in more layers of checking, making it harder to achieve the productivity target.

Karyn has attended morning huddles in many organizations where the leader is frustrated. Although the metrics seem to be improving for the type of task the manager has asked the team to focus on, the metrics for other processes are slipping. Since the members of the team are only focused on the ends of meeting the goal for each metric, they simply work harder, longer, or faster without changing the process, the means by which the work is completed.

Everyone I know who has worked with a Japanese sensei has felt frustration at one time or another when the sensei asks the seemingly very simple question, "Why?" I hear things like "We set up a beautiful pull system with color coding, and it became very clear what to work on next, and our sensei asked, 'What is the purpose?' This is basic lean. Doesn't the sensei know why?"

What the sensei is concerned about is a confusion of means and ends. Pull systems are a means, but setting up pull systems can quickly become an end unto itself: "We must deploy pull throughout the enterprise." Soon the lean group is mindlessly deploying things that it can call pull systems and see this as the solution to all ills: "Our organization doesn't respond to actual customer needs. We just push our services on to the next process whether they are ready or not and overwhelm them with paperwork. If we could simply get everybody to respond to real customer needs, we could solve half our customer complaints and improve our productivity."

It may be true that there is too much push in the organization, and there are many opportunities to improve through well-thought-out pull systems. But does the organization really know if that is going to get it to where it wants to be? Embedded in this frustrated rant are the assumptions that:

- Pull everywhere will lead to reduced customer complaints by 50 percent.
- Pull everywhere will lead to improved productivity.
- Reduced customer complaints and increased productivity are the main goals everywhere.
- Pull is the best generic solution to generic problems everywhere.

Continuous improvement does not mean applying generic solutions to generic problems. It means finding specific ways to move each part of the system in the direction of clearly established goals. We rarely know exactly how the new tool will work until we try. Therefore, we must experiment and learn.

KEY POINTS
MACROPROCESS PRINCIPLES

1. Process principles are not solutions. They help us think about what we want to accomplish and why; however, they do not solve problems.

2. In service processes, a generalized approach to value-stream mapping may be useful to help see the current state of the process from the customer's perspective and then develop the big-picture "macrovision" of where we want to go next. However:
   - Value-stream mapping is not a solution to a problem, but a tool to help us see.
   - Many service processes are highly variable, and it may not be useful or necessary to develop the level of detail such as takt time or the inventory between steps that is seen in many current-state manufacturing maps.
   - The real power of value-stream mapping is in developing targets to be achieved step by step through PDCA.

3. Lean principles can inform the target conditions we should be striving for and help us to identify possible countermeasures.

4. Determine what value means from the point of view of your customers:
   - All improvement efforts start with deeply understanding the needs of your organization's specific customers and what value they need you to add for them.
   - Customers don't always know what they need, so go to your customer's gemba and see what they actually do and what they need.

5. Strive for one-piece flow without stagnation by identifying and eliminating obstacles that are preventing work from flowing from one value-adding step to another:
   - Customers are only paying for value-added work, which we have defined as any concrete thought or action that advances the work toward satisfying the customer's need.
   - Each service organization and its customers are unique, so be creative in finding the ways that value can flow to customers. Lean concepts such as cells and takt might be applicable; however, they might not.
   - Look for places that work is stagnating and then find ways to eliminate that stagnation.

6. Level work patterns to achieve steady, stable processes with low variability.
   - Unevenness, or starting and stopping, leads to waste as we restart and also means that we will have a light workload sometimes and are overburdened at other times.

- Service providers often believe that it is impossible to level the workload; however, leveling can be accomplished by finding creative ways to reduce variability in customer orders or finding ways to adjust staffing.

7. Respond to customer pull by creating supermarkets and using visual management where that makes sense.

8. Use PDCA to learn how to apply the process principles creatively and in ways that make sense to satisfy your customers and meet your business goals.

9. Remember, there are no generic solutions to generic problems. Process principles are not solutions, but ways to guide our thinking about responding to the specific challenges we find in our service organization.

Chapter 6

Microprocess Principles: Make Work Patterns Visible for Continuous Improvement

Make your workplace into a showcase that can be understood by everyone at a glance. In terms of quality, it means to make the defects immediately apparent. In terms of quantity, it means that progress or delay, measured against the plan, is made immediately apparent. When this is done, problems can be discovered immediately, and everyone can initiate improvement plans.

—Taiichi Ohno, founder of the Toyota Production System

MICROPROCESS PRINCIPLES

Macroprocesses set the framework for microprocesses. Think of organizations as complex puzzles with thousands of pieces. We generally start a puzzle with the outer edges that frame the puzzle. Then we select big and distinctive objects like faces of people and build those. Finally, we get to the hard work of all the detailed pieces that are difficult to distinguish at first glance, like the sky. Microprocesses are like the detailed pieces in the center of the puzzle (see Figure 6.1). The macroframing is easier, but the tedious detail is what brings the puzzle to life, and this requires the hardest work and discipline.

In lean the macrolevel frame is the overall flow of material, people, and information through value streams—what we would draw as a value-stream map. Usually macroprocesses are the result of decisions about architecture and structure. How will we organize our supply chain? How do we lay out equipment and offices? How do we schedule the overall flow of work in the organization? For the microlevel we zoom into a process box. Macroprocesses establish the framework for daily work. The daily work follows a rhythm of activity, and this is where service excellence happens . . . or doesn't.

What should be found at the daily level are highly developed people who are passionate about serving customers, continuously improving how they do the work based on what they learn every day. To get to this we must thoroughly integrate process, people, and problem solving. The image we have of how the process

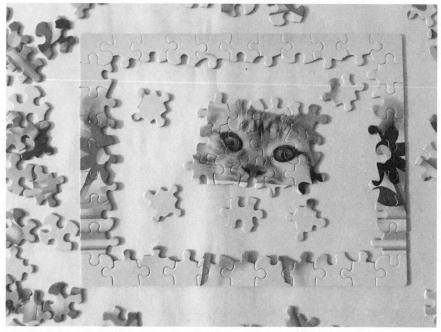

Figure 6.1   Macroprocesses frame detailed microprocesses.

should function (standard) provides the framework for excellence and highlights the next obstacle to overcome to get closer to an ideal process.

In this chapter we will talk about standardization, visualizing deviations from the standard, building in quality at each step, and using technology to enable people to perform and improve their work (see Figure 6.2).

The idea of voluminous standards and procedures might bring to mind a highly regimented bureaucratic process—the opposite of an empowered workforce creatively solving problems. Yet we will argue that bureaucracy has been misunderstood and misapplied, and if used properly, standard processes are the foundation for continuous improvement. This is difficult to accept, precisely because standards are so often used improperly.

PRINCIPLE 6: STABILIZE AND CONTINUALLY ADAPT WORK PATTERNS

We described leveling as one of the most misunderstood lean concepts in service organizations. Standards are the most abused lean concept by people who think they understand it. It seems remarkably easy to create rules and procedures, more difficult to enforce them, and really hard to embed them in a learning culture.

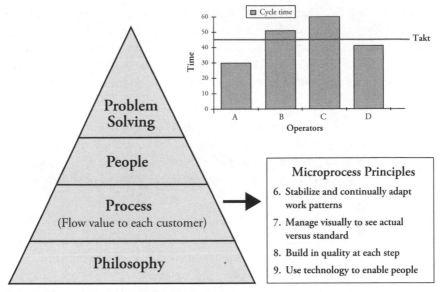

Figure 6.2 Microprocess principles

On the one hand, standards create order, and most of us would agree that without them we would have anarchy. How many people would enjoy a world with no traffic rules or property ownership rules or safety rules? In fact, rules are the foundation of civilization.

On the other hand, think of "bureaucracy," and what immediately comes to mind is red tape, waiting in long lines, filling out complex forms—in lean terms, "waste." We have been critical of mechanistic organizations because they fail to adapt to the rapidly changing world we live in. But we do not think the cause of this stagnation is rules. Rather, the way rules are used is a symptom of the deeper way of thinking of mechanistic organizations.

Coercive Versus Enabling Bureaucracy

My colleague Paul Adler made a breakthrough in organizational theory when he suggested bureaucracy is not necessarily limiting. He was not enraptured by Toyota, but as a Stanford professor he worked and lived near the Toyota-GM joint venture—NUMMI. He was intrigued with all that was written about it, and he made a visit, which led to an intensive study. He expected to see continuous improvement in action driven by empowered teams in a highly organic organization. What he actually saw surprised him. There seemed to be endless rules, or in Toyota's vernacular, "standards." They were visible everywhere you looked—signs, lights, standard work posted at the workplace, metric boards, signs indicating jobs that were critical to quality, visible safety procedures. Yet a deeper look confirmed what he had read about continuous improvement. Work groups, down to the individual worker, were empowered to alert management to deviations from the standard and to suggest improvements. Procedures normally owned by engineering were the responsibility of the work group. He concluded:[1]

> *What the NUMMI experiment shows is that hierarchy and standardization, with all their known advantages for efficiency, need not build on the logic of coercion. They can build instead on the logic of learning, a logic that motivates workers and taps their potential contribution to continuous improvement.*

Adler made a key distinction between coercive bureaucracy and enabling bureaucracy. Coercive bureaucracy is what we are used to seeing and is associated with all the negative stereotypes about the inefficiency of governments. In an enabling bureaucracy, rules, procedures, and standards support work groups in doing safe, efficient, high-quality work. Once standards are set, they are to be followed as they are the best we know today. But as Henry Ford extolled in his 1926 classic *Today and Tomorrow*:

> *Today's standardization . . . is the necessary foundation on which tomorrow's improvement will be based. If you think of "standardization" as the best you know today, but which is to be improved tomorrow—you get somewhere. But if you think of standards as confining, then progress stops.*

As we will see, enabling bureaucracy is empowering and a key to service excellence. But first, lets look in on an example of coercive bureaucracy at its worst.

Coercive Bureaucracy in Action at the U.S. Post Office

If we want to see coercive bureaucracy in action, there are fabulously horrifying examples at the U.S. Postal Service. A close friend, Fred (pseudonym), has worked for the post office as a postal carrier since 1997. He loves being outdoors and enjoys parking his mail truck in a neighborhood and walking around. He passed up opportunities to be promoted to management to continue the outdoor work he loves. Fred was never very political and did not have strong opinions one way or the other about the postal union for city mail carriers—the National Association of Letter Carriers. However, after repeated frustration with management, he got involved with the union and was elected to be a representative and eventually became vice president of the local. One of his pet peeves is the way the USPS handled standard work.

The post office first botched the introduction of standard work in the 1970s in what became known as the Kokomo Plan, named after the town in Indiana where it was tested. In order to try to develop a fast and simple way to develop standard work for jobs with standard timings, in 1974 the USPS timed routine tasks done by carriers such as reaching to pick up a package and placing it in a mailbox. Based on these times, the postal service constructed jobs under the assumption that the sum of the individual tasks would accurately reflect the time for the job. Known as predetermined time standards, the USPS could use these times to construct daily routes and assess the performance of carriers against the standard times.

It quickly became apparent to the union that these times were anything but accurate reflections of reality, and the union successfully fought the system. The union saw that there was far too much variation in actual routes to predict the time it should take using standard times. For example, letter mail to households is first put in sequence by machines, and the numbering of houses is straightforward with few errors. On a business route you have the street address and then many different suites, and the mail gets jumbled in the delivery sequence as the carrier walks from suite to suite finding the right mail. If you study the actual situation it will be clear that additional time is needed for these business deliveries, but this was not reflected in the standard times. There are thousands of variations on issues like these that make standard times guesses at best. In 1976 the post office proposed to take the standards nationwide, and this almost resulted in a nationwide strike. The experiment was scrapped.

Fred's personal experience with standard work was in a later wave in 2004 when a supervisor decided to change the delivery sequence of his route. There is an official route adjustment process in which a management representative walks with a carrier throughout the day and records data on a standard chart from point to point. Fred's direct supervisor walked with Fred, and also observed him covertly, and decided he could make Fred's route "more efficient." Changes were made with no input from Fred, and on the first day of walking the new route, it was clear to Fred that what his supervisor was proposing would take an extra 15 to 20 minutes.

Let's consider one part of the supervisor's idea for improvement, probably the worst part. Before the redesign, Fred's specified sequence for one part of the route was to park, then walk sequentially on one side of the street delivering to each house—for example, the even numbers 2, 4, 6—and then continue walking in a circle to get to the odd-number houses 1, 3, 5 and then back to his truck. In this particular area, one house was separated by about 250 feet from the other houses. So Fred would complete the circle and then get in his truck and drive to that house to deliver the mail (see Figure 6.3). His supervisor changed the walking sequence so Fred was zigzagging back and forth doing houses in exact order 1, 2,

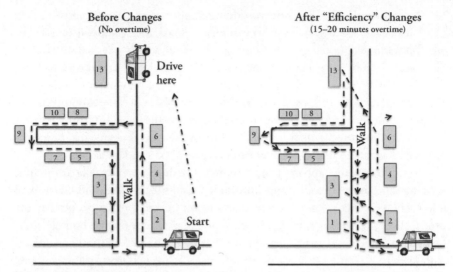

Figure 6.3 Example of before and after supervisor-imposed mail delivery pattern in a coercive bureaucracy

3, etc. Fred could only guess that his purpose was to eliminate the one dismount delivery (getting back in the truck) to the isolated house. If you look at the diagram of movement patterns, it is immediately obvious that the original pattern is more efficient than the new pattern, which involved wasteful zigzagging back and forth and then walking all the way to the isolated house and returning past houses that were already served. From a lean management perspective his supervisor had taken a pretty efficient process and inserted a lot of wasted travel into it.

As Fred expected, the supervisor's inefficient changes added 15 to 20 minutes a day, which turned into overtime pay for one year. Fred appreciated the extra money but did not think this benefited the post office in any way or the customers, who might end up paying more for postage to cover the extra costs of poor decisions. Fred decided to do the right thing and protest to the boss, explaining it added extra time, but the supervisor stuck to his guns. He seemed more determined to be right than to develop an efficient route. It was incidents like this that motivated Fred to become active in the union to stop ill-advised management behavior harmful to the workers, customers, and the USPS.

After one year of the overtime, the region got a new postmaster, and he decided to spend a day walking with Fred—highly unusual in the coercive bureaucracy of the U.S. post office. As they were approaching the changes with the zigzag route, Fred said to the postmaster, "At first I was concerned about spending the day with you, and then I realized this is a great opportunity to show you what one of your supervisors did." Fred soon started the zigzags, and the postmaster asked, "Why are you doing that?" Fred said, "You have to ask your supervisor. He is the one who made this change." The supervisor was not around much longer after that.

We should note that bureaucracies aren't always potent enough to be coercive. I remember working as a cooperative education student in the quality department of a company that built nuclear power plants. What we did was to write procedures—thousands of procedures and addenda. Presumably this would guide the design and building of the power plants, but our real customer was the Nuclear Regulatory Commission. We wanted to pass the commission's audits. I suspect the people there were the only ones who actually read these thousands of arcane procedures with headings and subheadings and citations. I never saw the site of a nuclear power plant, never went to the gemba, but I wrote great procedures. It is probably more accurate to call this "paper bureaucracy" rather than "coercive bureaucracy." I doubt many people were coerced by these procedure manuals. What was more concerning is that they were largely invisible to the people doing the work.

Standards in Enabling Bureaucracy

We constantly preach to organizations the power of using standards in an enabling way, and we often get pushback from management: "You mean standards become suggestions, and people without professional training can change them however they want?" One of the underlying causes of this concern is a misunderstanding of what we mean by a standard.

In *The Toyota Way Fieldbook* we separated different types of standards into a house structure, shown in Figure 6.4. As you can see, there are standards defined outside the organization adopting the standards. These include safety and environmental standards defined by the government. The standards are not to be tampered with, as they are the law. They are turned into standard specifications by internal specialists such as the corporate safety office and the corporate engineering departments. Again, specifications are not to be tampered with unless there is approval of the changes. What brings these standards to life is standard work, which very much should be tampered with to improve it.

Organizational learning not only can coexist with standards but actually depends upon standard methods. If there are no standards, then people have the freedom to do the job however they see fit. If they come up with what they think is a better way, they can use that method as an individual, while others can disregard the "improvement." Learning means we try something and study it, and if it is a better method, whoever does that job will follow the preferred method until a better one is identified. In an anarchy in which we all are "empowered"

Detailed work methods defined
to develop operators' knowledge
and skills (job breakdown)

General work methods
defined with an eye for waste

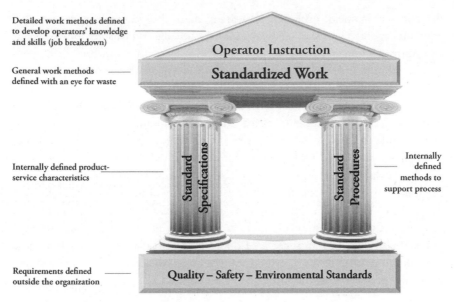

Internally defined product-
service characteristics

Internally
defined
methods to
support process

Requirements defined
outside the organization

Figure 6.4　Relationship and purpose of standards
Source: Jeff Liker and David Meier, *Toyota Way Fieldbook.*

to do our own work, individuals may learn, but this will rarely translate to organizational learning.

Robert Cole wrote an excellent essay arguing that the Japanese advantage through the 1980s was because of their capacity for organizational learning, whereas in the West we were better at individual learning.[2] He describes organizational learning as the process of turning individual learning into organizational routines, that is, standards that sit above any particular individual:

> *The process by which we transmit and evolve organizational routines is organizational learning. We, of course, can learn good and bad things. We want, however, to define organizational learning in terms of identifying and creating best-practice work routines, standardizing these practices, diffusing them (i.e., actualizing them) throughout the organization, and then renewing the process.*

In order to gain a better understanding of coercive versus enabling standards, let's check back in on NL Services, Inc. When we left the company, it was at a crossroads: continue to work organically with Leslie, focusing on satisfying the customer and teaching people how to identify problems and strive for constant improvement, or hire a big-box consulting firm to speed up the lean transformation and please shareholders who favor a quick return on investment. And as stated in Chapter 4, the cases below are a composite of experiences that Karyn has seen repeated across many different service organizations. In one form or another these things have actually happened, though the names have been changed to protect the well-intentioned but misinformed.

NL Services: Coercive Bureaucracy—Standards Are Something to Be "Adhered" To . . .

Unfortunately for NL Services, Sam McQuinn, the VP who championed the lean pilot project, decided to leave to take a job as a senior executive at the company where his former colleague Sarah Stevens worked. It was a smaller company, but he felt alive there. At NL Services, responsibility for companywide lean deployment was passed on to Mike Gallagher, who had taken on the role of executive vice president of Corporate Lean Strategy. Mike was brilliant and felt passionate about NL Services, but he knew nothing about lean beyond a few books he had perused. He had visited some of the people Sam worked with in the pilot and was impressed by their enthusiasm and accomplishments, but if he continued to spread lean using the deep pilot approach, he would retire before lean got serious traction across the company. He needed help from real experts.

After a competitive bidding process, NL Services decided to go with Lean Mechanics, Inc., a big-box consultancy specializing in implementing lean management systems for service organizations. Lean Mechanics seemed to have an impressive track record of quick, cost-effective deployments and promised that it would have its lean management system up and running across NL Services within six months.

After an initial investigative period in which a huge contingent of Lean Mechanics's certified lean experts swarmed the NL Services offices with stopwatches, the diagnosis was made that, like many other service organizations, NL Services' biggest problem was that it didn't have functioning standard work. Every credit transaction processor did the work differently, which, according to Ray Kensington, the Lean Mechanics Certified Master Lean Expert assigned to lead the work with NL Services, resulted in huge productivity losses. Ray promised Mike that implementing standard work for all the credit transaction processes would deliver at least a 20 percent productivity gain across the organization. When all the credit processors were doing the work the same, efficient way, it would be easy to share work across different parts of the organization, and the need for specialized regional training would drop dramatically. With the added efficiency, Lean Mechanics promised to deliver savings by eliminating jobs.

Creating the standard work would be a simple and painless process. Ray Kensington and his team of lean experts would time the credit transaction proces-

Process Name:	Role/Person:	
High-Level Process Step Description	Time to Do Step	Best Practice and/or Link to Other Roles
1.		
2.		
3.		
4.		
Created by:	Date:	Version:

Figure 6.5   Standard work template used by Lean Mechanics

sors in one office to estimate the amount of wasted time that could be eliminated using the standard work. They would then determine what the most efficient process would be. Once the steps were compiled and timing complete, the actual standard work would be created by the junior consultants, and the credit processors would be trained across the entire country and audited to comply with the new methods (Figure 6.5). Ray explained to Mike that there was no need to worry that credit transaction processors would resist following rigid procedures that would reduce their creativity, as the standard work was really just a high-level view of steps and handoffs between roles, nothing too detailed or specific.

In order to ensure that all credit processors adopted and adhered to the standard work, one credit processor per team would be designated as the team's standard work leader (SWL). As well as doing weekly audits to ensure that their team's members weren't deviating from the standard, the SWLs would meet on a biweekly basis to discuss any changes in the standard work that had been identified by any of the teams. If all the SWLs agreed with the change, then the office would implement the change in the standard work, and the SWLs would add extra audits to make sure the new changes were "adhered" to.

Lean Mechanics also suggested that a best practice deployment process be created across NL Services so that changes in standard work made in one area of the company could be easily shared and leveraged in other areas. Having the best-practice deployment process would also increase productivity by preventing regions from wasting time working on changes in standard work that had already been completed in other areas of the company. The best-practice deployment process would make for easy and swift adoption of those changes and ensure that productivity continued to rise.

Ray assured Mike that the best-practice deployment process would also be easy to implement: each office would designate two of their team SWLs as Level 2 SWLs, and they would attend monthly regional meetings. Each quarter, one of the Level 2 SWLs would prepare for and attend the national Level 3 SWL meeting. Changes approved at that meeting would be quickly spread to similar jobs across the country.

Mike Gallagher was a little concerned that between completing standard work audits and attending meetings, the SWLs would be taken away from processing credit transactions and serving their customers for quite a bit of time in the month; however, Ray reminded Mike that the positive gains in productivity from having credit transaction processors all doing work in the same efficient, standard way would outweigh any of the negative effects for the SWLs' teammates or customers. In fact, with the productivity gains from the standard work, it should be possible to reduce the workforce, the main basis for the promised cost reductions.

If Mike had any remaining reservations about how the use of standard work would be enforced across the organization, Ray explained the semiannual Lean Audit Review process: twice a year, a team made up of experts from Lean Mechanics and NL Services' audit department would visit each office to complete a Lean Audit Review, or LAR (see Figure 6.6). The LAR team would score the office on the adoption of various lean tools, including standard work; if credit transaction processors were not found to be "adhering" to their standard work, they and the SWL for their team would receive a written warning, and the LAR result would be noted in their annual performance appraisals. With all these levels of checking, there would be no possibility that credit transaction processors would be able to—or want to—deviate from their standard work.

Six months later, as promised, Lean Mechanics had created standard work for all the main tasks in the credit transaction process and set up the best-practice deployment process. By the end of the year, each region had had two Lean Audit Reviews. As Mike Gallagher reviewed the PowerPoint decks of the LAR results, the spreadsheets listed the changes that had been made to the standard work (mostly only changing words here or there) and the productivity numbers; yet something just didn't add up. And what didn't add up was the productivity savings that Ray Kensington and Lean Mechanics had predicted. Even after he ran the numbers for the third time, Mike had to admit that no matter how he calculated it, the 20 percent productivity gain that had been promised just wasn't there: when he looked at the cold, hard numbers, it was obvious that most offices had no productivity gains, and some even had losses. Even worse, when he talked to the regional managers, the CTPMs, and even the credit transaction processors themselves (when he had time to stop looking at the LAR report-out decks and get out from behind his computer screen), he heard a variety of disconcerting concerns about the standard work and best practice deployment process:

- Credit transaction processors were still doing their work however they wanted to; but not wanting to receive warnings or write-ups, they followed the standard work if they were being watched by the standard work leader for their team or during one of the LARs.

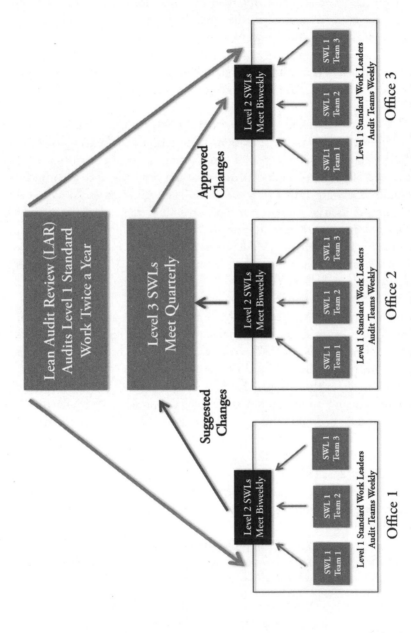

Figure 6.6 NL Services standard work audit process—it's as complicated as it looks!

- Very few improvements to standard work had been made at all. Standard work leaders complained that since most changes brought to them were simply the personal preference of the person who suggested it, it was impossible to get others to agree. And it took so long to move possible changes through the best practice deployment process, that most people were reluctant to even bring up a suggestion.
- Customers were complaining that it was harder than ever to get in touch with the credit transaction processor dedicated to their account if that person was a standard work leader. The number of team audits and amount of time for standard work leader meetings kept the SWLs away from their desks and customers for hours at a time.
- Since NL Services let go of 20 percent of its credit transaction processors in anticipation of the productivity savings that Lean Mechanics had promised, the numbers showed that accuracy and delivery times were down all over the country. And so were the results of this year's Employee Engagement Survey, as the remaining credit transaction processors struggled under the burden of managing the same amount of work using the same processes with 20 percent less help . . .

Mike Gallagher thought to himself, "It all looked so good on paper. When they presented their bid, the Lean Mechanics people seemed to know exactly what they were doing. If only I could ask them what went wrong." But Lean Mechanics's contract had run out at the end of the year, and once the company stopped getting paid, its lean experts had disappeared, moving on to the next deployment, at one of NL Services' competitors.

Take a minute to reflect on the rich, organic experience of the NL Services team that we described in Chapter 4, people like Kathy and Joe. Imagine what they experienced when Lean Mechanics came charging through, developing and imposing superficial standard work. "What a joke. Do they have any idea what they are doing? And why are SWLs responsible for changes when they have never experienced real standard work?"

Service 4U: Enabling Bureaucracy—Standards Support How We Learn to Improve . . .

Meanwhile, at Sarah Stevens's company, Service 4U, where Sam McQuinn had been working as the executive VP of Service Excellence for the past three months, the staff was learning about standards too. One of the things that Sam was enjoying most about working at Service 4U was the focus on finding unique ways to satisfy the company's customers. Just before Sam had arrived, Service 4U added a new service offering to provide electronic direct deposit transfers. Service 4U sales representatives actively partnered with their clients to find out what types of new services would help them run their businesses more easily. Once sales reps had brought the feedback that direct deposit transfers would be a service differentiator, new-product development had created the product, and IT had created a system enhancement.

Service 4U's credit processors had all received training on the new direct deposit capabilities of the transaction system and had been processing direct deposit transaction transfers for about four months. Everyone was expecting rave reviews from customers about the new service offering, but then came a cold dose of reality. Even after two levels of checking, between 30 and 50 percent of the direct deposits were failing the regulatory audit for various reasons, such as incorrect paperwork, missing bank documentation, and no customer signatures. The customer would then have to send in new information, and the direct deposit would have to be set up again after a waiting period. Also, on occasion, bank routing or account numbers had been entered incorrectly, and thus funds were direct-deposited into incorrect accounts. That didn't make customers very happy. Nor did the fact that customers had to send in all their direct deposit paperwork two days before their transaction processing date. What customers really wanted was to send in the paperwork at the time their transactions would be processed and have their direct deposit activated immediately. And that's where Sam came in. As VP of Service Excellence, it was his responsibility to make sure that Service 4U's underlying processes supported the delivery of service excellence.

One thing that Sam particularly enjoyed about his new position was the opportunity to regularly work with Leslie Harris, the lean management advisor who had helped him at NL Services. Unlike NL Services, which was focused on short-term results and quarterly dividends for its shareholders, Service 4U was dedicated to providing the best service possible for its customers over the long term. Sam knew that Leslie would be able to help him help Service 4U get to the bottom of the direct deposit problem.

After Sam explained the problem to Leslie and showed her the data the company had collected from the daily and monthly direct deposit audit process, Leslie suggested, as she always did, that they go together to the gemba to find out the facts behind the data and see what they could learn from the people who actually entered the direct deposits into the transaction processing system. As Sam and Leslie made their way through the six transaction processing teams, they heard the same thing from supervisors and transaction processors alike: no two processors had the same method for entering a direct deposit into the system. Some processors entered the routing and account numbers first and then checked the paperwork for accuracy, while others did it the other way around. And the transaction processors all had their own ways of explaining what was needed and of getting paperwork from customers.

After visiting all the teams, Leslie and Sam stopped to discuss the situation with Susan Jensen, the office's transaction processing manager. Susan explained that as soon as customers had started complaining, as Leslie had taught them and as was now their habit, the supervisors had gone to sit with the processors to see what they could learn. What they found out was exactly what Sam and Leslie were hearing on their gemba visit. No two processors did the work the same way, and there were various opportunities for errors. Susan said, "The problem seems to be that the methods used by various processors allow for errors that inconvenience customers. We are not providing anything like service excellence. We need to understand how the errors occur and work with the processors to develop a better method, then standardize it as a baseline for improvements."

Over the next few days, Leslie helped Susan and the supervisors put together time studies, just like the ones that Sam remembered from NL Services. After the supervisors had collected the data, they could see that a couple of the processors had excellent accuracy (their direct deposits rarely were on the daily Audit Fail list), and they also used the fewest steps and had the lowest repeatable times for the process. When the supervisors and Leslie and Sam looked at the steps that these processors followed, they could see that the first thing the processors did was check the documentation the customer sent for accuracy. Once they determined it was accurate, the processors scanned it into the WebDocs system so that it was available for the auditors immediately. Only after those steps were completed did the processor enter the routing and account numbers into the transaction processing system. The supervisors all agreed that following this process seemed to be the best way they knew to ensure accuracy and efficiency.

Working with the two processors and their supervisors, Leslie helped the team create a standard work document with a simple explanation and pictorial representations of the "Check-Scan-Enter" process, as they called it. At each step, the processors could easily see if what they had on their screen matched the picture on the document. It would certainly be easy for the processors and their supervisors to tell "good" from "not good." After they put together the first version of the standard work document, the two transaction processors brought it back to their teams and taught their teammates how to use it and the Check-Scan-Enter process. The processors each got a copy of the document to hang up at their desk, just beside their computer screen.

At first, team members were a little skeptical, but with support from both the transaction processor who had created the process and their supervisors, it soon became a new routine to follow the Check-Scan-Enter document. At the beginning of every day, the team's supervisor checked the Audit Fail list and if there was a failure went to understand what had happened. After a few changes to parts of the Check-Scan-Enter process and document, audit failures were virtually eliminated for the teams using the new process, and direct deposits were entered in less than half the time. The transaction processors on the two pilot teams were very excited . . . as were the processors on the four other teams. They were so excited that they begged the processors on the pilot teams to teach them how to use the Check-Scan-Enter process and standard work. Everyone wanted to be able to process work in a way that gave customers the quality results they expected.

Two months later, during their regular coaching time, Sam and Leslie reviewed the direct deposit Audit Fail results. They could see that there were rarely failures anymore. And as they worked their way through the teams in the gemba, supervisors and processors alike were excited to tell them about how happy customers were about the ease of direct deposit processing. Susan Jensen stopped them in the hall and told them that, working together, the transaction processors and supervisors had begun to create standard work for other processes as well. And as she reminded them, it was only the best way they knew how to do the work today, so they were still looking for better ways!

Standard Recipes at Zingerman's Mail Order

Standards and standard work are especially important at ZMO. Since the organization expands from 70 to 400 people in the busy holiday season in December, the staff knows it will be swamped with rookies for a matter of weeks. Before there was an established system, it was chaos. Now there is a clear system to follow at every level of detail. Standard work is the only way to ensure that people are properly trained and there is some consistency in quality and timing.

The Zingerman's community of food businesses does not have a problem with the concept of standard work. The employees refer to them as recipes. There is a recipe for everything at ZMO from how to pick orders from the shelf to how to place items in boxes to how to answer the phone. The standards for simple, repetitive manual tasks like picking are more detailed than for more customized tasks like answering the phone.

In Figure 6.7, we show page 1 of a two-page standard work sheet for ZMO, in this case for the initial job of picking items and putting them in a bin. For the detailed, highly repetitive tasks of a Toyota assembly line, there is a standard work sheet that includes times in seconds for each step and a separate job instruction sheet for training purposes that includes more detailed substeps along with key points and reasons.[3] ZMO's jobs have enough variability in them that the company uses higher-level steps and key points on one or two sheets, without specific times. Notice these are simple declarative statements like the first: "Read location of item to be picked from Work Order." The key point gives details on how to perform this step, in this case where to find what information: "Locations are list-

Process: Picking	
Create Date: 11/11/2009	Created By: Shalette Mays
Revised Date: 3/31/2016	Revised By: Kelly Nugent

Seq#	Operational Steps	Key Points
1	Read location of item to be picked from Work Order.	Locations are listed as... Rack - Shelf, Slot. Example: E3-B1
2	Touch location label, move hand *up* to item in location.	Multi-Lane locations are marked with pink labels; pick from open cases first.
3	Pick the number of items in the quantity field on Work Order.	For quantities greater than 1, the *item location* will be red, and the # of items will be in a red box.
4	Place item or items safely in tub, rearranging as needed.	**Frozen meats** go in a Wicketed Plastic Bag (up to 5 assorted meats per bag). **Large brownie bite picks, 15-50 bites**, go in Wicketed Plastic Bags
5	*Check off* single item picks on Work Order between the location and quantity field. *or* *Write number* of items picked for multiple quantities.	Example: **2** J4-A4 ✓ 1 / L1-E2 ✓ 1 / M1-B2 6

	Special Instructions	Key Points
A	**Kanban attached to item, or attached to empty cardboard box**... • Remove Kanban from item or box • Place Kanban in area's nearest Mailbox • Toss empty box under the pick line	Empty cardboard boxes should be removed from the shelf as soon as the last item is picked from them. Items in stacks, like empty wicker baskets and wooden crates, have a Kanban attached to the item on bottom.
B	**Empty Plastic Dry Good Totes**... • Remove Tote from shelf when picking last item • Remove Kanban from back, place in Red Mailbox • Stack empty Totes under midpoint bridge	Empty Dry Goods Totes may be set on top of pick line until they can be worked back down and stacked under the midpoint bridge. It might take several people to work tote back down the line.
C	**Empty Plastic Totes in Prep Areas**... • Remove Tote from shelf when picking last item • Slide Tote down Prep Area's Return Rack, *the same direction in was sitting on its shelf (Kanban faces away from you)*	Totes from Coolers, Bread, Pastry, Cheese! Kanbans stay with the plastic totes in these areas! Think of the entire tote as your Kanban! **"I" Coolers**... Totes are sorted by color around Kanban onto matching row of the Return Rack.
D	**Picking Lit (Literature)**... • Pick packets of Lit with sheet of colored paper on back • Return Kanbans from empty Lit boxes, return empty boxes to Lit rack	**Rack B4**... Kanbans go in "PRD" Mailbox at Order Release (*hand to person running Order Release*,) empty Lit boxes go on top of Rack **Rack N6**... Kanbans go in Red Mailbox chute, empty Lit boxes go in return slots at bottom of Rack.
E	**Picking by Product Code (Rack D5 and I1 - B1)**...	Most items on D5 will have a Product Code sticker on them for easy matching, but if not...

Figure 6.7   Standard work sheet for picking orders at Zingerman's Mail Order

ed as… Rack – Shelf, Slot. Example: E3-B1." The key point in step 5 illustrates how to check off items as you pick with a visual example.

It might appear rather obvious how to pick items off a shelf and put them in a bin. As you read down through the standard work it is surprising how much is involved in this apparently simple job. This is in part because of the lean systems. There are clear standards for where every item is located with distinct addresses and visual management identification. Consider the "Special Instructions" for non-recurring tasks. There is a kanban system for replenishing items and that needs to be understood. There is a standard for what to do with empty totes and one for dealing with empty dry good totes. In many warehouses all we would know is to look up the item on the pick list and find it, perhaps using some bar code technology. As ZMO developed visual standards, errors in picking were dramatically reduced, and at the same time there was more to teach in the "recipes." As you transform to lean there will be more detailed standard work and a greater need to do a good job of team member training. Some people say that lean does not work with temporary workers, but in fact, it becomes even more critical.

Standard Sales Processes in a Retail Chain

Inversiones La Paz owns two of the largest retail chains in Honduras: motorcycle sales and repair and Jetstereo consumer electronics stores. The executive board asked for help to bring lean to all its processes from warehousing, to motorcycle assembly, to motorcycle and consumer electronics repair, and even to back offices such as bill collection. One of the most critical steps in the value chain is sales, and the executives on the board were confused about how lean could apply to a process of individuals selling to a varied set of customers.

The executives had found a consulting company that coached salespeople in how to sell, including role playing, and store managers were quite rigorous about ensuring all salespeople were trained. But on a typical day salespeople were roaming around the store on the hunt for customers to help. Since salespeople are paid on commission, they can be a bit territorial about wanting their fair share of customers and then staying with those customers to the point of sale. They also tended to cherry-pick customers they perceived were more likely to buy something, leaving other customers just standing around waiting

One of my associates, Florencio Munoz, began working with the vice president of sales, and of course, he began by going with him to the gemba to grasp the current condition. As usual, it was eye-opening for the sales VP even though he had worked in the company for over a decade. The current condition was:

- A high number of walk-ins (customers) were not being engaged by salespeople, which led to unsatisfied customers and lost sales.
- Unbalanced workloads (average number of customers engaged per salesperson per hour) led to varying sales results among employees that were not directly attributed to skill level or effort.
- Not all the salespeople that came to work that day were available during peak hours.
- The store manager was not able to quickly identify what activities team members were performing at any point in time.

With the help of Florencio, the sales VP and his team concluded that the root cause was the fact that there was no system to plan or visualize which salespeople were available, what tasks they were performing, and whether all customers were being engaged by the staff. This may immediately bring to mind the need for some sort of surveillance with cameras and computers, but Florencio guided the improvement team in developing a manual visual system.

First, they had to visualize what they wanted to be happening (target condition) and then plan how it would work, including visual boards to display what was happening and the standard at a point in time. What they came up with was a visual display of the activities hour by hour of a salesperson at any given time (Figure 6.8). At a glance this showed which sales manager was in the store versus out, what training activities were scheduled (since the staff did a lot of training), and who was assigned to which "station" in the store.

Each station was a different position in the store with its own clearly defined tasks. A system of rotation was established for those who were on the floor (Figure 6.9). The managers wanted to make it clear who was working on what task and to identify the team member who was next up "at bat" to engage the next customer entering the store. The board also needed to communicate a state of emer-

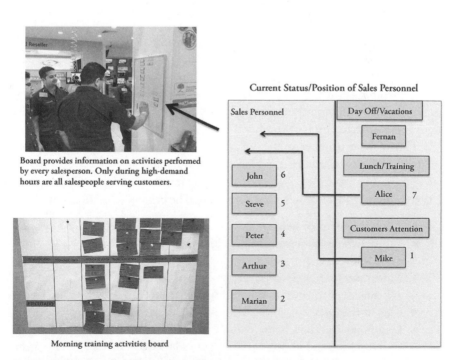

Board provides information on activities performed by every salesperson. Only during high-demand hours are all salespeople serving customers.

Morning training activities board

Current Status/Position of Sales Personnel

Figure 6.8 Visual management of salespeople's activities

One salesperson attends to any customer entering the store immediately, and the rest move to the next position. Anyone not seeing customers performs other activities, such as quoting, doing follow-up with customers, etc.

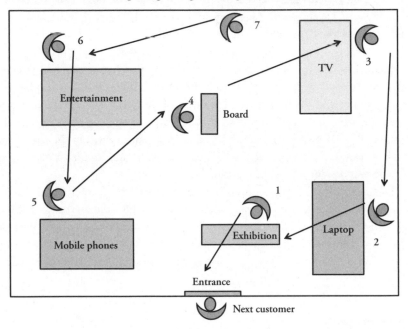

Figure 6.9 Standard rotation board for salespeople

gency when the number of customers in the store exceeded the number of salespeople so that countermeasures could be taken to avoid customers' leaving the store without having been engaged.

This may seem rather simple, but it was the first time the salespeople had thought through a system of any kind to split tasks among themselves, and certainly it was the first time it was made visual. This system was spread throughout Jetstereo stores, and the results were astounding:

- There were higher sales per store.
- Customer wait time was reduced from an average of 2 minutes to under 10 seconds.
- More customers were engaged per hour since all salespeople were made available at peak hours and wait time was reduced.
- Customer satisfaction measures improved.
- Understanding peak hours though visual signals of "emergencies" led to better staffing and better scheduling of nonselling activities.
- There was better coordination of administrative duties.

- Balancing of opportunities created comparable results between sales team members, which led to more focused and effective coaching and training.
- The practice of customer "picking" was eliminated.

Keeping Standard Work Alive Through Audits

To put it simply, if management takes standard work seriously, then those who do the work are likely to take it seriously—particularly if the manager is truly a leader. Taking it seriously means auditing the standard work, which can take on either a coercive or enabling flavor with dramatically different consequences.

Audits are often associated with coercive bureaucracy as we saw in the case of NL Services. The efficiency expert comes in with a stopwatch and a notebook, or perhaps a notebook computer, and observes people performing a process, all the while looking for inefficiencies or rule violations. The auditor then writes a report documenting the violations, which gets a lot of people in trouble. This can and does still happen, and the fear of audits is often justified. In a culture that supports a coercive bureaucracy, it is quite typical for any audits to become a tool for evaluation and rewards and punishments. This applies both to lean audits to see if the "proper" lean and six sigma tools are being used and to standard work audits. Unfortunately, this type of coercive culture is not likely to change quickly or easily.

However, as Paul Adler observed at NUMMI, standards and audits of standards can be a part of a totally different cultural context in which team members feel supported by management. NUMMI was the original documented enabling bureaucracy. What did a standard work audit look like? I happened to be visiting NUMMI the year it had introduced a more visible system for auditing standard work on what Toyota calls a *kamishibai board*. This means a "story board." For young children in Japan, it is common to have a book composed of a series of note cards. The parents can read each card one by one putting the card they read at the back of the pile so they can start on the next card the next time.

Figure 6.10 shows a board that NUMMI designed to train a group leader who has a certain number of processes to oversee. For each of the 15 assembly-line processes on the board, on each shift the group leader audits a team member performing the work. The group leader answers a series of yes-no questions that are written on a card, such as "Did the team member follow the specified sequence?" "Did the team member do the job in the prescribed time?" Completed audit cards are put into the slots to the right, and if an answer to any of the questions is a "no," the group leader will put the card in the slot with the back side, which is gray, facing outward and write down the problem on the problem tracking sheet. When the problems are addressed, the group leader writes down the corrective actions on the card and turns it to the front, white side out. Each shift the manager of the

Kamishibai Board (Story Board)

How it works:

- Group leader checks one process a day
  - Cards contain questions
  - Notes discrepancies/countermeasures
  - Moves card to slot in next row
  - Turns card gray side out if discrepancy
- Assistant manager checks daily
  - Randomly selects card
  - Obtains standard work sheet
  - Goes through audit with group leader

NUMMI had 90+ boards throughout the plant

Figure 6.10   NUMMI standard work audit story board

group leader comes down and selects an audited card to audit a second time to give feedback to the group leader.

We might assume the reason for this audit board was because the plant discovered that the workers were not following the standard work properly, but that was not the case. The problem was that the group leaders were not well trained in the fundamental skills needed to do their job. There was an exceptional amount of turnover leading to inexperienced group leaders, and the annual plan included a commitment to train group leaders in the fundamentals of TPS. This was part of their training. It also had the benefit of tightening up the use of standard work. Additionally, this forced their managers to go to the gemba and better understand the work while they learned to coach the group leaders. Thus, in an enabling bureaucracy, standard work is a collaborative tool that supports quality and consistency of work, continuous improvement, and effective coaching.

PRINCIPLE 7: MANAGE VISUALLY TO SEE ACTUAL VERSUS STANDARD

In a sense visual management is simple once we have determined the standards, and in another sense it is one of the most creative parts of lean management. We have seen in this book many examples of visual management, for example, from Menlo Innovations and ZMO. The Menlo work authorization board (Figure 5.20 in the previous chapter) is a great example. This is not standard work, but it creates a structure for the daily work. The story cards instruct the programmer on what features the customer wants that have been authorized for payment by the customer. The red, yellow, orange, and green sticky dots make clear to the project manager what the status is for each feature. Menlo is not simply displaying information on cards but using the story cards on a daily basis to organize the work. Ask Menlonians why they bother to create paper systems throughout the shop when software developers often hate paper. They will speak of the benefits of tactile manipulation of the paper and how it supports teamwork for communicating, planning, and tracking progress.

Our brains are hardwired to appreciate visual information. We remember more, and learn more, with less mental effort. Neuroscientist John Medina, in rule 10 of *Brain Rules*,[4] writes: "Rule #10: Vision trumps all other senses. Hear a piece of information, and three days later you'll remember 10% of it. Add a picture and you'll remember 65%."

Consider the table of data in Figure 6.11. Is it clear from the table what the pattern is? How about from the graph next to it? Which would you prefer?

True visual management shows at a glance when there is an out-of-standard condition, and then team members are trained in how to respond. In Chapter 5, we learned that at ZMO the employees work to an average takt and average time to perform a task, but in reality both are variable. The expected customer demand does not match the actual customer demand as the day proceeds, and the picking times vary with exactly what items are picked. In service organizations there are relatively few instances where time per customer can be precisely planned. Therefore, it is critical to identify when there is a deviation from our expectations and specify how to respond.

This?   . . . or This?

1	2487	7	3425	
2	2134	8	3750	
3	2756	9	2945	
4	3100	10	3260	
5	2950	11	3175	
6	3550	12	3525	

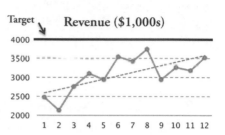

Figure 6.11 Why we like things visual

One clever use of visual management at ZMO supports what the business calls "help your neighbor." On the picking line there are flags along the conveyor (see Figure 6.12). On each side of the flag is an instruction like "Pull ONE BATCH of tubs from buffer." This indicates that team members should follow one-piece flow and not grab multiple tubs. The flags serve another function, as well. If a person downstream is taking longer to pick than a person upstream, then a buffer area between the two flags will start to fill up. When there are three tubs

Figure 6.12 ZMO picking line with "help your neighbor"

filling the buffer area, it is a signal for the upstream person to come and help her downstream neighbor get caught up. There is no value in continuing to fill tubs upstream when the downstream tubs on the moving conveyor are backing up. As you can see in the photo in Figure 6.12, there are two tubs in the buffer and the picker has just completed one tub and is placing it on the moving conveyor. If he had taken a few more seconds, there would have been three tubs, which would have signaled the person just before him to come to help. This buffer is also a mechanism for leveling the workload between associates.

Some tasks do not lend themselves easily to standard work. For example, the people who put items ordered by the customer into boxes for shipment must use their judgment. Each customer can order a different combination of items, and ZMO has not found a precise way of calculating the exact volume of box that is needed. So the boxers are trained to visualize how the items will be arranged and how large the box needs to be. However, ZMO found a visual job aid that enables the workers to use better judgment. Based on a rough estimate by the computer of the items to be packed and the volume they will need, the computer suggests a color-coded box size. A display shows the different box choices arranged with a color swatch on the box (see Figure 6.13). This is visual information supporting the judgment of the team member.

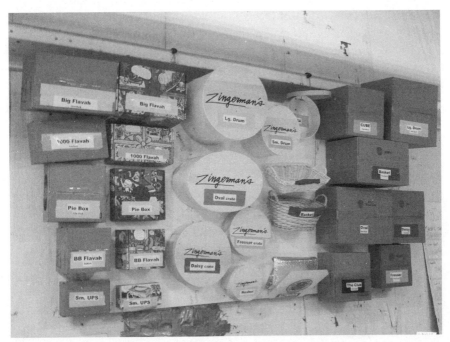

Figure 6.13 ZMO visual box-size guide

Another visual tool at ZMO is intended for "mistake proofing." There are many standard gift boxes that have the same collection of items ordered every day. For the popular boxes with standard items such as the "weekender," ZMO creates a single station to assemble them. ZMO also developed a template with cutouts the sizes of the individual items. Before loading the box the assembler will place each item on the template, and when each space is filled, she knows she has exactly what is needed for the box (see Figure 6.14).

When visual information is displayed for people to peruse at their leisure, as on a bulletin board, we call this "visual display." It seems nice to have, but it is not essential to doing the work, and as a result it is often not well maintained. When visual information is used as an essential part of the daily work to signal standard versus actual, we call this "visual management."

Making Daily Management Visual in an Aircraft Engine Company

It is always exciting to me to see real visual management, where the information is seriously used. I had the opportunity to visit MTU, a German company that builds and repairs aircraft engines. MTU has a large factory in Munich, and I visited it with a partner of Staufen, the consulting firm that supports the aircraft company. We spent time at MTU with a member of the board of directors, the senior vice president (SVP) of Operations. Staufen has been teaching executives the proper way to use visual management as a tool for coaching leaders.

The MTU factory in Munich has over 150 information centers on the shop floor, which are visual meeting areas for stand-up meetings. Displayed on whiteboards are various metrics and targets for cost, quality, delivery, inventory, safety, and morale. There are also human resource measures like attendance. Short meetings (10 to 15 minutes) are held every day, and the main discussions focus on what happened yesterday and what the group can improve on today and tomorrow. The SVP runs the plantwide meeting, and there are meetings at all levels down to group leaders.

At first the people from Staufen did the coaching, but they then trained internal full-time coaches—senior leaders and middle managers—to do daily coaching. Coaching means listening and watching and giving feedback. This was not a company that was new to lean; it had years of experience using almost every improvement tool imaginable. The company finally became convinced that the key to sustainable competitive advantage was leadership, and so it committed to developing lean leaders at all levels.

The senior vice president working with the head of lean began with a pilot area for about six months, and the SVP chose to use that time and more to persuade the managers to buy in. In fact, before deploying the information centers

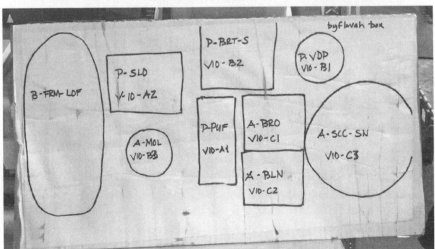

Figure 6.14 ZMO mistake-proofing template for items in a standard gift box

across the operation, he spent over one year holding regular meetings and bringing managers to see the pilot area firsthand. The result was that 100 percent of the managers bought in.

The SVP committed to spend time the first half of each day at the gemba. He simply refuses to allow anything else on his schedule before lunch. He explained that his coaching style had been more directive, telling people what to do. But he took his coaches seriously, learning to ask questions and challenge the leaders to grow. He admits it was difficult to shift from telling people things to asking them to think for themselves, but his progress was remarkable.

The results included impressive gains in productivity and quality and reductions in inventory. Morale and safety rose to levels never before experienced. But there are also intangibles that show how a culture of engagement is building. For example, the business tends to be cyclical, and there are slow periods followed by a lot of work. At some point in the week, it generally becomes clear that overtime and weekend work are needed to make the schedule. In the past the manager might ask for 10 volunteers, and people would look away or put their heads down. Now the visual display makes it clear to everyone what extra work will be needed, and team members work it out even before being asked by management. When I visited in November 2015, snow was forecast for the weekend with perfect ski conditions; yet the company already had volunteers to cover overtime.

The daily management system started in manufacturing, but the company was also holding daily meetings in information centers for service operations like purchasing and logistics. Product development had committed to piloting the system with daily meetings. The company has developed a breakthrough new engine that had five years of fully booked sales before it could even build the first production engine. The company's business plan was to grow sales by 20 percent with a 10 percent reduction in labor, using attrition to deal with the excess people. Nobody doubted it would succeed through the evolving culture of continuous improvement.

PRINCIPLE 8: BUILD IN QUALITY AT EACH STEP

Toyota became famous for its policy of stopping the line when there is a quality problem. What became known as the "andon" system began with a very practical problem when Sakichi Toyoda was working to develop a fully automatic loom. As the looms became more automatic, humans did not need to do much more than load in thread and unload cloth. Yet people had to stand by the machines to watch in case a single thread broke, which would lead to defective cloth. Toyoda had a very strict policy of not wasting people's time and felt that this was a case where the person was subservient to the machine when the machine should be serving the person. As Toyota president Eiji Toyoda later explained: "A person's life is an accumulation of time—just one hour is equivalent to a person's life. Employees provide their precious hours of life to the company, so we have to use it effectively; otherwise we are wasting their life."

To free up the person, Sakichi Toyoda developed a mechanical line-stopping method that caused the loom to stop itself when a single thread broke. However, with many noisy looms operating at once, it could be difficult to tell that a loom had stopped. Thus Sakichi introduced the *andon*, a metal flag that popped up when the loom stopped itself, in essence saying, "Help me!"

Today's andon in assembly is a more elaborate system of lights and sensors: when the assembly worker pulls a cord, a light identifying that workstation lights up and calls for help. The team leader has seconds to get to the station to see what is going on and has the right to decide to pull the cord again and override the line stop. If the car passes into the next work zone without the team leader pulling the cord a second time, then the line actually stops.

Andon literally means a light and is a form of visual control, like a traffic light (see Figure 6.15). All the lights are green when everything is okay. The light for Process 3 turns yellow, which means the andon cord has been pulled and there is some abnormality, but the line keeps moving. When the car enters the zone of the next process the light for 3 will turn red meaning the line has stopped. The standard within Toyota and much of the world: green is go, red is stop, and yellow is in between.

Figure 6.15 Andon requires a quick response

Stopping the line for any out-of-standard condition is rather dramatic. Talk to Toyota managers and workers about their first experience pulling the cord, and they will describe feeling reluctant and nervous, with many of the symptoms of severe stress. Announcing to the world there is a problem is seldom welcomed, but Toyota has built a culture that honors those who find problems. "A problem is a buried treasure," we hear.

Having an elaborate system of sensors and lights is not the main issue here. What's most important is building a culture of people who immediately alert leaders to any problems they notice and having a help chain in place so that well-trained people respond immediately to contain the problem and then solve it. If the problem is not contained within a process, one segment of the line stops and the problem is escalated to the group leader. If a small buffer of cars leading to the next work group empties, then the manager gets involved. Everyone has a role to play to support production when there is an abnormality. This culture has been painstakingly built in Toyota, and more recently it has been introduced in the labs of the Henry Ford Health System.

Quality Improvement at Henry Ford Health Systems Diagnostic Labs

No hospital can run without a lab analyzing blood and tissue samples. Every doctor working on a serious case is dependent on the results of lab tests. Unfortunately testing is often taken for granted, like breathing oxygen. As long as it is available, it is out of sight, out of mind. But when it does not function, it is a crisis, particularly if patient samples get mixed up and the wrong diagnosis is made.

Dr. Richard Zarbo, chairman and senior vice president of pathology and laboratory medicine at the Henry Ford Health System, decided he had had enough. He was not satisfied with the quality or efficiency of his lab, and he was not satisfied with his own leadership style despite decades of management experience. Moreover, he felt that he had let down Dr. W. Edwards Deming, who had influenced him years earlier about building in quality. Things had to change starting immediately.[5] Dr. Zarbo attended a course on lean management and he was hooked. He saw lean as a practical version of the philosophy Deming preached. He went to work on his lab immediately, first trying to lead it himself from the top down and then learning to engage leaders at all levels. It was a major professional and personal transformation for Dr. Zarbo and the results were spectacular putting his labs into the limelight as a global benchmark of lean management in practice.

The Henry Ford labs in 2015 generated $600 million in revenue and employed about 750 of the 23,000 people working in the Henry Ford system.

The labs serve six acute care hospitals and 30 medical clinics. Lives literally depend on the laboratory system. In large part because of its world-class quality, the lab in Detroit, southeast Michigan, has been steadily growing, taking on testing for the majority of Michigan, extending its services to clinics and healthcare providers outside the Henry Ford system. The quality is the result of a decade of both developing a culture of people who are seeking perfection and building systems to detect and eliminate defects.

With over 11 million lab tests per year, the lab depends on data analysis to identify common problems to attack. A new defect management system was initially based on human detection of nonconformances. This was eventually supplemented by specimen deviation data from the Henry Ford Health System's laboratory information system called Sunquest. The computer system collects data in real time as tests are being conducted and flags the defects immediately when they are discovered. This is like an automated version of the andon system of Toyota.

Zarbo decided to go after the top quality certification for labs, ISO 15189. The deviation management system was required for the challenging ISO quality accreditation, but Zarbo thought the system was already quite good. However, through working on the certification and setting up the Sunquest system, Zarbo discovered it was not as good as he originally thought. The team began tracking defects with 36 generic types selected from a menu. Zarbo and the members of his group quickly concluded the generic menu was not effective, and they needed more specific classifications. The "other" category was filling up. They looked at the most frequent defect classes and where they originated, e.g., from a provider group like hematology or from their own processes. They eventually developed 125 types.

They were ready to deploy the deviation management system and began by rolling it out to the anatomical pathology department, but it was not well received. There were many defect classification codes that were foreign to the pathologists, and as a result, they did not feel comfortable using the system. With a decade of lean management the laboratory culture was open to input from all and Dr. Zarbo was not going to impose an overly complex system onto the pathologists. He learned the hard way the harm caused by this type of coercive bureaucracy.

To tailor the system to the pathologists, Zarbo and the members of his group decided to survey the pathologists to identify the most frequent defects. Zarbo and his group developed a list of the 30 most common defects ranked by severity. Ultimately that number was reduced to seven of the most frequent and serious defects. The anatomical pathologists wanted a paper copy listing the defects so they could document where they thought a defect came from. In response, Zarbo's group designed a one-page form for the pathologists. But when they saw it, they said it was still too complex and in the past they only needed one-half page.

So the quality group reduced the categories further and got down to one-half page, more similar to the original list, but with different categories based on all the data the new system collected. The goal was not to create the most elaborate and comprehensive system possible, but to develop the simplest version that would be useful and used for actual improvement. And it did get used, and defects dropped day by day, month by month.

The Henry Ford Health System has been under great pressure to reduce costs based on generic cost reduction targets every year. Yet Dr. Zarbo's "lean program" focuses most heavily on reducing the time it takes to get results back to the doctors and on the quality of those results. Why is he so passionate about quality? According to Zarbo:

> As the head of the lab, if we get sued, I am personally liable. The license is in my name. With over 11 million tests in a year we need a quality system to show we are not perfect but we are making strides every day. We want to be a best in class laboratory. I know of a case where a surgeon removed the wrong breast of a patient as a result of a lab error. They are still being sued. I have never been sued. If we do get sued, we can show what we have been doing with hard data. We are at 99.73 percent accuracy internally, and virtually none of the defects get through to the customer. No other lab can tell you that. Others claim they run great labs. We can say it with data. And we have learned that great quality means higher productivity.

After 10 years of this intensive focus on quality, there are very few defects originating within the lab. Of the 0.27 percent, 90 percent comes from suppliers—those who collect the blood and tissue samples (0.18 %). But Dr. Zarbo is responsible, and so slowly but steadily he and his team have worked collaboratively with suppliers to standardize their processes and eliminate defects. Defects can include mislabeled samples, too little blood to conduct the test, contamination in the sample, and more.

We can see in Figure 6.16 the types of defects the labs had in 2014 using the defect categories that the members of the quality group created. They playfully call these the "Big 11 All-Star Team of Deviations." Nine of the eleven are "preanalytic," which means they originate outside of Zarbo's labs in the clinics and hospitals that collect the samples, like wrong test ordered, clotted samples, and insufficient quantity. These account for almost all the defects. The first response by his staff to this data was exactly what Dr. Zarbo did not want to hear: "It is not our problem."

Zarbo and his quality czar set up a process of working with suppliers to resolve problems identified in the data. In one example of working with one of the

2014 Big 11 All-Star Team of Deviations

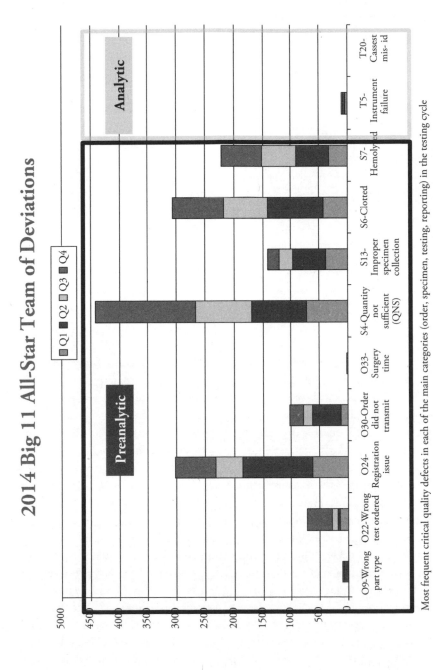

Most frequent critical quality defects in each of the main categories (order, specimen, testing, reporting) in the testing cycle

Figure 6.16 Henry Ford labs summary of quality defects by source

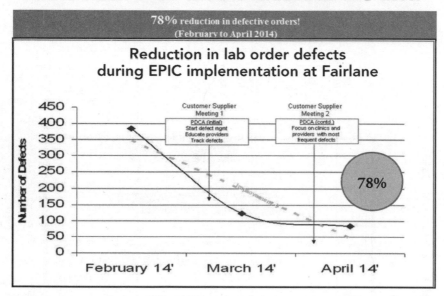

Figure 6.17   Henry Ford labs quality improvements with a branch lab supplier

branch labs, the Fairlane medical center, they were able to reduce order defects by 78 percent in three months after having the quality defect data properly categorized and visible and with coaching from Zarbo's team (see Figure 6.17). In one year, they reduced lab order defects preanalytic by 99 percent!

Even with this success they continued to work to improve their own internal processes. Dr. Zarbo had enough experience with continuous improvement to realize that automated defect detection systems do not solve problems—people do. Therefore Zarbo's team worked intensively to develop a daily improvement system at the level of the work group. Zarbo first saw how a daily management system can work when touring the labs of their equipment vendor, part of Danaher Corporation. Danaher is one of the pioneers of lean, as written about in *Lean Thinking*. Zarbo negotiated to have Danaher trainers help the labs set up a daily management system in 2013. It started with a day of training for all management about how to set up a visual tracking board and to hold daily work group meetings. Zarbo's leaders then figured out how to adapt the visual management displays to their own system. It is an integrated corrective action system and drives both daily problem solving and deeper problem solving for more complex problems on the same board. Every department has its metric board for QTIPS—quality, timeliness, inventory, productivity, and safety—and holds daily meetings. In the beginning the managers did not know how the system would be accepted, so they did a pilot. Within two months there was a flurry of activity, and within a year there were hundreds of process improvements. Over time there was a shift toward tackling bigger, more complex problems.

The first reaction to a defect is a rapid fix to get accurate results to the doctor, a rapid fix that contains the problem. This is followed by corrective action, which means going back to find the root cause and improving the process. The labs use an A3 process—one side of one sheet of A3-size paper—to work through the corrective action (discussed in Chapter 9).The various processes for improving the work are summarized in Figure 6.18. Each month Zarbo and a small panel select a team to present their best improvement project in a "share the gains" meeting of all employees and management to spread what has been learned and provide recognition to the teams.

I am pretty certain that any quality department in any company would recognize the fundamentals of the Henry Ford quality system. "We have had a similar quality system for decades and see regular improvements in defect reduction." I believe this is true but wonder how many organizations really have defect prevention built into their culture. In Zarbo's experience, most labs work

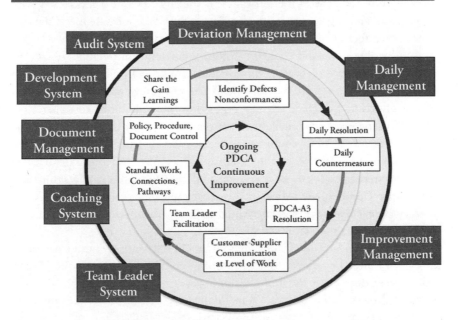

The Processes of Managing for Continuous Improvement

Audit System
Deviation Management
Development System
Daily Management
Document Management
Coaching System
Team Leader System
Improvement Management

Share the Gain Learnings
Identify Defects Nonconformances
Policy, Procedure, Document Control
Daily Resolution
Ongoing PDCA Continuous Improvement
Daily Countermeasure
Standard Work, Connections, Pathways
Team Leader Facilitation
PDCA-A3 Resolution
Customer-Supplier Communication at Level of Work

Figure 6.18   Henry Ford labs improvement process

on rapid fix and get on with it. Preventative action means changing the process so that it never happens again. This is where lean comes in—finding the root cause and changing the process. Zarbo notes: "We are among a few labs that always focus on changing the process. We can dominate anyone on quality and quality alone. With our culture we can innovate. Bring it on. We will get the cost reductions. And we can grow based on quality."

Designing Quality into Menlo Software

One thing not so visible on a tour of Menlo Innovations is its religious use of a best practice, which is rarely practiced by others, called unit testing. For each "unit" of code (generally a single function), the software programmer builds a test or tests that can reveal defective code. In a sense you are programming twice—one is the original code, and the second is code to test if your code is "fit for function." An added benefit of creating the test is that it forces the programmer to think deeply about the inputs, outputs, and error conditions and thus the unit's desired behavior. You can see on the wall near the work authorization boards a chart that records each of the unit tests designed and run, which can get into the hundreds of thousands for a complex project. The result is designed-in quality so the software rarely fails.

Unit testing also frees up Menlo's group of "quality advocates" from wasting time searching for defects. To get from an orange dot to a green dot, a quality advocate comes and checks the software. The quality advocate works closely with the technical anthropologists and is checking whether the software meets the customer requirements and is user friendly. In fact, some quality advocates were technical anthropologists and do not have software development training.

After the quality advocate approves, the team gets rapid feedback watching the customer attempt to use the software in the weekly reviews. Software that fails because of defective code, or software that is not satisfying to the customer, does not last beyond these rigorous tests. As we noted earlier in the book, years have passed without a customer complaint after the software has shipped. As a part of the pursuit of joy, Menlo wants any failures or customer concerns to be detected and resolved as the software is being developed. Of course, this requires some up-front money, but as quality guru David Crosby noted, "Quality is Free."[6] What he meant was that any up-front investments will pay themselves back in multiples due to much lower rework and customer pain.

Richard Sheridan tells an amusing story about the company's most successful project to write the software for a complex portable blood analyzer. Accuri Cytometers engaged Menlo Innovations to design and build the software that ships with each unit. He describes how Leo, Menlo's customer service guy, carefully packs up the unit and ships it to Accuri, anxious to learn if it will satisfy the customer. He intends to give detailed instructions on its use as soon as it arrives.

When he does not hear from his contacts at Accuri, he is desperate to know what is going on. Finally after waiting in agony all day and night, he calls them the second morning, and they pleasantly reply: "Oh yeah, we got the box yesterday morning. We just unpacked it and started using it right away. We've been doing science with it for two days. It is great!"

Customers who choose to work with Menlo are willing to pay for tech anthropologists in an extended up-front customer requirements phase, they are willing to pay for pairs of programmers, and they are willing to devote their time to weekly reviews. This is all costly, but the end result is lower-cost software, in large part because of avoiding all the costly rework that happens in traditional development processes. Richard calls this "lower cost, at a higher price," which means there are some higher prices but in large part because of built-in quality the overall cost of the software is much lower.

PRINCIPLE 9: USE TECHNOLOGY TO ENABLE PEOPLE

Information technology is the lifeblood of many service organizations. And as we saw in the Henry Ford labs, it can be a source of critical data to build in quality. But too often it becomes more of a barrier than an enabler to service excellence.

Like bureaucracy, technology can either be done to us in a coercive way or implemented to enable us to better do our jobs. Nothing feeds mechanistic thinking like technology. We are bombarded with it in the media. Software companies pop up like weeds, promising that their "solutions" will save the world from poverty, disease, and pestilence. If the Internet was not enough we now have the Internet of things to add sensors and gizmos to run everything by computers. One gets the impression we are like Mario living in a big video game.

Lean is very much about reality. "Go to the gemba!" is the battle cry of the lean practitioner. The gemba is reality, not a computer screen. We saw with Menlo Innovations that technical anthropologists go to the gemba and find computer users' needs that can be surprising to the customer and even the users themselves. Menlo technical anthropologists are not overdramatizing when they explain their mission is to "end human suffering as it relates to technology." Founder Richard Sheridan loves technology and finds it a crime against humanity to take such a beautiful human creation and turn it ugly and painful to use.

What is the attraction of technology to mechanistic thinkers, and why would they accept technology that is hard to use and maintain? I believe it is a result of the mindset of using technology to replace people. The way technology is often cost justified is through labor reduction. When that is the goal, we stop thinking creatively about the ways technology can improve quality of service and functionality, and we are myopic in thinking about how we can get the technology in and the people out as quickly as possible.

One of the top 10 reasons lean programs fail in my experience is because of the disruption of installing enterprise integration software systems like SAP. There is nothing necessarily harmful about these computer systems that prevents lean, but when we work with companies that are developing momentum in learning about lean, we often start to find engagements canceled because "we are having problems with SAP implementation and my team is now on 24-7 alert to help install SAP." Once SAP enters the organization, like a virus, its advocates want to use it for everything. It schedules operations that would benefit more from visual pull systems. If provides "workflow management" software to impose an artificial structure on the execution of projects. I worked with leaders at a product development organization that wanted to buy materials for prototypes in small lots, but the SAP protocol would not allow them to do it. They had to find a way to fool the system. This is a problem not just unique to SAP, but a disease of trying to make processes conform to the technology.

Karyn has worked with many organizations in which the "computer systems seem to run the people, instead of the people running the computer systems." She has often heard service representatives say to customers, "I'm sorry, we can't do that. Our system doesn't allow us to." And she has attended many huddles in which "computer system" problems were the only problems discussed. It seems many people now believe that the only types of problems that exist in services are computer system problems and that if the computer systems were only better, newer, faster, and more integrated, then all service problems would be instantly resolved. This, however, is an example of mechanistic thinking. In an organic lean culture, we recognize that our computer systems are never perfect and need to be continually improved as we learn from experiences working with them. A document that is received late by a customer, or a flight or hotel room booked improperly, is not necessarily the result of a computer system error. If we assume that it is, then we overlook the opportunity to develop our people's problem-solving abilities. (We will discuss this more in Chapters 8 and 9 on developing people and problem solving).

Technology Fiasco in a Healthcare System

One of my PhD students, Brock Husby, spent years working as a lean healthcare consultant as he was getting his PhD. One engagement, which turned out to be part of his dissertation, was to help a statewide system recover from a poor process of justifying and installing an automated, centralized laundry system.[7]

Toyota's predominate approach to technology is to use proven, reliable technology applied to well-defined and understood processes. They prefer to test the simplest solution, often on a pilot basis, before deploying more advanced technology. Often Toyota will delay new technology deployment until the site is ready, which means its processes are already lean and under control. The pilot program invariably reveals issues that the creators of the technology missed in the original design. Processes get fine-tuned, and the technology is adapted to support the process.

The hospital system that ultimately called Brock in for help did the opposite. It had laundries distributed through the healthcare system, and they worked well enough, but the processes to use them were not well defined and definitely not standardized. An executive commissioned a financial analysis that showed the organization could save millions of dollars per year if it centralized the laundry in one common facility that did the laundry for the entire state system. By using the latest technology, it would need a minimum of labor.

A total of $10 million was invested in a state-of-the-art facility. From the initial launch of the laundry, shortages of towels and scrubs were threatening to shut down the operating rooms at the main hospital (the financial engine), and the off-site laundry processing and onsite laundry distribution managers were not on speaking terms with each other due to animosity and finger-pointing about this poor system performance.

A fixed daily order for laundry was in place, with no system to react to variation in demand other than expediting orders or stealing from other departments. The chief operating officer (COO) of the hospital was getting 44 calls a day from angry department administrators, and most hospital employees were frustrated with the new process and wanted a return to the old system.

The $10 million investment (business failure), poor performance (technical failure), and low customer satisfaction (social failure) led to a call for help to Brock. The people at the healthcare organization thought that lean thinking might bail them out. Diving into the gemba, Brock observed and interviewed people for weeks and worked with a team to map the current state of the process, and then the team came up with a shared future-state vision and accompanying action plan. The team consisted of the on-site and off-site laundry managers, frontline staff, industrial laundry technical staff, truck drivers, and several internal customers. Brock facilitated the problem-solving process, but team members developed, implemented, and refined the process.

As the project progressed, the capability of the team members increased as they became more familiar with the approach and began focusing on process metrics (that weren't available at the beginning of the project). This was obviously a burning platform, and after completing 147 of the 150 action items, the process was working smoothly with no outages or calls to the COO. Also, the team reduced the workload per cart and improved other measures of efficiency. Frontline staff members who had never been engaged in creating their processes created a system of visual kanban replenishment (a pull system) to adjust orders to actual usage. Core process measurements were established and actively used for ongoing problem solving. The off-site and on-site laundry managers, who were not on speaking terms initially, were now friendly and communicating multiple times per day to dynamically coordinate the flow of laundry.

Improvements were not technically complex. An example of one of the improvements was shifting where the soiled linen was temporarily stored from the third floor to the basement. Before this change, the laundry staff had to take a heavily used elevator that only carried two carts to the third floor, which increased the number of trips and resulted in significant wait time for an available elevator. With the dirty laundry stored in the basement, a large freight elevator located at the loading dock could be used (which also greatly decreased the distance to be traveled to get to the elevator), which had a capacity for six or more carts and was only one level away from the basement storage room. This had a significant and immediate effect on the newly established metric of average time per cart.

Unfortunately this type of case is all too common—getting an abstract idea about the benefits of a new technology, building a business case, and then deploying without deeply understanding the reality. When we introduce any complex technology, there is a great deal of uncertainty, and yet technology providers often act like implementation is a routine process. Brock suggests a six-step process to effectively introduce new technology, which involves learning step by step as you go through PDCA:

Step 1. Clearly define the problem or need.

Step 2. Carefully evaluate the process and improve it as much as possible before leaping into new technology.

Step 3. Consider the skills required and develop a plan for training and involving the people affected by the introduction of technology.

Step 4. Introduce the technology first on a pilot basis to learn and work out the bugs and the process of introducing it.

Step 5. Introduce the technology into other locations in a stepwise fashion, with local management taking ownership and leading the process.

Step 6. Using an effective daily management system, expect the people responsible for the work to continue to improve the technology and process.

Automation at Henry Ford Health System Labs

These days fully automated lab work is the nirvana image. When Dr. Zarbo began the lean journey in 2004, he and his team benchmarked a lab nationally known for its labor efficiency. They discussed what they saw. They appreciated the efficiency as banks of automated equipment hummed away, but they agreed this was not the culture they were envisioning for Henry Ford. It was too sterile and mechanistic. People were appendages to the machines, not actively thinking and innovating.

As Zarbo and his team started down the lean road, they again looked at where automation might fit in. Before the lean transformation at the labs they were working toward a target to turn around blood samples in 60 minutes for the emergency room. Within one year on the lean journey, Zarbor raised that target to 45 minutes, and by 2015 his labs were able to complete 90 percent of what was ordered in 30 minutes. This was after thousands of process changes. They automated some processes, but most of what they did was tear apart the labs and reorganize them into manual cells in a clean flow. The labs were never fully automated. By streamlining the processes, humans were able to do a lot of efficient things to get samples prepared in sequence for the work cells and the material handling system to get completed results to doctors. The lab technicians were able to go faster than automated processing, and in fact automated lines, at that time based on batch processing, would have slowed them down.

Over the years automation has been enhanced, and the labs were in the process of switching to automated lines in 2015 working with the Beckman Coulter subsidiary of Danaher, which had selected the labs as a model for integrating lean culture with automation. As Zarbo explains:

> *There is a highway of multiple lines and crossovers, and bar codes tell us how to switch between lanes to get faster results. Now it is faster than we are. But we still have to get stuff to the line. We have a 10:30 meeting every week. We sit down with folks from the manufacturer. We designed the front end to shrink time to the line and the back end to speed results to our customers. The computer monitors have real-time andon built in. Beckman Coulter is using us as a global model for its other clients.*

People can get improvement from an automated line, but they will be limited by the 90 percent of problems that come to the line in the supply process. That is why Danaher selected Henry Ford as a center of excellence. It wanted to show how continuous improvement can streamline the process and get the most out of the automation, from taking the initial sample to giving results to the patient. As Zarbo explains:

> *I do not want to drop automated equipment in the middle of the laboratory and let it run. I want to design the workstations to support the people. Do we need different management and leadership systems for an automated system where we cannot see the process? We have been preparing people for*

*the last 8 months. We need the management level to understand everything
about the laboratory.*

Continuously Improving Automation at Toyota Machining and Forging

I will finish our discussion of automation with a remarkable example from Toyota. It is a manufacturing example, though not the usual image we have of a car being built on an assembly line. The Honsha plant in Toyota City is right next to the corporate headquarters and produces forged and machined engine and transmission parts for many vehicles. It is almost wall-to-wall automation. The company is fortunate to have Mitsuru Kawai, senior technical executive, running the plant. That job title is restricted to the best of the best in the Toyota Production System and in 2015 he was promoted to become a member of Toyota's board of directors. As an Ohno student, Kawai developed a passion for continuous improvement as well as the obligation to teach. Kawai attended the Toyota Technical High School and worked his way up from production team member. When I interviewed him he had already spent 50 years at Toyota, 40 years of that time in the Honsha plant.

The basics of TPS were already in place when Kawai joined the plant, but his job was more than to manage a well-functioning plant. His target was to improve production labor efficiency by 2 percent over the previous month, every month. That continued for his entire career.

One obvious approach to this relentless improvement was automation. But this provided a special challenge for Kawai. He had learned the skills of TPS through manual work, visualization, making knowledge explicit, standardized work, and simple intelligent automation. The younger people working in the plant only knew automation. He said: "I do not want workers and engineers who think all they need to do is push a button and a part comes out. They still need to deeply understand the process so they can improve it."

To teach TPS in this automated plant, Kawai devised a number of lessons. In one lesson he holds weekly, "my machine meetings," the students hand-draw each step of the process inside the automated machines using paper and pencil, recording every move and every time metal is cut. He believes this leads to a deep understanding of the process and identification of opportunities for improvement. One major focus was defect reduction. When the students started the drawing, there were 2,004 defects per year, and in one year this was reduced to almost zero.

Another lesson is to stop automation and have highly skilled workers do the processes manually. Doing the job manually leads to ideas for kaizen when they rebuild the machine. In this way they were able to reduce the line length in half, striving for one-piece flow. When the Great Recession hit, Toyota realized that much of the automation was inflexible, making only a specialized set of parts, and fixed costs were high. The company used the approach "Make it small and make it grow." The focus was on creating a multiproduct line, simplifying the automation, making the lines shorter, and making the process more flexible to adjust to demand. Note that although the equipment was provided by vendors who had their own experts, Kawai was leading hourly employees and engineers to redesign the vendor equipment to eliminate waste in the process.

One great opportunity for teaching became known as the "basic TPS line." This is an old assembly cell that was originally set up in Brazil 75 years earlier. These simple cells were set up to assemble transmissions using a lot of manual work and simple intelligent automation. In the 1950s the volumes in Brazil were low, and there was a decision to close down the forging and assembly plant. Ohno simply refused to accept that the plant could not profitably make low volume and high variety and personally went to Brazil to teach the people there. When Brazil volumes rose by the twenty-first century, the company decided to eliminate the old manual cells.

Kawai saw this as an opportunity to establish a simple manual line for training purposes. He had all the equipment moved to Toyota City and began working with his team to do kaizen on the cell. The team in the Honsha plant started immediately to do kaizen and was able to shrink the floor space of the lean line by 50 percent. The team reduced the number of people needed to assemble the transmission from 10 to 1 person who makes a continuous loop around the cell every six minutes. The assembly line is scheduled by a visual box with cards to level the daily schedule by volume and mix each day.

One of the challenges Kawai posed to his students working on this basic TPS line was to do everything they could without electricity. With the large variety of transmissions that run through the line, there are a lot of parts to pick. It is commonplace these days for such situations to use electronic light systems to prevent picking the wrong part. We would often see lights lighting up by the right part and a light curtain that will signal if the wrong part is picked. Kawai's students needed to design a simple manual way to do this. Someone came up with a "key kanban" (Figure 6.19). The color-coded key kanban is made of metal with a specific configuration and acts as a key opening only the cover of the bin containing the specific part that needs to be picked next. Each key kanban unlocks a different cover.

I have not seen this level of dedication to deep training of the workforce anyplace else. Typically the attitude is that the experts will design the equipment, maintenance will help install and repair it, and operators will be super-

Figure 6.19   Manual key kanban opens only the cover of the correct part to pick next

vised to run it. Kawai, to achieve his 2 percent per month objective, needed people on the floor to do daily kaizen. To do this he needed to school them in the basics of TPS and ask them to take responsibility for eliminating waste inside the complex automation. Mitsuru Kawai has a simple viewpoint: "The material should be flowing through the machines while changing the shapes at the speed of customer demand (takt). Everything else is waste."

SELF-SERVICE TECHNOLOGY FOR CUSTOMERS IS NOT ALWAYS SERVICE EXCELLENCE

By Karyn Ross

Often, on Tuesday evenings, my husband Brian and I eat out at a popular chain restaurant because it is across the street from where we have to pick up our dog from doggie day camp. On one visit, when we got there, there was a Ziosk table computer sitting on the table. The server said that we could use it to order our appetizers and drinks, pay, play games, etc., and that he would take our order for our main course. I looked at him in horror. "What if I don't want to do that?" I said. "Part of the reason I go to a restaurant is to interact with the server. The service component is important to me." "Well," said the server, "if that is the case, I can take your order for you." He then proceeded to pick up the computer terminal and hit the buttons as we ordered, focusing on the computer screen instead of us.

I then asked him why the restaurant chain had decided to go with the computer terminals on the tables (which really don't go at all with the ambience . . . they look like what you would see in a sports bar). He said that after trying a number of things to solve a problem with servers not bringing customers their bills quickly enough during lunch service, the chain had decided to go with the table computers as a full-time solution. So to solve a service problem in part of the process, the chain made a blanket technological choice.

A few weeks later we went to the restaurant again. Different server. I was already glaring at the machine when we sat down. The server came over, picked up the machine, and said, "Has anyone explained our Ziosk table computer to you?" (Of course, at this point, Brian had a stricken look on his face, concerned about what my answer might be!) I said, "I don't use Ziosk machines. I come to a restaurant to have a social experience. That includes the service experience I have ordering and paying for my food with a server." The server said, "We'll remove it from the table, then." It seems a lot of other customers don't like the experience either.

Self-service using computers is becoming increasingly common. Many types of service companies have created libraries of "self-service" reference material that customers can access online. Oftentimes this is intended to "reduce" the number of calls to a service center, under the guise of giving the customer access to everything at any time. The result is to provide a barrier between the customer and a live service provider. The is the opposite of the Zingerman's Mail Order call center, which is trying to find out more about the customer and provide the best possible customer service. I am not behind in my ability to use technology; in fact, I'm quite technically savvy. However, as a customer, do I really want to spend my valuable time searching for something that I then may not understand and end up having to call for an explanation after navigating through layers of technology trying to dissuade me from asking for a live person? Before choosing to implement any type of technology, service companies need to ask themselves, "How does this technology support and affect the service experience of our customers, and how does it connect our customer with our company and our company's purpose?"

KEY POINTS
MICROPROCESS PRINCIPLES

1. Macroprocesses set the framework for micro-processes, which can be described as the view from the process level: how the daily rhythm of process, people, and problem solving is integrated to deliver service excellence on an ongoing basis.

2. Standards are approached very differently in organizations with coercive or enabling (learning) bureaucracies:
   - In coercive bureaucracies, standards are seen as static, set-in-stone rules or SOPs to be followed mechanically; audits force compliance through rewards or punishments.
   - In enabling bureaucracies, standards are the best way known to do the work currently, and they provide the framework and basis for continuous improvement and organizational learning as the people doing the work actively look for better ways to do it.

3. Managing visually allows us to easily see whether what is actually happening is meeting the standard, what should be happening:
   - Using simple paper systems for visual management allows us to learn more easily, with less mental effort, while communicating, planning, and tracking progress.
   - When out-of-standard conditions are made visible at a glance, people can respond quickly and easily.
   - Visual job aids can be useful in cases where tasks may be too variable for more conventional standard work.

4. Building in quality at each step means creating a culture that allows people to identify problems and quickly respond to contain the problem, then solve it, before it propagates downstream:
   - People must know, and be able to easily see, if what is happening is in standard (what should be happening) or is out of standard (a problem).
   - Finding ways to identify and fix problems in a single-piece flow within a station is an integral part of delivering service excellence.

5. Use technology to enable people:
   - Although service processes are often highly dependent on computers, people run computer systems, not the other way around; computer systems need to support the work that people do to service customers in a timely and accurate manner.

- Not all problems in service processes result from computer errors; assuming they do limits our thinking and actions to develop our people's problem-solving abilities.
- Before adopting any type of new technology, including self-service apps or online libraries, determine whether the technology both supports the customers' service experience and connects them with your company's purpose.

Chapter 7

Macrolevel People Principles: The Context for Exceptional People to Provide Exceptional Service

Organization is a process, not a structure. Simultaneously, the process of organizing involves developing relationships from a shared sense of purpose, exchanging and creating information, learning constantly, paying attention to the results of our efforts, coadapting, coevolving, developing wisdom as we learn, staying clear about our purpose, being alert to changes from all directions . . . These are the capacities that give any organization its true aliveness, that support self organization.

—Margaret J. Wheatley,
author of *Finding Our Way*

THE ROLE OF ORGANIZATIONAL DESIGN

I seemed to have missed discussing organizational design in *The Toyota Way*. Interesting, since I taught organizational theory and design for over 30 years at University of Michigan. Perhaps this is because historically the organizational chart has not been emphasized in Toyota. A Toyota product development engineer once shared his business card with me and laughed as he said, "It is in Japanese; I am sorry. It says my name and 'engineer.'" His job was to work really hard to accomplish whatever challenge he took on, which varied over time as different needs arose. Working in what some call the white space—the spaces between boxes on the organizational chart—is more valued at Toyota than doing a great job inside your box.

Therefore much of the effort in Toyota is on setting challenging goals to achieve breakthrough business objectives, but equally important is to develop people to live the Toyota Way of thinking and acting. It is very fluid and takes place within a loosely defined organizational structure, in the spirit of what Margaret

Wheatley talks about as "the process of organizing." Toyota is more interested in "struggling to find our way" to the next big challenge than executing plans and policies within a tightly defined structure. On the other hand, under Akio Toyoda, organizational design became more important to Toyota. In just a few years, he led several reorganizations. These included a reorganization by region to create more self-reliance, with local CEOs appointed (in the past a Japanese executive was always at the top of the region). Then in 2016 Toyota reorganized again, this time by product family, in order to become more nimble and respond more quickly to the environment.

In this book we've decided to talk about macrolevel people principles because we believe they can be important to lean transformation. Perhaps in some sense it matters more in services where there are not clear physical boundaries for making things. The macrolevel creates one context in which members "find their way." We have summarized the macrolevel through three overarching principles (see Figure 7.1):

- Organize to balance deep expertise and customer focus.
- Develop a deliberate culture.
- Integrate outside partners.

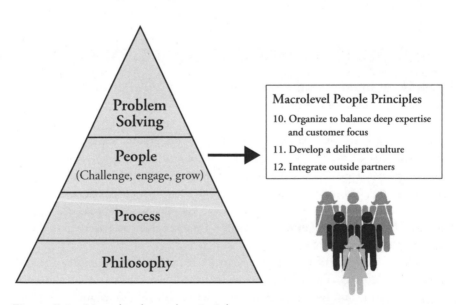

Figure 7.1   Macrolevel people principles

PRINCIPLE 10: ORGANIZE TO BALANCE DEEP EXPERTISE AND CUSTOMER FOCUS

The Challenge of Organizational Design

It was my first meeting with a new client. The COO pulled out an organizational chart to familiarize me with the organization's structure. He grunted and took out a marker. With an undertone of frustration, he began slashing, making new lines and boxes, and crossing out names and adding new ones. "This is a bit out-of-date, but it gives you an overview of our organization," he explained almost apologetically. I was not sure whether to make a mental note that this organization could not even keep up its org chart or be relieved that the org chart was not important enough to keep up-to-date.

Organizational structure has become somewhat of a joke popularized by comics like *Dilbert*. One now infamous quote, supposedly from Gaius Petronius Arbit in 210 BC, was actually published by an American journalist in *Harper's Magazine* in 1957. It continues to circulate widely, and people smile and nod. It hits home:

> *We trained hard, but it seemed that every time we were beginning to form up into teams, we would be reorganized. I was to learn later in life that we tend to meet any new situation by reorganizing; and a wonderful method it can be for creating the illusion of progress while producing confusion, inefficiency, and demoralization.*

There is widespread ambivalence, or even hostility, when it comes to the famed organizational chart. So many of us have lived through yet another reorganization that seems pointless and creates frustration and fear, while its architects were certain they were revolutionizing the organization to focus on the right things. While Margaret Wheatley wants us to understand that "organization is a process," the organizational chart presents a static structure. It provides a rough map of reporting relationships and who works together. A map gives you names and locations of places. We get some sense of place but know almost nothing about the big city over there, or the small village here, or the experiences of those parking on that bluff. However, although the organizational chart may be lifeless, it tells us something about how the organization sees itself, and as we all know, a picture is worth a thousand words.

What we can really learn from the organizational chart is the perspective of leaders about what they are trying to accomplish through a particular way of organizing—the purpose. Is it telling us about reporting relationships—who does performance reviews of whom and who has formal authority? Is it telling us about standard communication patterns like "follow the chain of command"? Or does it depict a chain of processes that add value to our customer? Sometimes in Toyota the organizational chart is flipped upside down with the value-added workers at the top, an image suggesting those closest to the customer are at the top, served by their leaders whose only influence on the customer is indirect through the value-added workers.

Common Types of Organizational Design

Functional Organization. As Frederick Taylor was working to develop scientific management at the microlevel of individual workers, there were similar efforts to develop a scientific approach to macrolevel organizational design. One of the leading figures in this body of work was Henri Fayol, who worked his way up as a mining engineer to become the managing director of a large mining company. He retired and became a scholar, writing about what he learned as an executive.[1] He approached the task as a scientist and developed 14 principles of management (sound familiar?). Like Taylor, he was searching for the one best way to organize. He found it in traditional command-and-control principles such as:

- **Unity of command.** Subordinates receive orders from one and only one boss.
- **Authority.** Power to give orders and exact obedience.
- **Division of work.** Organize by specialty.

Fayol did allow for some flexibility in the application of the principles depending on the situation. Nonetheless, the organizational design that arose from his principles was the command-and-control, functional organization. This is still with us today in most large organizations.

The functional organization puts people together by purported expertise—all the accountants under an accounting boss, all the architects under a managing architect, and so on. The idea is to build expertise and exercise control. The accountants will share practices and learn from each other. The accountant boss will know what the individual accountants are supposed to do and how they are performing. In a command-and-control environment, perhaps the latter is more important—knowing enough to control the people who report to you.

The problem is that departments become like little castles with moats around them, fighting for resources to take home and defend against other functional groups (see Figure 7.2). People focus on climbing the functional ladder, and in many cases in this organizational structure, the poor customer seems to be an afterthought. There is a huge amount of waste between departments, and there are often competing priorities between functions.

Figure 7.2   Departments are like castles

Customer-Facing Organization. To become customer focused, we often see organizations flip from a functional to a product organization. In order to do this, they define product or service groups and create vice president or director positions that might even have profit and loss accountability. They might split up customer bases by commercial versus private home offices, region, or size. There are endless ways to slice and dice the customer base. The point is for all the specialty functions that are needed for a customer base to align toward customer service. At the same time the organizations may be parsed into smaller organizations that run like minibusinesses, with accountable leaders who think and act like CEOs.[2] This might also be thought of as organizing around value streams.

Matrix Organization. The customer-facing organization, or organizing by value streams, seems like the ideal structure; yet we have seen cases where it limits people development. Consider Chrysler before it was taken over by Daimler. Chrysler had made dramatic improvements in the appeal of its vehicles by transforming product development from a purely functional organization to a product organization that the company called "platform teams." The company was reorganized around a set of platforms—large cars, small cars, trucks, minivans, Jeeps. It built a brand-new R&D center in Auburn Hills (Michigan) arranged so hundreds of engineers representing all the functional groups could sit on the same floor of the building to develop vehicles for a common platform. Chrysler even had financial analysts and purchasing representatives assigned to the teams (dotted-line reporting). It literally erased the functional organization and replaced it with the customer-facing platform teams leading to a rapid boost to the desirability of the company's vehicles and sales. Unfortunately, as time went on, Chrysler realized it was losing functional depth—engine engineers were not learning from each other, body engineers were not learning from each other, and so forth. The company tried "technology clubs" so that functional groups could compare best practices, but they rarely met and it did not work. People focused on where their core work was and on the people they reported to. After about a decade, the company began to shift toward a matrix organization.

Toyota has used matrix organizations for decades. In product development, the functional groups, like body engineering and chassis engineering, report to a general manager within their technical specialty. The general manager is responsible for developing engineers with deep technical skills, assigning them to projects, and doing their performance reviews. The engineers work on development projects, reporting to a chief engineer for a vehicle, like Camry. The chief engineer is the CEO of that vehicle program and is, in essence, renting the engineers as contractors. Although the chief engineer works to develop the engineers as well, the chief engineer does not want to be distracted by personnel administration issues. This reporting structure works extremely well in large part because of mutual respect between the chief engineer and general manager of the function. The chief engineer trusts the general manager to provide highly developed engineers, and the general manager sees the chief engineer as the most important customer. In this way, matrix organizations seem to be the best of both worlds, and they can be seen all over Toyota.[3]

In *Toyota Culture* we describe how the human resource department at Toyota's manufacturing operation in Georgetown, Kentucky, faced a major crisis when a number of female supervisors were sexually harassed. This led to deep reflection, and management concluded it was a failure of HR to build trusting relationships with team members on the factory floor. One result was to move HR professionals to the factory floor and make them responsible for a geographic region of the factory. Before this, the HR professionals had hard-line reporting relationships to human resources and dotted-lined reporting relationships to manufacturing. Now it was reversed: the primary reporting relationship was to the general managers in the factory so they could focus on building relationships in a specific part of the factory. It made a large difference in rebuilding trust and developing a strong connection between the people in human resources and their core job—developing people; but like any reorganization, it does not fix all the human resources problems for all time. For example, later in that same plant, when Gary Convis became president, he found weaknesses in human resource development because many key people had been hired away by other firms. He had to mount yet another major effort to develop leaders, even bringing in people from the outside.[4]

Matrix organizations "seem" to be a win-win, but in reality they are very difficult to manage. Now instead of having one boss, team members have two or more, which can lead to confusion and conflicting direction unless (1) the bosses communicate effectively, (2) they are aligned toward common goals, and (3) they respect each other. Toyota works hard to develop these types of relationships so it can make them work, but many other organizations, which do not spend as much time developing people, find it a very difficult structure to manage.

Networked Organization. This is one of the newer forms and appears to be loosely structured anarchy. Empower people, make the organization's purpose clear, and allow them to ebb and flow with those they need to work with on their own. Remove barriers to effective communication. Do not presuppose there is a best way of organizing on any given day.

In principle this seems utopian, but we have seen it devolve into chaos. One company that is making it work is Menlo Innovations, as we will discuss later in the chapter. Menlo's CEO, or formally "chief storyteller," Richard Sheridan, likes to say that when he and his partners formed the company, they forgot to create an organizational chart and assign people to bosses. He says there are no bosses, only people doing work for customers.

At Menlo there is evidence of a high-performing networked organization. For example, programmers with a huge range of experience pair together to write code, and the pairs change every week. Calling a meeting is as simple as shouting out in a big room where everyone works, "Hey Menlo!" The response will be everyone shouting back, "Hey Jeff (or fill in name)!" Then you are on the spot to say what you have to say or ask what you want to ask.

On the other hand, Menlo actually has very clear structures, and there are many of them. Pairing is not a choice of people floating around a room; it is a formal requirement to write code. Pairs are assigned every week by a manager, not self-selected by participants. Rich Sheridan can call himself what he wants, but he and two partners are the senior executives, both formally and spiritually. Nonetheless, Menlo functions as a highly customer-focused and productive custom software house without a lot of evident hierarchy and with clearly defined roles and responsibilities that do not appear on organizational charts.

While organizational structure matters, we still believe that how people think about customers and their work and their relationships with others, and how they think about the purpose of the organization and where they fit in, is far more important than where they sit in the organization. The most important thing is to focus intensely on understanding changing customer needs and work to align all the people in the organization in ways that allow them to serve customers to fulfill the organization's purpose. In that way, customer focus and deep expertise remain balanced across the organization.

ORGANIZATIONAL DESIGN AND HIGH-PERFORMANCE ORGANIZATIONS

In the 1980s I helped facilitate "open-systems workshops" with senior managers that started with identifying key environmental changes that would affect the organization, then defining the organization's purpose, then understanding the fit between the people, technology, and organizational systems. This led to envisioning a desired future. These workshops were effective in getting people to think about how to design their internal organization to fit the organization's purpose and environment. The focus was mainly on the human system, and the solution almost always was to develop some form of self-sufficient teams with all the functions needed to accomplish the work. For example, if a manufacturing group needed operators, supervisors, quality experts, manufacturing engineers, and maintenance to function, an attempt would be made to assign all these functions to the team. Unfortunately, there was a gap between the thinking and the doing, and the teams often did not have the leadership skills to perform at a high level of efficiency and effectiveness.

More recently there have been efforts to combine the macroview of open-systems theory with the microview of lean thinking, incorporating concepts like standard work, andon, visual management, and problem solving into self-sufficient teams.[5] Some companies that follow the high-performance organization approach have embraced the improvement and coaching kata that we will detail in Chapters 8 and 9, and the daily process of developing people can help bring the concept of a self-sufficient team to life.

Elisa Reorganizing Around Value Streams

Elisa is a provider of telecommunications services, one of the best in service excellence in Finland.[6] The company had different functional groups supporting different services—cable TV and Internet, wireless phones, and sales of devices. Customers expect their service to work on demand every time. If there is a failure, they want it to be fixed correctly and at lightning speed. Elisa needs great technology and great people who can maintain and improve the technology, and it needs well-informed customer service representatives who clearly and efficiently walk customers through various technical processes. The company falls mainly in the category of mass goods distribution (Internet, phone, cable, hardware).

Elisa went through a major transformation when it realized that many parts of the company were broken and customer satisfaction was disturbingly low. Management used all the principles we talk about in this book to increase the level of service quality, with Toyota as a model. The people in the company put a good deal of effort into improving the technological infrastructure, the types of physical systems that are more like manufacturing. They also worked intensely on customer-facing services. Elisa improved markedly on all key performance indicators. For example they achieved 4 out of 5 on an empowerment measure and reduced the number of network disruptions by 30 percent while the network was growing. In 2014 Elisa was honored as the best B2B sales organization in Finland by the Finnish Quality Centre. Profits have grown steadily year after year. But it was not profits that drove the transformation—it was customer satisfaction and a philosophy of engaging associates in a journey toward excellence that drove profits.

Elisa was fortunate to have a visionary CEO who was committed to the values of the high-performance organization. He was passionate about providing excellent customer service and about developing people. In 2009, Petri Selkäinaho, vice president of business development, took over the leadership of Elisa's transformation to business excellence with Toyota as the model. Petri started to work with the senior leadership team teaching lean concepts and problem-solving methods. This started their lean transformation. In 2010, Elisa's lean transformation was broadened including training all managers in problem-solving methods. This training was later made available and recommended for all personnel, and Elisa developed facilitation methods, e.g., for "learning from mistakes" and "learning from success."

Petri then recommended finding help in identifying their core business processes and brought in Kai Laamanen who was skilled in facilitating macro-redesign to achieve high-performance organizations. Kai focused on the bigger-picture level using the HPO approach. Kai Laamanen helped Elisa to look beyond the functional organization and identify the core customer-focused business processes, sometimes called value streams. Each value stream was assigned to an executive in charge, and Kai led workshops with executives who defined in greater detail their core process. Following this Petri led them in improvement workshops to drive to targets for customer satisfaction, quality, and efficiency. The executives were taught the PDCA process—investigate the current condition of each business core process, set targets, identify improvement actions, lead implementation of those actions, check on results, and reflect on what was learned.

It was the Elisa executives who actively led the improvement process rather than delegating it or outsourcing it. For example, the consumer services team found that a top customer complaint was billing errors. The team went to work to eliminate these errors using data and solving problem after problem while customer satisfaction quickly rose.

The combination of macro organizational change and local development of people as problem solvers turned out to be a winning combination. Customer satisfaction steadily increased, leading to the national Finnish award. It became clear to me that the broad organizational design approach of HPO, with the right leadership, could be complementary to the lean approach of developing people to continually improve processes.

PRINCIPLE 11: DEVELOP A DELIBERATE CULTURE

The Role of National Culture

Let's start with a basic truth. Culture is darn complex. Culture refers to *shared* values, beliefs, and rules of behavior. Try to get any two people to think alike and then multiply that by 10, 40, 10,000, and we get a sense of the complexity. There is far more diversity of thinking in any collectivity of people than we want to accept. And to make matters worse, people come and go, and some of those who stay have the audacity to change their thinking over time. In some ways culture is a theoretical concept that does not really fit the vagaries of the real world.

On the other hand, culture seems to be a powerful construct. On the whole, looking at central tendencies, we can see large differences across regions, nations, and different organizations within nations. Anyone spending time in other countries will quickly notice vast differences. One of the most comprehensive studies that quantifies national culture was led by sociologist Geert Hofstede over decades. He identified six dimensions that distinguish national cultures, and on his website you can select from among many different countries and get a country's scores on these dimensions and a description for that country, along with comparisons.

We will focus on three of Hoftstede's broad cultural dimensions that seem particularly relevant to lean—individualism-collectivism, long-term versus short-term orientation, and uncertainty avoidance versus risk taking. One of the concerns we repeatedly hear in companies looking to adopt some version of lean is that there is something peculiarly Japanese and Eastern about a continuous improvement culture that cannot be transplanted to the West. Let's compare Japan with the United States, one of the most Western countries (see Figure 7.3).

Japan, like other Asian countries, ranks relatively high on collectivism. Contrast that with the United States, which is among the most individualistic countries in the world. The strong American value of individual rights and freedom from control by organizations (or government) makes Toyota Way culture difficult to imitate. Working in teams, identifying with the organization's purpose, and following standard work are difficult. Early in the 1980s when U.S.

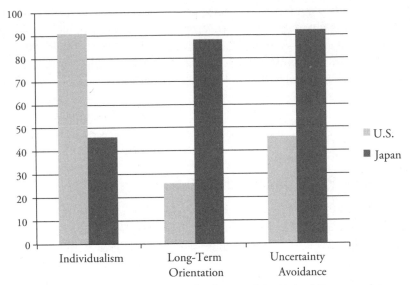

Figure 7.3   A comparison of the national cultures of the United States and Japan
Source: http://geert-hofstede.com/countries.html

auto companies were studying the Japanese companies, we would hear derogatory remarks like "We do not want to be an army of obedient robots like the Japanese." The Japanese all wore the same uniforms, they exercised to music at the same time in the same way, and they sang the company song. They acted like a collective—something totally alien to American workers (though not so different for those at Menlo).

We described long-term thinking as the foundation of the Toyota Way. Having a strong sense of purpose focused on achieving something great for customers and society depends on long-term thinking, as does developing people patiently. The United States is relatively weak on long-term thinking, and Japan is very strong.

Complementing the individualistic tendencies of American culture is the tolerance for uncertainty. In combination, individualism and risk taking may be a reason for the success of entrepreneurial business start-ups in the United States. In many ways becoming an entrepreneur, earning riches, and doing it our own way without a boss is the American dream.

The Japanese are quite averse to uncertainty, which may be a reason why so many go to work for a large company for life and strongly identify with that company. Japan is a country fraught with uncertainty. It is a small island nation with few natural resources and is regularly buffeted by environmental threats including earthquakes and tsunamis. The Japanese must struggle to maintain a balance of international trade that depends on producing innovative, high-quality products. It is a matter of survival to gain some modicum of control over the environment. A Toyota mantra is "We defend our own castle," which means the people at Toyota act as though they are self-sufficient as a company and must learn to navigate the rocky environment, gaining as much control as possible over their own destiny. Through collective action Toyota has conquered a myriad of threats from the environment and against the odds has become one of the world's leading companies.

The Role of Organizational Culture

Organizations are said to have their own culture, to some degree independent of the national culture. Toyota's culture is reflected in the artifact of the Toyota Way 2001 house. The purpose is contributing to society and customers, which in turn will lead to revenue to sustain the economic well-being of the company. The people at Toyota value both respect for people and continuous improvement and believe this is the only true path to sustainable growth. They believe challenge, kaizen, go and see firsthand, teamwork, and respect are the way to develop people so that they can meet the many challenges thrown at them by a complex and sometimes even hostile world.

These values and beliefs in Japan are all supported by the collectivist culture, long-term thinking, and a desire to avoid uncertainty by controlling whatever is possible to control. Since Toyota considers culture the source of its competitive advantage, the company is devoted to building its culture any place it sets up shop. Accepting that its culture was peculiar to Japan and could not be established in other countries would have meant giving up. And that would have meant that Toyota could not become a global company. Therefore the company accepted the challenge of developing the Toyota Way throughout the world.

For the most part it has succeeded. How? Through working hard, experimenting, learning, and above all persevering. A pivotal learning point was at NUMMI, the joint venture between Toyota and General Motors in California. Toyota set up the joint venture for the purpose of learning how to establish its culture with Americans. If it could do it in the United States, it could do it anywhere.

The company did not leave the culture to chance, but invested heavily in NUMMI in order to learn. The people at Toyota carefully selected American managers who seemed to fit Toyota's culture, intensely socialized them first in Japan and then at NUMMI by sending over a Japanese coordinator for every executive and manager and Japanese trainers for group leaders and team leaders. The mentors coached daily, and Japanese coordinators called the parent company in Japan every night to report on what they had learned. They did not try to transfer every aspect of their culture in Japan, adapting some aspects to local culture. When they got resistance, they reflected, tried to understand the cause, and experimented with a variety of countermeasures. Again, this was one-on-one mentoring of all leaders for years!

One senior Japanese leader explained that his biggest challenge was establishing a culture of openly discussing problems. At first he would do what he was used to doing in Japan, which is ask everyone he was coaching, "What is the problem?" Americans responded defensively, even with hostility: "Are you saying I have a problem?" He would explain that "we all have problems, and by addressing them that is how we improve." No luck. After deep reflection and some tutoring by the American leaders, the Japanese mentors concluded that they needed to say two to three positive things before bringing up a problem that would be viewed as negative. It worked for a while, and eventually enough trust was built to openly discuss problems.

Toyota's persistence paid off—NUMMI became the best automotive plant in North America—comparable to Toyota's plants in Japan on key performance indicators. And Toyota took what it learned and applied it to a successful launch of its own plant in Georgetown, Kentucky. Every plant, every sales office, every technical center was launched with a strong focus on building Toyota Way culture. It was not 100 percent though. Some Americans got it, others not so much. Developing Toyota culture was most successful in manufacturing and product development. But there was something distinctively Toyota-like in all parts of the company. Toyota's experiences support the hypothesis that organizational culture can be sustained globally through persistent effort and learning. The best learning is direct one-on-one with a coach. Classroom training simply does not work to develop the right daily behavior.

Build a Deliberate Culture and Then Find People Who Fit

One of the big questions in the technical world is whether it is better to hire a competent person who can be developed to fit the culture or find the most talented individual star even if their personality is contrary to the culture. The individual star generally means great credentials—prestigious university, high grades, and fast tracker. We have observed many companies that go for the fast trackers and give them a quick pathway through different departments to get to a management position. According to a *Harvard Business Review* article on creative development work, star players can be up to six times as productive as others.[7] So why not pay three or four times as much to get them?

It may not be a surprise to learn that Toyota in fact avoids star players, or at least people who think of themselves as stars. Toyota wants high performers, but its system is designed to develop people to be exceptional at what they do—some of course more exceptional than others. Toyota will always work to protect its system of human resource development and promotion and avoid people who are individualistic. It wants coachable team players who are excited to get their hands dirty and learn. For example, the company routinely passes over engineers from top universities, who have strong egos and ambition to fast track, often in favor of those from lesser-known engineering schools who have a clear passion for automobiles. One vice president had a favorite interview question: "If you could afford any car, what would you buy and why?" Someone who would talk excitedly about his childhood dream car and describe buying an old model and personally rebuilding it scored a lot of points.

Menlo also is obsessive about its culture of "Menlonians" and refuses to even do one-on-one interviews. Résumés are not terribly important—they show you have a pulse and have done well in academic courses. Richard Sheridan likes to say, "An interview is two people lying to each other." It is more difficult to pretend to be something you are not when you are in an actual work situation, particularly when there is some stress involved. So Menlo interviews groups of people at once and gives them a variety of timed tasks. Since Menlo expects everyone to work in pairs all the time, the exercises are done in pairs. The person who grabs a pencil away from his partner or dominates the pair is not likely to be invited back. Those invited back then return to spend a day doing paid work paired with a Menlonian, and if they survive that, they are paid for several weeks and pair with several people. There is intense discussion about each potential employee by all those who worked with the person, and through a form of consensus final decisions are made.

One thing Menlonians fear with a passion is "towers of knowledge." A tower of knowledge comes about when a brilliant software programmer is the only one who knows how a particular piece of software works. You coddle the person, hire the secret service to provide protection, insure them through Lloyd's of London, and sweat at their every cough. The project will crash and burn without that programmer. Menlo does not want to be dependent on any one individual. Teamwork is the name of the game at Menlo. Enter its office and look around, and teamwork is in the air (see Figure 7.4).

What you are actually seeing are pairs of people working together, enthusiastically (see Figure 7.5). They are sharing their knowledge. Richard talks of kindergarten rules. Be nice to your neighbors. Help them when you can. One-upmanship is unacceptable. In fact, in what Menlo calls the "extreme selection process," interviewees are told they will be judged by how good they make their partner (competitor) look. People rotate every single week. Of course, if there are people with a lot of experience, they will tend to rotate within the project, and an experienced person in the latest version of Java may be paired with someone with little Java experience. Teach each other. Learn together. Avoid towers of knowledge.

Figure 7.4   Enter and see and feel teamwork

Figure 7.5   Working in pairs multiplies creativity, error detection, joy

Working in pairs is exhilarating, and there is joy in accomplishment. Finish a story card, and you have a sense of accomplishment. Get a green sticker from the quality advocates, and there's a buzz. But get the customer to come in week by week and use your program flawlessly or give useful feedback, and that is priceless. On the other hand, for some people pairing is their worst nightmare, and they prefer to work alone. So be it. They have their choice of the vast majority of other IT firms in the world that are not Menlo. We have seen other companies with individualistic cultures that try to adopt paired programming—it rarely works.

One way Menlo's culture caters to the common values of software programmers is its approach to meetings. Meetings can be distractions from the joy of accomplishment, so they are kept short at Menlo. Every day there is an all-employee meeting, but it is not a bunch of people packing a conference room and competing for the good chair, coffee and doughnuts in hand. It is a stand-up meeting in a huge circle—70 people holding a meeting (see Figure 7.6). Two people report out at a time, each holding a horn of the infamous Viking helmet that Rich and his wife, Carol, brought back from a trip to Norway. It became a symbol of collaboration and it is fun. Those holding it have the floor and report out. The helmet circulates around the circle. Everyone gets to speak, in pairs. Others chime in if they have something to offer. And the meeting is short and ends on time— usually 12 to 15 minutes after it starts. As visitors to Menlo have experienced, buying lots of Viking helmets will not reproduce Menlo's culture. It is deep in the hearts and minds of Menlonians.

Is Toyota's culture Japanese and oppressive? Is it unfair of Menlo to expect all members to conform to its apparently loose culture, which in reality is loaded with strict role expectations and codes of conduct? Rich Sheridan says he and his partners created a "deliberate culture." They had a vision, and they are continually working toward that vision. A deliberate culture will almost by defini-

Figure 7.6 All-company meeting: the Viking helmet is the tip of the iceberg of shared culture

tion feel oppressive to people who do not fit in. Those who do not belong, but manage to slip through the selection filters, will feel alienated and will often complain . . . until they leave. When this happens, the culture is functioning as intended. If you want service excellence, do not compromise your deliberate culture that is working to fulfill its purpose in order to accommodate everyone's personal vision of a desired culture. Find people who fit and then socialize them into the culture.

Of course, not all organizations have the luxury of renewing themselves through hiring. What do you do if you already have entrenched employees who do not fit the culture the organization decides it wants to change to? Then you have to work to socialize them into the new culture and develop them, which is the subject of Chapter 8. What you will notice is that some will develop faster and farther than others. Those are the ones you want to promote. Selection does not end at hiring, but rather it continues as people are developed and promoted, or not.

PRINCIPLE 12: INTEGRATE OUTSIDE PARTNERS

As open systems, all organizations must continually work with outside organizations whether they be customers, suppliers, government organizations, joint venture partners—the list goes on. Toyota is famous for its tight-knit supplier network tied together in a just-in-time system, but Toyota treats all key environmental actors as partners important to the success of the enterprise. In *The Toyota Way* I wrote of the company's relationship with a lawyer who relearned how he practiced law based on the way Toyota worked with him and taught him. It was transformative. He learned to study the details of the case at a level beyond anything he had done in law school, question his every assumption, and work to collaborate even with hostile accusers. Service excellence depends on the performance of all people connected to the company to do their part at a high level of excellence and to fit the company's processes and even culture.

Toyota's Supplier Partnership Model

The Japanese *keiretsu*, a closely knit network of businesses that operate under an umbrella company, has received a great deal of attention in the popular press and management literature. There is a certain fascination with collections of companies that work together, selling shares to each other, meeting regularly to plot strategy, and doing a degree of exclusive business together. To some, it sounds like some sort of closed club colluding to take down the competition.

Over time the formal keiretsu were broken apart in the name of antitrust, with reductions in cross-ownership. Yet networks of companies that work with each other, or act under a broad umbrella like Mitsubishi Heavy Industries and the Toyota Group, continue to exist. Antitrust seems like an odd designation for the Toyota group since they are a collection of different companies—vehicle design and assembly, components manufacture, a trading company, a finance company—rather than a merger of competitors.

Ford, Chrysler, and General Motors all had large internal component groups, which in fact they spun off as separate companies when it became clear there were benefits to purchasing from outside suppliers competing with each other. Ford begat Visteon. General Motors begat Delphi. In a sense they were following the Japanese model of having a small number of outside suppliers in competition for their business. But the American companies did not know how to partner. And these internal component groups had high costs and lacked the skills to compete. Both these spin-offs ultimately went through Chapter 11 reorganization under bankruptcy law. This opened up competition, which reduced cost and put pressure on component suppliers for higher quality and service. But it was intense pressure from the customer organization, not collaboration, that drove cost reductions and quality improvement.

Decades ago, Toyota spun off its electronics department into Denso, which has grown to become the second largest global components supplier, selling to many non-Toyota companies. But Toyota has maintained a close relationship including some ownership and executives who leave Toyota to help lead Denso. Why maintain this tie to a longstanding partner? There are a variety of reasons, but at least one is the vision of an integrated enterprise with compatible cultures.

Denso fought for its independence to grow its non-Toyota business, but despite this, over time Toyota's and Denso's culture have become similar. Both believe in respect for people and continuous improvement. Both have invested heavily in lean systems in manufacturing. Both are obsessive at meeting new challenges through innovative products. Denso, like all suppliers who design components to fit Toyota vehicles, has many "guest engineers" who spend several years housed in Toyota R&D working side by side with Toyota engineers. This is obviously helpful for knowing what components Toyota will want in future vehicles, but it also leads to excellent communication and coordination between Toyota and its suppliers. They are building a compatible culture.

There are many ways that Toyota and its direct suppliers are integrated.[8] There are supplier associations with regular meetings, annual themes of topics to focus on improving, and committees to work on special projects. Purchasing is much more than buyers who negotiate on price. The purchasing departments have many people skilled in TPS and quality who teach the suppliers—and bring ideas back to Toyota. Since first-tier suppliers are delivering just in time, with very little inventory, any issue that might threaten production becomes immediately visible and leads to intense discussion about why it occurred.

It is very difficult to become a Toyota supplier. Toyota's general policy is to have two to three suppliers for a commodity in a region, for example seats in the United States, and they are locked in intense competition. When Toyota has this, there are no openings for additional suppliers. When Toyota moves into a new region or when there are new items to purchase because of technological innovation, the company starts by giving small contracts to a supplier. Over years, if the supplier proves itself, it will get more contracts until at some point it is part of the Toyota extended enterprise, and then it is difficult to get fired. However, it will have to compete and intensely improve quality, cost, and delivery. If it does not improve, it may lose a portion of its business to the competitor suppliers until it shows improvement. For those who get into the supply chain and perform, it is a stable and profitable business. They become partners and enjoy success with Toyota and go through bad times with Toyota, though generally Toyota's lows are not as low as those of the rest of the industry. They increasingly learn over time respect for people and continuous improvement through Toyota's tutelage and experience.

Toyota's Call Center and Its Partners Were Vital in the Recall Crisis

The recall crisis of 2009 to 2010 was a major blow to Toyota's self-image as a highly reliable automaker that always puts the customer first. We detailed what happened in *Toyota Under Fire*, and there was more speculation than facts about electronics problems causing sudden unintended acceleration. In fact, the U.S. National Institute of Highway Safety hired NASA, which did all it could to make Toyota vehicles fail, bombarding them with electromagnetic interference, and concluded there was no evidence the phenomena existed. Virtually every case of vehicles careening out of control where there was real data showed it was because of driver misapplication of the pedals. In other words, the driver pushed hard on the gas pedal when he or she intended to brake. Nonetheless, the media had a field day, and Toyota's reputation was gravely in question. To Toyota it was a major crisis, and it wants to be sure the pain continues to motivate learning.

What was not visible to outsiders is that the first line of defense when a company like Toyota is publicly accused of potentially deadly safety problems is addressing the concerns of the anxious customer calling the company help line. When it was announced that Toyota would stop selling vehicles because of "sticky pedals," the call volume went overnight from 3,000 calls per day to 96,000 calls per day. Call center personnel were dealing with anxious customers questioning whether they could safely drive their vehicles.

As Nancy Fein, then vice president of Customer Relations, described, calling it a difficult situation to manage through is an understatement:[9]

> *It was a very tough time with our customers, because our customers had periods where they didn't trust us, or they felt like we were lying to them, or they felt that we were misrepresenting ourselves. Being in customer relations, that means that we had a really difficult role of not just taking care of an individual customer problem with the vehicle, but needing to rebuild our customers' trust. We needed to fix our customers' problems, and we needed to help them have belief, and have confidence in Toyota, the way we have confidence in Toyota.*

Toyota had one big advantage in dealing with this crisis compared with many other organizations. It had decided many years ago to invest in its own call center rather than outsource it to low-wage countries. The careful selection and intense training of customer service representatives (CSRs) also made a huge difference. The employees in the call center at Toyota Motor Sales have been specifically screened for skills in building relationships with customers over the phone. While this is an entry-level job, it is not an easy job to obtain. Those who have the basic skill set go through a 4-week training course, followed by 6 to 18 months of close supervision before "graduating" as a full-fledged CSR.

Each of the Toyota CSRs is empowered to make decisions on the spot to help resolve customer issues. In addition to being directly connected to dealer service centers, a CSR working through the recall crisis could also immediately approve such expenses as having a car towed to the dealer, reimbursing a customer for renting a car or arranging a loaner vehicle from a dealer, or extending a warranty to cover other issues that a customer might be having. Once a customer talks to a CSR, an attempt is made to connect that customer to the same CSR on any follow-up phone calls. For every five CSRs, there is a supervisor who monitors selected calls, coaches the CSRs, and can authorize more expensive solutions.

Another somewhat unique feature of the TMS call center was the use of quality circles, even during the height of the crisis. Every call center supervisor had a quality circle of 8 to 10 CSRs, meeting once a week to talk about problems, solutions, and best practices. These quality circles were led by senior CSRs as a way of giving them experience in leading quality circles and of continuing to ramp up the skills and training of the outside personnel.

A second critical advantage Toyota had is the close partnerships it had fostered with trusted subcontractors whom Toyota developed almost as if they were inside employees. Over the years, Fein had built long-term relationships with three call center staffing agencies that had trained personnel on hand. By the end of the first week, all three of the agencies were providing supplementary staff to the call center. These supplementary staff had already had training as customer service representatives, but they still underwent up to three days of specific training to prepare them to handle the often emotional calls during the recall crisis. As well, the outside agency personnel were integrated to a degree into the Toyota processes. Group leaders listened in on random calls to coach the subcontractors, as they did with regular employees. The outside contractors were even invited to participate in the quality circles to help resolve issues that arose and develop their problem-solving skills.

Still, in order to ensure the highest quality of service, TMS had the CSRs from the outside agencies primarily deal with information requests, such as a customer calling in with his Vehicle Identification Number to confirm whether his vehicle was or was not part of the recall. If a customer had more serious questions or believed that he had experienced sudden acceleration or a sticky pedal, the outside agencies were able to transfer a call to the TMS call center immediately, so that the more experienced Toyota CSRs could work with the customer.

One measure of the effectiveness of this group was in customer satisfaction. To Toyota's surprise the customer satisfaction of those whose cars were recalled was even higher than those whose cars were not recalled. Apparently the additional attention they received from the highly skilled CSRs, as well as very accommodating dealerships that went out of their way to address customer concerns, increased customer satisfaction.

The Risks of Outsourcing Services

It has become fashionable to outsource services—bundle together services into centralized "shared resources" and then contract them out. Outsource human resource services, IT services, call centers, and anything else that leads to a reduced cost per piece. There are short-term savings, and it is certainly attractive. Often new CEOs of service organizations use outsourcing as one of their strategies to turn around the company. But there is a risk!

Unlike Toyota, which carefully sifts through opportunities and experiments on a small scale, gradually developing suppliers up to Toyota standards, most service organizations seem to treat outsourcing as though they are holding an auction. Who will be the lowest bidder? We saw what happened in Chapter 6 when a healthcare system centralized laundry services in a highly automated system. It was a whiz-bang impressive system that simply could not clean enough laundry to keep the hospitals running.

As much of an investment as we need to make in people and processes inside the firm, we need a similar effort outside the firm. The process of improvement is fractal. The same thinking and systems are needed at every level, inside and outside the firm. We have seen companies take years to develop their own lean cultures, only to expect suppliers to change through a few one-week lean workshops. It simply will not happen.

This is why Toyota will first build its own internal competency and then gradually outsource until it can build highly reliable outside capability that it can rely on as if the supplier were integrated into the culture. We saw that Toyota invested heavily in its own internal call center and then partnered with and developed outside services for additional capacity in peak periods.

This is not to say that Toyota invests heavily in developing every supplier of nuts and bolts and safety gloves. Before outsourcing to the relatively low bidder that has an acceptable quality record, consider: Is it truly a commodity where one quality service provider is as good as another and location does not matter? What are the coordination requirements? How much customization is needed? Consider the service typology from Chapter 1 (Figure 1.10). In general, suppliers of standard services are more likely to provide commodities that can be outsourced at arm's length compared with suppliers of customized services that need to be closely integrated into your company culture. The outside call centers used by Toyota were providing something between a standard experience and a personalized one. Mostly Toyota sent them customers with standard questions, though the crisis heightened the need for a personal touch for all customers.

Integrating Customers into the Culture at Menlo

Menlo truly operates as an open system. For example, Menlo gives hundreds of tours each year involving thousands of people. Customers regularly come to plan the project or attend "show-and-tells." Classes are held to teach Menlo's system to other companies. Even babies and dogs are welcome. Human interaction is visible everywhere all the time. Toyota also openly shares its system through daily tours of selected plants. People often ask, "What's in it for Toyota to openly share what it does?" There are many answers, but one looms above the rest. Opening yourself up to outside visits, and scrutiny, can strengthen your culture.

As noted earlier, Richard Sheridan's job title is chief storyteller. This seems like a cute joke, but he is serious. His biggest asset to the company is telling stories. Externally his book and presentations help sell the IT work and the training business that Menlo does. But what Menlo is selling is its culture. And stories are part of the lifeblood of culture. Stories help us create a collective identity. Hearing our stories repeatedly told to outsiders helps reinforce our culture. Having a constant stream of visitors motivates us to sustain our culture, including keeping artifacts up-to-date and visible. Being open to outsiders at Menlo both rejuvenates the culture that is Menlo's chief asset and rejuvenates customers who find joy in being part of the community.

Customers cannot help but be integrated into the Menlo process and culture. They are part of the Menlo team from selecting the primary and secondary user personas that we described in Chapter 5 to selecting the story cards they are willing to pay for week by week, to show-and-tells to review the software week by week. The customers are often IT folks who come from a more traditional culture. They do not use folksy language like "show-and-tell" meetings; they do not make critical quality decisions with colored sticky dots; they do not use dart board images to select key users. Menlo is an energizing and fun environment, and often customers do not want to leave. One IT manager who cannot bring his dog to work because of legitimate hygiene concerns in a closely controlled environment asked to bring his dog to Menlo, and the answer was "Certainly." He wears jeans to meetings on Menlo days. He is relaxed yet energized at Menlo. Sometimes he asks if he can continue to hang out and do his work at Menlo after the meeting. For some period of time he is part of the Menlo culture.

The weekly show-and-tell is critical both for getting rapid feedback and for engaging customers with the culture. Each week the customer comes to Menlo, is handed the story cards coded that week, and is asked to operate the system with the newly programmed features (see Figure 7.7). The customer is in control. She is not given voluminous instruction manuals. If the software is not intuitive, it needs improvement. In systems theory we learn that the speed of feedback is critical to self-correcting loops. PDCA depends on rapid feedback and equally rapid responses to the feedback. Week by week the software is written, tests are written to check the software technically (does it do what it is sup-

Figure 7.7   Customer show-and-tell

posed to), and quality advocates check to see if the software meets their understanding of what the customer wants. But the customer is the final check. By the last week of a three-year project, all that is really being checked is the last week of work. Is it a wonder that the customer will take the final software and often use it for real work the same day it arrives, flawlessly? Customer complaints are an ancient relic of a past life.

An even more direct way that Menlo integrates its customers into the business is through equity ownership. When Menlo contracts with new clients for work, the company offers to accept half the bill in equity in the company. Menlo figures if it is truly committed to helping clients, and believes its software will make them better, then it should put its money where its mouth is.

One of the pioneering efforts, which turned out to pay off handsomely, was taking equity in a start-up firm that developed the Accuri flow cytometer. Flow cytometers are used to analyze cells in both research and clinical settings for cancer, AIDS, leukemia, and various other immunological disorders. Jen Baird and Colin Rich were two Ann Arbor entrepreneurs with an idea. They had licensed their technology out of the University of Michigan Office of Technology Transfer, and their intention was to revolutionize the world of flow cytometry by creating an affordable, easy-to-use, and very compact personal flow cytometer. This type of product had been on the market for 30 years, but the existing products were big, cumbersome, difficult-to-use maintenance nightmares and very expensive.

One thing the people at Menlo had learned early on was that they had to teach their process to their clients. At the outset of the project, Accuri was asked to attend a full-day class in the Menlo process so it could learn what to expect and what role it would play in the project's success. In this case it was more of a joint development project than a separable software task—the hardware and software were being developed in parallel.

Menlo taught Accuri about the various failure modes of development projects, software or otherwise, and how Menlo's process avoided those failures. I interviewed Richard about this experience, and he explained the failure modes and Menlo's countermeasures:

1. *Projects often get off track, and no one realizes it until it is too late. Our solution was a weekly Show & Tell where Jen and her team could try out the emerging software to witness firsthand the tangible progress. This grounded the progress report in reality rather than typical status reports, Gantt Charts and percent completion statistics which are impossible to verify in a software project.*

2. *Failure often occurs because budgets are not well tracked and money runs out when the project is "80 percent complete" and unshippable. Our iter-*

ative and incremental approach meant we always had working software that could be shipped, if needed, even if all the features weren't present.

3. *Projects often technically succeed, but end up unusable by the target audience and thus fail to achieve the widespread adoption necessary for a profitable business. We taught Jen and her team about our High-Tech Anthropology approach to user experience design. We would ask them to introduce us to real end users who were already using existing flow cytometers from their competitors. Our High-Tech Anthropologists would study these users in their native work environments to understand their struggles and design those struggles out of the user experience. Our goal was to produce software that did not need user manuals, training classes or help text and could be used immediately by the typical end user.*

4. *A very typical failure mode of software products is their overly ambitious goals to be "all things to all people." We combat this through the use of personas and persona maps which prioritize the types of user so that we have exactly ONE primary type of user we are trying to serve better than anyone else. They chose an inexperienced graduate assistant who currently is not allowed to use the existing flow cytometers because the error rates were too high and thus only lab directors would use the current products in the market. While this choice may seem unusual at first, there were 10 graduate assistants to every lab director and thus, if we succeeded in addressing this audience the target market would be larger by an order of magnitude. It was a bold move.*

5. *Even if all this goes well, software quality can still suffer and the product fail due to unreliability. This is often manifested in the later stages of a product development effort when time and budget are being exhausted and an overworked team puts the pedal to the metal and starts working tons of overtime including weekends, all-nighters and delayed or cancelled vacations. Many, many bugs are introduced at this stage due to fatigue, and it is often impossible to overcome this onslaught of quality issues after the product is released, as first impressions can doom a new product if it continually crashes or creates errors. We had to teach the Accuri management team about our paired-programming approach and our hard rule of no more than 40-hour work weeks, our automated unit testing practice, and the consequent positive effect all of this would have on the final product.*

One other problem emerged quickly. Phase one of the project as defined by the project leader Jen was estimated to cost $600K, and she only had $300K to spend on her software team. As good as everything felt to Jen and her team, the reality was they could not afford us. I suggested we cut our cash price in half and trade the rest for equity. Jen was shocked that an outside vendor

*would be willing to place that big a bet on a start-up client. I confirmed for
her once again our relational model and said if we were not willing to bet on
the outcome, we shouldn't do the project in the first place. The deal was done
and we began work. Throughout the nearly three and a half years of product
development we continued to trade cash for equity as we had in that first
project. We also struck a deal to trade cash for a future royalty on the product
once it shipped. We were all in.*

The first unit shipped after 3½ years, and it worked beautifully right out of
the box. That first customer was able to plug it in and start using it without user
manuals, help text, or training classes, just as Menlo had predicted. Orders began
to flow in. Within three years after the first unit shipped, Accuri had captured
nearly 30 percent of the worldwide market in flow cytometry, and the company
was purchased by one of its largest rivals for $205 million. Menlo made millions,
the Accuri founders got rich, and everyone was happy, especially the users who
now had a flow cytometer they loved to use.

START WITH MACRODESIGN OR BUILD CULTURE PERSON BY PERSON?

This is a difficult question to answer in generic terms, as it is very organizationally
specific. New CEOs brought in from the outside to turn around the company will
typically spend a good deal of time with their close inner circle redesigning the
organizational structure and envisioning the new culture—which not surprisingly
will often resemble where they came from. They pore over boxes on charts. "We
are organized by region, but we should be organized by product group with profit
and loss responsibility." "The product organization has become so cumbersome
we need to refocus it with four major groups instead of twelve and build in strong
financial and marketing functions." "The organization has emptied out the corporate office, and running this organization is like herding cats—we need to
strengthen the corporate office and all work for one company." If the organizational design is A, the new CEO will shift to B or C.

The culture is even more amorphous. "I have interviewed dozens of people,
and my conclusion is that we have a broken culture." "This is an 'I' culture. We
need a 'we' culture." "This is a culture of 'it's not my job.' We need a culture of
'accountability.'"

Perhaps these CEOs are correct that there needs to be some realignment of
priorities and even stronger shared values, but how will they achieve this? In command and control organizations the CEO is putting in place levers to control profits—higher sales and lower costs. Where can the CEO create the highest leverage

points for results? Develop new service offerings, business models, promotions, advertising? Eliminate low performers—services and the people associated with them? If there are different groups of people in different parts of the organization responsible for a similar service offering, then organizing shared services in one unit can allow for head count reduction, consolidation, or outsourcing. And someone at the helm of each service unit becomes the go-to person to squeeze for results—sink or swim—and by the way find his own lieutenants to squeeze, and so it goes on down the line until we have a culture of "accountability." "Get results or else" becomes the unofficial mantra of the new culture.

Contrast this with what Elisa's CEO did. At Elisa he asked, "How can we create core customer-facing units where we can have the maximum leverage on customer satisfaction?" It was clear he was interested in accountability. But his was accountability to the customer. Get someone in charge who can be the first to be coached on how to solve the customer's problems—one by one. Eliminate those nasty billing errors that cause angst. Get the service outages fixed fast and find the root cause so they do not come back. Elisa then enjoyed a rapid rise in customer satisfaction. But the folks at Elisa were not done. They had just begun. After spending over five years developing people at the local level and defining core processes to get end-to-end value streams focused on customer satisfaction, the people at Elisa turned their focus to continuous improvement, and so every day in 2014–2015 they worked on the core values of the company. The goal was to develop a picture of their target culture. Ranta-aho Merja, executive vice president of Human Resources, led the effort and explains:

> We engaged our whole personnel in dialogue about what we feel is important to us. We integrated our excellence principles into our core values, that now contain five distinct values, each being explained by three behaviors that we want to cherish and develop. We find that the only way to reach excellence is to consciously build a culture that supports passion for the customer, continuous learning and improvement, and mutual respect.

In the meantime, Petri was focused on creating daily management systems so small groups of frontline supervisors and their team were solving problems every day. Petri then was put in charge of sales to bring the daily management system to the sales organization with great success. The macrolevel context had set the stage for the hard work of building a culture of continuous improvement.

In our experience a culture based on quick results, fear, and generous rewards for a few can be rapidly established, though it lacks depth beyond the executive suite and a few senior levels of management. A culture of service excellence is slow to build, takes constant vigilance to sustain, but is the only true path to greatness.

KEY POINTS
MACROLEVEL PEOPLE
PRINCIPLES

1. Organizational design is particularly important in services because, unlike manufacturing, there aren't clear boundaries for making things.
   - Macrolevel people processes create a context for people to understand where they fit into the organization and "find their way."
2. Organizing to balance deep expertise and customer focus allows the organization to be flexible to the changing needs of customers:
   - Common types of organizational design include functional organization, customer-facing organization, matrix organization, and networked organization.
   - Over time, organizational design can—and should—change, based on changes in the environment, including markets, and an ever-deepening understanding of the needs of customers and the business.
3. Culture is extremely complex, and each organization's culture develops over time; culture can just "happen," or it can be cultivated *deliberately* so that every person understands the nuances of the culture and how to act in accordance with the culture, whatever the person's role:
   - Creating a deliberate culture means hiring deliberately: carefully interview and screen for cultural fit during the hiring process.
   - Make sure that the hiring process itself reflects the culture of the organization.
   - Creating a deliberate culture means making sure that all key aspects of the culture and expectations are understood and practiced in all functions.
4. Integrate outside partners (suppliers and customers) into your organization's culture deliberately since suppliers' services and products will ultimately touch and affect your customers, and customers should be providing continual feedback about their needs.
5. Building a deliberate culture of service excellence will take time, effort, and a deep understanding of your customers' needs and your organization's purpose.

Chapter 8

Microlevel People Principles: Develop People to Become Masters of Their Craft

They're (traveling teachers) useless sir. They teach us facts, not understanding. It's like teaching people about forests by showing them a saw. I want a proper school, sir, to teach reading and writing, and most of all thinking, sir, so people can find what they're good at, because someone doing what they really like is always an asset to any country, and too often people never find out until it's too late.

—Tiffany Aching (town witch) pleading the case
for a new school to the Duke,
in Terry Pratchett, *I Shall Wear Midnight*

DEVELOPING PEOPLE AS AN ORGANIZING PRINCIPLE

Limitations of Organizational Design Approaches to Change

The high-performance organization approach is humanistic and has led to impressive results. But there is something missing. The starting assumptions seem flawed: that a good design, meaning an elaborate sociotechnical systems plan, can be faithfully executed if only management will get behind it. In this approach, most of the organizational design activity is done in several-day workshops led by external or internal consultants, with senior managers who get "educated" and develop a paper design that they then try to implement throughout the organization.

The Finnish consulting firm Innotiimi began to learn about lean management and saw how it could complement the broad HPO design concepts. In its magazine called *Change*, it vividly describes what happens when the broad HPO design characteristics are combined with rapid-change methods based on scientific experimentation:[1]

Just remember a situation (in your private or professional life) where really great things happened: situations where nearly impossible, brilliant results were achieved, where positive energy was high and people felt some kind of flow. What happened? Typically, people describe it like this: "We had a clear, challenging goal to which we all were committed. We felt trust in our team, and each of us acted out of our own personal judgments for success. It was easy to find the right person for the task without any power games. The processes were smooth, without bureaucracy. The focus was on short planning, doing, short reflection, easy adoption and doing again. And at the end, we were proud of our success and were not the same as at the beginning. Our culture, the way we do things, has changed."

Despite this deep insight, however, Innotiimi continued to focus heavily on the workshop approach. The company added a longer "three-month Rapid Results . . . series of workshops to implement the changes" to the macrolevel workshops. This seems like a useful addition to the theoretical design workshops, but it still is far short of the extended period of daily practice needed to change behavior and mindset. As they describe for one engagement:[2]

The first workshop was held for the management team. In this one-day meeting, the three percent direct cost decrease, the main organizational framework of the process and the management roles for the project itself were decided. This was followed by functional mini workshops with the key people of each function: three-to-four-hour discussions about the interpretation of the goals for each functional area and the preparation of a process roadmap. . . . In a second half-day management workshop, the potentials found by the functional subteams, who had reviewed their own cost structures, were summarized, and people for the Rapid Results teams were appointed. Afterwards, bi-weekly how-to-workshops were held. . . . Through the initiative, a cultural change started. . . . The Hungarian site achieved savings of 3.3 percent in direct production costs.

In other words the senior management developed a plan for the cost reduction and in a cross-functional team found the cost savings. We certainly believe a well-facilitated team of managers can identify cost savings, but this is far short of any intervention that will deeply change culture. Nonetheless, the macrolevel planning of HPO can provide a framework for microlevel change that is often missing from many lean approaches, which can have the opposite problem of getting caught up in improving specific processes without seeing the bigger, organizational picture. We are not out to criticize this consulting group for which we have deep respect, but short bursts of decisions at meetings is simply not how culture change works. If only cultural change were so quick and easy as creating plans on paper during workshops and then implementing them according to plan.

We believe this common mythology holds many organizations back. There is something missing. And that something, we believe, is the development of the skills and mindset needed for continuous improvement, which focuses on continuously learning, not on rapidly implementing well-defined conceptual plans in short workshop bursts.

We saw in Chapter 7 that Elisa got great value from the work of Kai Laamanen, a consultant of Innotiimi. But his work was specifically focused by Elisa VP Petri Selkäinaho on a specific task—facilitating an executive team to identify the core customer-focused business processes. Then Petri and Elisa people took over facilitating improvement, teaching problem solving, establishing daily management systems, and leading the long and arduous process of changing culture. After six years Petri will tell you that they are still scratching the surface.

Our three microlevel people principles focus on developing people who are coached by leaders with the skills and mindset for improvement (see Figure 8.1):

- Develop skills and mindset through practicing kata
- Develop leaders as coaches of continually developing teams
- Balance extrinsic-intrinsic rewards

From the very beginning, organizations serious about lean transformation need leaders to have the scientific mindset and skills to lead the transformation. As we will see, changing how we think and act is very challenging. We might learn the concepts in training sessions and workshops, but we deeply change how we think and act through repeated action and repeated experiences, and we generally

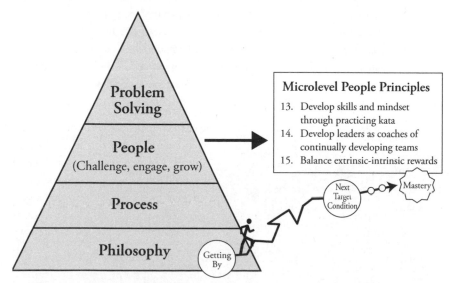

Figure 8.1 Microlevel people principles

need a coach to guide us. A relatively new approach to developing leaders, introduced in the book *Toyota Kata*, is a powerful way to develop the scientific mindset. Let's consider how the fictional company Service 4U came to realize that leaders who were not committed and lacked skills were holding back the lean transformation process.

Services 4U Learns to Develop Leaders Using the Improvement Kata and Coaching Kata

Sam McQuinn and Sarah Stevens had just finished eating lunch in Sarah's office. It was hard for Sam to believe that almost a year had passed since he left NL Services. Leaning back in his chair, Sam shook his head and said, "Well, what they say about time moving more quickly as you get older really must be right! Looking at the calendar, I can see a year has passed, but it really seems like it's only been a moment that I've been here!"

Sarah laughed, "That's because we've done so much work and made so much progress! At NL Services, even when we'd put in a lot of time and effort doing 'things,' it always seemed like we just ended up in the same place—exactly where we started!" Sam laughed as well. Sarah was right. At NL Services, no matter how many long hours he had put in and no matter how many "initiatives" were put in place, the company never seemed to make any progress.

"That's a great observation," Sam said as he finished folding up the last bit of paper from his sandwich. "And it's a great segue into our meeting topic for this afternoon. Just how much progress have we made this year at Service 4U?" Sarah and Sam spent the best part of the afternoon reviewing the targets and results for the different regions: customer satisfaction, client retention, new client growth, and productivity. They were pleased to see that there had been a great deal of progress in many parts of the company. But as they reviewed the graphs for each business unit, they noticed there were a few stars that exceeded expectations, a good number of units that barely made the numbers, and some laggards who seemed hopelessly behind.

"Interesting," said Sarah as she moved some of the graphs around on the table and lined them up beside one another. "The Northwest Division is on fire, while the Southeast and Southwest Divisions seem to be making steady progress. But the Northeast really seems to be lagging behind. I wonder why that is?"

Sam was silent for a moment reviewing the graphs. "Hold on a minute," he said to Sarah as he searched on his computer. "Look," he said, pulling up a copy of the company's org chart. "I've just completed my annual reviews with the regional presidents. Doug Barns, the regional president for the Northwest, just couldn't stop talking about all the lean work that's been going on in his regions. And I know that he really 'knows' what's going on—the facts, not just data from reports—and he is always in the regional offices . . . going to the gemba to see for himself. He's even been out on sales calls with his sales managers and their reps."

"Yes," agreed Sarah. "That's definitely true! I approve Doug's expense reports, and when I asked him about all the travel, he told me that it was a small price to pay for what he was learning and how he was able to help his managers and supervisors develop themselves and their people."

Nodding in agreement, Sam went on, "Unfortunately, it doesn't seem to be the same for the Northeast. Maria Canson, the regional president for the large Northeastern region, just doesn't seem to be as actively involved in the lean efforts. When I asked her about how she was monitoring her region's progress and teaching her leaders how to use lean principles, she could give me a few examples of lean projects that she had read reports about, but it didn't seem to me that she was as committed, as excited, or as personally invested as Doug was."

Sarah thought about it for a minute. "I think you may be onto something," she said to Sam. "I've noticed the same thing. When I ask her how her people are doing, she seems to give the right kind of answers, but then often follows up with something like, 'This lean stuff is harder than it looks. I miss the good old days when we just told people what to do and they did it.' I wonder if she's really focusing on developing her people's capabilities—and if she isn't, maybe that's one of the reasons her region isn't making the same sort of progress that Doug's regions are."

"Yes," said Sam, "I agree. And thinking back on it, too, I guess I've spent more time with Doug and his leaders because he calls more often for my continuous improvement team's help. I haven't spent the same time focusing on Maria and her region either."

Sam and Sarah were silent for a few minutes. Overall they were pleased with the company's results, and they were excited that management culture seemed to be shifting to a long-term focus on developing people, but it was also clear to them that most of the company, the regions in which leaders were just playing with lean and were really relying on their past history of traditional command and control, wasn't progressing like the one part of the company with a passionate leader who was learning to lead with the right combination of understanding lean processes and knowing how to motivate people toward a common goal.

"Sam," said Sarah, "I think that if we want to continue to make progress—and not end up just like we were at NL Services in the long run—we're going to have to do some more work on this leadership thing. For the most part, we still have a lot of the leaders we started with, and we certainly don't have any strategy for promoting or choosing new leaders. And we seem to be focusing our efforts on helping the leader who is already 'getting it' and paying less attention to those who don't. It seems to me that to really become a culture of continuous improvement, we're going to have to make a plan for developing our leaders so that they can develop their managers and supervisors too. I just wish I knew how to do that. Can't say that I do right now."

"Well, Sarah," said Sam, "I can't say I know how to do that either. But I bet I know someone who does!"

Two weeks later, Sam and Sarah had a conference call with Leslie Harris, the lean advisor whom they'd grown to trust deeply. Leslie listened carefully to their story. "Great observations and learning," she applauded Sam and Sarah. "What you're noticing is a very common problem, and as you've found out, unless you have the right leaders in place and they are learning and teaching others, you're going to see the uneven development that you're having now: some areas blossoming and some areas stagnating. I'd like to put you in touch with a colleague of mine, Dennis Garrett, who's very involved in a recent movement in lean toward a practice called Toyota Kata. Toyota Kata is an approach to developing people that fits the way adults learn. Dennis is a real 'kata geek,' and I think he'll be just the right person to help Service 4U progress on leadership development—give the leaders the tools to change instead of just expecting them to figure it out."

PRINCIPLE 13: DEVELOP SKILLS AND MINDSET THROUGH PRACTICING KATA

The Research Behind Toyota Kata

Mike Rother was my student in a master's program and worked with me at University of Michigan, but then we went separate ways professionally. I was writing books, speaking, and developing the conceptual basis for the Toyota Way, and he was on the shop floor learning by doing. We both faced the challenge of trying to shift managers from a lean tools orientation to more of a focus on developing people, but in different ways. I wrote about the concepts with case examples. Mike was trying to develop a practical countermeasure. The countermeasure he developed was Toyota Kata. Before we delve deeply into Toyota Kata, let's consider the problems it was trying to solve.

What Mike observed were a number of weaknesses in lean transformation:

1. **Mindless tool deployment.** People deployed tools to take out waste without really understanding the reasons for using the tools. They were using "tools for tools' sake."
2. **No clear direction.** There was no clear direction to waste elimination, just a kind of random walk, so the often frenetic activity did not add up to meaningful business results.
3. **Lack of scientific method.** Although lean professionals all learned about PDCA, few had a really deep understanding of the scientific method

behind it; therefore, they were doing a lot of work that had weak planning, checking, and learning.

4. **Unclear leadership and accountability.** Although improvement teams did this and that, it was not always clear who was responsible for what targets and areas of improvement.

5. **Start-and-stop, episodic improvement.** There were bursts of improvement activity, followed by business as usual, particularly in companies that used kaizen events as the main deployment mechanism.

There were some positive results from these bursts of activity to deploy tools. Things would get better in certain respects—better flow, less inventory, more organized work patterns, better quality, higher productivity, and on-time delivery, and people were deeply engaged . . . at times. But the process was always jerky, and most of the great ideas produced in those flurries of activity led to changes that degenerated over time. Even when "improvements" led to longer-term changes in the flow of work, there was little adaptation to changing conditions, and eventually the improvements were out of step and less effective. Moreover, management was not really changing the way it thought or acted to support the new systems. Lean became one more improvement program to work on until the next program came along.

The Root Cause: The Way Our Brains Work

Mike concluded that in most cases well-intentioned people were doing what they thought was right for the company based on existing habits and mindset. He delved into research on neuroscience and cognitive psychology. This was not a Toyota thing; it was a matter of the way humans work and learn. It turns out that the part of our brain that our prefrontal cortex cannot access—the unconscious—plays a far greater role in how we operate day to day than we generally believe. Some estimate 70 to 80 percent of what we do comes from deeply rooted habits that we find difficult to change or do not try hard to change.

The need for habits, or routines, evolved out of the instinct for survival in prehistoric times. People hunting deadly prey did not have the luxury of time to reflect and reason when faced with what they hoped would be their next meal. They had to read and react—see the animal, predict where it would be when the spear arrived, and throw the spear. Those who did this well survived and spawned children, and those who were very contemplative died—and their genes died with them. In modern life there is still a need to read and react, for example in driving. And read-and-react is also very helpful in getting through the day—to get dressed and washed, get to that meeting, get our coffee, perform the routine parts of our daily work, and much more.

Whatever is stored in our brain as routines does not require the use of our most energy-intensive and valuable real estate—the prefrontal cortex. This is our conscious reasoning center where we think through what to say and do. This is where we reflect on what happened and try to learn from it. And it is where we try to control that unruly unconscious part of the brain—most often to little avail. Roughly speaking it is estimated that the brain is about 2 percent of our body volume, yet takes about 20 percent of our energy. The real energy hog is the prefrontal cortex, while much of the brain coasts on automatic pilot. In fact, some argue that what freed us up to develop the human part of the brain that reasons was shifting from moving on all fours to walking erect on two legs, thereby reducing energy for movement and allowing us to develop our brain through evolution. In other words those with developed prefrontal cortexes (the energy hogs) could use their wits to survive and reproduce.[3]

This is a terribly simplistic explanation, but it provides a general picture, and neuroscientists now know a great deal about how the brain works and are learning more every day. When we are learning something new, we have to forge new connections—synapses —between individual neurons. It is these connections that allow us to remember. These then become our storage for memory and the basis of our semiautomatic routines that we execute. Complex tasks require very dense networks of connections between neurons. Building up these networks of connections takes a lot of work, mainly through repetition. As Mike Rother concludes from his research:[4]

- The brain learns to favor whatever we focus on repeatedly.
- As this information is reinforced through repetition, it becomes wired in the brain and solidifies our thoughts and actions. It becomes who you are. Think about that the next time you're angry at something or someone.
- Due to these preferred pathways in the brain, we are led into using them again and again, like walking a trail in the snow, which strengthens them even more. Try brushing your teeth with your nondominant hand.
- We can alter our mindset! A way to rewire your brain is to deliberately practice a new pattern. In so doing the existing pathways eventually lose their strength and are replaced with new neural pathways and behaviors.
- A sense of optimism will be important. To develop new habits and a sense of self-efficacy through practice, the learner should experience successes and the positive emotions, like those produced by dopamine, that come from them.

Those of us who have learned to play a musical instrument, in my case classical guitar, know the hard work necessary to build these neural networks. When I begin to learn a challenging piece for the first time, it is downright painful.

Twenty minutes of practice and I am spent. My teacher has carefully guided me on how to practice:

1. Break the overall musical piece into small sections, or phrases.
2. Learn to play a phrase at a time, starting with learning individual measures.
3. Play a single measure repeatedly until it is done correctly five times in a row, then move to the next measure, then play the measures together, then move to the next measure, then play the two measures together, and continue to build outward from there into the phrase. Then advance to the next phrase.
4. Play slowly, then more slowly, then more slowly until it is barely recognizable as music. Doing it slowly and correctly is more effective than speeding through it and making mistakes. It turns out our brains will build the pattern just as well slowly and can easily then speed it up when the synapses start getting developed. The brain will also learn the mistakes made when going fast and try to reproduce these "bad habits."
5. Keep practice sessions short and frequent. Three 20-minute sessions with breaks between are more effective than a continuous 60-minute practice session. The first part of the practice session, when I am most fresh, should focus on learning something new, and then the later part could be playing already learned pieces to enjoy them and to maintain them in my brain.
6. With a degree of mastery of the notes and rhythm of each section, it is time to put it all together and begin focusing on expression.
7. Get corrective feedback from the teacher as often as possible, in my case weekly.

To be honest, what I desire to do is play pieces I already know how to play. This is pleasant, and apparently my brain is doing a lot of self-rewarding through shots of dopamine. However, what I hope to do is to continue to learn, and that is hard and painful. Giving in to playing, rather than learning, means stagnating. I do not develop as a guitar player. And my teacher routinely, year after year, reminds me: "Start with a section that you are having difficulty with and practice it repeatedly, and very slowly, in the way I taught you."

Kata to Practice Toward Mastery: Sword-Making Example

Kata are the practice routines that allow us to build effective habits. The more I practice a musical piece in the proper way, the more easily I can access what I learned from memory and execute it with little energy expenditure. It is now fun. And it frees me to focus on expression of the music. But I need to know what to practice and how in order to develop these priceless routines. And I need to know what it feels and sounds like to play it in the right way, which I could not do effectively without my teacher's information inputs.

The Japanese term "kata" is used routinely in the martial arts, which evolved through the master-apprentice relationship. Many people saw the original film *The Karate Kid* when the master, Mr. Myagi, orders the student, Daniel, to clean his car—wax on, wax off—for many hours.[5] He orders him to sand a floor with a similar repetitive motion. He orders him to paint a fence with a repetitive motion. Daniel cannot imagine why he is mindlessly repeating these menial tasks day after day. Exhausted and frustrated, he finally has had enough and confronts Myagi. Finally Mr. Myagi asks him to repeat the motions for sanding a wood floor, for waxing the car, and for painting a fence. He then engages him in a mock fight and tells him to sand the floor, now wax the car, and now paint the fence! Daniel uses the exact same motions to defend himself against Myagi's attacks. The lightbulb comes on. He was mastering patterns through practice routines that on the surface had little to do with the desired skill but actually were basic skills for karate.

One "karate kid" who decided to submit himself to this process in real life is Pierre Nadeau, a French-Canadian blacksmith, who learned sword making in Japan as an apprentice to a master sword maker.[6] After five years of intense study, submitting himself to the teachings of the master, he still came away feeling like an apprentice, and years later he refuses to call himself a master. He realizes how much more there is to learn.

Pierre began his journey with a desired outcome. He loved the swords made by the hands of masters and wanted to learn to make this beautiful product. So he decided from the start that he would do whatever was necessary to develop the skill. He was aware of the rituals in the initial stages of learning from a master, the mindless work that appeared to be meaningless, but he committed to doing whatever he was asked with energy and enthusiasm.

He discovered that we often overemphasize learning concepts with the mind. Think about all those classes and workshops to "explain the concepts and change people's minds" that most companies start with to begin their lean transformations. Pierre learned that we underemphasize how our mind can learn from what our body does. In fact, the master early on refused to answer any of Pierre's questions because it would be a waste of time, and it might give the apprentice the impression that hearing an explanation is the same as developing a skill. As Pierre Nadeau explains:

> The first aspect of traditional learning in Japan (and, I realized later, anywhere else in the world as far as craftsmanship is concerned) is that one should learn with one's body instead of one's head. Narau yori narero. *Don't understand intellectually, but assimilate with your whole body. In the beginning*

many questions were left unanswered (literally, like you ask a question and my master would keep working like I wasn't there at all). The idea is that even if he explained it to you in detail, since you haven't had the experience, it would not make any sense to you other than give you a false feeling of having gotten it. Understanding is actually considered dangerous for it prevents the open-mindedness and full-body experience of someone doing something without any prior knowledge. Even if given the exact recipe, someone with only an intellectual understanding wouldn't be able to replicate the same sauce. But an experienced chef could guess the right preparation without even knowing the recipe.

Pierre also explains something that I admit was kind of embarrassing to me as someone known as a Toyota Way expert. He says:

If you try to take knowledge (that is, the real learned-with-body kind) and write it down, put it in a box . . . as is done in most school systems nowadays, and you try to pass knowledge around (that is, teach), you're losing the essence, you're losing the important subtleties that make this knowledge useful.

And here my main professional accomplishment has been putting the Toyota Way into a box. I can hear my readers, "Now you tell us!" Pierre further explains:

That's why martial arts (and many other practices) are learned through kata, the actual repetition of the movement, not the explanation of the movement. During kata, the role model (the sensei) watches and corrects; he refines your practice until your kata is perfect.

When writing *The Toyota Way to Lean Leadership*, I was excited when I discovered the notion of *shu-ha-ri*, which are three phases of mastering a skill. Pierre describes this as a Western construction that you rarely hear about in Japan and can be misunderstood as a linear process. The idea is that in the *shu* phase you are copying the role model exactly without questioning. You are imitating a specific pattern. When you practice it enough in the *ha* stage, it becomes natural, like the basic skills of riding a bike. You do not have to think about the basics—they are now routines embedded in long-term memory. In the *ri* phase you begin to innovate with new ways of doing things. Pierre agrees you have to start someplace in the *shu* phase, but after that you could be alternating between the *ha* phase and the *shu* phase or even the *ri* phase and returning periodically to the *shu* phase to brush up on basic technique.

The *shu* phase is where the concept of kata comes in—basic practice routines. This he says is also to a degree a Western construction of trying to make sense of Japan, but he likes the idea. As he explains:

I love the expression "fake it until you can feel it." If you do not agree or you do not understand something you can still do it, just accept to do it, and at some point it may become natural for you to do it and you will be the first to say that this is the best way to do something. This is why learning with the body and learning with the mind are very different. When you learn with your body you have a whole set of senses and emotions that come into play which doesn't happen when you learn with your mind. . . . The idea of kata is very interesting because instead of trying to convince somebody to adopt managerial or work practices, you get them to fake it at some point or just do it, without asking questions, or maybe without agreeing. But they get to assimilate and do it naturally. . . . They get to assimilate continuous improvement practices into their routines and then reach the goal without any specific effort—it becomes natural for them.

When Pierre was explaining his experience to me, he made one thing clear. To begin his immersion in learning sword making, he needed a high level of trust in the master teacher. Early on he had to prove to the master he was worthy of being taught. Often it seems the other way in the West—the teacher must convince the students he is worthy of teaching. For that reason Pierre sees an advantage in Japanese culture for the type of mentor-apprenticeship model we are talking about. "Trust your mentor, trust your community. People trust those older than them all their life. The craftsmanship culture is alive throughout Japan."

Skill Development Cycle

By now the notion of 10,000 hours of deliberate practice to mastery is practically a cliché. Who knows if it is 10,000 hours of practice or half that or three times that—what we can be sure of is that it is a lot of practice. But the key word here is "deliberate." My son, a professional musician, regularly reminds me not to "play through my mistakes." He hears me practicing, and I continue through mistakes because I am enjoying playing. He thinks I should be working to learn, not playing around. The usual exchange:

> JESSE: Hi dad, what are you doing?
> ME: Practicing guitar.
> JESSE: Oh, that's nice. What are you trying to learn?
> ME: I am practicing a new piece I am working on with my teacher.
> JESSE: Oh, so what is it you are working on?
> ME: Getting better at the piece.
> JESSE: If you keep playing through your mistakes, do you think you will get better?

You can extrapolate and imagine how much fun I am having talking to Jesse. I want to get back to "practicing." Playing is not practicing in music, sports, or any craft. Playing is executing what you have already learned, incorrect or correct. Deliberate practice means you know what you are trying to learn, what good performance looks like (excellent is even better), and where there are deviations from good performance.

This is where my teacher comes in. His corrective feedback helps me to understand how I am doing compared with an excellent performance. I am not great at giving myself feedback, and I often do not even know how well I am doing until he explains it.

The process of developing new skills and habits can be thought of as a cycle, or some would say a spiral increasingly deepening your skills and understanding. The cycle can be somewhat simplistically thought of as four steps (see Figure 8.2):

1. **Starter kata.** To learn a new skill it helps to have a beginner's kata—something to practice to develop the pattern in your brain.
2. **Practice.** You then practice the kata repeatedly, ideally at least daily, in short bursts working to build the complex synaptic structure to make it a routine.
3. **Coaching.** An experienced coach really helps to get the corrective feedback so you are burning into your brain a good way of executing the routine, rather than practicing mistakes.
4. **Self-efficacy.** It is unlikely we will put ourselves through grueling practice sessions without getting some type of reward that is best when it is

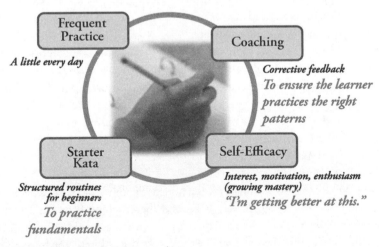

Figure 8.2 Skill development cycles
Source: Mike Rother

intrinsic—within our brain. This triggers feelings of self-efficacy—I can do this, and I can make a difference. Self-efficacy is the emotional experience that comes from learning with your body, not only your mind. It can trigger amazing sensations as your brain rewards you for a job well done.

In the center of the skill development cycle shown in Figure 8.2 is the hand of a person learning to write. This act is related to a simple exercise that you can do right now. Please sign your name five times and time it from start to finish. How does it feel? Now use your *other* hand and sign your name five times and time it. How does that feel? If you are like me, you have highly developed neural pathways for your dominant hand and very weak ones for your other hand. For the nondominant hand it probably takes longer, the quality of writing is lower, and it feels strange and frustrating. Now imagine if you deliberately practiced with your nondominant hand every day for a few weeks. I bet it will feel more natural, the time will go down, and the quality will go up.

The Improvement Kata Model

Learning a scientific approach to continuous improvement is similar in many ways to learning to write with your nondominant hand. It does not come naturally, but the habit can be developed with a lot of deliberate practice. Few people can be expected to go through the grueling ordeal that Pierre endured, but we can learn important lessons from him. As Pierre says, you cannot develop deep skills from books, and the learning process cannot be packaged in a box. It is a fluid, dynamic process with a skilled teacher. In this spirit Mike Rother wanted to create effective aids to learning for those of us not willing or able to spend five years at the feet of a master.

These aids are what Rother calls "starter kata," and as the apprentices are developed and coaches are developed, they will naturally elaborate on the kata. The starter kata come from decades of deep-practice learning and coaching by Mike, as well as five years of research refining the kata by trial and error. Mike observed that the conditions for effective learning involved a coach and a student he called the learner. The coach used practice routines, kata, to teach the learner step by step. Without a coach or practice routines, the student will tend to fall back to bad habits.

What Mike came up with fits well the underlying thinking of the Toyota Way. Like Toyota, the improvement kata (IK) and the coaching kata (CK) focus on developing people through actual experience improving processes—learning by doing with a coach. Like Toyota and like the experience of Pierre, the most effective way to develop a mindset, in this case a scientific approach to improvement, is through deliberate practice. Like Toyota, the ultimate goal is respect for people and continuous improvement, including improving ourselves. Where the IK and CK go a step further is in developing explicit practice routines so we can systematically develop both the skills and the mindset. We will discuss the approach in more detail in Chapter 9. We will introduce the model here.

There are four high-level steps in the improvement kata (see Figure 8.3). Together these make up a meta-pattern. By this we mean the kata can be applied to any type of improvement goal, from business goals like quality, lead time, safety, and cost reduction to personal goals like losing weight or stopping smoking. The kata is a higher-level scientific process that is agnostic about the specific content of the problem. It can be applied to any challenge and goals, but following the basic pattern is very important. Let's consider each step with a simple illustration of trying to lose weight.

1. **Understand the direction or challenge (Plan).** This is the first step in planning. In Lewis Carroll's book *Alice's Adventures in Wonderland*, the Cheshire Cat and Alice have the following conversation:

   > *"Would you tell me, please, which way I ought to go from here?" asked Alice.*
   > *"That depends a good deal on where you want to get to," said the Cat.*
   > *"I don't much care where—" said Alice.*
   > *"Then it doesn't matter which way you go," said the Cat.*

A systematic, scientific pattern of working

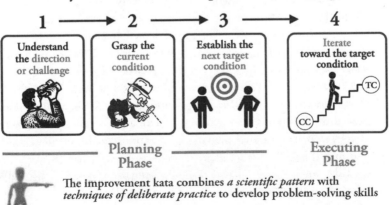

Figure 8.3   The four steps of the improvement kata model
Source: Mike Rother

"—so long as I get SOMEWHERE," Alice added as an explanation.

"Oh, you're sure to do that," said the Cat, "if you only walk long enough."

It seems like many lean practitioners are taking the same page out of the book:

"Would you tell me, please, which wastes I should chase first?" asked the lean practitioner.

"That depends a good deal on where you want to get to," said the Cat.

"I don't much care where—" said the lean practitioner.

"Then it doesn't matter which waste you chase," said the Cat.

"—so long as I get SOMEWHERE," the lean practitioner added as an explanation.

"Oh, you're sure to do that," said the Cat, "if you only chase wastes long enough."

To get beyond randomly "eliminating wastes," we have to decide where we want to get to. We discussed this in Chapter 3 when we talked about purpose-driven organizations. Asking "What is your purpose?" leads to a general, abstract answer. It is what we might call a vision. A strategy, like that of Southwest Airlines, makes the vision more concrete. But to motivate groups of people toward collective action requires a challenge statement, one that is inspiring, concrete, and measurable, or at least observable.

Assume you have a friend, Fred, who wants to lose weight and seeks your help. He has tried in the past with limited success and any weight he lost immediately returned. You have learned about the kata at work and decide to practice using it as a coach helping Fred, the learner, with his weight loss goal. First you ask him what he would like to accomplish. Fred is 55 years old, is 5'11", and currently weighs 250 pounds, and his challenge is to get to and sustain 200 pounds. He decides he wants to do this over a two-year period. There are plenty of quick-results weight loss programs out there, but Fred wants to achieve a sustainable change in lifestyle and read that this is more likely if you change your habits over a longer period of time. You emphasize to Fred the power of defining the challenge in crisp, motivational terms. He comes up with "50 in 2."

2. **Grasp the current condition (Plan).** If we want to improve toward a challenging goal, we have to understand our starting point. Can't we simply measure where we are on the challenge metric? "We want to double sales, and we are at $100 million in sales. The current state is done." This

is useful information but not enough. The question remains: What in the process is producing the current outcome? That is why this is called a current "condition" rather than current "results."

The concept of a condition versus results is perhaps the most difficult to understand in the IK. We are so used to results-oriented thinking. "What do I need to accomplish to get a good performance review? Give me the target, and I will chase it." In some senses chasing a target is no better than chasing wastes. What am I likely to try to change if I am making a mad dash for the target? I am likely to go after the low-hanging fruit using methods that I am already good at. "If it worked for me in the past, then it will work for me in the future."

Unfortunately what has worked in the past in some other condition may not work in your current condition. And this mad sprint to results kills creativity. So we ask in the IK that the learner describe the current condition. Where am I compared with the desired result? What is my current operating pattern?

Understanding the current operating pattern was the goal of Taiichi Ohno's famous teaching device known as the Ohno circle. He simply would draw a circle on the shop floor and ask you as a learner to stand in it and look. About one hour later he would come by to ask what you see. You describe it, and he says, "Please keep looking." He repeats this throughout the day. At the end of the day if you have done well, he says, "You are tired. Please go home." The unlucky students were asked to come back to the circle tomorrow.

What Ohno was teaching was the power of real observation, with a "clear mind." He wanted the learner to strip away assumptions and see the reality in great detail. He knew this was an experience few had, as most of us run from place to place without really seeing. As you observe, you will understand the operating patterns of all the various actors and the equipment. You will see patterns where at first glance you saw what appeared to be random events.

Back to Fred, he is raring to get started toward his new lifestyle, but as his coach you slow him down a bit. We know he weighs 250 pounds, but there is more to learn. You ask him to establish his current condition by keeping a log of what he eats for one week. He finds he is taking in just over 3,000 calories a day on average. There is about an equal split between high-carb foods, meat and fish, and fruits and vegetables. In addition Fred likes to have a dish of low-fat ice cream before he goes to sleep. He rarely exercises and is in a sedentary job.

Understanding the current condition grounds us in today's realities. We begin to understand the operating conditions we might have to change to approach the challenge. At this point many "solutions" come to mind, but there is one more critical step in the improvement kata before we run off eliminating wastes and implementing things.

3. **Establish the next target condition and define obstacles (Plan).** We are still in the planning mode and need a series of shorter-term goals between us and the challenge. The challenge provides direction, but there are many obstacles between us and this big challenge, so we are still wandering through an uncharted wilderness. Expecting to jump from where we are to the challenge suggests an unrealistic degree of certainty in our solutions.

What is perhaps unusual about the target conditions is that we are not going to lay all of them out as a road map to get from here to there. In fact, we are going to start with only one, the first target condition. When we achieve that, we will look at where we are and where we are going and identify the second target condition, and so on.

We need to define a near-term next target condition that we can see clearly from where we are and set an achieve-by date. The key words here are "next," "condition," and "achieve by." It is not enough to say my challenge is to get to a 50 percent customer satisfaction improvement, and my first target condition is a 5 percent improvement. It is like telling Fred who wants to lose 50 pounds that he should start with 5 pounds in the next month. Okay, but how? "Eat less and exercise more," you answer. The response is likely to be, "I think I knew that, but I still do not know how."

Assume you are Fred's kata coach and he is your learner. Instead of giving him useless generic advice, you ask him to set his first target condition. It should include a desired result like a three-pound weight loss but also include the change in desired living pattern—the condition—by some specific date. Generally speaking, novices should have shorter-term achieve-by dates than those with experience in scientific thinking. The more the learners have mastered the kata, the more disciplined they will be in experimenting systematically with that target condition in mind. For a novice, three months out might as well be three years out. So we suggest a target condition two to three weeks out.

Fred sets as his first target condition that he wants to lose three pounds in three weeks. You as a coach ask him what he expects to be different about his eating or exercising pattern in three weeks. You suggest that he think of himself as traveling by time capsule to three weeks from now and describing what he sees in his eating or exercising habits that he believes will help him lose three pounds. It should be a condition he observes, like the current-condition analysis, but after stepping three weeks into the future. He thinks about this and projects that in three weeks he will be going to bed without a snack and eating 20 percent fewer carbohydrates daily. Now he has a target condition:

- **Target results:** Three pounds
- **Target daily process:** No bedtime snack, 20 percent fewer carbs
- **Achieve by:** 21 days out

There is strong evidence from psychology research that Fred has greatly improved his chances of succeeding by defining a short-term target condition. Goal setting generally distinguishes between outcome goals and process goals. A sports psychology definition is that "Outcome goals are a result you'd like to achieve, and process goals are the processes you will need to repeatedly follow to achieve that result."[7] Outcome goals should give clear, measurable outcomes to aim for, but process goals give a desired pattern you can begin to work on right away.

But even this is not enough. There is one more step before execution. We identify obstacles to this first target condition. What will we have to overcome in order to achieve the desired pattern? In this case Fred thinks about it and develops the following obstacle list:

- Knows few low-carb dishes
- Low willpower at bedtime
- High-carb foods easily available
- Weekly pizza with friends

Finally Fred has completed the initial planning phase and is ready to begin execution. In these coaching sessions with Fred, you have asked him to document his plan on a learner's story board that tracks the steps of the improvement kata (see Figure 8.4).

4. **Iterate toward the target condition (PDCA Cycles of Learning).** Finally Fred gets to do something. He is excited. He meets with you as his coach, and you explain that he will begin by planning an experiment. Fred screams—"Arghh!!! I thought we were done with planning." You, as his coach, explain, "We are done with planning where we want to be in the next three weeks, but we are not done with PDCA. We still need to think carefully about each experiment, rapidly try it, and then check on results and think through what we have learned. PDCA is going to be our pattern for execution, but now we are in a rapid PDCA mode. Planning the first experiment involves picking one obstacle and then testing ideas for overcoming that obstacle one by one." Fred, a bit reluctantly, plays along. He chooses "Low willpower at bedtime." His first experiment will be to get rid of ice cream from his freezer.

Focus Process: Fred's Weight Loss		Challenge: 50 in 2
Target Condition	**Actual Condition Now**	**PDCA Cycles Record**
Achieve by: 21 days out Target Results: 297 pounds Target Daily Process: No bedtime snack 20 percent fewer carbs	250 pounds 3,000 calories daily Food Wheel: 1/3 carbs 1/3 meat or fish 1/3 veggies + ice cream at bedtime	Step and Date: Removed ice cream from house, begin tonight Expect: Eliminate night snack Result: Ate other junk food Learned: Still have habit
		Obstacles Parking Lot • Knows few low-carb dishes ➤ Low willpower at bedtime • High-carb foods easily available • Weekly pizza party

Figure 8.4   Learner storyboard for Fred

You, as a coach, respond, "Great start, Fred! Please explain to me what you expect to happen when you try this?" Fred says he expects to skip his snack before bed. "Great," you say. "When can you run this experiment, and when can we next meet to discuss the results?" Fred says it would help to run the experiment for two nights, so let's meet in two days. You respond, "I look forward to learning about the results of your experiment in two days."

Two days later you ask Fred how it is going. Standing in front of the learner storyboard, you ask him to remind you about the first target condition. You then ask him what the actual condition is and the obstacle he chose to work on. He reads his first target condition, describes his current condition, and reminds you of the experiment he chose to run and what he expected to happen. You then ask the big question: "What actually happened?" Fred looks disappointed. Without ice cream to turn to, tired and feeling hungry before bed, he found a junk food stash and ate even more calories of sweets and potato chips. "The first experiment failed," he explained, obviously disappointed. You as the coach respond that no experiment is a failure if you learn from it. "What did you learn, Fred?" He responds that he learned that he did not break the habit of an unhealthy snack before bed but simply made one snack unavailable. You exclaim: "Great learning Fred!!! Now we can plan our second PDCA building on what we learned."

What we are doing is developing a new pattern, a new habit, of iterative learning. We are learning to experiment, and for each experiment we explicitly define expectations, try one thing at a time, define the results of the experiment, and reflect on what we learned. Real learning happens when we compare expectations with reality. This forces us to confront the fact that there is much we do not know until we try. It starts to eat away at our fear of uncertainty. It begins to reinforce our comfort with failed experiments. In our experience, reflective trial and error will overcome obstacles and get us closer to our goals in a sustainable way.

What Mike Rother concluded from years of studying Toyota, and from practicing what he learned, is that there are limitations to revering Toyota as a model and worshiping "sensei" who in some way learned from Toyota. He explained this to me in a personal communication (March 2016):

> In hindsight (and this is all conjecture), it seems like the Lean community had long been practicing a mindset of "certainty," using Toyota as a mythical organization where everything that glitters is gold. It was actually our two trips to Japan that helped me get beyond this attractive but completely fabricated mental image. How healthy it was to learn that Toyota has all sorts of struggles and messes too. They just approach them a little differently. I think there is a danger in perpetuating a "guru" mindset in the community which, again, makes its followers believe that there is a right answer and that the gurus and Toyota know what that answer is. That's a comforting, religious-like feeling for people, and probably a comforting "I'm great" feeling for the gurus. You can see this reflected in the behavior and words of many Lean specialists out there.

PRINCIPLE 14: DEVELOP LEADERS AS COACHES OF CONTINUALLY DEVELOPING TEAMS

Often in a seminar I ask, "What are the characteristics of a great coach?" Most of us either have direct experience with a coach we admire or know of a famous coach of a sports team. The groups have no trouble generating marvelous lists that include characteristics like:

- Passionate about vision of success
- Follows a disciplined process
- Clear communicator
- Motivates players
- Listens to players

- Understands the game in detail
- Patient
- Firm
- Fair

Then I ask the group to think about any great coaches among the management team of their organizations. Total silence. We think about management as something different from coaching. Yet what do great coaches do? They get the best out of all of their people and develop them as a team. Don't we want our managers to do that? Isn't that important for twenty-first-century management?

Like culture, great leadership is a complex topic. We know it when we see it. Different organizations have different ideas about the ideal leader. Most work hard to identify personality profiles to select their ideal. But are great leaders born that way or developed? Ask a Toyota executive, and that person would probably say both.

Toyota works hard to select people with high potential, but it recognizes this is a hit-or-miss process. Since Toyota employs people over long periods of time, often a full work life to retirement, it can be patient to see how people evolve. The company uses the same skills for deeply observing processes to observe people in actual work situations. Some rise to each challenge living Toyota Way values step by step and get promoted. Others get results, but by working around people rather than developing people—they do not get promoted to further leadership positions. Over time the cream does not naturally rise to the top, but through challenging goals and nurturing by managers as coaches, people learn and develop. Those who develop faster and better and show true leadership skills at the gemba will rise the fastest and furthest.

There is no standard definition of great leadership at Toyota, but the people there know it when they see it. As we discussed in Chapter 2, Toyota Business Practices training is one way to identify those with potential for further leadership roles. It is Toyota's improvement kata. After that, leaders are expected to coach others to complete a TBP project through On-the-Job Development. This is Toyota's coaching kata.

Kata to Learn to Coach

The coaching kata that Mike Rother developed exactly parallels the improvement kata (see Figure 8.5). Ideally the coaches will meet with the learners at the storyboard every day and ask them questions about where they are and what they did since yesterday. What the coaches ask them will depend on where they are in the improvement kata. At first it is about the challenge and then moves to the current state, target conditions, obstacles, and PDCA cycles.

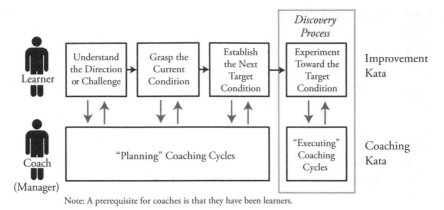

Figure 8.5   The coaching kata mirrors the improvement kata
Source: Mike Rother

The challenge is actually provided to the group by management so the learners do not need to be coached about this. There is a fair amount of work to coach the learners through the current-condition analysis, and there are many failure modes. Learners collect and analyze outcome data until the cows come home and do not spend enough time at the gemba observing the facts. Learners do not develop good run charts (timed cycles and observations to identify work timing and patterns). Learners have difficulty figuring out the customer demand rate or takt. The type of process they are working on is not simple and repetitive, and it is not clear how the basic kata tools apply (see Chapter 9 on current condition analysis). At some point the coach needs to get a little directive and take this as an opportunity for some training on how to collect and analyze data. Setting the target condition is even more challenging as we will discuss in the next chapter. There is plenty of opportunity for teaching, and it takes repeated practice until the student gets it.

Once we get past the initial planning stage—challenge, current condition, target condition, obstacles—we move on to execution through PDCA cycles, and the coaching becomes more routine. This repetitive part of the coaching kata is simple and structured. What has become known as the five-question card provides the script for the early learner of the coaching kata (see Figure 8.6). At the very beginning the coach should follow the script exactly, like any kata. Simply ask the questions. Now the student may not have great answers. Getting the student on track may require further clarifying questions, as we illustrate here when the coach is trying to understand what the learner expected to happen in the last step taken:

COACH: What did you expect?
LEARNER: We expected improvement.

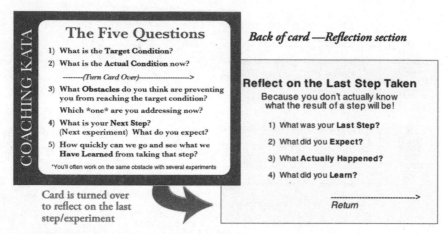

Figure 8.6   The question card is the standard work for the coach
Source: Mike Rother

COACH: Good. Can you be more specific about what you expected to improve and by how much?
LEARNER: We expected a 3 percent drop in missed customer calls.

In some cases the learner will be off track on the kata, and the coach will have to bring him back on track. In these cases it is often best to explain in simple terms what is being missed and ask the learner to think about it overnight.

COACH: Which one obstacle are you addressing now?
LEARNER: We are not addressing any specific obstacle. If we solve this problem, we will overcome a number of obstacles.
COACH: In the improvement kata the experiments should be against an obstacle. Can you get with the team and think some more about this so we can return to it tomorrow?

Is that it, you might ask? Simply ask the questions on the card along with a few elaborating questions, and you become an expert coach? Clearly that is not the case. This is still at the starter level where the coach in training is following the kata exactly. As the coach advances, she will learn to develop questions that go beyond the card, as well as approaches to corrective feedback.

The coaching kata is a bit less structured than the improvement kata, by necessity. There are so many situations, it is impossible to account for them all, or even a large percentage. So the stripped-down basics are provided to get the new coach started. Some companies have developed more extensive cards that include notes and clarifying questions. This is great! As you begin your journey, follow the kata exactly. As you mature in your learning by doing, please do modify and expand to improve it for your use. But do not abandon the underlying pattern of improvement.

The difference between clarifying questions and completely new impromptu questions is important. What we are trying to teach through the kata is a pattern—a pattern of improving using the scientific method. It is important to keep the learners focused on the pattern of the improvement kata, or it will not become a habit. If the coaches begin making up questions on the fly, the questions are likely to take the learners, and the coaches, out of the pattern. Often when the coaches feel free to make up their own questions, the questions become directive: "Is that really a difficult enough target condition?" "Did you consider this other solution?" "Was that the real root cause?"

In these cases the coaches were likely trained in some problem-solving methodology and have their own ideas and begin to impose their known methodology, and their ideas, on the learners. It will distract the learners, and the learners will shift into a passive mode, thinking: "Yes, boss. Right, boss. If you wanted it your way, why did you pretend to want to coach me?"

Toyota Work-Group Structure: Layers of Leadership, Not Supervisors

Toyota believes strongly in the power of work groups, but unlike the high-performance organization movement, the company does not believe in self-directed or even self-sufficient teams. Toyota believes strongly in leadership. When a work group is not functioning properly, Toyota management officials almost always will look at weakness in the group leader as the source of the problem. They will focus on developing group leaders as the countermeasure.

Toyota views its managers as leaders who develop other leaders and team members. And the manager of the group leaders will be expected to coach them. The managers' primary role is to act as coaches. They have figured out the ideal span of control of a work group based on this coaching role. A supervisor who is mainly checking for compliance and dealing with those who break rules might be able to manage 30 or more people. But a leader can coach about five people at a time, so that became the goal of Toyota's work-group structure. This of course leads to a taller structure, while the rage in businesses today is to flatten the structure. The concept of self-directed teams is attractive if it can mean eliminating a whole layer of management and saving money. Since Toyota believes in leaders developing people, it is willing to pay the extra cost of this apparently nonlean management structure.

I first saw an organizational chart of Toyota's work-group structure when it was drawn for me by Bill Costantino, one of the first group leader's in Toyota's Georgetown, Kentucky, plant. He drew it upside down by usual standards, with

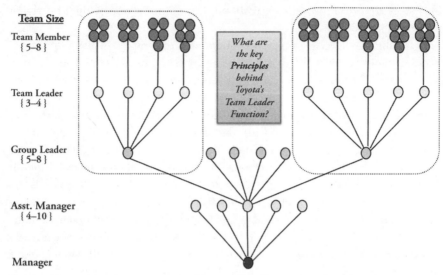

Figure 8.7   Typical organizational structure of Toyota assembly—trim
Source: Bill Costantino, W3 Consulting

hourly production workers (called "team members") at the top of the chart and senior managers at the bottom (see Figure 8.7). He had been taught this by his Japanese trainers. It represents a version of servant leadership where leaders serve those whom they lead by coaching and developing them. That was how he saw his role at Toyota.

It is often said in Toyota that the group leader is like the CEO of a small business. What this means is that the group leader is accountable for everything that goes on in the group, from safety, to discipline, to business results, to human resource development. Nothing is "implemented" in her area that is not led by the group leader. An engineer trying to deploy new technology cannot just walk in and start doing his work. He must inform the group leader, schedule his visits, and serve the work group. Ultimately the members of the work group will be responsible for operating and maintaining any new equipment, and so they must lead its introduction.

The work-group size is about 25 to 30 people, so there is a need for more leaders to get closer to Toyota's ideal 1:5 ratio. To do this, the company created an assistant role called "team leader." Team leaders are hourly employees with a natural leadership capability that is cultivated by the group leader. The group leader sees potential and encourages the hourly team member to go to training classes to become a team leader. The group leader finds opportunities to put that team member into leadership positions such as heading up the safety committee or running a quality circle that meets weekly for several months to solve a significant problem. Every day at work there is an on-the-job training opportunity for future team leaders.

Group leaders have formal authority to discipline team members, but team leaders do not. Team leaders normally support a specific number of people doing jobs, usually five to eight. They have done all those jobs and can perform them as needed, for example, if a team member is out sick. They get to the work area early to make sure everything is where it should be, in good working order. They support the team member if she pulls the andon cord, they do quality checks, they collect data for improvement activities, they substitute for team members who need a break, and they stay overtime to clean up and prepare for the next shift. In an ideal situation two of the team leaders are working production on a given day, and two are offline in a support role for the shift.

This model is quite standard in Toyota manufacturing, and variations of this model are used in all functions. Does this mean that it should be copied? Absolutely not! Toyota does not copy it exactly in other parts of manufacturing such as stamping and plastic molding. These are equipment-intensive processes, and the roles and responsibilities are somewhat different. What the company does insist on is following the principles.

Bill Costantino explained further to me that there are certain operating assumptions that are carried out by the work group (see Figure 8.8). Toyota's assumption in manufacturing is that every car scheduled to be built in a shift will be built. Since Toyota encourages team members to pull the andon when they see an abnormality there is almost always some overtime needed to complete the build schedule. There are no extra people to staff the line if a team member is out for

- **Line support for 100% daily schedule attainment**
  - 100% staffing of operations; instant absentee replacement
  - Process support: 10 seconds/hourly/daily/weekly checks
  - Routine maintenance, machine adjustments
  - Team member training/cross-training
  - Continuous improvement
    - Time to conduct experiments
    - Time for mentoring by group leader

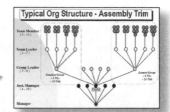

Figure 8.8 Principles behind Toyota's work-group structure
Source: Bill Costantino, W3 Consulting

some reason—the team leaders will act as flexible resources for staffing. Team leaders will perform regular, standard checks of the process—standard work checks, tool checks, product checks. Team leaders will perform routine preventative maintenance of tools and equipment. The leaders will train the team members so they know enough jobs to rotate throughout the shift. And the group leader and team leaders will facilitate continuous improvement and develop team members' improvement skills.

Work Groups Need to Be Developed, Not Deployed

When the people at General Motors first attempted to implement work groups like those they saw at their joint venture NUMMI, they copied blindly.[8] They exactly copied the structure, but they missed the critical role of leadership development. When GM conducted an internal study to understand how team leaders spent their time, it was found that they focused on emergency relief of workers (e.g., so workers could use the restroom) and quality inspection and repair. When there were no immediate problems and no fires to put out, they went to a back room for a break. In fact, only 52 percent of the time the GM team leaders did anything that you could regard as work, while NUMMI team leaders were actively supporting the assembly-line workers and spent 90 percent of their time doing work on the shop floor. Some of the things the NUMMI team leaders were actively doing:

- 21 percent of their time was spent filling in for workers who were absent or on vacation. GM team leaders did this 1.5 percent of the time.
- 10 percent of their time was spent ensuring a smooth flow of parts to the line. GM team leaders were at 3 percent.
- 7 percent of their time was spent actively communicating job-related information. This was virtually absent at GM.
- 5 percent of their time was spent observing the team working, in order to anticipate problems. This did not happen at all at GM.

I advised one large multinational manufacturing company, starting when the company first introduced its version of lean. The vice president in charge was very diligent about going to see top lean benchmarks. He told me that he was assembling the company "recipes" (his word) for the production system. With over 90 manufacturing sites throughout the world, he believed a key to success was a set of recipes organized around my Toyota Way principles. Flattering, but I was concerned.

He came back from one trip excitedly exclaiming: "Every success story has in common work groups. They all build around work groups with group leaders and team leaders who are responsible for standard work, visual management, respond-

ing to andon, and continuous improvement. We need a recipe for work groups."
At that point the company had supervisors with a span of control of 30 to 40 people who were traditional command-and-control managers. He explained that he
had already met with human resources in each country his company operated in
to develop legal job descriptions and pay scales for group leaders and team leaders,
and he wanted all plants in the world to begin to "roll out work groups" by the
end of the year.

By now it should be clear that this is a mechanistic approach to deploying
something that is inherently organic. My personal andon was going crazy saying
stop, stop, stop! This will fail! As I thought about it, I realized the recipe should
not be about putting bodies into job roles, but developing leadership. This personal transformation cannot be mandated. It is something that must be developed, and it takes time and patience—two things missing from this company's
view of deploying lean.

As expected, the teams got "deployed." Also deployed were very well
designed standard visual boards that served as a meeting place for daily huddles
and also were used for monitoring suggestions for improvement. I recall touring
a plant when an hourly production worker politely asked if he could ask me a
question. He pulled me aside and said: "Dr. Liker, I understand the idea behind
these teams. But they are not working. The group leaders and team leaders don't
know how to lead, the morning meetings are a joke, and people put up bad suggestions just to get management off their back. Is this really the way teams are
supposed to work?" I felt uncomfortable in this situation because I believed he
was right and the approach to deployment was fundamentally flawed, but I
could not say that. I apologetically explained that senior management was sincerely trying, and there would be growing pains.

Contrast this with the leadership development approach used in the launch
of a Toyota service parts warehouse described in *The Toyota Way* (Chapter 16).
Senior leaders reflected on what they had learned in launching a similar warehouse
and concluded that they had prematurely assigned group leaders and team leaders,
giving them too much responsibility too soon. As a result they developed bad
habits, and for years the organization had to backtrack and try to retrain these
leaders. The head of the new warehouse explained, "We had one chance to get the
culture right in the new warehouse." He knew there was an early window to do it
right, and if the company did not properly develop the leaders, it would mean
years of rework.

He took a somewhat radical step within Toyota. He launched the warehouse
without team leaders. The work groups started with group leaders, but they acted
in a more directive way, like supervisors. The group leaders were intensely taught
Toyota Production System principles and were responsible for applying them.

Leadership was situational, and as the culture matured it would evolve from directive to participative. As the work groups developed to a certain level of proficiency and potential team leaders emerged, management would consider allowing the group leaders to appoint team leaders group by group as they were ready. Appointing team leaders was something to earn, not an inherent right. It was a multiyear process before all the group leaders had team leaders—years of intensive development.

Applying Principles of Toyota Work-Group Structure: Hospice Nursing Example

Bill Costantino served as a coach to a hospice that served terminally ill patients starting with the executives in charge. They made great progress in the initial stages, but realized their limitations. They had an admirable mission of "Here for Life" and devoted people at all levels. But managers were fighting fires every day and not improving. Each coach could at most develop five learners of the kata at a time, and that was pushing it. Developing coaches would take even longer. It could take years to get through even the management levels of the organization. The leadership team needed a more efficient way. This led them to think about the organizational structure.

The hospice was traditionally organized with anywhere from 13 to 32 nurses reporting to a supervisor. Bill described to the executives the Toyota group leader and team leader system, along with the underlying principles. He emphasized that they should focus on the principles rather than copying the Toyota structure. To his delight the team of executives wanted to approach the problem of organizational structure as a set of kata experiments. They wanted to identify a direction, understand the current condition, set a first target condition, and then experiment.

The initial condition is shown in Figure 8.9. The improvement team found that nursing directors and managers already felt overwhelmed with their workload. They spent all their time chasing problems and never felt like they had enough time. It became clear that layering improvement and coaching onto their existing responsibilities would be too much. If the hospice used a Toyota-like team leader model with a ratio closer to one leader per five team members, there would be time for each manager to become proficient at leading improvement and coaching others to lead improvement.

The hospice decided to focus on the largest group with the largest span of control reporting up to a director of client care (see Figure 8.10). The director, Kristin, had 25 direct reports, including Amy, a home care manager, who had 13 of her own direct reports. Both were overwhelmed with their daily responsibilities of managing mostly by exception and coordinating with other parts of the organization.

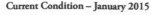

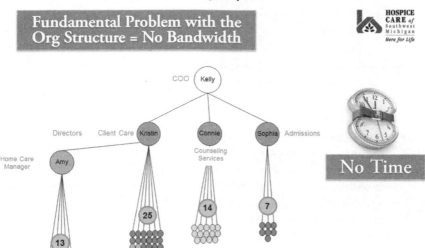

Figure 8.9 Current condition for the Hospice Care of Southwest Michigan nursing organization
Source: Hospice Care of Southwest Michigan

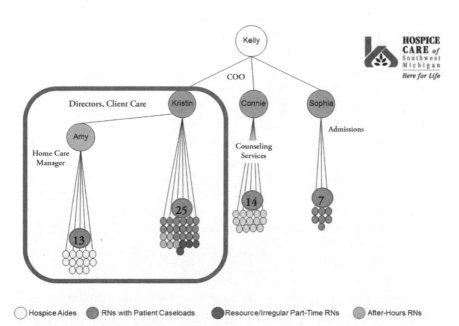

Figure 8.10 Kata pilot for the hospice care nursing organization
Source: Hospice Care of Southwest Michigan

The hospice team developed a variety of new organization concepts and in each case got broad input into strengths and possible limitations. The first concept sent up as a trial balloon looked virtually identical to the Toyota model with one team leader for every four team members. This was viewed as promising yet impractical. It would require a significant increase in the number of positions in the organization, and there was already a shortage of clinician talent available, and of course cost was always an issue. The second concept had larger groups with a mix of registered nurses and hospice aides and included a senior leader assisting the team leader. Each team leader would have six to eight registered nurses and six to eight hospice aides. Each team would also have at least one senior registered nurse with a lighter caseload to support the team leader. The nurses chose as their first target condition a third concept, similar to the second concept but without the senior registered nurse assisting (see Figure 8.11).

The team thought deeply about the responsibilities of their team leader role. The leader was not supporting a repetitive operation located in one place like the Toyota team leader. Clinicians were spread around mostly going to patient's homes and the caseload varied day to day. They identified the team

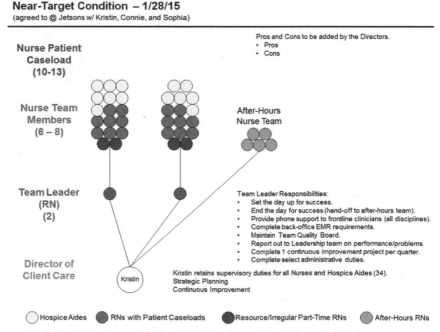

Figure 8.11   The third concept was chosen as the target condition for the hospice
Source: Hospice Care of Southwest Michigan

leader responsibilities in a way that borrowed some ideas from the Toyota model but fit better their situation:

- Set the day up for success
- End the day for success (hand-off to after-hours team)
- Provide phone support to frontline clinicians
- Complete back-office EMR (electronic medical records) requirements
- Maintain Team Quality Board
- Report out to leadership team on performance/problems
- Complete one continuous improvement project per quarter
- Complete select administrative duties

A fourth organization concept was put in place in April, 2016 (Figure 8.12). By then they had decided to call the "team leaders" registered nurse managers. It was really a combination of what Toyota calls the team leader and group leader. They had a smaller span of control than the Toyota group leader, but larger than a team leader. They estimated that the ideal number of direct reports for this management position was 10 to 13, and they were close to this ratio at 9 to 14. Notice that their concern about difficulties filling these leadership positions was justified. One of the three management positions was open, with a number of other vacancies, as turnover was com-

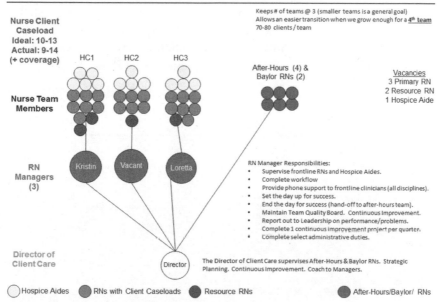

Structure – as of 4/14/16

Figure 8.12 Hospice Care of Michigan, fourth concept
Source: Hospice Care of Southwest Michigan

mon. Also notice that Kristen was "elevated" from director to manager. She discovered she really enjoyed practicing the kata and being closer to the front lines and did not enjoy many of the administrative duties of a director. The turnover meant that whoever was put in the vacant position needed a great deal of kata training. On the other hand Kristen was right there as a resource and one of their most experienced kata coaches.

The results in two areas more then justified all the resources put into learning the improvement kata and coaching kata. First was the preparation for deaths. At some point it is clear when the patient will die. There is a great deal of preparation required in paperwork, funeral arrangements, contacting all the right people, and more. Clinicians were overwhelmed with daily work and most of the time did not do this preparation as shown in Figure 8.13. Through the improvement kata, experiment after experiment, they were able to increase the percent of patients who were properly prepared for from about 20 percent to reach their goal of 80 percent.

Improvements through the kata that went right to the bottom line were in the use of generic drugs, rather then "non-formulary" drugs that are not reimbursable by Medicare-Medicade. We can see in the graphs in Figure 8.14 that these costs were reduced overall, and particularly for drugs for dementia and statin, or lipid-lowering drugs.

The hospice ultimately had success in developing an effective team leader role that broke the logjam of nursing directors and home care managers fighting fires all day. True coaching began to emerge. The key to success was carefully considering a variety of new organizational structures and then viewing the selected structure as a target condition. A target condition is something to strive for dyamically, not a static structure to be copied and implemented. Many experiments were run and many adjustments made as the hospice learned how to develop the

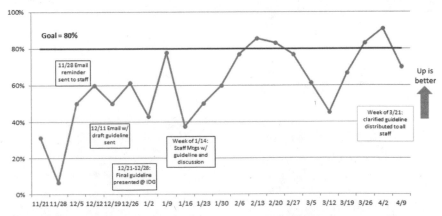

Figure 8.13 Number of deaths that were preceded by a zip or on-call report
Source: Hospice Care of Southwest Michigan

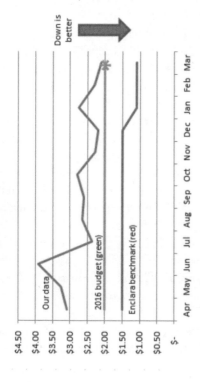

Non-Formulary Med Costs per Patient Day

Down is better

Our data

2016 budget (green)

Enclara benchmark (red)

$4.50
$4.00
$3.50
$3.00
$2.50
$2.00
$1.50
$1.00
$0.50
$-

Apr May Jun Jul Aug Sep Oct Nov Dec Jan Feb Mar

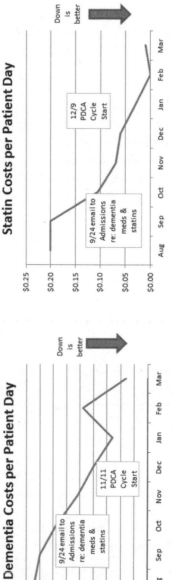

Statin Costs per Patient Day

Down is better

12/9 PDCA Cycle Start

9/24 email to Admissions re: dementia meds & statins

$0.25
$0.20
$0.15
$0.10
$0.05
$0.00

Aug Sep Oct Nov Dec Jan Feb Mar

Dementia Costs per Patient Day

Down is better

9/24 email to Admissions re: dementia meds & statins

11/11 PDCA Cycle Start

$0.45
$0.40
$0.35
$0.30
$0.25
$0.20
$0.15
$0.10
$0.05
$0.00

Aug Sep Oct Nov Dec Jan Feb Mar

Figure 8.14 Reduction in non-reimbursable medicine through improvement kata

Source: Hospice Care of Southwest Michigan

leaders into their new roles. This organic approach based on a scientific learning process required time and struggle, but it was effective.

PRINCIPLE 15: BALANCE EXTRINSIC-INTRINSIC REWARDS

People Are Not Like Machines

It is a well-known adage that "you get what you measure." What this suggests is that if you measure the right things, you will get the right results. Comforting thought, but far from the truth.

The simplest and most efficient assumption about what drives people is that we are all like computers programmed to maximize our expected utility. This is the assumption underlying most economics models, and it seems to be predictive to some degree, at least at a macrolevel. We crunch numbers in our head and figure out the costs and benefits of alternative actions and select the path with the highest payout. Thus, people are thought of as rational actors, which means that what motivates us is easily quantifiable. Since economists deal with money and since money can be counted, the assumption is that almost everything that motivates us can be converted to units of money. That was the original assumption of Frederick Taylor and scientific management, and along with the more efficient work methods that the experts designed, Taylor was able to motivate people to dramatically improve productivity.

The idea that you get what you measure and what you reward is deeply rooted in the psyche of most management throughout the world. It is particularly rooted in Western countries that have highly individualistic cultures where the individual wants to know, "What is in it for me?" Many consultants and business books educate us on how to answer this question, which they describe as the key to unlocking motivation. Yet Toyota goes out of its way to try to weed out hiring people who ask "What is in it for me?" The company seems to violate yet another fundamental tenet of management thought.

Conditioned Responses and Habits Are Powerful Motivators

Our trusted sensei Dr. Deming, in a somewhat cynical mood said, "People with targets and jobs dependent upon meeting them will probably meet the targets—even if they have to destroy the enterprise to do it." Deming preached against numerical targets, annual performance appraisals, and pay by the piece. What is wrong with incentive pay, and how can management possibly motivate people if it is not through contingent pay?

We learn a lot about contingent pay through the field of psychology known as behavior modification. One of the formative events in this field is the famous Pavlov's dog response. Pavlov was studying the physiological digestive process when he observed a curious phenomenon. He noticed that the dogs in the experiment began to salivate in the presence of the technician who normally fed them, even when there was no food. He explained this as a "conditioned response." The dogs were fed by the technicians, and their brains came to associate the technician with the food. He observed "anticipatory salivation" even when no food was present.

This important discovery suggested that a reward does not need to be provided for each instance of a desired behavior. Rather, once we become conditioned to expect the reward, we will behave in the desired way in anticipation of the reward. You can say we have formed a habit. Now this habit will die out over time if there is never a reward. Psychologists have experimented with many stimulus-response tables to understand the conditions under which different patterns of rewards have the greatest chance of creating and sustaining desired behaviors. In a simplistic sense the pattern is to reward every instance of the behavior early in the reinforcement process, as close as possible to the time of the behavior, and then begin to randomly reward instances to sustain the behavior.

This makes life easy for managers. Identify a reward that matters to the worker, make it contingent on desired behaviors, and use the correct reinforcement pattern. People, like dogs, will do what you want without even realizing they are being manipulated.

There are some problems with this. One of the most powerful barriers to lean transformation is precisely this type of system of reinforcement. I have seen a number of cases of companies that had a long history of piece-rate systems. This was straight out of Frederick Taylor, and people were paid proportional to the number of pieces they produced. It worked to motivate people to want to make a lot of pieces. But with real lean systems, we are not interested only in producing many pieces. We are interested in the right pieces, the right quantity, the right timing, and the right quality. Overproduction is the fundamental waste. Try telling that to someone paid by the piece. "When this buffer is filled, please stop producing and we will reduce your pay." Good luck with that!

These same companies were trying to introduce ergonomics to reduce repetitive trauma injuries. Workers were being told to change the way they do the job to put less stress on their hands, wrists, and backs. But at least at first, the new ergonomic way slowed them down. Good luck with that! Moreover, these companies had learned about the power of work groups and wanted workers to be part of a team that rotated jobs. Reward people as individuals for their own output and then ask them to work as a team doing different jobs and potentially reducing their own individual output, and again you have a recipe for frustration and rebellion. I know of cases where unions threatened to strike when lean was introduced in piece-rate companies. After pushback by the union, each of these companies went back to the drawing board and, after years of concerted effort, got agreements to eliminate the piece-rate system. They had to reset base pay at a higher level so people did not lose money in the new system, but they had determined the benefits for overall system performance were well worth that cost. Finally lean had a chance!

Habits created with the help of contingent rewards are real and actually can be the foundation of the behaviors desired for continuous improvement. The *Power of Habit*[9] is an easy read and simplifies behavior modification to three elements: cue, routine, reward. We need a discernible cue that triggers a routine or habit, which is then reinforced with a reward. The reward can be extrinsic or intrinsic but needs to be something that feels good to our brain.

Habits are developed through repetition, as in Pavlov's dog. They become conditioned responses, so the need for an actual reward diminishes over time. Scott Adams, the *Dilbert* cartoonist, describes how he got himself to exercise every day.[10] One cue for him is simply putting on his running sneakers. Once he puts on his sneakers, his brain seems to be saying, "We might as well go to the gym." The key to developing the habit is simple—repetition. The more repetition, the tighter the connection between the cue and the routine. At some point exercising simply feels good to your brain, and the absence of it feels like something is missing.

Almost all of the process principles in Chapter 6 depend upon forming the right types of habits in our employees. An andon system is one example. The light goes on acting as the cue. The team leader comes running and executes the proper routine for responding to the andon. As we discussed in Chapter 6, often companies imitate the andon through some sort of visual or audible signal when there is a need for help, and either nobody comes or a manager runs over steaming mad because of the disruption. Many of my Toyota associates had the opposite experience, getting pats on the back, "atta boys," or even applause when they first pulled the andon. It was like a rite of passage. It is important in the early stages of andon to have a quick response and positive reinforcement until it becomes a habit (see Figure 8.15).

Similarly, if we look under the hood of standard work, pull systems, visual management, daily huddle areas, and all the other lean processes, it will become clear that in the center are people who must do the right thing in the right way. There are no fully automated systems in lean that can operate independently of the right human intervention. Even automation itself requires disciplined maintenance that depends on people responding to the right cues with the right routines at the right time.

Figure 8.15   Andon and habit forming

The most basic form of behavior modification is that I perform behavior A, and it leads to desired outcome B, and I receive reward C. It works when there is a direct and simple relationship. At the dawn of the industrial revolution, the workplace was simple—make a lot of shoes or shovel a lot of iron ore or assemble a lot of Model Ts, and they will sell and the company will be profitable. This is why the piece-rate system of pay worked so well. Make a lot of pieces per person, and life will be good for the owner of the business.

There are still examples of relatively simple cause-and-effect relationships today in services. One great example is Uber's taxi service. Uber says, "Drive your own car and be your own boss." With relatively little vetting, drivers are enlisted to drive their own car and pick up fares determined by transactions through the Internet. The drivers are not managed or indoctrinated into the Uber culture. They are directly rated by customers, who need to have a smartphone to use the service. The drivers do not immediately see the current passenger's rating, to protect the anonymity of customers. They and the customers see aggregate ratings and any customer comments. And you as a customer can turn down a driver who you notice has low ratings. In some locations Uber can even require the low-rated drivers to pay for costly training to continue their livelihood. Uber drivers complain about not knowing who gave them a bad rating or why they got it. In fact, this is a risky business model. For example, there is a risk of a violent person becoming an Uber driver, but in the vast majority of cases, it has worked to satisfy customers enough to want to continue to use the low-cost, reliable service.

The reason this relatively weak behavior modification system works at Uber is because there is a direct relationship between what the drivers do and how they are rated. They need to pick up customers quickly, drive them to the destination safely, and treat them respectfully, in a car that is not offensive. If they do this, they are likely to get five stars. If they violate any of these basic expectations, they get less than five stars, and it hurts their ability to get more work. As long as this is all that is expected of the driver, even a weak reinforcement system is effective.

In the modern age we have much more complex work, even in manufacturing, and more need for situational behaviors—the right behaviors under the right conditions. Trying to set up rewards and punishments for everything we want an employee to do under every condition ends up being an impossible situation. We might need an artificial intelligence program to figure out whether the employee should be rewarded or punished in a given instance.

Contrast Uber with a personal transportation company that Karyn has been working with, National Taxi Limo (NTL). Although NTL has an app like Uber through which customers can book their trips, track their driver, and pay for their rides, the similarities end there. NTL is focused on fulfilling its long-term purpose of helping independent taxi owners grow their businesses and develop as business owners and people through delivering personal, personable service, one taxi ride at a time. NTL is very particular about who becomes part of its web of drivers, and the company is developing itself and its drivers by striving toward its vision of "Every Ride. On Time. Every Time. Working Together." We'll learn more about NTL's story in Chapter 10.

People React to Extrinsic Rewards but Can Become Innovative with Intrinsic Rewards

One of the most consistent and counterintuitive findings in psychology is that extrinsic rewards can actually harm certain types of performance. One set of experiments that demonstrated the limits of extrinsic rewards is the candle problem first developed by Karl Duncker and published posthumously in 1945.[11] In this clever experiment participants were asked to take a candle, a box of tacks, and matches and find a way to attach the candle to the wall. They would be timed for how long it took them to succeed.

There were two experiments, one in which tacks were provided in a box, and the other in which tacks were outside the box (see Figure 8.16). In both experiments the members of an experimental group were told they would get money if they succeeded (extrinsic rewards), and the members of a control group were told to do their best in order to advance an understanding of problem solving (intrinsic rewards).

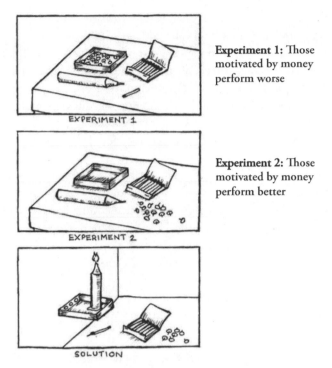

Experiment 1: Those motivated by money perform worse

Experiment 2: Those motivated by money perform better

Figure 8.16 Candle experiments with extrinsic rewards and intrinsic rewards
Source: Duncker, Karl (1945). *On Problem Solving.* Psychological Monographs 58. American Psychological Association.

Models of humans as utility maximizers would predict those subjects who could earn money would be more highly motivated and thus the fastest in each task. Yet those who were not offered any money were significantly faster in experiment 1. Notice that in this experiment we have a box of tacks and a match to attach the candle to the wall. The first attempts are often to try to find a way to melt the candle wax or to use the tacks to attach the candle to the wall. They fail. The right solution is to empty the box of tacks and then use the tacks to attach the box to the wall, melt the candle at the bottom, and attach it to the box. The problem with those in the experimental group motivated by money was that they were rushing to succeed and thus focused on obvious solutions. Duncker called this "functional fixedness." The participants saw each object as having a fixed function, like the box holds the tacks, and their focus on the reward blinded them to alternative uses.

On the other hand, in experiment 2, when the tacks were removed from the box, everyone in both groups could see the box as just a box, not a container for tacks. In this experiment those offered money took much less time than those doing the task for the sake of science. The conclusion: *money does motivate, but it can limit our creativity.*

There have been many more recent studies that suggest that when people are motivated by something they find inherently rewarding, intrinsic rewards, they will be more creative and continue doing the task even when offered a break. Those motivated by money will use already well-learned approaches to quickly get to the result and will gladly take a break when offered. If money is our motivator, it also means that without the contingent money, we will stop, even doing something we otherwise enjoy. It is as if we are saying to ourself: "I am getting paid to do this, so I must be doing it for the money, therefore I will not do anything I am not being paid for."

If we consider the Uber case, the taxi drivers are doing something they already know how to do, and what is measured (customer ratings) is directly related to their performance. Do the job and get the reward of more business. But National Taxi Limo wants more from its drivers. The company wants the drivers to feel like a part of NTL, to share its vision and values, and then to contribute to improvement. This requires a deeper commitment and creative thinking about how they can improve. This in fact is the vision of continuous improvement of services. We cannot depend on carrot-and-stick rewards to get people to invest their souls in the company and find creative ways to better serve customers.

Reward Holistically, and Make Work Visible

Accountability, accountability, accountability! "We reorganized under regional presidents to have the right people in the right positions to be accountable." "We are building a new culture of accountability for key business results." "We used to be all cost centers, and now we are profit and loss centers, and leaders will be judged by profitability." The subtext: "We are putting ambitious and competitive people in charge and measuring their performance, and they will get rich or get fired based on results!"

We have seen this work in environments where senior leaders have become comfortable and complacent. The new CEO comes in, reorganizes so there are distinctive business units with profit and loss responsibility, streamlines key performance indicators, and develops aggressive business plans, and within months profits are up. They must believe there is not enough time to change the culture of the organization other than through incentivizing top executives who cut costs through restructuring and layoffs, growing revenue by entering new markets, and pressuring all their direct reports to perform or else. A comfortable culture of people doing what they know how to do, coasting through the workday, turns into a culture of discomfort and fear. The KPIs make results visible so that appropriate rewards . . . and punishments . . . can be applied. What is missing from this equation is a serious effort to understand the customer and make the way people work visible. Fear as a motivator replaces engagement. People development means produce or else.

Toyota also believes in accountability and transparency, but with a twist. The company wants people to be accountable for highlighting problems in the system and participating in improving processes to improve the customer experience. Gary Convis, former Toyota executive, loves to say, "There are only two things that could get people fired at Toyota—failing to show up for work and failing to use the andon to surface problems." This is sort of tongue-in-cheek, but he is serious that one of the most egregious offenses at Toyota is hiding problems. It undermines the entire system of respect for people and continuous improvement.

The most visible performance I have seen in a Toyota assembly plant was a group leader board showing the number of quality defects produced by team member. It was the Georgetown, Kentucky, plant, and the team members rotate within their team to work on four jobs per shift. The diagram showed circles for each team member, and you could see where there were defects by person and by job. If one job had relatively high defects, which only occurred when one specific person was working on that job, it was a red circle. The chart was posted on a board for quality issues and visible to everyone.

What is the purpose of a board like this? In a command-and-control environment, it would be clear: find the underperformers and pressure them to improve or face punishment. In this plant the intent was to surface problems. If everyone performing that job had the problem equally, then it was clearly a problem with the system, not the person. If it was a problem one person had on that job, then it was still first assumed to be a system problem. Even if it was a problem of how the person performed the job, it raised questions like "Why has this person been allowed to do that job if he is not properly trained?" "Is there a weakness in the training system?" "Is there some way of changing the job so that everyone can perform it with high quality such as creating a mistake-proofing device?" Identify problems and solve the problems begins with the assumption that it is a problem with the system which is within management control.

The underlying assumption of Toyota's system is that people will trust management not to use visual management systems against them. Even when a document highlights people by name, the goal is not to find the guilty party, but rather to improve value to the customer. This is a fine line when a person's reputation and self-confidence are on the line. It depends heavily on the reward system, not only what is rewarded but what is punished.

The piece-rate system, which has been so damaging to companies trying to transform to a lean, customer-focused system, is even more scary if we publicly post individual performance. In that case having a red circle around your name may mean that you do not get the performance bonus, a form of punishment.

Workers will then do anything they can to hide any problems that may get them a bad grade.

A system based on openness—surfacing problems regardless of the cause so we can all improve—tends to go along with transparent systems that reward team members for the performance of the whole. One type of transparent reward system is open-book accounting as practiced by Zingerman's. The figures that go into profit and loss, that are normally reserved for accountants, tax professionals, and owners of the business, are openly shared with everyone.

All of Zingerman's businesses proudly display key figures on whiteboards for anyone to see. These are organized as "Department Operating Reports" (DORs). Like all Zingerman's businesses, Zingerman's Mail Order holds monthly all-staff meetings focused on finances. The company presents sales versus plan, labor costs, material costs, gross margin, net operating profit, and all the elements of income statements and balance sheets. The year-round employees have training on what these mean, which means accounting 101.

Each department has its own DOR reviews weekly with all team members. The department DORs focus on five to six key metrics on the board. Each department selects the metrics most important to it. The weekly metric board for the warehouse of Zingerman's Mail Order is shown in Figure 8.17. We can see the forecast, plan, and actual numbers for revenue in dollars, boxes shipped, minutes

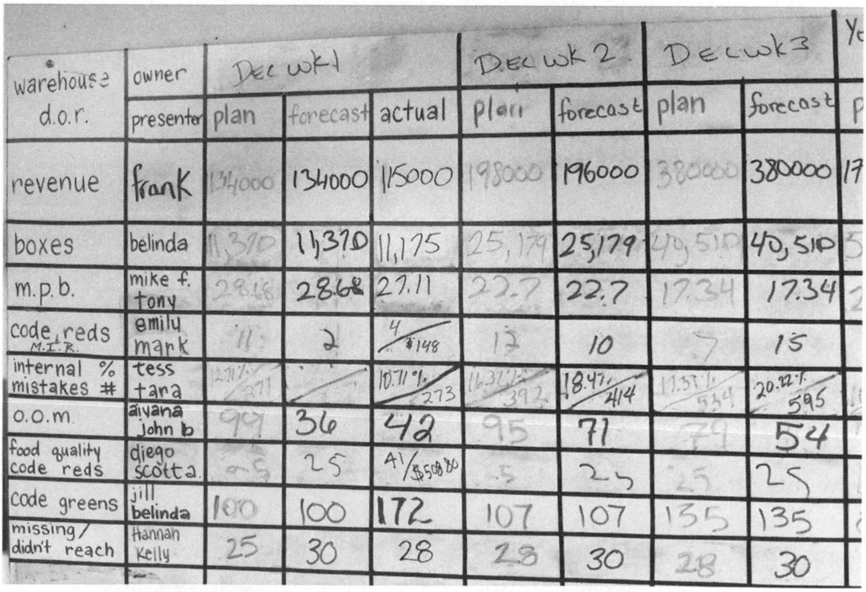

warehouse d.o.r.	owner	Dec wk 1			Dec wk 2		Dec wk 3		Yr
	presenter	plan	forecast	actual	plan	forecast	plan	forecast	p
revenue	frank	134000	134000	115000	198000	196000	380000	380000	17
boxes	belinda	11,370	11,370	11,175	25,179	25,179	40,510	40,510	5
m.p.b.	mike f. tony	28.68	28.68	27.11	22.7	22.7	17.34	17.34	2
code reds M.I.R.	emily mark	11	2	4 #148	12	10	5	15	
internal % mistakes #	tess tara	2.31% 271		10.71% 273	16.36% 392	18.47% 414	11.35% 534	20.22% 595	
o.o.m.	aivana john b	99	36	42	95	71	79	54	
food quality code reds	diego scott a.	25	25	41 /$50880	5	25	25	25	
code greens	jill belinda	100	100	172	107	107	135	135	
missing/ didn't reach	Hannah kelly	25	30	28	28	30	28	30	

Figure 8.17 Weekly metrics for Zingerman's Mail Order December warehouse performance

per box, and quality indicators. Note that for each row on the board, there is an accountable person's name. These people are not accountable for results, but rather for presenting that indicator at the meeting. There are many people who present results to get broad involvement.

There are also real-time dashboards for each department posted on flat panel displays. The dashboard for the call center is pictured in Figure 8.18. Shown are the key performance indicators that ZMO has chosen to focus on. We see three indicators with actual versus plan. The indicators start with bookings in thousands of dollars, which is a sale for future delivery. When this board was filled in, it was early morning, and the company had so far made $1,000 in new sales toward its target for the day of $22,000. The average order size in dollars is displayed; at this time it was $118 versus a target of $90. An interesting measure is a personal energy rating, which is on a 1-to-10 scale based on team members self-assessing how they feel. The overall bar across the top reflects capacity for handling phone calls versus the current volume of callers. It was at 100 percent at this time, which meant 100 percent of the call staff were available with no customers currently on the line. If half the staff were occupied with phone calls, it would read 50 percent.

The dashboard is the most immediate set of indicators and the ones focused on throughout the day. A common experience is that on days that are short of the sales target, people on the phones work harder to sell extra items. One might assume that those answering calls are paid a bonus based on bookings. But that is

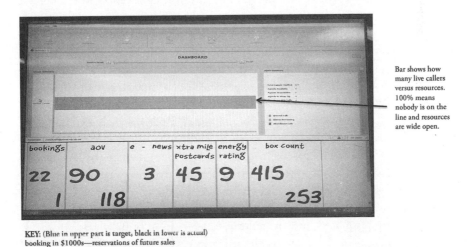

KEY: (Blue in upper part is target, black in lower is actual)
booking in $1000s—reservations of future sales
aov—average order size in dollars
e-news—new subscription requests to e-news
xtra mile postcards—a handwritten thank you or personal message to a customer
energy rating—3 self-assessments of personal energy—physical, emotional and vibrational 1–10 scale
box count—orders shipping same day

Figure 8.18   Live dashboard for Zingerman's Mail Order call center

not the case. In the Zingerman's culture every person you talk to is "the best part of my day." You give each customer your undivided attention for as long as needed. If you were paid by the booking, your incentive would be to get that customer off the line as soon as a sale is made and get on to the next potential sale.

Zingerman's people feel a direct connection to the company and to customers, and this is reinforced by the company's holistic pay system. When people become full-time employees at Zingerman's Mail Order, from day one they get medical and dental coverage, a flexible medical spending account, and a 401(k). They also participate in the gain-sharing plan, which is a percentage of profits shared among employees. More recently Zingerman's added Zingshare. Employees can purchase one share, and only one, of Zingerman's privately held stock for $1,000, which can be paid for by payroll deduction. (If you leave the company, you are guaranteed your $1,000 back.) This money is then used within the Zingerman's family of businesses to fund start-ups.

Another unusual feature of Zingerman's is its clear target for operating profits. Each business in the family has a commitment to the holding company to earn 5.25 percent net operating profit. Any profits over this target are reinvested in the business and the people. Each individual business has a two-day management meeting to put together a wish list of what to do with any extra profits, which can include investing in renovation of the building, buying equipment, or investing in team members through bonuses, wage increases, and field trips.

The intrinsic rewards of working at Zingerman's come, not from the daily tasks that can be repetitive and dreary, but from the connection to the culture and customers. Talk to full-time employees who work in the warehouse year-round, and you'll discover that they have come from a variety of jobs, some that would seem more challenging. One member of the warehouse crew worked in repair of robotics and later in sales. He hated working at these places. He loves working in the ZMO warehouse at what seems like a menial, repetitive job. He appreciates that his ideas are listened to and that he helps shape the company. He appreciates that he continues to learn and grow. He loves all the training the company provides and the chance to learn new skills through the improvement and coaching kata. He prepares all year for being a captain when the busy season rolls around and he needs to teach and support the temporary workforce.

The overall message is that every employee at every level is a valued member of the Zingerman's culture. No full-time employee is cheap labor. Year-round employees are integrated into the culture. They even informally refer to themselves as "Zingernauts." Of course, the temporary workers hired during the holiday season are not full-time employees and are not eligible for all these benefits, though they are treated well. For example, they get a free meal prepared by a top chef every workday at ZMO.

Work Role \ Work Culture	Individualistic	Collectivist
Routine Execution	Individual pay for performance	Intrinsic motivation and bonuses for group and company performance
Innovation	Reward star performers	Intrinsic motivation and holistic rewards

Figure 8.19 Use of extrinsic and intrinsic motivators

We have summarized the role of different types of intrinsic and extrinsic reward systems in a 2 × 2 table in Figure 8.19. We argue that the best types of rewards depend on the culture you are trying to create and and one dimension distinguishes between a culture centered on the individual and a collectivist culture. In the second dimension we distinguish between rewards for routine execution of clearly defined tasks and rewards for innovation.

As we have noted, extrinsic rewards at the individual level work best when the tasks are limited to routine execution of what we already know how to do. This fits with an individualist culture. For frontline staff in these organizations, it is effective to make pay contingent on specific performance indicators. If we want true innovation to work in an individualistic culture then we need to identify the star performers, the creative geniuses, and pay them handsomely. In this case it is not likely to be pay for the piece, but more broad rewards like large salaries and stock options.

On the other hand, we have seen that this extrinsic reward system can actually be counterproductive if we want people to act in concert with others in a collectivist culture characteristic of lean systems. At Toyota, even the team member performing a simple one-minute repetitive job is expected to contribute to the team and think creatively about how to better perform the job.

Previously in the book, we mentioned that Toyota tries to avoid hiring those who are focused on their own achievements and rewards. Toyota is very dedicated to building a collectivist culture. Companies like Menlo and Zingerman's are also focused on deliberately building a collectivist culture. These organizations focus more heavily on intrinsically rewarding work and use holistic reward systems tied to how the business as a whole is doing. Even frontline employees are expected to contribute to continuous improvement, and paying them by the piece would limit their creative contributions.

THE REAL MEANING OF RESPECT FOR PEOPLE

Respect for people and continuous improvement are the two pillars of the Toyota Way. They are totally integrated. Respect for people means more than treating people nicely and fairly. It means investing in people to be partners in the business and investing in their development. In *Toyota Culture* we drew an analogy between value-stream mapping of processes and a people value stream. In the people value stream, value is added whenever the person is learning something new. Waste is when people are simply executing what they already know.

Any good teacher knows that learning can be painful. It involves all the elements we presented in the "skill development cycle." It includes structured practice routines, or kata, frequent practice, coaching to provide corrective feedback, and feelings of self-efficacy. Performing routine tasks is always easier than learning new skills. Being pushed by a coach to critically examine the current condition and strive to meet a new target condition is not necessarily fun. Being pushed by a coach to exercise your body at a push pace beyond your current comfort level is not fun. You are using muscles in ways they are not used to, and they answer back with pain signals. When we push our brains, they answer back with pain signals. We will only work to overcome this pain if we truly believe we are working toward a larger vision that matters to us—a purpose and a set of goals we care about.

Michael Ballé has been working hard to answer the question, "What does respect for people mean in practice?" In the business novel *Lead with Respect*, he illustrated a model through a semifictional story.[12] Its seven elements are *go see, challenge, listen, teach, support, teamwork,* and *learn*. It is another way of defining what we have called lean leadership. In the book he argues that this is a radically different way of managing that for most people requires a personal transformation with a coach.

In Mike Rother's work we learned about an explicit step-by-step methodology for developing these types of leaders using an improvement kata and a coaching kata. Learning this method requires all of the seven elements of Michael Ballé's lead with respect model and provides opportunities for daily coaching—plan, do, learn with corrective feedback over and over and over again. It is continuous improvement of ourselves.

Our conclusion is that respect for people is a continuous process of striving for a vision. Like lean processes it is not something to implement but rather something to aspire to. It provides a true north vision that we can never fully achieve. We can only do our best to get better and learn from our successes and failures. We must be open to critical feedback, something else that naturally causes pain. It is not easy to work in an organization dedicated to respect for people striving for customer service excellence. Easy does not equal respect. Respect is committing to a learning partnership, to collaborating, to working together toward the next challenge so we can all benefit by working toward a purpose we care about.

KEY POINTS
DEVELOP PEOPLE TO BECOME MASTERS OF THEIR CRAFT

1. Changing an organization's culture is not simply a matter of creating plans on paper in workshops and then implementing them rigorously and exactly. In order to change culture, the skills and mindset for continuous improvement must be developed over time through continuous learning, preferably with a coach.

2. Fundamental scientific mindset and skills are developed through kata.
   - Concepts and theory can be presented in training sessions, but real learning—changes to the way we think and act—only takes place through repeated action and experience.
   - Learning something new through repeated practice, with the help of a coach, creates new connections—synapses—in our brains, which, over time, become habits.
   - Kata are practice routines that are used to build effective habits and can be applied in many areas of life, including continuous improvement in organizations.
   - Having an experienced coach to give corrective feedback helps the learner stay on track and practice correct habits.

3. The improvement kata consists of four high-level steps that, when repeated over and over again, create a routine for continuous learning and improvement:
   - **Understand the direction or challenge.** A specific and compelling challenge statement is needed to motivate groups of people toward collective action.
   - **Grasp the current condition.** A deep understanding of the process that produces the current outcome, as well as the current outcome, is needed.
   - **Establish the next target condition.** Set a series of short-term goals, one by one, to work toward the challenge.
   - **Iterate toward the target condition.** Experiment by trying one thing at a time to learn by comparing expectations to reality.

4. Develop leaders as coaches of continually developing teams:
   - Organizations serious about lean transformation need leaders who have a scientific mindset and the skills to lead the transformation and coach teams for continual development.
   - Using the coaching kata regularly allows managers to develop their coaching ability and fulfill their primary role of developing their team's mindset and skills for improvement.

- Team structure and leadership need to be developed according to each organization's specific needs.
5. Balance extrinsic and intrinsic rewards:
   - Habits created with the help of intrinsic and extrinsic rewards can be the foundation of behaviors desired for continuous improvement.
   - Extrinsic rewards work to motivate and reinforce specific, habitual behaviors.
   - Intrinsic rewards lead to greater creativity and learning new skills.
   - Work toward finding the correct balance between extrinsic and intrinsic rewards that motivates people in your organization to be accountable for highlighting problems in the system and for improving processes to improve the customer experience.
6. Respect for people means fully investing in their learning and development through frequent coaching with structured practice routines (kata) and corrective feedback so that they gain self-efficacy and become full partners in striving toward your organization's purpose.

Chapter 9

Problem-Solving Principles: Strive Toward a Clear Direction Through Experimenting

One area where I think we are especially distinctive is failure. I believe we are the best place in the world to fail (we have plenty of practice!), and failure and invention are inseparable twins. To invent you have to experiment, and if you know in advance that it's going to work, it's not an experiment.

—Jeff Bezos, Amazon founder

PROBLEM SOLVING AS SCIENCE

Toyota Business Practices (Chapter 2) is Toyota's problem-solving method. When someone says "I am a problem solver," they often mean they are fire fighters—fixing things that are broken. This is not what we mean by problem solving. There are several common understandings in Toyota about problem solving. First, there is no problem without a standard. A standard can be a policy, an engineering specification, or an aspirational target, and it can come from inside or outside the organization. The current state is then compared with the standard, and the gap is a problem. The focus of problem solving is striving to close the gap between the actual condition and the standard. It goes far beyond fixing things that are broken.

Second, a problem is not an opportunity. It is a "problem" because there is a gap that needs to be closed. Closing the gap is not some nice opportunity in Toyota. It is an obligation.

Third, problem solving should be a focused search in the direction of the target. Those who have been students of a Toyota master trainer quickly tire of the incessant questions: "What is the purpose?" and "Why focus on this instead of that?" "There is waste, and we want to eliminate it" is never a sufficient reason. There must be a defined need, ultimately defined as a measurable or observable target.

But Toyota Business Practices is more than a problem-solving method. It is an approach to developing people to think deeply about their goals and how to achieve them. It is a teaching method to develop a way of thinking, a pattern. The way of thinking is drilled into the student until it is a habit that will automatically be drawn on to address any problem, big or small.

If we follow a standard method that becomes a habit, we do not have to think deeply, which conserves energy. When we strive toward an ambitious goal, we will need to discover new information and innovate, which heavily taxes our prefrontal cortex. But if we draw on an established routine for approaching the improvement, one that we have practiced many times, we will have less of a burden on our brain. We still have to navigate through uncertain territory, but we will not have to, in parallel, teach ourselves an approach to navigating.

Our lives at work and at home are full of routines (see Figure 9.1). When we are performing tasks using a standard method that we have practiced, we are using an execution routine—getting dressed, driving a car, balancing our checkbook, checking our e-mail, and the list goes on. Daniel Kahneman, the Nobel prize winner, called this fast thinking. It is as if we are on automatic pilot. Ever had the experience of arriving at work and you can't remember anything about the drive there? You are doing fast thinking, almost in the background, to drive this well-practiced route. Your brain loves it—it conserves mental energy to be saved for your survival.

The mental work of striving for a new standard requires a lot of activity in the prefrontal cortex—what Daniel Kahneman calls "slow thinking," deep and intensive. As we have repeatedly emphasized, slow thinking is painful and requires a lot of mental energy, and therefore we tend to avoid it if possible. Kahneman calls this "the law of least mental effort." Unfortunately, as a result, we attempt to use fast thinking even when slow thinking is called for. That is why we must work so hard to develop the habits of scientific thinking.

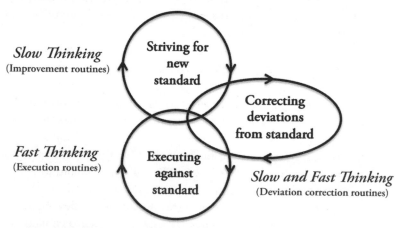

Figure 9.1   Standards and problem-solving routines
See Daniel Kahneman, *Thinking, Fast and Slow*, 2011.

Correcting deviations to an already standard method that we have practiced is somewhere in between. Again we will draw on our habits. For example, one manager may think there is an easy solution to every case of a slippage in production or quality or safety and run in to implement the known solution. On the other hand, a manager who has learned a more deliberate improvement process will see this as yet another gap between the standard and actual, and his improvement routine will kick into gear. Therefore, we are always using routines either to conduct work that we are familiar with or to face a challenging goal that requires innovative thinking. Tough problems will require routines for "slow thinking," deep and intensive, while simple problems that we already know how to solve can draw on existing routines or "fast thinking."[1]

We caution that correcting deviations from the standard is very different from striving for a new level of performance. One of the greatest systems thinkers, Russell Ackoff, made this distinction very clear:[2]

> *A defect is something that is wrong . . . When you get rid of something that you don't want you do not necessarily get what you do want. So finding deficiencies and getting rid of them is not a way of improving performance of the system.*

What Is Scientific Thinking?

I always had a bit of slow thinking in me, which is why I pursued a PhD and wanted to be a professor. Getting a PhD in sociology at the University of Massachusetts in the late 1970s put me at the center of debates about the nature of social science, a decidedly slow thinking process. Sociology, the study of people in groups and social systems, is perhaps the most complex science, with many variables interacting in complex ways. My PhD advisor, Peter Rossi, was known as one of the leaders in quantitative sociology. His focus was applied sociology to inform policy. Like the Toyota folks, he valued managing by facts, which to him was mainly large data sets. He believed the ultimate test of the efficacy of a policy was a large social experiment comparing a treatment group with a control group, such as experimenting with different forms of unemployment insurance.

A number of other sociology faculty were violently opposed to Rossi's approach. They believed there were severe limits in our ability to understand social phenomena through the lens of statistical analysis. There were various tribes that did qualitative social research—observing and meticulously recording notes and seeking to build theory from the ground up. Ohno's admonition to stand in one place and observe without preconceptions would resonate with these faculty members. As you might imagine from this book I have increasingly grown to appreciate the qualitative researchers and wish I had spent more time learning from them when I was in graduate school.

A Practical View of Scientific Thinking

Karyn sent me an eye-opening article by Robin Wall Kimmerer about the nature of science. Kimmerer is a Native American woman whose PhD dissertation was on moss, and her first book was called *Gathering Moss*.[3] Compared with sociology, what could be a simpler application of the traditional scientific method than to study moss? It turns out there is much more to the study of plant life than I ever imagined.

Kimmerer's father was forced off an Indian reservation in New York State and sent to a school designed to assimilate Native American children. Over time her family bucked this trend and worked hard to rekindle tribal connections, which included getting close to nature. Robin Wall Kimmerer was well educated in traditional American schools and earned her PhD in botany. She describes her learning journey as a circle. She loved plants as a child, observing them with awe and living among them, then conformed to the traditional scientific view of studying plant life from a distance, and then returned to learning through the senses in a spiritual connection with nature. She now spends much of her time living among plant life and observing it with childlike awe.

Kimmerer writes about "two ways of knowing."[4] One is the traditional scientific method of isolating samples in a lab, studying the world as an object, and attempting to make generalizations. The other is an observational approach, like that used by qualitative social researchers, based on interacting with, and sharing learning with, the life-form being studied. She explains this in a deep and personal way:

> *Western science explicitly separates observer and observed. It's rule number one: keep yourself out of the experiment. . . . In the traditional way of learning, instead of conducting a tightly controlled experiment, you interact with the being in question—with that plant, with that stream. And you watch what happens to everything around it too. The idea is to pay attention to the living world as if it were a spider's web: when you touch one part, the whole web responds. Experimental hypothesis-driven science looks just at that one point you touched.*

Her patient, direct observation of nature has led to many surprising findings, such as "Plants certainly do communicate, primarily through exchange of chemical signals. They inform one another of insect and pathogen attacks for example, which allows them to mount defenses."

Detailed observations of nature also have practical value for the very preservation of life. For example, salmon fishermen will not survive very long if they do not learn about the mating and migration habits of salmon and about specific environmental conditions, such as the presence of mosquitos and how they will affect the stock of salmon and where they will be at a particular time.

We can see parallels between the way Kimmerer came to learn about plant life and the way Pierre Nadeau learned sword making. Kimmerer's teachers were the plant life. Pierre learned from a master sword maker, but actually his most important lessons were learned by his body, in the process of working with metal.

Both Kimmerer and Nadeau were learning a science, but it was a practical view of science. Their goal was to deeply learn and understand, not to poke and prod and divide and compartmentalize the subject in order to test generalizations.

Lean Management and Scientific Thinking

At the heart of lean management is scientific thinking. It was not a casual decision for James Womack and Daniel Jones to call their seminal book *Lean Thinking*.[5] They could have called it *Lean Processes*, or *Lean Implementation*, or *Lean Deployment*, but they called it *Lean Thinking*. In the book they tell a story of a Japanese sensei practically being begged and cajoled into coming to America to teach about the Toyota Production System. He was invited to advise a division of Danaher Corporation that made brakes. The sensei at first refused to come, then came to the plant and immediately went back to Japan. He said the Americans were "concrete heads" and would never understand.

After further cajoling by the president, who flew to Japan, he agreed to come back to America and warned that if anyone questioned anything he said or did not comply, he would be on the next plane to Japan. The people at Danaher did everything he asked, and he continued to teach them. He was brutal, for example, using a chainsaw to cut down shelves of inventory and then asking his students to place all the inventory on the floor and spend day and night over the weekend figuring out what to get rid of and how to organize the rest so they could continue manufacturing on Monday. Danaher calls these dramatic displays "kaizen theater," and the company still practices this internally. The point of the theater is to open people up to a new way of thinking, instead of accepting things as they are.

Danaher's business model is to buy underperforming companies and use the Danaher Business System to raise their performance level and profitability. It works. Danaher is very profitable and keeps growing year after year. For example, in 1994 its total sales were $1.29 billion, and by 2014 they reached $19.9 billion. What Danaher's leaders learned was a new way of thinking, and they have used it repeatedly to elevate the performance of companies they purchase.

Taichi Ohno provides some perspective on the deep thinking at the core of the Toyota Way: "The Toyota style is not to create results by working hard. It is a system that says there is no limit to people's creativity. People don't go to Toyota to 'work'; they go there to 'think.'"

From the early days the Toyota Production System was equated with the scientific method. One of Taichi Ohno's star students, Hajime Ohba, explained it this way: "TPS is built on the scientific way of thinking. How do I respond to *this* problem? It is not a toolbox. You must be willing to start small, and learn through trial and error."

If you watch Ohba work, you will see that a project with a new client who desires to learn TPS always starts with a big challenge, but then the work itself focuses on a very small area. A client who wants to start by implementing a future-state value-stream map will be asked instead to start work in one area without spending money. "Let's start small, and learn through trial and error." The reason is that the learner cannot accurately guess at all the problems and appropriate countermeasures entailed in a major transformation of all the things shown on the future-state value-stream map. The client company must discover the value of learning by trial and error and learn that it knows much less than it thinks it knows.

Ohba is like Nadeau's sword master teacher who refused to answer questions if he thought it would encourage the student to think he knew before he actually learned through the body. Ohba refused to show his students in companies the value-stream maps because it would confuse them—"they will not understand." But even worse, they might think they understand.

View of Scientific Thinking Underlying Kata

If lean is based on scientific thinking, and our brains punish us for trying to think slowly and deeply, what are we to do? The answer is practice. Mike Rother describes the improvement kata as "a process of deliberate practice to develop more scientific thinking in groups of people who work together."[6] He is not interested in turning people into scientists for the purpose of developing universal theories. His goal is to develop practical scientific thinking to improve toward a clear vision of what we need to achieve to be successful. Practical scientific thinking is a *life skill*.

The improvement kata pattern is designed to address common weaknesses in how adults respond to problems. This includes observing only superficially and filling in blanks in our understanding by making assumptions without even realizing it. It includes jumping into a waste-elimination mode before clearly understanding our direction. And it includes implementing "solutions" without taking the time to predict what will happen so we can compare the prediction with what actually happens and reflect on what we learned.

Earlier in the book, we introduced the 4P model and called the fourth P problem solving. We do not mean fighting fires or reacting to all the problems we notice. For us problem solving is a deliberate process of learning our way to achieving a clearly defined vision (see Figure 9.2). Ultimately it is a process of continuous learning at the individual level, group level, and organizational level.

We borrowed from Rother in mapping PDCA to the common process of scientific experimentation. In the final analysis the Plan leads to a prediction, or

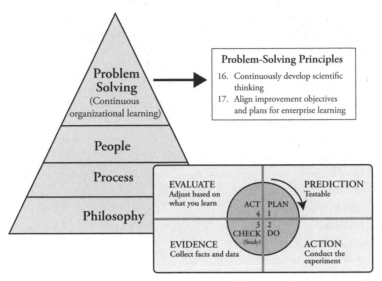

Figure 9.2   Problem-solving principles

hypothesis. The hypothesis is the countermeasure that we expect will move us in the direction of the challenge. It is a hypothesis because we do not assume we know it will work. At this point it is a theory to be tested. The Do means we run the experiment. Let's try it and see what we can learn. As Jeff Bezos notes, it is not an experiment if you know what is going to happen. If you actually know then just do it. The Check (or Study, if the process is PDSA) is when we collect the data and facts to assess what happened. Finally we move to the Act stage, where we evaluate what we learned, which prepares us to plan our next experiment, and the cycle continues.

The starting point is to "continuously develop scientific thinking" of the practical variety. We will consider Toyota's approach to developing scientific thinking and relate this to the improvement kata and coaching kata. As the skills and mindset of scientific thinking mature, the organization is better able to "align improvement objectives and plans for enterprise learning."

PRINCIPLE 16: CONTINUOUSLY DEVELOP SCIENTIFIC THINKING

Managing to Learn Through True A3 Coaching

John Shook was the first foreign national to become a manager for Toyota Motor Company in Japan. He wrote and spoke Japanese and was hired in 1983 as Toyota was preparing to launch NUMMI. At the time TPS was not well documented, and John had to piece together the knowledge to develop training materials to teach the Americans hired for NUMMI. In this unique position John was taught and coached by many of the best in Toyota. He was exposed firsthand to Toyota's unique culture, including the role of A3 reports, a report on one side of an A3-size paper. His first boss emphasized that he needed to learn how to "use the organization" to get anything important accomplished. A3 was one tool to help in using the organization.

There are a variety of types of A3 reports ranging from the highly structured problem-solving story to the very unspecified format for an information story.[7] An example format of a problem-solving A3 is shown in Figure 9.3. This is one I got from Toyota. It is curious that after the Do box there is one box which would include the Check and the Act which leaves little room for documenting results. We are presenting this as a common A3 problem solving format, but there are many variations.

A lot of information can be jammed into a well-constructed A3. In fact, the project plan for NUMMI was on an A3 signed off by vice presidents and cascaded down to department managers who then had to develop their own A3s on how they would support the plan. At each step there was a deliberate and exhaustive process of discussion, debate, and revision after revision. One person was respon-

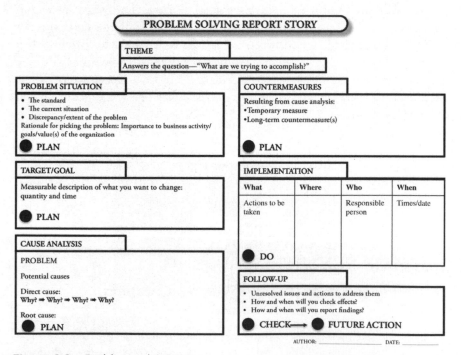

Figure 9.3   Problem-solving A3

sible for each A3, including gathering and using input from appropriate people. *Nemawashi* is the process of seeking information and ideas from many people, often one by one, and the "A3 story" evolves through investigation and synthesis. The A3 is a living document to be used in dialogue with others. Its power is in quick communication with others.

The final A3 is a snapshot of the overall process of planning or solving a problem, but it does not give any insight into the learning process that produced it. To better understand the full story, one would have to view the multiple iterations that got torn up, torn down, and revised and follow the evolution of the writer's thinking, discussions, and experimentation.

The A3 report came to be a hot tool used by lean practitioners outside of Toyota. After all, Toyota was the benchmark and used A3, so lean companies should use A3. When John saw how it was being used by "outsiders," he shuddered. He had gone through many years of training and practice on how to define a problem, how to deeply observe the actual process, how to ask questions, and how to conduct *nemawashi*, while constantly responding to questions and challenges from his various coaches. It was always intense and exhausting—lots of slow thinking. The A3 can be a powerful tool to summarize thinking at the moment and to continue to work through the organization—when this tool is used within the context of coaching by an experienced mentor. But writing an A3 does not somehow transform the writer into an excellent thinker or leader (see Figure 9.4) any more than handing someone a laptop would make him or her a great author.

The thinking and behavior patterns at Toyota are held in their seasoned coaches, not in the A3 tool format

The A3 Tool

The desired pattern of thinking and acting is here

Experienced Mentor

Figure 9.4 Learning A3 thinking requires a seasoned coach; the A3 tool format is not enough

Source: Mike Rother

John Shook wrote *Managing to Learn*[8] with the intention of correcting many misconceptions about the role of the A3. As John writes in the book:

> *I discovered the A3 process of managing to learn firsthand during the nat-*
> *ural course of my work in Toyota City. . . . My colleagues and I wrote A3s*
> *almost daily. We would joke, and lament, that it seemed we would regu-*
> *larly rewrite A3s 10 times or more. We would write and revise them, tear*
> *them up and start over, discuss them and curse them, all as ways of clari-*
> *fying our own thinking, learning from others, informing and teaching oth-*
> *ers, capturing lessons learned, hammering down decisions, and reflecting on*
> *what was going on.*

Managing to Learn tells the story of a young manager, Desi Porter, who is assigned to improve Japanese documentation for a major plant expansion. The last time this was done, there were many problems in the translation causing signifi-cant project delays. He is asked by his boss to develop an A3 for the preliminary plan to address the documentation issue. He did have some experience writing simple problem-solving A3s, but this was a much more complex assignment.

Buckling down he launched into developing an A3 that would get quick approval and impress the boss. This would allow him to then dive into imple-mentation. Desi Porter used the scant information that he already knew to "write the report." This began an odyssey that Porter could not have imagined, as his boss, Ken Sanderson, incessantly questioned everything, driving Porter to the gemba to learn and challenge his thinking about even the smallest detail of the project. He was being mentored in A3 thinking to learn how to "use the organization," not simply write a report.

The learning process began when Desi proudly presented what he thought was his completed A3 to Ken Sanderson. Ken focused in on the goals and targets that were to simplify and standardize the process and reduce costs by 10 percent. Ken wondered why Desi assumed he had to standardize the process. Was that real-ly a main goal or an assumed countermeasure? And how did Desi decide the main goal was cost reduction and come up with a 10 percent target? It seemed that qual-ity of the translation work was the priority.

Desi Porter was flabbergasted by Ken's questions. Of course, he believed he understood the problem and had good ideas on how to solve it. He had learned from his research that in the last project the company had used multiple vendors with vary-ing cost and performance, so it stands to reason this needed to be fixed with a more rigorous selection process. Ken replied rather harshly to Desi's defensive responses:

> *That is all very general and vague. Do you know how the process actually*
> *works? Can you tell me what is causing the problems and delays? What is*
> *actually causing the cost overruns?*

This intensive questioning led Desi Porter to more carefully study the process at the gemba where he discovered most of his preconceptions were wrong. This led to rethinking and rewriting and more and more questioning from Ken. It was not simply an issue of vendor selection for cost reduction. Many of the translation problems originated in the IT system. The bigger issue was the quality of the translation, as the cost of delays was many times more than any savings that might come from a cheaper translating service. The final A3 bears little resemblance to the original. In the process of digging deeper and deeper and being forced to think and rethink, Desi Porter grows immensely as a manager and a thinker. In fact, he can never go back to naively assuming so much when confronted with a new problem.

Desi was beginning a personal transformation in his way of thinking. It would never have even started if his boss had simply accepted his initial A3 or had just made some minor edits. It was the deliberate feedback and challenges by Ken that forced Desi to go back and question his assumptions and approach over and over. Ken had a general picture of the A3 process and what he wanted Desi to learn. We rarely can effectively challenge our own thinking. Desi needed Ken to coach him and in fact needs continued coaching, or his start at scientific thinking will atrophy.

A3 Coaching by the Real Leslie in a Payroll Company

The real Leslie, whom NL Service's lean advisor is modeled after and who was Karyn's first lean mentor, has evolved an approach to developing leaders through A3 that is very much in the spirit of the Toyota Way. Her goal is to change thinking, not simply deliver one-off business results. She does not assume that she can teach people in a classroom and send them off as experts. Here is how she helped one region within a payroll company go from worst to best on key performance indicators through leadership coaching using A3 . . . and then watched them fall backward.

Each month the payroll company's corporate office sent out a report of overall performance by branch. There were a variety of KPIs rolled into one that created that list, with high performers at the top and low performers at the bottom.

The region at the bottom that Leslie worked with had about 500 people in total. The senior leader was the regional manager responsible for 10 branches. Each branch had a branch manager and a service manager, for a total of 10 branch managers and 10 service managers for the region. Each branch also had about 10 customer satisfaction supervisors (approximately 100 in total for the region).

The regional manager had previously been in a different position and had worked closely with Leslie, so he already had experience with lean in his operation. When he moved to the regional manager position, he wanted to incorporate what he had already learned and also continue learning. He also wanted to develop the leaders that reported to him from the branches.

His challenge was to raise the scores in his region, which was in last place overall for KPIs measuring business performance (including customer satisfaction) for the country. The regional manager brought together the branch managers and service managers, and Leslie provided a one-day overview of lean learning. They used a Lego airplane simulation and created "practice" A3s from the exercise.

At the end of the day of lean learning, the regional manager tasked each of the branch and service managers to go back to their branches and create A3s focusing on KPIs with the two biggest gaps. The branch manager and service manager were each responsible for their own A3, with coaching from Leslie and the regional manager. The challenge—a formidable one—was to move from last place into first by the end of the fiscal year.

Figure 9.5 shows the A3 for one branch for one of the two KPIs that it was worst on—single dial resolution. Single dial resolution was measured by three sub-KPIs:

1. **Workable percent.** Percentage of time in the day that the service reps were available to answer customer calls or were talking to customers
2. **Abandoned percent.** Percentage of customers who hung up without the phone being answered or without leaving a message
3. **Speed to answer.** Amount of time from when the phone first rings to when the service rep picks up phone

Leslie held weekly meetings to coach the regional manager. In their coaching sessions, they reviewed the A3s of the branch and service managers that the regional manager would be having one-on-ones with that week.

Each branch and service manager had a biweekly one-on-one in which the regional manager would review and coach them on their A3 and on the rest of the KPIs. For the first quarter, Leslie joined those one-on-ones to evaluate and coach the regional manager on his coaching. As the regional manager's coaching experience and strength increased, Leslie joined less frequently.

During Leslie's weekly coaching sessions with the regional manager, she would ask him questions such as "How do you know that?" and "How can you find out?" as she was teaching him the questions to ask the branch managers and service managers. The regional manager, in his one-on-ones with each branch manager and service manager, was coached by Leslie to ask questions about both process and results for the A3s, such as "Were the results of what you did what you expected? What did you learn?"

These questions focused largely on the KPIs and the progress toward the KPIs and whether the managers were following up. We asked Leslie whether the

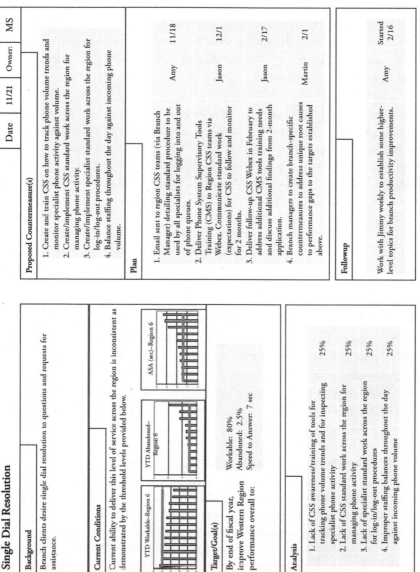

Figure 9.5 Single dial resolution A3 for one branch manager

writers of A3s experimented as the improvement kata would suggest. Leslie explained that she was not teaching the improvement kata, but she coached the learners to develop countermeasures which built on one another. As each countermeasure was put into place, the KPI shifted (or didn't shift). Once the learners saw what happened, the coaching revolved around creating the next countermeasure based on understanding what previously happened. Leslie didn't use the exact word "experiment"; but she did use the term "PDCA cycle." She also taught people to use the word "countermeasure," and not "solution," as the process was iterative and experimental.

The individual branch and service managers were responsible for developing their people by creating a team and coaching the team members through the work on their A3. The regional manager coached this during the biweekly one-on-ones. The branch and service managers were in the beginning stages of learning themselves and did not suddenly become seasoned coaches, but those who took it seriously were on a fast learning curve.

Finally, the regional manager made follow-up calls each month to check on the status of the KPIs. At the end of each month, after the regional KPI results were available, branch and service managers were responsible for updating the status of their A3s—red, yellow, or green based on KPI targets—in preparation for the call.

Approximately four months into the work, the regional manager called the branch managers and service managers together for another day of lean learning, again led by Leslie. This time, the participants included the 100 or so customer service supervisors, and the group redid the Lego simulation, etc. Many of the customer service supervisors had been working on the A3s with their branch and service managers, and so they already had practical experience. Now they would have the "theory" behind it, and they would be expected to take the thinking and start working on A3s at their levels and teaching the frontline team members.

After six months the region was excited to find that its hard work had paid off. It had moved from last place overall to first place overall. It wasn't first in every KPI, so it continued to create A3s for those that still had gaps to target. Until . . .

The regional manager was, yet again, moved to another area. Unfortunately, the new regional manager who took over the leadership of the region didn't have the same interest in lean and didn't continue the coaching and A3 process . . . so . . .

Over the next six months or so, without someone to coach the managers on a continual basis, old habits returned and the branch and service managers stopped using the A3 process . . . and . . .

The region returned to its original position . . . last.

What does this case teach us? We could easily jump to a number of different conclusions:

1. The use of A3 for coaching and learning does not work. After all, it was not sustainable.
2. The whole idea of creating a culture of continuous improvement is not possible in most organizations because it depends on the fragile role of particular leaders.

I would propose a different set of conclusions:

1. **It is fragile, unless . . .** It does seem fair to conclude that if building a learning culture depends on people leading in a certain way, the culture is inherently fragile unless we develop enough of a critical mass of people who deeply learn the way of thinking to survive changes in leaders.
2. **It takes time . . .** Six months certainly was not a lot of time to change the habitual way of thinking and alter the leading style of 100 people. It was not enough time to become a new culture, so when the leader driving it stepped away, it disintegrated fast.
3. **It did get results . . .** As an experiment testing the efficacy of developing people through an A3 process with strong coaching, it was quite impressive. When we perform an experimental intervention, we would like to see that there is a big change from before to after in the treatment group compared with a control group that did not get the intervention. In this case the treatment group went from last to first in a large company compared with the control groups of other regions. This was a convincing result. And the performance of the treatment group falling down when the leadership coaching ended also demonstrates the efficacy of the coaching and learning process. Without that, superior performance ends.

Leslie was working with the opportunities presented to her, which were actually exceptional. It is rare that you start out with so engaged and enlightened a senior leader who provides this opportunity for intensive coaching over a six-month period. Yet even this was not sufficient to create a self-sustaining change in culture. In fact, it can be argued that there is no self-sustaining cultural change—just a culture continually reinforced and rebuilt by passionate leaders.

Managing to Teach: Do We Have the Coaches?

Not all teaching of A3 in real life resembles the intensive coaching that John Shook received or that Leslie was able to provide. Karyn has worked with many organizations and has experienced firsthand the limitations of trying to treat A3 as a classroom training exercise. As Karyn explains:

> Many of the service companies that I've worked with have "lean training groups" that create "training" materials and courses for the internal lean

change agents. Because *Managing to Learn* is such a powerful story, it is often used as the basis of A3 training courses that the lean training groups put together. Having attended a number of these classes in different organizations, I've often been quite surprised at how the rigorous people-development process described in *Managing to Learn* gets lost in translation in the classes. Here is how most of these classes go:

Before the class, all the attendees are asked to "choose a problem to bring to class" . . . any problem they want. Of course, in *Managing to Learn*, Desi Porter doesn't pick his own problem to work on; Ken Sanderson assigns it to him.

When I go to class, I usually find that the "coaching" part of this is going to be "peer to peer" only. The people attending the class—who have absolutely no more knowledge or skill than each other—are going to be practicing coaching each other—in groups. As the class mechanically goes over each section of the A3, class participants take turns trying to "coach" each other through their problems. Unfortunately, since they don't have deep experience coaching, or understanding of the business conditions of the problems, it's usually just a disaster . . . what else could it be?

To add to the problems, these classes are often held in a central training facility that the participants must all travel to. How are the participants going to work on their A3s without being able to go to the gemba and see? The result is that the participants sit around conference tables in the training room and discuss "assumptions" they have. This only serves to reinforce the behavior of sitting around in conference rooms discussing assumptions.

Classes wrap up with the instructor tasking the students to "please finish the A3" when they go home. Of course there is usually no expectation that they will have coaching from their manager or anyone else from the lean training group as it will take too much time.

I often hear students as they leave say things like, "Now we really have a much better understanding of A3 thinking and we'll be able to use A3s to solve problems."

A3s don't solve problems . . .

Now in all fairness, Karyn is not saying that the trainers did a bad job on organizing the class or on delivery. The students appreciated the classes because they were well done. But sitting in a conference room, working with fake data, being coached by other beginners, and then going off with no coaching to apply what you have learned is far from the experience John Shook had in Japan . . . like night-and-day difference. Unfortunately Karyn's experience is all too typical. We acquaint people with the tools and somehow expect the tool itself to make people into great problem solvers.

The A3 is a Toyota tool that the company uses in the context of corrective coaching by an experienced mentor. When A3 gets used in other organizations without this skilled coaching, the probability of A3 developing systematic, scientific thinking and acting is low. The improvement kata and coaching kata provide the structure for bringing novices to a basic level of competence.

The Improvement Kata and Coaching Kata in Services: Sales Example from Dunning Toyota

Dunning Toyota is a family-owned and -operated business that has been part of the greater Ann Arbor community for more than 40 years. One might assume that it follows all the principles of the Toyota Production System and the Toyota Way, but as an independent business it only began learning this from Toyota recently through a pilot project to create express maintenance—dedicating repair bays for rapid turnaround, routine service like oil and tire changes. The company already had strong values to support its customers and respect people, but this had not translated into managers and team members trained in continuous improvement.

In 2014 Dunning Toyota agreed to participate as a host site for a team of students in my graduate course on lean thinking. The students in class, and Dunning Toyota managers at the same time, practiced the improvement kata and coaching kata. Dunning participated again in 2015 and then in 2016, expanding the number of projects and managers trained. One of the 2016 projects focused on the sales process.[9] As we all know, sales is not a routine process and will vary with each customer. Yet we will see that it is still a process that can be improved with impressive results. Let's walk through the steps of the improvement kata using the sales process example.

1. **Direction.** Dunning's challenge was "Number 1 in Michigan." The vision was to become number one in Michigan in new car sales in three years. This was of course too big a challenge for the student group to take on in one semester, but I always advise companies to select a big challenge and then begin learning the improvement kata focused on one part of the value stream with its own challenge. Dunning had experience with the kata, but not in sales. It considered the overall value streams of different customers purchasing cars and decided to focus on what is often the first stage in sales, the phone call to the dealership. The challenge for this process became "making every phone call count."

2. **Current condition.** This turned out to be a much bigger part of the improvement project than anyone would have imagined. The general sales manager,

Lowell Dunning was leading the activity and exclaimed, "I thought we would just knock off the current-state analysis, but the more we dug in, the more we realized we had no idea what the condition of the process was!"

The dealership had data from new CRM (customer relations management) software and was quite proud of this relatively new system it had purchased. But it soon discovered it was garbage in, garbage out. There were serious problems with data quality because of very basic issues like no common definition of concepts. For example, the business was interested in turning "fresh calls" into sales but there was no common definition of a fresh call. If a husband calls in after his wife had previously purchased a car, is he a fresh call or a referral?

When the process was documented, it became clear that there were a number of handoffs among people all entering data into the CRM. The call came into a receptionist, who entered some data and handed the customer over to a salesperson, who entered some data and handed off the customer to a sales manager, and then the customer might call back any of these people. The result was often inconsistent information or maybe missing information, as one party thought the other had taken care of it.

For the focus on "making every phone call count," the sales management team needed accurate measures of the process, which required that all participants use a consistent approach to entering data. The management team chose two metrics for "making every phone call count" and needed to establish an accurate baseline for comparison. The management team, with my students' support, spent a lot of time on measurements of the current condition and found the following:

- **Fresh calls to appointments.** March 16–22: of 39 fresh phone-ins, 24 appointments were made (61 percent).
- **Appointments to actual visits.** March 23–29: of 30 appointments made by phone, 14 led to visits (47 percent).

3. **First target condition.** The process of making every phone call count was broken into two stages: converting calls to appointments and converting appointment to visits. The first target condition was to be achieved in one week: convert 70 percent of phone calls into appointments to visit the dealership, based on a common process and definition of terms, and achieve accurate input of data in CRM.

   Obstacles to the first target condition:
   - Differing definitions of key terms
   - Variation in how people are trained
   - Customers who do not commit to a specific time

4. **Experiments.** The PDCA cycles for the first target condition are summarized in Figure 9.6. The team first took on the obstacle that there was

Target Condition 1: Achieve 70 percent conversion of fresh phone-ins to appointments with a common process and definitions of key terms and accurate date in CRM

PDCA CYCLES RECORD *(Each row = one experiment)*

| | **Process:** Convert phone-ins to appointments | | |
| | **Learner:** | **Coach:** | |

Obstacle 1: Variation in how people are trained			
Date, step, & metric	**What do you expect?**	**What happened**	**What we learned**
Create training document in less than 1 week	Training document would clarify process and definitions	Created one-page document and salespeople used it	A one-page document can be easy to create and very useful
Obstacle 2: Customers who do not commit to a specific time			
Train to set up dummy time in CRM with a note	Increase appointments for those without specific time	Appointments increased from 61 to 71%	Even a simple note can help. Easier to change system than change customers

Do a Coaching Cycle
Conduct the Experiment

Figure 9.6 Dunning Toyota sales process experiments to achieve the first target condition

"variation in how people are trained." The sales manager agreed to put together a simple, one-page sheet to define key terms and specify how to enter data into the CRM. He sat down and went through the information on the sheet with each of the CRM users. It worked and only took one week to complete. Each person referred to it when taking phone calls. Everyone concluded that it was simple to follow and useful as a reference.

The second obstacle addressed was "customers who do not commit to a specific time." Oh, those customers are always messing things up! The team analyzed the problem and realized the problem was in the CRM system. The system required the user to select a specific appointment time, or else it would record that no appointment was made and mess up metrics on percentage of calls converted to appointments. The team figured out how to get around the system and trained users on how to set up dummy appointments when the customer did not want to commit to a specific time. This immediately increased appointments made from 61 to 71 percent, achieving the first target condition. More important, the team realized that there is no benefit to blaming the customer, and it is more productive to find something to improve in the system that supports the customer. The team was excited. Two experiments, two successes!

5. **Second target condition.** One week out: Convert 70 percent of appointments into actual visits to the dealership with all visits accurately recorded on CRM.

   Obstacles to the second target condition:
   - Salesperson had only 30 minutes from scheduled appointment to click button, or CRM would record as missed.
   - No reliable way to confirm visit with customer on morning of appointment (75 percent of calls go to voice mail).

6. **Experiments.** The PDCA cycles for the second target condition are summarized in Figure 9.7. The team first took on the obstacle that the "salesperson had only 30 minutes from scheduled appointment to click button, or CRM would record as missed." That is, if the user does not push a button within 30 minutes, the system records the customer as a no-show. In reality some customers show up late, beyond the 30-minute window. A simple fix was to increase the buffer time to 90 minutes. Implementing the fix, though, was not simple since nobody at Dunning had made changes in system settings like this before. Fortunately, my students figured it out. The change had an immediate effect, increasing visits recorded from 47 to 54 percent. The Dunning folks realized that not all automation is productive. They needed to be in control of the system, not let the system control them.

Target Condition 2: Achieve 70 percent conversion of appointments made to dealership visits with all visits accurately recorded on CRM.

PDCA CYCLES RECORD (Each row = one experiment)

Process: Convert appointments to visits

Learner: ___ **Coach:** ___

Obstacle	Date, step, & metric	What do you expect?	Do a Coaching Cycle / Conduct the Experiment — What happened	What we learned
Obstacle 1: Records as no-show 30 mins after scheduled appointment				
	3. Change CRM setting to allow 90 minutes from appointment	More accurate data would show increase in visits as a percentage of appointments	Visits recorded went from 47 to 54 percent	Automation of system can create problems if does not fit the process
Obstacle 2: No reliable way to confirm visit with customer on morning of visit				
	4. 48-hour system alert and get customer-preferred method of contact	More accurate data would show increase in visits as a percentage of appointments	Appointments increased from 54 to 63 percent, and customers appreciated thoughtfulness	Customization is critical in the service industry

Figure 9.7 Dunning Toyota sales process experiments to achieve the second target condition

The second experiment addressed the obstacle of "no reliable way to confirm visit with customer on morning of visit." The system would ping the receptionist the morning of the visit to remind her that the appointment was coming up. She would in turn call to remind the customer but often the call would go to voice mail. It was too late to do anything about it. Again a simple system change addressed the problem. The system was reset to remind the receptionist 48 hours in advance. The staff also asked the customers how they preferred to be contacted—phone, text, or e-mail? This increased the rate of getting customers into the store from 54 to 63 percent, and some customers commented that Dunning was very efficient and they appreciated that the staff was courteous enough to ask for their preferred communication method.

Dunning Toyota Results and Reflection

As the improvement process progressed, there was a steady increase in calls turning into appointments, visits, and ultimately sales. There was an increase of 27 percent in the calls leading to appointments and a whopping 90 percent increase in appointments leading to visits to the dealership.

Of course, the bottom line is sales. In February 2016, 12 percent of fresh calls were converted to sales. By March, the conversion rate rose to 16 percent, and by April, a solid 22 percent of fresh calls resulted in sales.

There was also a great deal that was learned. Dunning Toyota learned the value of continuous improvement starting with understanding the current condition. When the CRM was first installed, Lowell Dunning was excited about what it did for the business and assumed the process of entering data and using it effectively was just fine. When Lowell and his staff took a close look at the current condition, they found they were wrong on both counts. The process was not well developed, it varied from person to person, and poor data quality meant the CRM was not as effective as they assumed. This new understanding led immediately to experiments that dramatically improved data integrity and the goal of the system, which was to get customers into the showroom and increase sales. Among the lessons from the experiments:

1. Understanding the current condition with reliable and useful metrics is critical to guiding improvement.
2. Technology can support people and a good process, but only if it is effectively used.
3. Technology off the shelf requires continuous improvement to maximize its effectiveness.
4. When it appears that the problem is the customer, one should look carefully at internal systems and processes for improvement.

5. Experimenting by changing one factor at a time leads to deep understanding of how to improve the process.

An astute observation from my students about what they learned borrowed a quote from educational reformer John Dewey: "We do not learn from experience. We learn from reflecting on experience." They also learned a good deal about lean in sales. They learned that applying generic lean solutions to sales would be a lot of wasted effort, but rather they needed to systematically work toward a challenge, experimenting at each step. They intentionally avoided setting a goal that involved improving how salespeople sold. First, the salespeople were already well trained, and this did not appear to be the bottleneck. Second, this would be a very difficult project for those first learning the improvement kata. Therefore they focused on the systems and processes supporting the salespeople.

The students also got insight about the role of the consultant. They provided coaching support for the core team led by the senior sales executive, but the ownership and ideas came from the Dunning team. This led to a great deal of learning by the Dunning team and a process of learning that is continuing beyond the student project. Among other benefits the salespeople involved and the receptionist felt good about being involved and using their brains to improve the sales process. The receptionist was ecstatic about her involvement because usually "nobody pays attention to the receptionist." With the various experiences Dunning had with my student projects, it now has assigned all managers to lead improvement activities using the kata.

One disappointment to the students was how easily each experiment accomplished the intended goal and ultimately the target conditions. They referred to a graphic by Rother displaying three zones of target setting—apparent certainty, learning zone, and danger zone (see Figure 9.8). The Dunning project was mostly in the

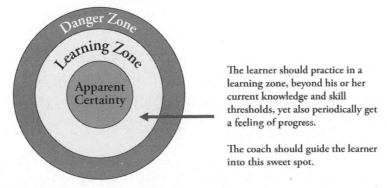

The learner should practice in a learning zone, beyond his or her current knowledge and skill thresholds, yet also periodically get a feeling of progress.

The coach should guide the learner into this sweet spot.

Figure 9.8   Three zones of challenge for the learner
Source: Mike Rother

zone of apparent certainty. This is not challenging enough to push the learners beyond their current knowledge threshold, and the lack of challenge limits enthusiasm and learning. This is the responsibility of the coach, and in this case I did not coach the new learners sufficiently to push them beyond their comfort zone.

Improvement Kata Pattern and What Each Step Intends to Teach

A mantra of the improvement kata could be "It is all about practicing the pattern." The IK is designed to teach a meta-skill, which becomes a habitual pattern of how we think and act. Here is one useful explanation of a meta-skill:[10]

> *A meta-skill is a kernel of pragmatic knowledge that applies to a wide variety of circumstances including ones you have never directly experienced before. Because meta-skills are portable across many environments, they are extremely valuable. . . .*

The meta-skill taught by practicing the routines of the IK is a pattern of scientifically approaching how to navigate your way through obstacles in the direction of a challenge. It applies to the pursuit of virtually any challenge. We saw for example how it was used effectively to improve the sales process at Dunning. Typically we hear statements about how lean does not apply to us because our work is not repetitive, manual tasks. We do not hear that once people get started down the path of the improvement kata. They are focused on improving their process, not trying to imitate someone else's very different process. As the improvement pattern starts to become a habit, it changes the thinking of people to a new way of approaching any goal.

Consider the life-changing experience of Tyson Ortiz and his wife when they discovered their newborn son had a very rare condition, half a heart. Tyson was being trained in the improvement kata at work and almost naturally began to use the pattern to save his son's life. Tyson and his wife succeeded, and their son lived to get a successful heart transplant when he turned three, as you will read below.

HOW WE FOLLOWED THE IMPROVEMENT KATA PATTERN TO SAVE OUR SON'S LIFE

By Tyson Ortiz

My wife Sarah and I were devastated to learn that our newborn son, Michael, would be born with a heart defect so severe that roughly half of children affected do not live to kindergarten. Michael had an especially serious form, the complete absence of the left-side chambers of the heart. We were told that in the best case, he would need three open-heart surgeries in the first few years of life to allow him to survive with his single-ventricle heart. Sarah and I spent weeks in surreal disbelief, with no idea how we would face our future.

Fortunately, this discovery came as I was making a career transition to begin practicing Lean. Specifically, my work would involve learning about Toyota Kata from my manager who is an exceptional scientific thinker. Sarah and I quickly concluded that we could not passively assume the healthcare system would provide the best possible care for our son and we needed to be proactive to give him the best chance of a quality life. As I learned about Toyota Kata, I naturally began using the scientific method as Sarah and I engaged in the daunting effort of managing our child's care.

Today (May 2016) our son, Michael, is three years old. He's happy, active, and very smart—an absolute treasure for our family. Across five open-heart surgeries and over a dozen procedures totaling several months spent inpatient, with daily effort Sarah and I have sought to actively manage his care. The big turning point was last December. We seem to have guessed correctly (despite the doubts of the experts) about the benefits of a heart transplant, which has changed all of our lives. We continue to struggle a bit with feeding and some anomalies, but the big picture has changed dramatically with the new heart (which continues to work great). He's got endless energy and has blossomed into a full-blown "threenager."

What got us through this was the use of the scientific method. We had a clear challenge to get Michael to the point that he lived a healthy life into old age and had a normal childhood growing up. We then studied every decision, independent of doctors' recommendations, looking deeply at Michael's current condition at the time, the alternatives the medical knowledge to that point provided, and then ran a series of experiments for each of our target conditions. We did not think about it precisely in these terms but this is what we did.

For example, one of the major obstacles in Michael's life has been persistent feeding intolerance, hindering his weight gain despite starting life with a feeding tube. His weight gain first stalled around three months of age, with an open-heart surgery planned just three months out. The medical team recommended various standard protocols including a dangerous medication and a drastic surgery. After extensive discussion we found that these solutions were based on questionable assumptions. We slowed down the medical staff jumping to these conclusions, and collaborated with them to experiment with alternative approaches. Through daily effort and teamwork we were able to iteratively modify Michael's feeding regimen to safely test suspected factors behind the intolerance. In this way we discovered ways to help him gain weight and he did well in his second surgery, recovering quickly despite the fact that the surgery was done a full month earlier than planned.

When his weight gain stalled again about one year later, the medical team recommended surgery to transition from the nasogastric tube originally implanted to a more permanent gastronomy tube. However, again we felt that the underlying assumptions were unsound, and rather than cement his tube dependency we discussed the possibility of first pursuing a transition to oral feeding. Although the team agreed that this was the ideal outcome, they expressed doubt that it could happen. With the improvement kata mindset driving us, we persisted, and they somewhat grudgingly agreed to let us try. After several challenging weeks of Sarah's intense daily effort, including trial of countless small changes that seemed to hold potential, Michael was tube-free and gaining weight with oral feeding at a rate at least double the best he'd ever gained with tube feeding. As an unexpected benefit, this effort also saw Michael enter a developmental explosion in which he quickly grew from a somewhat immobile baby to a walking, talking, trouble-making toddler.

The intimacy of working so closely with Michael in managing his care has created a situational awareness that often exceeds that of his clinicians. His second surgery occurred a month earlier than planned because of various qualitative and quantitative shifts we noticed at home, largely invisible to his cardiologist despite weekly clinic visits. A year later, we began noticing concerning changes and asked the team for help understanding them. After several weeks of our insisting there was a problem, finally an anomaly was discovered—and largely written off. We continued to see degradation that worried us—but with which the medical team was fairly unimpressed—so we continued to push for deeper understanding. Four months after we began noticing changes, a potentially serious and unexpected complication was discovered that explained our observations.

In response the medical team put forth a surgical plan; however, by that time we had developed a fairly sophisticated mental model of Michael's physiology and an understanding of his condition that led us to question the recommendation. We felt that the proposed surgery was likely to fail, and even if successful, carried unacceptable risk down the road. Reaching out to two of the top surgical centers in the country for second opinions, our suspicions were supported and one of the centers offered a surgical plan that seemed to offer more promise.

Our health plan flatly refused to refer us for the preferred treatment, as it was offered by an uncontracted center on the opposite side of the country. Any other path that we could see to obtain this treatment required accepting serious unwanted consequences. Still, Sarah and I, inspired by our previous successes, spent the next month urgently exploring possibilities and avoiding the urge to give up and settle for an inferior plan. Literally one day before our cross-country flight a key discovery was made that revealed a hidden path, enabling us to get Michael the preferred treatment and get it paid for. The surgical plan was far superior to what the original physicians had proposed and it turned him around.

Personally working with Sarah and Michael has been the most fulfilling part of my life so far. After 15 months as a full-time dad working to save Michael, I started a new job as Lean Champion at a medical device company that makes ventricular assist devices to recover failing hearts. Ironic?

We should recognize that the underlying pattern of the IK makes assumptions about the elements and sequence of an effective improvement process. It is trying to teach good habits and in the process defines what good habits are. Another representation of the pattern of the IK is shown in Figure 9.9, and our experience is that people find the steps intuitive and logical. We will walk through each step and describe what it intends to teach (summarized in Figure 9.10):

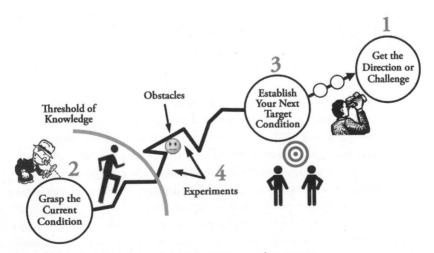

Figure 9.9   Another view of the improvement kata pattern
Source: Mike Rother

Kata step	What are the skills the learner develops?
Direction/challenge	• See improvement efforts as part of a larger whole
Current condition	• Systematically using direct observation and data to understand current operating patterns
Target conditions	• Set one interim goal at a time on the way to a bigger challenge • Envisioning a future operating pattern that is predicted to lead to desired outcomes • Developing both process and outcome measures
Obstacles	• Understanding the limits of our ability to "find the root cause"
Experiments (PDCA)	• Viewing each step as an experiment • Comparing recorded expectations with reality • Understanding the limits of assumptions • One experiment builds on learning from the last one • Internalizing the value of learning at the gemba

Figure 9.10   Core skills taught in improvement kata

1. **Direction/challenge.** How do my improvement activities contribute to a larger goal that matters to the organization? How do I know what problems to pay attention to and which are lower priority? We discussed strategy and purpose in Chapter 3 as part of the philosophy of the organization. Clarifying the organization's purpose and defining a clear and distinctive strategy are critical skills to learn. Creating challenge statements that motivate us and help us achieve our purpose, and are consistent with our strategy, is another vital skill set that must be developed. We can think of challenge with the sentence "Wouldn't it be great if . . . ?" What would be a difference maker? What could you provide your customer that would distinguish you from the competition for years to come?

2. **Current condition.** Fancy whiz-kid manipulation of data is not enough. Ohno admonished us to learn to deeply observe at the gemba without preconceptions. What is really going on? The more deeply that we observe, the more that current operating patterns, or routines, become clear.

3. **Next target condition and obstacles.** The key word is "next." It is not the final target condition, but the next one in the near term on the way to the longer-term challenge. Most people find it pretty easy to state an outcome they desire on key performance indicators. Few are good at defining the operating pattern that they believe will help achieve the outcome. Think of traveling in a time machine to a certain future date (say three weeks out) and describe what you expect to see as the operating pattern and outcomes. Then ask what obstacles stand between where you are and where you want to be.

4. **Experiments.** This is where Plan-Do-Check-Act comes together as a series of rapid learning cycles. The fun part is fast thinking to brainstorm possible countermeasures and then "just doing it!" The slow thinking part is explicitly stating what you expect to happen before you run the experiment and then after the experiment reflecting on what happened and what you learned. We find that people do not naturally do the slow thinking without good coaching.

Comparing the Underlying Improvement Model of A3 and IK

Managing to Learn teaches us that the intended role of the A3 is as a living document that is rewritten and torn up many times as the student is being coached. The underlying model of improvement at Toyota is very similar to the improvement kata, which is not a surprise since the IK was, in part, modeled after what Rother observed from top Toyota coaches.

On the other hand, if we take the perspective of a novice learning to improve and we look at the A3 problem-solving story, we can infer some differences in the pattern compared with the IK. We have summarized the similarities and differences in Figure 9.11.

1. **Direction/challenge.** The A3 starts with the background. This could be in the form of a challenge statement, but this is not as explicit in the methodology as it is in the IK.

2. **Current condition.** We typically see in A3 reports the current condition expressed as the baseline on KPIs. These KPIs might include both outcome metrics and process metrics, or they might not. The small space of the A3, and the desire to use graphics, leads to charting a few metrics. The IK storyboard, by contrast includes a whole column for current condition analysis and explicitly asks the learner to look for both outcome metrics and operating patterns.

3. **Next target condition and obstacles.** The A3 asks for the overall desired project results, but it does not emphasize setting a series of "target conditions" one by one that include outcome metrics and desired operating patterns. Nor does it explicitly suggest an iterative approach to identifying the next target condition—and the next and the next.

   A core assumption of A3 thinking is that it is important to find the root cause. Ask why many times, and keep digging until you find the root cause. The IK makes the almost blasphemous assumption that it is not realistic or necessary to find the single root cause. Instead brainstorm "obstacles," and pick one at a time to overcome through experimentation. As you experiment, you will discover which obstacles are more important to overcome.

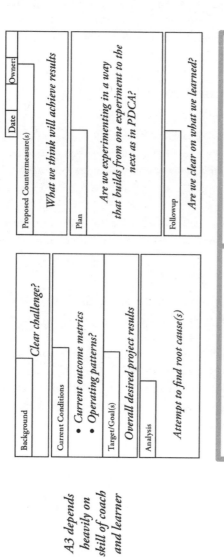

Background   Date | Owner:

Proposed Countermeasure(s)

Clear challenge?   *What we think will achieve results*

Current Conditions
  • *Current outcome metrics*
  • *Operating patterns?*   Plan

Target/Goal(s)   *Are we experimenting in a way*
Overall desired project results   *that builds from one experiment to the*
                                                       next as in PDCA?

Analysis   Followup

Attempt to find root cause(s)   *Are we clear on what we learned?*

*A3 depends
heavily on
skill of coach
and learner*

Focus Process: *Nested Levels*	Challenge: *Overall Direction*	

Target Condition
Achieve by:
	Current Condition	**PDCA Cycles Record**
		Each Experiment:
		  Plan
		  Expectation
		  Actual Result
		  Learning

Next Interim Goal: • Outcome metrics • Desired operating patterns	*Actual Condition:* • Outcome metrics • Operating patterns	**Obstacles Parking Lot** *Evolving list of obstacles that are experimented against one by one*

*Improvement
kata has more
built-in
structure but
also depends on
coaching skill*

Figure 9.11   Underlying improvement process of A3 compared with IK

4. **Experiments.** A3 is not explicit about iterative learning through a series of experiments. The learner seems encouraged to identify all the countermeasures and to schedule their implementation, which the IK explicitly avoids. There is no clear pattern of PDCA cycles with predictions and reflection for each cycle in A3. By contrast, the IK's PDCA cycles record explicitly calls for one experiment at a time, in each case recording expected results, actual results, and what was learned.

One way to think about the improvement kata is by returning to its purpose—to provide starter practice routines to develop positive habits for learning to improve to meet a challenge. In the learning phase it is important to document each step so it is clear to the learners as they are coached. The kata storyboard does this well.

The A3 is a way to document something on one side of one piece of paper to summarize the logical thought process. A good A3 tells a story, whether it is a problem-solving story, a proposal story, or a story presenting the status of a project. Think of the A3 as a snapshot at any point in the improvement process, or a summary at the end, that gives a picture of the whole and is a useful communication vehicle. The kata storyboard is a way of documenting each step of the learning pattern as the project unfolds, and also provides a forum for the coach to keep the student focused on the correct pattern (see Figure 9.12).

The A3, as it is used to train people at Toyota, and the improvement kata/coaching kata (IK/CK) are aimed at the same purpose: developing scientific

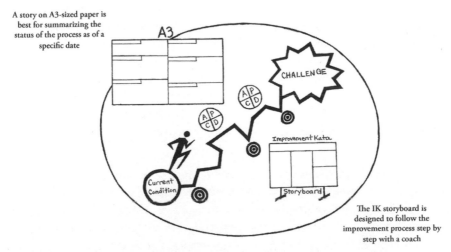

A story on A3-sized paper is best for summarizing the status of the process as of a specific date

The IK storyboard is designed to follow the improvement process step by step with a coach

Figure 9.12 The A3 documents the whole process, whereas the IK storyboard documents each step of the process

thinking skills (achieving clarity of objective, conducting experiments, striving based on facts and data).

The A3 *alone* is more of a summary of a problem-solving process. If used correctly, the learner is going through it with coaching, and hence practice, at every step. At Toyota the coaching is less structured than the kata, and it is not necessarily daily. There is no formal coaching protocol and no protocol for daily practice. It is up to the coach to determine the frequency and approach. This means the A3 requires a higher level of coaching skill.

The improvement kata and coaching kata make this process more explicit, teachable, and transferable, especially for beginning learners. The purpose of the IK and CK is to systematize the practice—as in sports and music—that's more implicit in Toyota's already-strong culture of improvement. Practicing the routines of the improvement kata and coaching kata teaches foundational thinking that makes the A3 effective at Toyota.

Creating Your Own Approach

While the IK is a great approach for beginners, as you mature, you should develop your own approach to improvement that still maintains the high-level pattern. That's the point of the improvement kata approach. Mike Rother even calls the practice routines of the improvement kata "starter kata." One experienced group of coaches used elements of the kata, but developed their own approach to teaching Michigan physician practices to improve their processes.

Blue Cross Blue Shield of Michigan funded a program called the Lean Collaborative Process Initiative (lean CPI), run out of University of Michigan, to help physician practices increase their focus on preventative healthcare. Healthcare reimbursement, particularly from Medicare-Medicaid, is increasingly tied to measurement of quality of care. One element of this is to make full payments contingent on regular screening for early detection of serious diseases. Physician practices are often not very good at this and have a strong incentive to learn how to improve.

Whitney Walters leads the center out of University of Michigan. She describes the challenge these small organizations have, which lack the staff for extensive measurement:

> *The targets are constantly going up and their processes have to keep getting better. There are so many things being measured that it is becoming difficult for the physician organization to really manage that. They are accustomed to relying on state-provided outcome measures, which are typically sixty days lagging. So you are not getting anything right away that is telling you whether this process is getting better. If I am working on colorectal screening in my office today, how do I know at the end of today how well I performed? So they*

are looking at their calendars at the end of the day and highlighting those over
50 and checking: Did we ask them for a screen? Did we schedule them for a
screen? Did they get the screen?

Whitney's group was fortunate to have funding for six months just to develop
and pilot the approach. The general evolution was to start with a very rigorous and
complex process and repeatedly simplify it as they practiced and learned. For
example, the group members began with an approach they were trained on—
using value-stream mapping. They spent a lot of time tracking the patient, or in
some cases the test, through the current-state value stream and then developing a
desired future-state map. As Whitney explains:

> *We were very by the book when we got started. And what we found out was*
> *that they just needed to get the gist of what is happening and what is going*
> *on in each role. So now we have them pick a type of patient. So for one of the*
> *teams they are looking at well visits, so it is going to be someone coming in for*
> *a well-patient physical. It is really loose. They do not need precise measures.*
> *It is ranges, like how long does it take the patient to check in? 30 seconds to*
> *5 minutes. We had spent a lot of time getting really specific about those things*
> *and found that there wasn't a lot of return on that.*

Whitney's group developed an approach similar to the A3 method Leslie
used, but the group members put the information on whiteboards. They found
that however much they simplified a step, they needed to simplify it further to be
used by office managers and nurses who did not have experience documenting
processes and measuring things.

The process started with high-level mapping to see the current state and
develop a vision of the future state—the direction. Then the improvement team
broke down the problem setting a series of goals and began to measure the current
condition using run charts, measuring outcomes and process, cause and effect dia-
grams, and using simple forms for Pareto analysis of the relative frequency of different causes. They intentionally talked about targets, rather than target conditions, as they found the office managers and nurses found the concept of target
condition confusing. At first they had difficulty getting the staff to feel comfortable experimenting. They added the PDCA cycles record and the coaching kata
and they could barely slow them down to experiment on one change at a time. It
worked, especially the experimentation, unleashing creativity and energy among
the office managers and staff. Experimenting took off and percent of people
receiving screening went steadily up.

Their largest client was a company with many physician offices, the Bronson
Healthcare Group of over 7,800 employees. The client had gone through an earlier phase of lean and designed a standard KPI board and deployed daily manage-

ment boards everywhere with little coaching. But that did not meet Bronson's objectives. When the people at Bronson worked with Whitney's organization, engagement and results went up dramatically, so Bronson replaced the standard boards with the kata approach.

The overall UM model is a series of three learning cycles, each 16 weeks long, with initial training, then Plan-Do-Study-Act coaching sessions, then monthly shared learning meetings. This at first seemed daunting to those at Bronson, but after the first of the three learning waves, the results were so compelling and enthusiasm so high that the most senior leadership asked to be trained. Dr. Elizabeth Warner led the effort inside Bronson, and she explained what happened:

> Relatively early in the 2nd wave of training sessions, one of the directors stated, "I am not sure how to best support this work, what kind of training do I need?" This prompted an entirely new curriculum that was developed with University of Michigan, and tested as lean leader training. This was piloted with 6 leaders including the COO of Bronson Methodist Hospital, Vice President of Physician Development, Medical Director of Continuous Improvement Support, System Director of Continuous Improvement Support, and the System Director of Center for Learning. The impact of this training was immense, providing learners the opportunity to practice humility, self-discovery, and personal willingness to change.

The experience changed Dr. Warner's view of improvement approaches—and in fact, the opportunities within our healthcare systems:

> As a physician, being able to look at a process, with a process to really see the patient's experience, was humbling. To see the confounding variation in our current processes, the elaborate strategies (work-arounds) that we had created, usually for provider-centric processes, and legacy processes and systems which never have been challenged prior to this context because "that's how we do things" was a goldmine of improvement opportunities. It solidified my commitment to this methodology for life. The American healthcare system is so broken, and I believe that lean thinking, and the principles which can build and drive positive behaviors, will help us rebuild it.

The Role of Coaching in Improvement

I gave a talk and was asked how important coaching is for effective development of problem-solving skills. I answered that a tiny percentage of people can teach themselves basic skills with a book, whether it is playing a musical instrument, learning to bake, or learning to do basic home improvement. For the more than 95 percent of the rest of us, we need someone to teach us, on the job, providing corrective feedback. Without that, we will run out of steam and stop learning, or we will continue to practice the wrong thing, developing bad habits. It is that simple.

The coach and learner roles are not as explicit in A3 thinking, though clearly that is the intent. There is no explicit coaching kata in the A3, though Toyota has worked to address this internally through OJD training.

What we repeatedly see outside of Toyota is that A3 is introduced in a course and then students are on their own with little or no coaching. Does this in fact lead to people development? In our experience, no.

Without effective coaching any method becomes a blunt tool wielded without skill. Probably the best situation is one-on-one mentoring from the very best, such as learning to make swords from a master or being taught by Ohno on the shop floor. Master coaches will adjust their methods based on the student and the situation at the moment. With novice to intermediate coaches, there is an important role for a more structured approach such as the kata. But these simple kata do not compensate for impatience, lack of persistence, lackadaisical coaching to meet the corporate mandate, etc. Bad or no coaching leads to little learning and skill development.

PRINCIPLE 17: ALIGN IMPROVEMENT OBJECTIVES AND PLANS FOR ENTERPRISE LEARNING

We have learned a good deal about how to coach continuous improvement. Continuous improvement is a skill and mindset of always searching for something better, not randomly, but with a clear direction guiding the search.

An effective search follows a defined meta-pattern. When the direction is clear, we open our mind to the reality of our current condition. Then we do not plan endlessly to imagine the single best solution, and we do not plot a detailed road map to get from here to there. We define a short-term target condition that includes what we want operating patterns to look like and what outcomes we want by a certain near-term date. At that point we think about the obstacles that will get in our way. And finally we start testing countermeasures to overcome the obstacles and reach our next target condition. When we have reached it, we look back to reflect on what we learned and where we now are, then set our next target condition.

Think of climbing a steep mountain, and the overall task seems overwhelming. But we set the next stake a certain distance up, struggle to get there, then reflect on what we learned about the mountain and look ahead to further obstacles and our next step to overcome them. We cannot possibly anticipate in advance all the obstacles we will face. We have to face them one by one. At some point we are on the top of the mountain, and then we search out another mountain to climb.

Now that we understand the skills that can help us strive toward a challenge, we can ask, "How do we identify the challenge?" In fact, the challenge will be different for different people in different departments and positions. Therefore we need nested challenges that connect from the very top of the organization to all its parts. That is the role of what in Japanese is called hoshin kanri and in the West is often called policy deployment.

Hoshin Kanri at Toyota

Hoshin kanri was first experimented with in Toyota in 1961 as part of a total quality management program. President Eiji Toyoda identified the need to modernize Toyota's management practices in order to move from a provider of automobiles inside Japan to a global company. He identified two specific needs:

- The need for top management to clarify targets (especially quality) and engage employees
- A management system that promoted cross-functional cooperation

A challenge to mobilize the organization was to win the highly coveted Deming Prize for quality in three years. In 1965 Toyota won the Deming Prize. By 1972, after a decade of continuous improvement, Toyota matured hoshin kanri so that it is now a standard annual practice throughout the company globally.

Toyota works on a fiscal-year calendar from April 1 to March 31. At the beginning of January the company president makes an important speech reflecting on the last year and laying out the vision of the board of directors for the coming year. He enunciates three to five high-level challenges for the year. This leads to a flurry of activity, as these somewhat abstract challenges cascade down through the organization to concrete plans level by level.

For example, the global executive vice presidents of each function, such as sales, are asked what the challenges mean for their organization. How will they support the president's objectives? What is the current condition? They have intensive discussions, fed by data, with their direct reports, who confer with their direct reports. So at any time there are at least three levels of the organization involved. When the executive vice presidents have committed to their targets and taken a first pass at the means to work toward the targets, the process is then cascaded to the next level down—leaders of the function in each region of the world. It ultimately continues down to the work group.

Some of these goals can be handled within a function, vertically, and others require leading horizontally across multiple functions (see Figure 9.13). For cross-functional work, one leader in one function is assigned the lead role. Learning to lead horizontally is considered the highest level of leadership skill at Toyota. The leader cannot fall back on command-and-control authority to get the team ener-

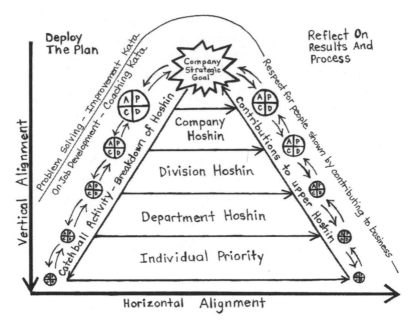

Figure 9.13 Hoshin kanri is a top-down and bottom-up learning process

gized and directed toward the challenge. It requires true leadership! In fact as we look at the development of Toyota leaders, we see them starting out by working within one specialty and learning it deeply, then getting leadership responsibility for that function where they have formal authority, and then branching out to horizontal leadership responsibility, all under the watchful eyes of coaches.

Toyota identifies two skills that are at the center of the hoshin kanri process—problem solving and OJD. We have discussed how Toyota teaches these, and we drew a parallel to using the improvement kata and coaching kata to develop fundamental skills. Toyota sees the hoshin kanri system as further developing these skills. To achieve increasingly difficult challenges as one rises in the organization takes greater mastery of problem solving and OJD.

Catchball in Developing the Initial Plan

Many companies have gotten the memo that hoshin kanri is more than top-down deployment of targets on KPIs. It requires a dialogue between boss and subordinate about the goals for the year. The process of catchball (throwing the ball back and forth) is often used in the planning process so that targets are bought into by each level of management. It is often viewed as a kind of negotiation session, but this is a very small part of the process of coaching and feedback. Each step in hoshin kanri has two objectives: (1) Get results aligned to the company needs.

(2) Develop people. The catchball process is part of developing people. It begins in the planning stage that leads to aligned challenges, but then it continues at least as intensely in the ongoing execution process that follows PDCA.

What happens if we take the hoshin kanri method and introduce it into an organization whose managers rely primarily on formal authority and do not have the skills of scientific thinking? The answer is the same as asking what happens to the A3 report. It does not work like it does at Toyota. Targets get cascaded down the chain as orders, and managers are expected to make the numbers or else. Even if the managers participate in setting the targets through catchball, they are basically helping to create the noose that can be used to hang them. Making the numbers is very different from systematically learning your way toward a challenge through continuous improvement.

The X-Matrix in Henry Ford Medical Labs

Henry Ford Health System pathology and laboratory medicine under Dr. Richard Zarbo began using hoshin kanri about 10 years into its lean journey. By then all managers and supervisors had been taught problem solving and used it repeatedly, and every manager had an established daily management system with daily meetings to review the status of KPIs.

The X-matrix is to hoshin kanri what the A3 is to problem solving. Both are simple visual representations on one side of one piece of paper. Both can be powerful tools, or they can be superficial information displays. For the Henry Ford labs, building on the years of developing a culture of improvers, it became a powerful tool (see Figure 9.14). It allowed them to focus their improvement efforts toward a common strategic direction.

Richard Zarbo and his executive team spent weeks meeting, discussing, and crafting their strategy and the first annual plan for the business. The healthcare environment is in turmoil and very stressful for managers trying to navigate through it. Quality care—a basic expectation! Patient safety—a must! Cost reduction—continuous pressure! Cost reduction has been the biggest challenge for the labs because of their dedication to developing a continuous improvement culture.

A foundation of the pact made with employees was that Dr. Zarbo would fight tooth and nail to protect their jobs. They would go forward and work intensely to learn and improve and prosper together. Zarbo managed to hold up his end for many years as other parts of the healthcare system were laying off and shrinking, but at some point he had to succumb to the pressure. It seemed that growth and profitability did not protect any part of the enterprise from mandatory targets for head-count reduction. This did not stop Zarbo from focusing on growth and total cost reduction as a way to reduce any layoffs.

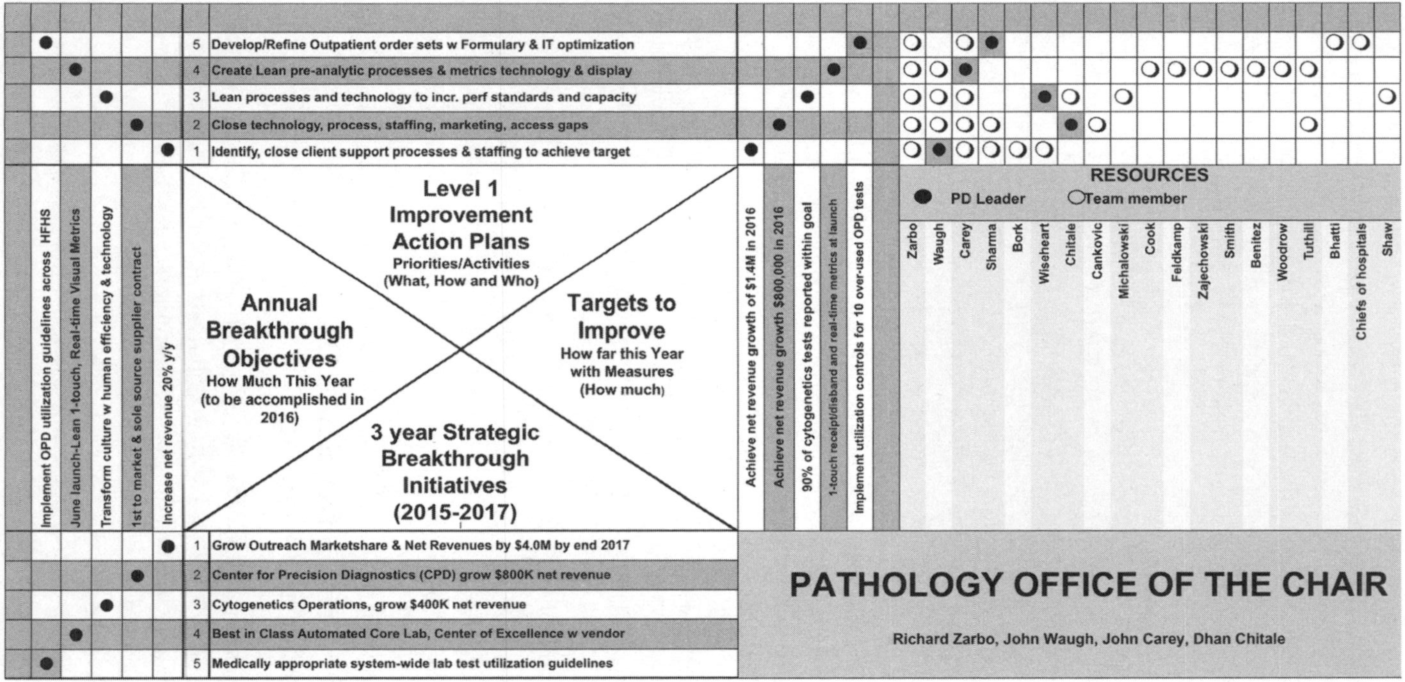

Figure 9.14 Hoshin kanri X-matrix for Henry Ford Health System pathology and laboratory medicine

PATHOLOGY OFFICE OF THE CHAIR

Richard Zarbo, John Waugh, John Carey, Dhan Chitale

RESOURCES — ○ Team member ● PD Leader

Team members: Zarbo, Waugh, Carey, Sharma, Bork, Wiseheart, Chitale, Cankovic, Michalowski, Cook, Feldkamp, Zajechowski, Smith, Benitez, Woodrow, Tuthill, Bhatti, Chiefs of hospitals, Shaw

Level 1 Improvement Action Plans — Priorities/Activities (What, How and Who)

5 Develop/Refine Outpatient order sets w Formulary & IT optimization
4 Create Lean pre-analytic processes & metrics technology & display
3 Lean processes and technology to incr. perf standards and capacity
2 Close technology, process, staffing, marketing, access gaps
1 Identify, close client support processes & staffing to achieve target

Targets to Improve — How far this Year with Measures (How much)

- Achieve net revenue growth of $1.4M in 2016
- Achieve net revenue growth $800,000 in 2016
- 90% of cytogenetics tests reported within goal
- 1-touch receipt/dashboard and real-time metrics at launch
- Implement utilization controls for 10 over-used OPD tests

3 year Strategic Breakthrough Initiatives (2015–2017)

1 Grow Outreach Marketshare & Net Revenues by $4.0M by end 2017
2 Center for Precision Diagnostics (CPD) grow $800K net revenue
3 Cytogenetics Operations, grow $400K net revenue
4 Best in Class Automated Core Lab, Center of Excellence w vendor
5 Medically appropriate system-wide lab test utilization guidelines

Annual Breakthrough Objectives — How Much This Year (to be accomplished in 2016)

- Increase net revenue 20% y/y
- 1st to market & sole source supplier contract
- Transform culture w human efficiency & technology
- June launch-Lean 1-touch, Real-time Visual Metrics
- Implement OPD utilization guidelines across HFHS

349

Zarbo's X-matrix focuses on strategies for growth and profitability. The five 3-year breakthrough initiatives are all focused on strengthening the lab system and growing. For example, one goal is to grow cytogenetics testing by $400,000. This is a new field focusing on the number and structure of chromosomes. Having extra or missing chromosomes is a cause of many chronic diseases. One application is in fetal testing to predict if there will be birth defects or a serious health threat. This is a potential growth area. As Zarbo explains:

> *Growth and new areas of testing will not protect us from cost reduction targets, but will allow us to get a more meaningful recognition of the lab's role. Our real goal is growth. Our first target is to grow outreach business, beyond the Henry Ford system, 30 percent year over year. This will provide another million dollars per year in net income. This is the era of personalized medicine, precision medicine. These are tests tailored to the individual based on the DNA profile. We developed a new business starting with personnel recruitment, technology, informatics, marketing, and a business plan. Another goal is to grow the molecular business. We are negotiating to be the sole source provider for the second largest insurer to cover 800 thousand lives. Molecular informatics for a large population. We are not thinking small. This is all survival.*

The X-matrix then breaks the three-year goals down to one-year breakthrough objectives and high-priority (level 1) actions, and it identifies who is accountable. This is not a replacement for the ongoing effort to develop a culture of problem solvers continually improving. Zarbo sees continuous improvement as the way to achieve these large, complex goals:

> *With our lean culture, collaboratively, we break these complex problems into small problems so everyone is pulling at the oars. The decade-old culture we have worked so hard on is what allows us to succeed. We can take on anything. Any stress. We just figure out how to solve problems as a team.*

Using the Kata to Develop a Chain of Coaching and Learning

What enables hoshin kanri to shift from a way of cascading targets to a way of scientifically working toward breakthrough goals is the coach-learner relationship. When there is an ongoing dialogue, and people step back and begin to systematically work toward the goal through small PDCA cycles, we can move toward the ideal of simultaneously achieving business objectives and developing people.

This is illustrated in a case example that describes the chain of coaching using the improvement kata.[11] The simplified example, Acme Gear Box Manufacturing, takes us from the top strategic level of the business to the individual machining process. At the top level the senior executives conclude that the company needs to increase product variety and reduce the time to meet customer demands. This is communicated to Nancy, the head of gearbox manufacturing, who develops a current-state and future-state value-stream map. The future-state map gives Nancy her challenge—what needs to change so manufacturing can deliver on the required variety and lead time reductions.

The future-state map is parsed into sections and loops, and each manager of a loop gets a challenge, including Steve, the manager of the gear machining loop. To achieve the future-state challenge, Steve needs Roger, who is supervisor of gear broaching, to improve cycle times, reduce downtime of equipment, and reduce changeover time. Now each level of the value stream has aligned challenges to support the business plan (see Figure 9.15).

Since this company is in the midst of learning the improvement kata and the coaching kata, each level is expected to use the kata to work toward its challenge. In the hoshin kanri planning stage, the managers worked to understand what needs to change in manufacturing to support the business plan. This led to a better understanding of their current processes and what they need to work on, as well as some metrics and targets. The managers are not expected in the hoshin planning stage to come up with solutions and action plans. That would violate

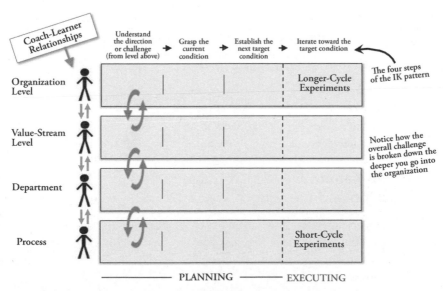

Figure 9.15 Hoshin kanri aligns challenges that are achieved through the improvement kata pattern

Source: Mike Rother

basic tenets of the improvement kata. Now that they have the challenges—the what—they need the how, which is provided by the improvement kata—grasp the current condition, establish a first target condition, iterate toward the target condition, and continue this cycle over and over until they meet the challenge.

As the ongoing improvement process moves forward, there will be daily coaching. The chain of coaching literally means that every person in the chain of command is both a learner being coached and a coach developing learners. The participants are all learning the same pattern of improvement. The dialogues do not stop because they have hoshin plans. If anything, the dialogues will get more intense in the ongoing improvement phase.

The metrics are different at every level. The business plan is in terms of finances, amount of product variety, and overall delivery lead times. The value-stream map focuses on how to deliver the lead time and variety within this manufacturing stream. By the time it gets down to Roger, who supervises a machining process, the targets are in terms of cycle time, equipment uptime, and changeover time. These challenges and activities will all be aligned, but not because the same things are being measured at all levels. A standard set of KPIs could actually hamper progress toward the specific business plan that Acme is now working toward.

In *The Toyota Way to Lean Leadership*, Gary Convis and I developed a model of leadership development (see Figure 9.16). The model was developed from what we learned about how Gary was developed first as the plant manager of NUMMI

Figure 9.16   Model of lean leadership development
Source: Jeffrey Liker and Gary Convis, *The Toyota Way to Lean Leadership.*

and eventually as a senior executive within Toyota. Over and over his challenges grew more difficult, and he had to go back to the basics, which begins with self-development. How could he develop himself, with a coach, to live the core values at an even higher level? It was self-development because the inner drive had to come from him. He could not be coerced by extrinsic rewards to have the necessary passion and commitment to learn to achieve ever more difficult goals while patiently developing others.

The more Gary developed himself, the better he was able to coach and develop others. As senior management develops middle management, middle management can also develop work group leaders to think scientifically as they do daily kaizen. When this chain of coaching is well developed, management can align its challenges through hoshin kanri. A weak link will break the chain of coaching. Notice that some development of improvement skills in the chain of leaders is needed to effectively align goals and actions through hoshin kanri.

There is an obvious chicken-and-egg problem here. If there needs to be a chain of competency to work the right way toward challenges, and we need challenges to give us direction, what comes first—the challenges or the skills? The answer is that to some degree both must evolve in parallel. When senior managers are first in the learning stage, it is better if they learn on individual processes. There are many ways to get their challenges—drawing from business plans that almost all organizations already have or using a clear pain point as the basis. As the organization matures in learning how to improve, we can begin to cascade challenges down through the organization. The challenges can become more of a stretch, and they can be more tightly connected.

How do we learn and capture best practices as the organization experiments and learns to achieve its targets? In many cases best-practice sharing is not a good use of time and resources. My best practice is my countermeasure for my specific situation and may or may not be of great value to others. Each person responsible for improvement must carefully think through what new knowledge should be shared and with whom. Often direct sharing at the gemba is superior to developing huge databases of best practices. We will discuss this more thoroughly in the next chapter.

DAILY WORK AS PROBLEM SOLVING

In lean we often view problem solving as improving how we do our work. Yet in services most people are problem solvers in their daily work. Ask medical doctors what they do, and they may well say they solve problems for patients. Lawyers are solving problems for clients. Customer service representatives are solving problems for customers.

This thought crystalized when I started thinking about Menlo Innovations as solving problems for users. Each product is itself an innovation—custom software that the world has not seen in this precise form. Menlo's chief storyteller Richard Sheridan spoke to my graduate course on lean and almost apologized for not being as scientific as they could be about improving Menlo's processes. Yet the Menlo system is highly effective and based on innovation.

The lightbulb finally went on weeks later. Menlo is following the scientific method every day as it develops new software. I recast the Menlo development process in terms of the improvement kata (see Figure 9.17). Menlo's technical anthropologists spend a lot of time up front developing a vision for the software through the interplay of observing users deeply, employing techniques such as mind mapping, and developing user personas. Pairs of tech anthropologists are in constant dialogue with users, customers, and each other crafting this vision. Then they write out a vision statement that provides the direction for all subsequent work.

The deep observation in which they act like "flies on the wall" helps them grasp the current condition as a starting point. When they finally get to the detail of writing out story cards that define different features of the software,

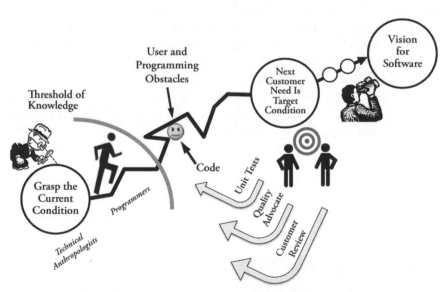

Figure 9.17 Menlo system as innovating toward a vision

they are in a sense defining target conditions for the software. But these target conditions are not "implemented." Rather they must be authorized by the customer as the customer decides which cards to play in the project-planning game. Then programmers do a lot of PDCA hour by hour as they find ways to achieve the target conditions represented by each story card.

Then week by week the customer reviews what has been done in the past week and which cards to play the next week—the next target conditions. The programmers read the next card on the wall, and that gives them the desired characteristics of the software for the next iteration. Then, still working in pairs, they experiment to overcome obstacles, constantly challenging each other, considering alternatives, testing them out, and critiquing the code, until they have something that they believe will work.

There is a remarkable amount of rapid feedback as the programmers write code. They are required to develop unit tests for each unit of code so they get immediate feedback on whether the code does what it is supposed to do functionally. They then get feedback from quality advocates, generally within the day, on whether the code will satisfy the customer. Then each week they get feedback as the customer attempts to use the code, and they can observe what happens and listen to the customer's feedback. The technical anthropologists are also regularly circling back to represent the end users.

Through this iterative learning process, the software goes live, generally with little training for the users and without bugs. Users are surprised and delighted because they are accustomed to getting new software that blocks their processes and Menlo software enables their processes instead. A bit more joy has been added to the world!

It is useful to think of service work as solving problems for customers. We can apply the scientific method to our daily work of serving others. At another level we can improve the way we do our work. So we are using the scientific method both to do the work and to improve how we do the work.

This all assumes that scientific thinking becomes a habit. We know positive habits have to be learned through continual practice and reinforcement, with a coach. The role of leadership then becomes that of coaching others to be diligent in how they approach problems. The kata are practice routines, so we can shift to a scientific mindset and periodically return to the basics of maintaining this mindset.

KEY POINTS
STRIVE TOWARD A CLEAR
DIRECTION THROUGH
EXPERIMENTING

1. Problems are gaps from standard, meaning they are deviations from what should be happening—whether related to a policy, an engineering specification, or an aspirational target—and can come from inside or outside the organization. The focus of problem solving is on closing the gap between the actual condition and the standard. Problem solving is a process of continuous learning at the individual, group, and organizational levels.

2. Scientific thinking, practical learning through deliberate experimentation, is the method underlying lean thinking such as TBP, OJD, and A3 thinking of how to close gaps from the standard in order to improve toward a clear vision. The improvement kata is designed to teach a meta-skill, the pattern of scientifically approaching how to navigate your way through obstacles in the direction of a challenge.

3. Experimenting to improve toward a clear vision involves practicing deliberately with a clear routine, such as the improvement kata, and with a coach. Simply using forms such as the A3 to record and document the steps of the problem-solving process does not solve problems or develop people's scientific thinking abilities.

4. The underlying pattern of the improvement kata defines and teaches good practice habits for the improvement process:
   - **Direction/challenge.** How do my improvement activities contribute to a larger goal that matters to the organization?
   - **Current condition.** Deeply understand the current operating patterns at the gemba from direct observation and use data to further understand what is happening.
   - **Next target condition and obstacles.** Define the next operating pattern that will get you closer to the challenge and the obstacles that are standing between you and the next target condition.
   - **Experiments.** Plan-Do-Check-Act comes together as a series of rapid learning cycles in which predictions are made about what is expected to happen for each experiment, after which the results of the prediction are compared with the hypothesis.

5. The learner storyboard from the improvement kata and the A3 can work together. The learner storyboard provides the framework to teach and record the meta-pattern of the improvement kata. The A3 is an overall

summary of that improvement process that can be used for communication with others.

6. Hoshin kanri (policy deployment) is the process used by Toyota to align improvement and learning across the enterprise. Toyota uses it as the system to attain organization-level challenges by developing the problem-solving skills of people across all levels of the organization through layered coaching; everyone is being coached, and everyone is coaching someone.

7. In service organizations, most daily work is problem solving. Doctors solve problems for patients; lawyers solve problems for their clients; customer service reps answer questions and solve problems for their customers. Applying scientific thinking allows individuals in a service organization to improve the lives of the customers they serve while improving their capacity to innovate.

Chapter 10

The Long Journey to a Customer-Focused Learning Organization

Transformation is a process, and as life happens there are tons of ups and downs. It's a journey of discovery—there are moments on mountaintops and moments in deep valleys of despair.

—Rick Warren, theologian

INTRODUCTION

We organized our service excellence principles around my 4P model of the Toyota Way—philosophy, process, people, and problem solving. We described in great detail how these four simple ideas work for service excellence organized around seventeen principles. We illustrated these principles with many case examples, some real and some fictional, some manufacturing and most from services.

We do not expect these principles to translate directly into a things-to-do list or into a road map where you can plot out your transformation over the next five years. That would be contrary to the models we have presented of improvement. Improvement is an individual and organizational journey and requires skill development over time. You need to learn your way, not "implement" principles.

This presents a conundrum because you would like some advice. We decided that instead of a laundry list of implementation tips, we will use stories to illustrate how these principles apply in several situations, beginning with a start-up service company that Karyn has been joyfully advising. She is using all the principles in this book to coach taxi drivers, who have a lot of driving experience but little previous business experience. During weekly meetings, Karyn has been coaching them as they work their way through the process of building an exceptional taxi business focused on collaboration and 100 percent customer satisfaction. We will then revisit our fictional cases of NL Services and Service 4U one last time to address the question: How can we engage and develop leaders at all levels in a journey to become a high-performance, customer-focused organization?

These examples will leave you with a vivid picture of what is possible when serious people dedicate themselves to excellence with the help of compassionate and experienced coaches. It will be difficult to conclude that lean does not apply to services. It will be difficult to argue that it takes super people who are Japanese to follow this model. Ordinary people with extraordinary vision and persistence are doing remarkable things throughout the world following the simple guidance of the Toyota Way—respect for people and continuous improvement. Let's listen in while Karyn tells us the story of NTL's journey in light of the 4Ps and 17 principles.

NATIONAL TAXI LIMO AND THE 4Ps

I travel a lot so I take a lot of taxis. That's how I met Joe Draheim, one of the owners of National Taxi Limo, a new personal transportation service near Chicago. Joe is in his early thirties, and when I first met him, he was dressed in jeans and a hoodie. The little bit I knew of Joe's background came from clues from other drivers: "Joe's a great guy, but he doesn't seem to want to work really hard. He likes to 'hang out,' and he's not always reliable."

One day, when Joe picked me up at O'Hare Airport, he excitedly told me about his new venture: "I'm working with a couple of other guys to start our own personal transportation company. We know it's going to be hard, but we have an idea that we think is pretty different. Taxi drivers live ride to ride. And they're always worried that someone is going to steal their ride. If customers ride with another company, even once, they'll probably never come back. So if you own your own cab, you can never take a day off. And drivers sometimes answer the phone while they're driving so they don't miss a customer's call, and that's not safe. What we want to do is create a network of 'driver partners' that will work together. We'll have an app, like Uber, so customers can book, track, and pay for their ride through the app, but we're going to combine that with an actual taxi dispatch service. And we're only going to work with licensed taxi drivers who have their own cars and commercial insurance. That way we can help small, independent taxi company owner-operators support each other so that they can grow their businesses cooperating and helping each other out. We also want to help them become better businesspeople. Right now they're so busy driving, they don't have time to work on their own development as business owners."

As Joe and I continued to talk, Joe told me more about the vision for the new company: "Taxi drivers are a pretty independent lot—that's probably why they're driving taxis! They don't like being told what to do. Funny thing is, though, they don't seem to mind telling other people what to do, so there's often a lot of bad communication going on. We don't want our company to be like that though. We want to create a different culture, a culture where we work together with our driver partners. That way we can take care of our customers and take care of each other. Problem is, it all seems good in theory, but we're having a little trouble really getting it all going."

That's how I got started working with National Taxi Limo. Could the principles of the Toyota Way—respect for people and continuous improvement—apply and work for a personal transportation company? How could someone like Joe, a 32-year-old taxi driver with a spotty track record and no previous leadership experience, develop himself and develop others? And how would the typical lean tools work? How could something like visual management be creatively adapted for taxi drivers who need to keep their eyes on the road driving? How could I help Joe and his partners use the Toyota Way to develop themselves professionally and personally so that they could help other taxi drivers improve their circumstances by continuously delivering service excellence to ensure that their customers were satisfied? It helped that Joe was on fire with passion for the business, and reading *The Toyota Way*, which I gave him, just fueled the fire even further.

Philosophy: Long-Term Systems Thinking

Principle 1. Passionately Pursue Purpose Based on Guiding Values

Like all journeys, NTL's began with a single, very important step: the definition of its purpose for existing in the world. Joe and his partners Todd VanderSchoor and Ken Kaiser determined that their purpose was to create a personal transportation service that actively worked with their driver partners to help them become better businesspeople so that they could grow their businesses while offering all customers the best in personalized, personable service at a reasonable price. This was a mouthful, but it did provide a starting direction.

"This all sounds good," said Joe during a meeting with the partners and me. "However, how do we actually do that? And how do we make sure that we are on track to reach our goals? The app isn't ready, and we're not even dispatching yet. How are we going to make sure we get to where we want to go and don't get sidetracked? If only we had a map to get us there."

"Funny you should bring that up," I said, pointing to the large piece of blank paper taped to the wall. "What we're going to do today is create a way for us all to see where NTL is now and where you need to be in the next year, so that you're making the right progress toward your purpose. If we had not taken the time to identify the purpose, we would not even know what direction we want to go."

"We'll call it the 'NTL road map'!" Joe exclaimed. After working together for a few hours, Joe, Ken, and Todd had drawn out the path for NTL's first year in business (see Figure 10.1). The 'road map' was not a detailed action plan with dates and assignments, but rather a set of milestones to work towards, quarter by quarter. Each milestone was written on a Post-it. For example, one Post-it read "Dispatch First Ride." Joe and his partners then worked to figure out how to overcome the obstacles needed to make that happen. As well as having a good idea of their current state (see Figure 10.2), where they were right now, they also defined where they wanted to be at the end of their first year (see Figure 10.3).

Figure 10.1   NTL road map

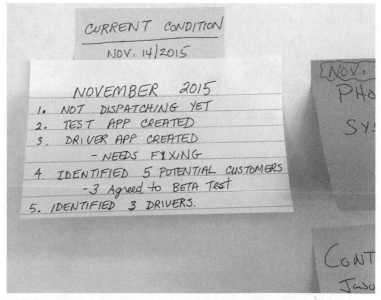

Figure 10.2   NTL road map, current condition

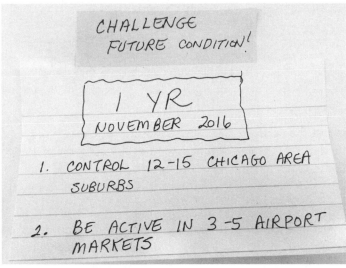

Figure 10.3   NTL road map, future condition

Finally, they created a challenge statement to reflect how they wanted to get to their future condition: "Every Ride. On Time. Every Time. Working Together." Now Joe and his partners would have a yardstick against which they could measure all ideas, decisions, and solutions. Any investments or ideas that would not move them closer to their challenge of "Every Ride. On Time. Every Time. Working Together" would be a distraction. At first Joe was concerned about the challenge and could not see how a taxi company could possibly achieve it. He was uncomfortable with the uncertainty. But as he and I continued to talk about how important it was to have a challenge to strive toward, he started warming up to the idea.

Joe lamented, "But we'll never really be able to pick up and deliver every ride on time . . . in reality, that would just be impossible, wouldn't it? There are so many things that can go wrong. Cars breaking down, road construction—too many to name," said Joe.

"Really?" I challenged. "You're pretty committed to caring for your customers and driver partners. If you don't pick up every ride on time, what's the consequence? What's going to happen to your business?"

"You're right," said Joe. "We won't be here long." Thinking for a moment he added, "Maybe we don't know how to do it now, but working together we'll have to learn to solve the problems that we know are going to occur. We'll simply figure out how to get to 'every ride on time.' We'll just have to strive toward that goal." Joe and NTL now had a challenging future-state vision to work toward together, for as Joe said, "Now you see it. Now you do it."

Process: Flow Value to Each Customer

Principle 2. Deeply Understand Customer Needs

Joe and his partners had worked for a variety of taxi companies over the years. Having spent countless hours talking with customers as they drove them for other companies, they started out with a pretty deep understanding of customer needs and what service excellence meant to them:

1. Safety first—a safe ride was always most important.
2. On time, every time—customers want to be picked up and dropped off on time.
3. Clean cars and personable, friendly drivers—delightful in-car experience.
4. Reasonable price.

With that understanding, NTL could begin to form some hypotheses about what delivering that service excellence would look like. For example:

1. Drivers won't text or answer the phone while a customer is in the car. Ever.
2. Drivers will use the app to give real-time status updates to customers and dispatch about pick-up and drop-off times.
3. Drivers will wear suits and tuck in their shirts.
4. Cars will be cleaned—inside and out—on a regular schedule.

As well as having a good understanding of their customers' needs and the opportunity to gather feedback from them on an ongoing basis, each and every ride, Joe and his team also used their taxi driving experience to start thinking about how to keep all the rides "flowing" and to work on leveling their workload.

Principle 3. Strive for One-Piece Flow

Think about it; although it may not seem obvious at first, taxi drivers actually have an innate understanding of flow! They are on the road every day, so both flow and barriers to flow—which the partners decided to call "roadblocks"—are a huge part of a taxi driver's everyday experience. Anything that stops or slows down the ride once it's started is a roadblock and a barrier to flow. And taxi drivers know how important flow is: neither they nor their customers want to stop moving once they get going! So finding ways to keep the ride moving, from the moment the customers are picked up to the moment they are dropped off, is of the utmost importance in delivering service excellence in the world of taxi driving.

They also know that, in general, Monday mornings and Thursday nights will be busiest for airport drop-offs and pick-ups, as that is when the majority of business travelers are heading to the airport and coming home. Striving to be on time, every time, would mean paying careful attention to ride patterns and determining the right number of drivers during those times. In order to do this, the partners decided to track each day's ride destinations and times on a visual board so that they could identify patterns and trends. And they started a spreadsheet to track ride "target" and "actual" times: what time was a customer supposed to have been picked up, what time was she actually picked up, and if she wasn't picked up on time, what was the cause? In this way, Joe, Ken, and Todd would be able to begin to identify the roadblocks and barriers to flow. Once they identified them, they would be able to start to use PDCA to figure out the causes and identify potential countermeasures that they could experiment with daily.

Principle 4. Strive for Leveled Work Patterns

After a month of keeping close tabs on what was happening day in and day out, Joe and his partners realized that they needed to set up separate drivers and systems for airport rides and local rides. Most airport rides were booked in advance by "regulars," business travelers, on a fairly predictable schedule; however, local rides tended to come from customers "pulling" for immediate pick-ups: they wanted to go to the grocery store or to their friend's house, and they wanted to do it right now. It simply took too long to get drivers from the airport back to local, suburban destinations to be able to have on-time pick-ups. And it was difficult and stressful for the drivers.

Separating "airport" drivers and "local" drivers substantially improved "traffic flow" and reduced driver stress from having to rush back from the airport to pick up a local ride. Joe and NTL learned that it was possible to take a positive step toward leveled work patterns, even in a business of erratic customer demand. The flow of work became much smoother for the drivers. And customer satisfaction improved too. "Having a whole separate set of drivers and processes wasn't what we had envisioned when we started out, but having our challenge statement of 'Every Ride. On Time. Every Time. Working Together' really helped us to think differently about how to solve the problem," said Joe. "It's a lot easier for us to cover every ride this way, and customers get picked up when they want to be picked up."

Principle 5. Respond to Customer Pull

Just as they have an understanding of one-piece flow, taxi drivers also have an innate understanding of customer pull. In fact, customers pull for their services 24 hours a day. "It's important that our customers are able to reach us whenever they want to and however they want to," Joe told me when we started working together. To that end, NTL customers can pull for airport or local rides by booking in advance through the app (which is what most regular business travelers do), using the online booking function on NTL's website (used most often by customers booking rides to the airport for vacations), calling NTL on the phone (customers wanting local rides usually call), or sending an e-mail directly (customers who have questions about timing of rides or who have special requests). As Joe said, "Making sure our customers can reach us anytime using whatever method works best for them is one of the most important parts of delivering service excellence. If they can't reach us immediately, they'll just call another company. Then we'll lose the ride. And that will be bad for our customers, as we won't have the opportunity to wow them with our service, and it's bad for our business too."

Principle 6. Stabilize and Continually Adapt Work Patterns

"I think we're having a problem," Ken said during our weekly meeting. "Some customers have said they're frustrated because they haven't been getting text messages when they land, so they don't know if their driver is at the airport and available to pick them up."

"I've heard that too," said Joe.

"And I've had that experience," I chimed in.

"Do you think that everyone is following the same process using the app and in picking up our airport customers?" asked Joe. Ten minutes later, after they polled each driver partner about his process, it was obvious that everyone was doing things differently. "We need to have a standard way to use the app when we're picking up customers so that they get the information that they need," said Joe. So, working together, the guys created a first-version standard to try (see Figure 10.4).

"This makes perfect sense to us, but how can we make sure that all our drivers are aware of the standard and will use it?" Todd asked. After a few minutes of discussion, the partners decided that they would try the simplest solution first— experimenting on themselves. They would photocopy the piece of paper and keep it in the car with them. That way they wouldn't have anything electronic that they would have to use their phone to reference, and they could jot down notes on the page if something didn't work well or if they had another idea.

"And since it's written in pencil, on a piece of paper, it's really easy to change as we find better ways," said Ken.

"Gentlemen, try it out next week, and let's see what happens. We can discuss what happened during next week's meeting," I suggested.

"And," said Joe, "we can look at the problem log for airport rides and see if we had any customers who didn't get the text message at the right time. We'll have a great opportunity to learn."

Principle 7. Manage Visually to See Actual Versus Standard

Joe gushes about visual management and how it has helped National Taxi Limo. Since taxi drivers spend a lot of time driving, it is sometimes difficult for them to

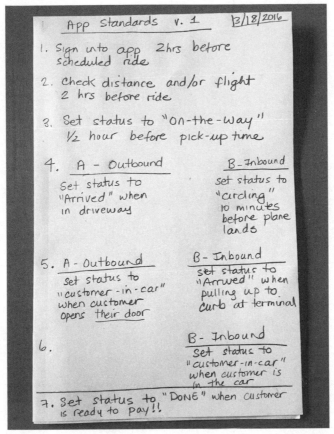

App Standards v. 1   3/18/2016

1. Sign into app 2hrs before scheduled ride

2. Check distance and/or flight 2 hrs before ride

3. Set status to "on-the-way" ½ hour before pick-up time

4. A - Outbound   B - Inbound

    Set status to   set status to
    "Arrived" when   "circling"
    in driveway   10 minutes
                                    before plane
                                    lands

5. A - Outbound   B - Inbound

    set status to   set status to
    "customer-in-car"   "Arrived" when
    when customer   pulling up to
    opens their door   curb at terminal

6.   B - Inbound

                                    set status to
                                    "customer-in-car"
                                    when customer is
                                    in the car

7. Set status to "DONE" when customer is ready to pay!!

Figure 10.4   NTL app used for airport rides, version 1, standard work

have time to stop and "see" the big picture. Just like their rides, their business is coming at them 24 hours a day, 65 miles per hour! However, as in many other service businesses, if they can't see what is actually happening, everything seems to be random. And if everything seems to be random, how can it be managed so that customers receive the service they need and the business reaches its targets?

NTL's visual management systems helps Joe, Todd, and Ken see what is happening on a day-to-day basis so that they can make sense of it and visualize any problems in real time during the day. Joe updates rides, drivers, pick-up times, and revenue throughout the day on a whiteboard in the office. Color coding makes it easy for everyone to see the source of the ride: green is an NTL direct customer, and blue is a ride sent to NTL by another company (see Figure 10.5).

Since NTL is working to grow its own customer base, it's important for the partners to be able to see how close they are to their target of "NTL-generated"

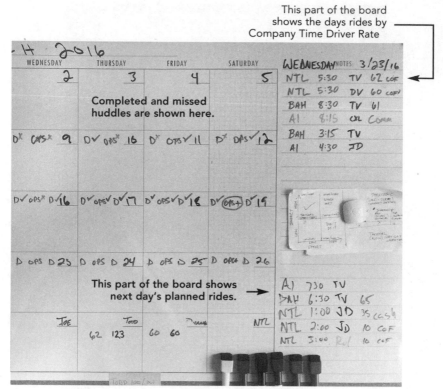

Figure 10.5   NTL daily visual management board

rides each day. If there's a dropped or canceled ride its noted in red. Beside each dropped or canceled ride is the "reason code." During the three daily huddles, Joe and the team can quickly review any dropped or canceled rides and make sure that they have countermeasures in place to prevent the problem from recurring. The team is experimenting with three-times-a-day huddles (remember, NTL is a 24-hour-a-day operation), and there is a green check mark or red X beside each, noting whether the huddle took place and whether the standard was followed.

"Being able to see whether we are huddling or not has really helped us get better at it," says Joe. "And what we've found out is that if we don't huddle, rides don't get covered or aren't picked up on time, so huddling is a *really* important part of our process. Being able to see which ones we're completing and which ones we're not has helped us change what we do. Like I said before, 'now you see it, now you do it!'"

As well as using visual management to understand and manage on a daily basis, Joe, Todd, and Ken also use it during their end-of-week partner meeting to check to see that they are making progress toward their road-map goals (see Figure 10.6).

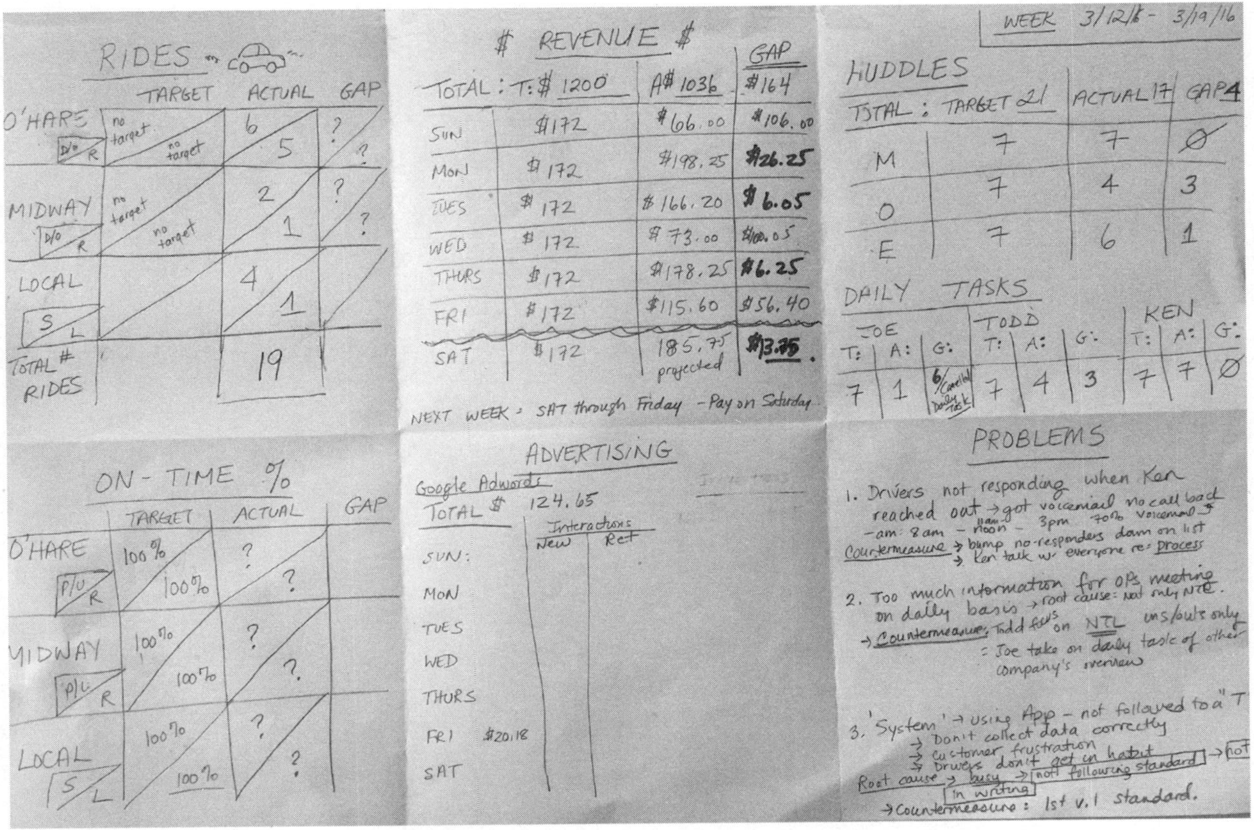

WEEK 3/12/16 - 3/19/16

RIDES "⌐"

	TARGET	ACTUAL	GAP
O'HARE P/R	no target	no target	?
	6	5	?
MIDWAY P/R W/R	no target	no target	?
	2	1	?
LOCAL S/L	4	1	?
TOTAL # RIDES		19	

$ REVENUE $

TOTAL: T: $1200 A: $1036 A: $164

			GAP
SUN	$172	$66.00	$106.00
MON	$172	$198.25	$26.25
TUES	$172	$166.20	$6.05
WED	$172	$73.00	$100.05
THURS	$172	$178.25	$6.25
FRI	$172	$115.60	$56.40
SAT	$172	185.75 projected	$13.75

NEXT WEEK = SAT through Friday - Pay on Saturday

HUDDLES

TOTAL: TARGET 21 ACTUAL 17 GAP 4

M	7	7	0
O	7	4	3
E	7	6	1

DAILY TASKS

	JOE	TODD	KEN
T: A: G:	7 1 6 (actual week)	7 4 3	7 7 0

ON-TIME %

	TARGET	ACTUAL	GAP
O'HARE P/R	100%	?	?
	100%	?	?
MIDWAY P/R	100%	?	?
	100%	?	?
LOCAL S/L	100%	?	?

ADVERTISING

Google Adwords
TOTAL $: 124.65

	Interactions New	Ret
SUN:		
MON:		
TUES:		
WED:		
THURS:		
FRI	$20.18	
SAT		

PROBLEMS

1. Drivers not responding when Ken reached out → got voicemail - no call back - then 70% voicemail → 3pm - 2am - 11am no-responders down on list. Countermeasure → bump no-responders re: process → Ken talk w/ everyone re: process.

2. Too much information for O/E meeting on daily basis → root cause - will interpret only → Countermeasure: add on NTL on/out only. = Joe take on daily basis on topic of company's overview.

3. 'System' → using App - not followed to a "T". → Don't collect data correctly → customer frustration → Drivers don't get on habit → not following standard → NOT in writing. Root cause → busy → Countermeasure: 1st v. 1 standard.

Figure 10.6 NTL weekly summary document

369

Each week, targets for number of rides, revenue, huddles, and advertising for the next week are set. These targets roll up to the longer-range NTL road map goals. During the meeting, the partners review whether they reached each target, and they go over the problems that occurred during the week. They review the effectiveness of countermeasures that were put in place, and if targets are missed, countermeasures are created for the next week. Everyone can easily see where NTL is compared with where it wants to be. "It's really easy," says Joe. "And it will change over time. You don't have to have a complicated system. You just have to see where you are and where you want be. Then you can figure out how to get there."

Principle 8. Build in Quality at Each Step

A few weeks ago, during the weekly partner meeting, Joe said, "I think that we need to talk about jidoka."

"Jidoka?" said Todd, with a puzzled look on his face. "What's jidoka?"

Now perhaps you wouldn't think that taxi drivers would be using terms like jidoka; however, as Joe explained, "The idea of jidoka is really simple, Todd. We have to have a way for all our drivers to recognize a problem right away and tell us about it so we can figure out what went wrong and how to fix it before it happens again. If we don't do that, our flow is going to stop."

"I don't know," said Todd. "Seems to me that if we stop driving to report a problem, then that is what is going to stop our flow. We're not a manufacturing company. We can't just 'stop the line' in the middle of driving down the highway!"

"You're both right," I said. Then I explained to them that when a problem is detected on the line at Toyota and a team member pulls the andon cord, the whole line doesn't immediately come to a stop. What happens is that the team leader rushes over to see what the problem is and works to understand the cause and contain it immediately, so the production line doesn't have to stop.

"How do you think that we could do something like that while safely driving customers?" I asked. After thinking for a while, Todd, Ken, and Joe came up with a plan. "Since on-time pick-up is the most important for our customers, let's find a way to figure out what is preventing us picking up customers on time first," suggested Ken.

"Good idea," said Joe. "If drivers are using the app correctly, as soon as they pick up a customer, whoever is dispatching should be able to see the time in the system. As long as the dispatcher is monitoring the rides as he should, he should be able to see right away if there is a problem or not." Joe continued, "Then whoever is dispatching can contact the driver and ask why the pick-up was late after the ride is dropped off. That way we don't have to have people stop driving or use their cell phone to text or answer the call in the car. Then we could discuss what happened during our next huddle in the day so we can make sure the problem is fixed for that day."

"What if we also created a problem log for late rides?" asked Ken. "Then we could collect all the data about the late rides and the reasons why for the week. We could review the data during our weekly partner meeting and figure out what to try next week to prevent those problems from happening again."

"And we will know what we need to work on in our standard work too," said Joe. "When we can see the problems, we'll be able to fix them and get better at preventing them from ever happening in the first place."

As Joe, Ken, and Todd have found out, if the customer experience is your top priority, with a little creativity it's always possible to find ways to build in quality at each step.

Principle 9. Use Technology to Enable People

"Since Uber came on the scene, everyone expects a taxi company to have an app," said Joe. "Problem is, many of our driver partners aren't comfortable using all that technology, as they just haven't used it before. Our customers want it, though, and it's a great way for us to keep track of our regular rides, so it's really important that we get everyone used to it and using it regularly."

Like many other companies in this day and age, NTL is finding that it's very important to consider the effects of all choices about technology, both for customers and for those working in the business. To make sure that NTL's technology is enabling both customers and drivers, Joe and the team have a process for testing each piece of technology with a select group of customers and driver partners. All information on the website is available on a single page, so customers don't have to click through many screens to book a ride. And after gathering feedback from a number of customers who used the website, changes were made in how the booking screens worked.

In addition, any changes made to the customer interface of the app are tested with a select set of customers, and changes to the driver interface are tested with a set of driver partners. If the functionality of the app doesn't support NTL's challenge statement of "working together," then it's back to the drawing board! "We control what technology does for our customers and our company," says Joe. "The technology works for us. Not the other way around."

People: Challenge, Engage, and Grow

Principle 10. Organize to Balance
Deep Expertise and Customer Focus

When I first started working with NTL, the partners' roles and responsibilities were vague at best—everyone would do everything. And this seemed like it might work . . . until . . . NTL actually started dispatching. Once it began, Joe realized that he and Todd and Ken needed to have a better division of company responsibilities. As noted earlier, the taxi business is a 24-hour-a-day one, and in order to make sure that rides weren't missed because the person who was scheduled to answer the phones fell asleep, the partners needed to create a daily schedule of who was responsible for intake and who was responsible for dispatch.

They also realized that they needed to each take primary responsibility for a business area, so that tasks such as bookkeeping and marketing were completed in a timely manner. Joe became the VP of Operations, Todd became the treasurer and VP of Finance, and Ken became the president. Ken, who has the greatest access to potential driver partners from his long tenure in the taxi industry, is responsible for working with the driver partners to make sure they have the correct airport and local coverage; Todd, who has a background in business, is responsible for keeping all the finances in order, including ensuring that NTL is reaching its daily "ride" goals so that all the driver partners and the business are taken care of financially. Joe, who enjoys analytics and web design, takes care of the app, website, and advertising and is in charge of finding ways to get new customers for the business. Joe is often the dispatcher, as well.

The three daily huddles came out of this division of labor. To make sure that the partners were communicating and "working together," they determined that they would have three quick daily check-ins, or huddles, two "dispatch huddles" to make sure their driver partners were organized and on track to pick up all customers on time, and one midday "operations huddle" with all three partners to make sure that revenue and other goals were being met each day.

Each partner is also responsible for completing a standard set of daily tasks as well as updating the visual management spreadsheet at the weekly partner meetings. So far, this has been working well to balance customer needs and ensures that each partner is working in an area that is his strength. As Joe says, "Once we decided to split out our organization this way, it really helped us to make sure that 'every ride is on time, every time' and that we're working together."

Principle 11. Develop a Deliberate Culture

"Taxi culture isn't always the most pleasant one," Joe said to me when I first started working with NTL. "There can be a lot of yelling and bad communication, and people don't trust each other because they think other drivers are going to steal their rides. That's not what we want our culture to be like at NTL, though. But I'm not sure how to make sure that doesn't happen to us. I really want us to be successful at creating a different kind of culture, where people care about each other and work together to take care of the customer, but I'm not sure how to do that."

"It's not going to be easy," I said. "The people that you are working with are used to the old taxi culture. But it can be done. Remember your challenge statement: 'Every Ride. On Time. Every Time. Working Together.' You are going to have to make sure that every decision you make and every interaction you have will support that challenge statement. And you are going to have to make sure that Todd and Ken understand that as well. When problems happen—and they are going to happen all the time—you're going to have to create your culture of 'working together' by working together to solve those problems." Joe smiled and nodded, but I wondered if he really understood.

Luckily, a day or so later, we had an opportunity to turn theory into deliberate practice when I got a text message from Joe about a situation that had happened earlier that day. A customer had complained to one of NTL's suppliers about one of NTL's drivers. The customer hadn't liked the way the driver partner was driving, and the supplier was threatening to stop sending its overflow rides to NTL.

"I'm not sure how to handle this," Joe said to me when I gave him a call. "I'm not used to having this kind of conversation. In the past, I would just ignore the problem or yell. That never really helped anyone though, and it's definitely not the kind of culture we want." So, for the next half hour, Joe and I talked through the different strategies he could take to deal with the driver partner and the supplier so that they could work together. Once Joe settled on the approach, talking first with the driver partner and then with the supplier, Joe and I practiced both conversations until he felt comfortable that he knew what he was going to say. Joe then decided that he would have both conversations the next day when everyone was fresh and some time had passed, so that any initial anger would have dissipated.

You can imagine how happy I was when Joe called me the next evening. "Everything went great," he said. "The driver partner was certainly happy that no one yelled at him, and he was very open to take the suggestions about how to improve. He really wants to continue to work with us and make sure our customers are satisfied. It was a really great experience. And our supplier was even happier. He really felt we cared about him and his customers. Instead of not sending us any more of his overflow rides, he decided to send us more! This is what I dreamed of when we started NTL: everyone working together so our customers can be satisfied!"

Since then, Joe and the team have had many other opportunities to create their culture deliberately, as problems occur constantly. And for each problem that they have to solve, and for each decision that they have to make, if they aren't sure what to do, they reflect on whether it is going to get them closer to the goal of "Every Ride. On Time. Every Time. Working Together."

Principle 12. Integrate Outside Partners

Just like every other decision NTL makes, the choice to work with an outside business partner is made through the lens of NTL's purpose. I was so proud when Joe,

Ken, and Todd parted ways with an auto dealer because the dealership did not fit their values.

A few weeks earlier, Joe had called me on my cell. "I'm really excited," he said. "We're about to buy a car for NTL. Todd and I have spent a lot of time looking, and we think we've finally found the one that our customers will really like and that's within the budget. I'll text you a picture after we buy it."

I didn't receive any picture, so the next day I gave Joe a call. "Just want to say congratulations on the new car!"

"Oh," said Joe. "We decided not to buy it. The longer we stayed at the car dealership, the more we realized that the people there just didn't have the same values that NTL does. It seemed fine at first, but then we realized that they didn't really understand what we meant by 'working together.' And they didn't seem to be interested in solving problems either. Since we plan to buy a lot of cars as our business grows, we want to make sure that we are working with a dealer that shares our values. If the dealer doesn't, how will we be able to reach our challenge of 'Every Ride. On Time. Every Time. Working Together'? What if we need a new car and the dealer can't get us one quickly enough? Or what if the quality isn't good and it breaks down, and so we miss rides? Problems are always going to happen, so if the people at the dealership didn't want to work on solving problems during this first transaction, what's going to happen later on? If we want to be sure to satisfy our customers, we're going to have to make sure that all the people we work with understand and share our values and philosophy—or are willing to learn!"

Principles 13 and 14. Develop Fundamental Skills and Mindset and Develop Leaders as Coaches of Continually Developing Teams

"We've missed a couple of rides this week, and I think I've figured out why," Joe said at the beginning of one of our weekly meetings. "I think that there are a couple of things going on. First is that we don't really have a set plan about who is going to contact our driver partners to schedule the rides. Sometimes Ken does it, and sometimes I do it, but sometimes one of us thinks the other is going to do it, and then nobody does.

I think I've come up with a plan to test this week: Ken and I will split the driver partner list in half, and each of us will call the driver partners on our list first thing every morning. Then, when we get together for the morning dispatch huddle, we'll know that each driver partner has received a call. The other problem is that Todd hasn't dispatched before, so he's just learning. He's doing a good job, but I think that he needs more training so that he can be more confident. I've already set up some time for him and Ken, who's really the dispatch guru, to get together."

"Both ideas sound great," I said. "You, Todd, and Ken all have different skills and a different amount of experience driving taxis and dispatching. It's going to take some time to understand and then help each other develop skills in the areas that you need to learn more about. Then, as you get more driver partners on board, each of you will be able to help develop them as well."

Joe agreed and then said, "It's interesting. I never realized how much of running a company was about teaching and developing people. But each of us is good at some things and less good at others. We're all helping each other learn and grow, and that's what's helping our business develop and helping us solve the problems that come up."

In order for NTL to grow and develop, Joe has learned that his role as a leader is to coach and develop—and be coached and developed by—his business partners.

Principle 15. Balance Extrinsic-Intrinsic Rewards

"I've never been happier in my life," Joe said to me the other day. "And it doesn't have to do with money, because there have been times when I made more money just doing straight taxi driving. And I'm working harder than I've ever worked in my whole life. I used to really look forward to just 'hanging out,' but now if I have any spare time, I use it to do something for NTL. It's not what I expected."

"Interesting," I said. "Why do you think that is?"

"Well," said Joe, "I think that it is because, before, I was making money and taking care of myself, but now I'm responsible for lots of other things: for our driver partners earning a living so that they can take care of their families; for our customers, making sure that they are having the service experience they deserve; and for Todd and Ken, my business partners, making sure that they are getting what they need. It's not easy turning our vision of 'On Time. Every Time. Every Ride. Working Together' into reality, but it's a lot more rewarding than I ever expected it to be."

Problem Solving: Continuous Organizational Learning

Principle 16. Continuously Develop Scientific Thinking

"Tell me again what it stands for?" Joe asked.

"P is for 'plan,' D is for 'do,' C is for 'check,' and A is for 'act,'" I said.

"And it's a circle, right?" said Joe. "It just keeps going, and it's never ending."

"Yes," I answered. "It's never ending. It's the way we can solve every problem and make sure that we reach our goals. When we have a challenging goal, we don't know how to reach it. That's okay. We need to learn our way toward the goal and figure it out as we go."

"And we do that by spinning the PDCA wheel over and over again!" exclaimed Joe. "I get it! Makes total sense to me," he said as he reviewed the

Post-it note I'd given him. "I'm going to keep this and put it where I can see it every day."

Joe and I have been working together for the past six months. And during that time, Joe has been learning to use PDCA to solve a variety of problems that have gotten NTL up and running and progressing toward its goals. Getting the app completed and in customers' and drivers' hands, finding new customers, figuring out how to balance local and airport rides are just a few. To make sure that Joe is learning and making progress, we have weekly coaching meetings—and Joe can always reach out in between if needed! During our coaching meetings, I ask him questions and listen as he struggles thinking the answer through. When the need arises, based on the challenge being worked on, I teach him a tool or concept. During the meeting we review progress toward goals and deal with any roadblocks. Then we set the challenge for the next week. And Joe's daily huddles with his partners are an opportunity to rapidly spin the wheel as problems arise that day.

Spinning the PDCA wheel daily, Joe is learning through doing, with me as his coach, and he is also learning through coaching others. He has explained and taught PDCA to his business partners and driver partners, and he coaches them through solving problems that they are having. We have not approached this strictly following the practice routines of the improvement kata and coaching kata, but we use a similar pattern of improvement, and it is working.

Principle 17. Align Improvement Objectives and Plans for Enterprise Learning

Every improvement that any of the guys at NTL undertakes is prioritized against the original NTL road map that they created to see where they are going. As they progress along the road map, sometimes forward and sometimes sideways or backward, they are figuring out how to overcome the obstacles that are keeping them from reaching their next target condition.

And with every ride, every day, they are solving problems for their customers. One customer asked about booking a ride from a regional airport to a suburb. When Joe saw that the suburb was over two hours from the airport, he called the customer back and asked if she had the right airport. The ride would be exceptionally long and expensive. The customer then realized she could make a different airport choice and was extremely grateful to Joe and NTL for helping her avoid a potential problem. What Joe and the guys at NTL understand is that solving problems for customers, with each and every ride, is simply the business that they are in.

What Did We Learn from NTL?

There is no doubt that Joe and the guys at NTL are actively and "passionately pursuing their purpose" based on the guiding values that support our service excellence 4P model.

Challenge

As the partners in a new start-up company, Joe, Ken, and Todd don't know how to reach their goal of "Every Ride. On Time. Every Time. Working Together." There is a lot of competition in the personal transportation industry from established regular local taxi companies as well as from other models such as Uber and Lyft. In order to differentiate themselves and consistently deliver service excellence while keeping prices low and competitive, Joe and the guys have to challenge themselves to think—and do—in new and different ways, every single day.

Systematic Improvement

The partners of NTL embrace continuous improvement. "Everything is constantly changing," says Joe. "As we get more and more new customers, each of them wants different kinds of things, and new problems keep coming up. And I just read an article that said that Lyft and Google are going to have self-driving car services in the next few years. We've got to make sure we keep up with what our customers are going to want in the future. And we've got to start thinking about that now. It's like Henry Ford said, 'If we'd asked our customers what they wanted, they would have said faster horses.' We want to be around and helping our driver partners grow for a long time. And if we don't keep improving our service and our service offerings, we're never going to be able to keep up."

And continuous improvement starts with each leader. Previously, Joe struggled to finish things—now he isn't having that problem anymore. Now he wears a suit and is reading books and is totally engaged. He has a vision of himself as an entrepreneur and is looking forward to starting and owning more businesses!

Workplace (Gemba) Learning

Although Joe, Ken, and Todd all have experience in the taxi industry, NTL is new. And although they can rely on some of the experience they have from the past, in order to create NTL, they need to learn, one ride at a time, what their customers want and how to solve the unique problems NTL faces on its journey to fulfilling its purpose. NTL is not Uber, it's not Lyft, and it's not any of the taxi companies that Joe, Ken, and Todd have worked for in the past. It's NTL, and the only way it will be able to become the unique company that NTL's customers and driver partners want is to learn what works and what doesn't, through experimentation, in the gemba, on the job.

Teamwork and Accountability

Taxi culture is not one that is often associated with teamwork or accountability. Many people become taxi drivers because they like and want the independence, and they don't want to have to answer to anybody else. Before starting NTL, Joe shied away from what he called "tough conversations." Now, however, he's having them regularly with software companies, driver partners, and vendors. Customer needs are first, so he has to be accountable and make sure that others are accountable as well. The "working together" part of the NTL challenge statement is the glue that holds the rest together. If the solution to an "every ride, on time, every time," problem doesn't involve "working together," the NTL guys don't do it.

Respect and Develop People

This is right in the company vision of working together for 100 percent customer satisfaction. Every time the partners solve a customer problem, or solve an internal team problem, or learn to deal with outside partners, they are referring to this vision. Collectively this learning brings them a step toward the ideal of respecting and developing everyone in and affected by the enterprise.

WHY LIMITED LEADERS PRODUCE LIMITED RESULTS

It would be a wonderful world for consultants if all of our clients were as open-minded and eager to learn as Joe and his partners. Unfortunately, that is just not so. Leaders generally get to where they are because they have drive and passion, which often means they have egos and can be a bit stubborn. They know what made them successful and they want to keep on doing that. As we have learned, habits can be replaced with better habits, but it takes a lot of work.

NL Services: Training Classes with PowerPoint Don't Change Leadership Behavior

It was Monday evening. It had been a long but satisfying day at Service 4U. Sam McQuinn was in the car heading out to meet Mike Gallagher, who had taken the position of EVP of Corporate Lean Strategy for NL Services after Sam had moved over to Service 4U. Mike had texted that he would be a few minutes late; a last-minute phone call from corporate was putting him a little behind schedule.

"Funny how things work out," Sam thought to himself as he swung his car into a parking space. "A year-and-a-half ago that's exactly where I would have been." As he walked into the restaurant (coincidentally, the same one where he and Sarah Stevens had met before he worked at Service 4U), he realized how long ago and far away those frantic Mondays at NL Services seemed to be. Sam was looking forward to seeing Mike. They had kept in contact for a little while after Sam had left but then lost touch. Sam had been a little surprised when Mike gave him a call out of the blue and asked if they could meet for dinner, but he had to admit to himself that he was quite interested in hearing how NL Services was doing.

"Sorry I'm late," Mike apologized as he reached out to shake Sam's hand.

"No problem, Mike," said Sam. Laughing wryly Sam said, "I know it's been a while, but I guess I haven't quite wiped from my memory all those crazy Mondays at NL Services."

"Yeah," said Mike, shaking his head and sitting down heavily in his chair, "I guess not much has really changed since you left. Still fighting with corporate about those numbers every Monday and spending more time on the phone begging and pleading with the regional managers than I would like. It's exhausting! And since we haven't been doing any lean work over the past six months, things have gone backward real fast."

"Sorry to hear that," Sam said. "I didn't realize that NL Services has stopped doing lean. Last I had heard, the work with that consulting company, Lean Mechanics, was moving right along. They're a big, well-established company. I'm surprised to hear that you aren't working with them anymore."

"Yeah," said Mike. "I'm kind of surprised too. Everything seemed to start out so well with them. We were really impressed with their sales pitch, including all the other examples of companies like ours that they had worked with who claimed great successes with their Standard Implementation Program. The whole thing seemed so easy on paper. Their senior lean experts would come in, they'd run two-day training classes at our corporate officers for the execs and senior managers on lean tools, and then the senior managers would each get one of Lean Mechanics's lean experts to help them implement the program in their area. Lean Mechanics supplied us with everything they said we would need, and they had great-looking PowerPoint decks on all the tools: 5S, value-stream mapping, standard work, and problem solving. We licensed all the training materials so that once our people were trained, they could take the material back with them for reference when their lean expert wasn't around to help."

Sam could see that Mike was getting more and more uncomfortable as he told the story. "Well," said Sam, "seems like they were very organized and had everything well laid out. Lean Mechanics really seemed to have a plan. What happened?"

Shaking his head, Mike said, "It's like the old saying goes, I guess—even 'the best laid plans' . . . As I said, the plan really did look great on paper. The problem is that after all the senior managers finished their training classes and went back to their areas, they just didn't stick to the plan, and they just led the implementation however they felt comfortable. Once they got back to their areas, they said that the material in the PowerPoint decks didn't apply to what their business unit did and that they didn't have any time to work on their leader standard work."

As Mike stopped for a minute to drink some of the wine that he had ordered, Sam thought to himself, "Sounds so different from the work we did with Leslie. Doesn't seem like Lean Mechanics even cared about any of the problems each of the areas might be having. This just sounds like a cookie-cutter, one-size-fits-all kind of thing. How could anyone expect that it could fit every area of NL Services—or any company for that matter? They are quite different, and the problems they have are different as well."

Just as Sam was about to ask Mike to tell him more, Mike started up again. "And to make matters worse, the senior managers didn't want to pay any attention to the lean experts that Lean Mechanics assigned to coach them after the training program was finished. The senior managers complained that the lean experts didn't know anything about NL Services' business and that the huddle boards, dashboards, and metrics that they designed for the teams to use didn't make any business sense at all. No matter what the lean experts said or did, the senior managers just did whatever they wanted and didn't seem to change at all. And since they didn't buy in to the whole lean implementation, no one else did either."

Mike sighed, leaned back in his chair, and took another drink of his wine. Then he went on, "Finally, after arguing with the senior managers for months, getting very poor results on our annual Employee Engagement and Experience Survey, and coming to the conclusion that we weren't getting any real business results for our shareholders either, we decided to let Lean Mechanics go. After all the time and money we put into it, it certainly was an expensive lesson for all of us at NL Services."

Sam thought for a moment and then asked, "And what do you think that the lessons were?" Mike finished his glass of wine, frowned, and concluded, "When we started the whole lean thing, we had such high hopes. After the work that you and Leslie did, all the managers and leaders in the other regions really seemed excited to give it a try. I thought it would be easy to get them to all do what they were supposed to do and put Lean Mechanics's plan in place, but I guess it wasn't as easy to get them to change after all. The biggest lesson was that deploying a plan is not like spreading peanut butter on bread. One size certainly doesn't fit all in our case. The approach has to be tailored in order to grow competency in lean."

Why Changing Leadership Behavior and Thinking Is Difficult

Karyn has been a lean consultant for firms like NL Services, Inc., more times than she would care to remember. Her main contributions as a professional have been working to shift executives in service organizations from managing by command and control to leading the development of people. Over the years, she has found some common threads that seem to underlie the difficulties of changing leadership behavior. Let's pause, look through the eyes of successful senior leaders who grew up in careers in command and control cultures, and consider what it is that would make them seem so insulated and hard to change.

1. Lack of Understanding of the Work Area That They Are Leading

Many of the executives and managers haven't actually had any work experience in the area that they are leading; for example, one executive Karyn worked closely with (we'll call him Bob) was promoted to a very senior leadership position, overseeing the operations of a number of regions. Bob had previously been in leadership roles in a variety of different support functions for the company, but the promotion was to lead a functional group that worked directly with the company's most important customers. Bob had only a theoretical understanding of the department and the customers' needs from his experiences in other departments. Although this might seem daunting, to Bob it wasn't! There was never an expectation, by him or his superiors, that his leadership role depended on a deep understanding of how the work was done. His job was to make sure that his unit got the *results* it was supposed to . . . end of story. As long as he got results, nobody higher up asked or cared how those results were achieved, nor did anyone ask or care whether or not he had an understanding of how the work was done to achieve those results.

Karyn started as a worker in a call center and, and as a result of her experiences, always believed that as a consultant it was critical to understand her customers and the work their unit did. It seemed rather obvious. Yet it was anything but obvious to the leaders of the companies. In one company she worked with, ignorance of the work was almost considered a virtue: "Leadership is leadership." If people had the potential to become a leader and aspired to it, they would be rotated broadly to get exposure to the company and would be expected to take any opportunity in any area of the company, regardless of their experience or understanding of the work of that area—and they would then be held accountable for results. It was common to hear executives say, "I don't know how the work gets done, but it doesn't matter, as long as we're getting the results our shareholders need each quarter."

Although this attitude might be acceptable in a command-and-control environment, in a lean organization developing people's capability through the work they do is the primary responsibility of a leader. Executives with no experience doing the work find it extremely difficult to develop their people's skills through doing, as they themselves do not know how to "do." As our sensei, Dr. Deming, reminds us: "Management should lead, not supervise. Leaders must know the work that they supervise. They must be empowered and directed to communicate and to act on conditions that need correction."

Karyn has been asked to support many executives like Bob. One might wonder how she could possibly move the needle to convince them to invest in understanding the work, let alone the customer. How can she get them to the gemba—

to where the service representatives are creating the services that customers want and need? It is important to empathize. They are worried that the people they are supposed to be leading will see their lack of deep knowledge as a weakness. They may be embarrassed that it could become obvious that a frontline worker might know more than they do. After all, if they are the leader—and especially an executive—shouldn't they be the one who knows everything? Karyn has seen many top-down, command-and-control leaders who are afraid that they will lose "control" if the people they lead can see their lack of knowledge about how value is created for customers. As we will see later, "convincing" is not a matter of telling them things, but rather creating a safe place where they can experiment and learn for themselves.

2. Command-and-Control Thinking Is Reinforced by the Executive's Isolation from the Masses

Over the years, Karyn has noticed that many executives and senior leaders are physically located far from the people that do the work to satisfy customers and create results in their area. Their offices are in distant home office locations, or if they are actually located in the same building as the people they are leading, their office is still far removed from the gemba. Take Bob, for example. Although he sat in the same building as the people he led, his office was in a separate, walled-off, high-security area of the complex, labeled "Executives Only." This may appear to protect him from the danger posed by the riffraff workers. In reality it is to provide an aura of power and control. Think about kings and their castles and the moats that surround them.

In Bob's case, like many of the executives in services, he had always had a person reporting to him, such as an "operations manager," whose job was to understand the work and manage the people who did it. Bob did not actually lead an entire organization. He led a small number of subordinates who acted as his eyes, ears, and hands. Bob's main job was to hobnob with other executives in "important" meetings. This isolation provided Bob with comfort and affirmation—he was one of the chosen ones who were too busy to be involved with routine operations. Bob struggled when lean was brought into the company, and there now seemed to be an expectation that he learn the daily work that he had mostly bypassed in his own rise to the top. This was actually scary—leaving the safety of his walled-off "Executives Only" area to go and see at the gemba!

3. Being in the Same Old Environment Promotes and Reinforces the Same Old Habits

The lean initiatives that Karyn has supported have almost always started at the bottom or "service floor" level. Someone hears about how lean has worked in manufacturing or a similar service environment and decides to give it a try. It is robust enough that even the basic use of tools can produce initial results that get the attention of higher levels, who then decide to make lean a corporate program to be spread across the company. In these cases, although workers and managers who are closer to the front line develop some experience of working in the new, lean culture, senior leaders, and especially executives, are the last to go through the cultural change. And because senior leaders don't directly provide customer service, there is often confusion about how lean applies to their roles.

This isolation is further reinforced by the way leaders are selected. In many organizations, executives and senior leaders have reached their positions by being promoted through the old boys network, or else they have been brought in from the outside by the old boys because they got results in a similar management culture. We talk about the "old boys club," and like any club, the members identify with each other and reinforce their shared values and beliefs. This reinforces the same old habits, which gets the leaders rewarded since those giving the rewards think as they do. These habits are extremely entrenched and very hard to break. One senior executive who was determined to change himself as he learned about lean expressed his own frustration:

> *How can I change when I am in the same environment that encouraged these bad habits? Habits are so hard to change. As a leader, I know that I need to focus on our customers—theoretically—and I try to practice that—but then I spend the majority of my time in an environment that is the "old culture," so I revert back to the old habits of how I thought and did things before. Then I do my best to pull myself out of that and I do something to try to get new habits started. Every day I have to work in the old culture environment, so the new habits just never seem to get going enough to get strong enough to overcome the old ones.*

4. Most Old-Style, Command-and-Control Leaders Are Not Systems Thinkers

Most of the executives that Karyn has worked with over the years are not systems thinkers. They have developed a mechanistic mindset that seeks to optimize results, not interrelated people and processes. They are paid and promoted to make their numbers, and they look for the most direct path to getting there. Since these results are almost always financial, the most direct path is efficiency in their area, which leads to cost reduction. Simple formula; systems thinkers stay away! However, as we know, that siloed view is not good for the service organization as a whole, or for customers.

CHANGING LEADERSHIP BEHAVIOR AND THINKING

Some of the questions that we are frequently asked are about how to begin the process: "Where should our lean efforts start? Should we start with the executives right at the top?" Should we start with the supervisors and service providers in the gemba working directly with our customers where value is created? Or with middle managers? Which level of leadership should we start with first?" In our experience, the best answer, as we shall see, is to take a systems view and begin all together in one relatively self-contained area, as all parts of the system need to function together. The higher the level of leader you can engage in that pilot the better. To see how that can work, let's check back in on Sam McQuinn and Mike Gallagher as they continue their dinner discussion.

Service 4U: Learning Lean Leadership by Self Development and Developing Others

"Mike," Sam said, "sounds like you and NL Services have been going through a really rough time. And you're right. It's not as easy to get leaders to change their thinking or their behavior as it seems that it should be. You'd think that with all the money we pay them and all the skills that they seem to have, change would be easier for them. But it just doesn't seem to be. We've noticed that some of our leaders are having problems changing and that some aren't. It's really interesting.

First we spent a lot of time trying to figure out if some of them are just more natural lean thinkers or if it was the environment they were in. Were the leaders that were involved from the beginning having an easier time changing? After a while, though, we realized that we couldn't really figure it out, and that instead of spending more time trying, we just needed to find a better way to get all our leaders on board. Improving for our customers is the most important thing for us at Services 4U, so we need all our executives and managers to be able to lead in a way that helps the whole organization improve."

Mike nodded and laughed, "I agree. You'd think with all that money we're paying them, our execs would be really motivated to change to the new way. But obviously they aren't! And I'm tired of trying to figure out why. If you don't mind my asking, have you made any progress with Service 4U's leaders?"

"Actually we have," said Sam. "And I don't mind sharing how. It's not a secret. After Sarah Stevens and I determined that the areas that were really surging ahead in satisfying our customers and improving business performance were the same areas that had leaders who were acting in the new lean way, we realized that we had to try something new. So we reached out to Leslie Harris, who recommended we work with a colleague of hers, Dennis Garrett. Dennis is really into something called Toyota Kata, and since we've started working with him, our leaders have made remarkable progress developing themselves and others. And the progress is showing in their business results too. Funniest thing is that many of them have even started calling themselves what Dennis refers to himself as—a kata geek!"

Mike was impressed by the enthusiasm and excitement that he heard in Sam's voice. "Wow," he said, "there really must be something special in what Dennis is doing with your execs if he's getting that kind of response from them. As I said, we couldn't get ours to give the Lean Mechanics's lean experts the time of day. What's Dennis doing that's so different?"

Sam thought for a moment, and answered, "At first, we were a little skeptical about his approach, but Dennis has really gotten our executives thinking in a different way by actually having them do things differently right away. Dennis doesn't have people go to training classes, and he doesn't use long PowerPoint decks. In fact, he doesn't usually use PowerPoint at all. Just simple charts and graphs that people can fill out with pencil and paper, right in the area where the work is being done on a kata storyboard. He's simply teaching our executives how to act differently by getting them to act differently. And that seems to be changing how they are thinking. I know it sounds strange, but it's really not as complicated as it sounds."

Mike Gallagher shook his head. "I don't really understand," he said. "Changing execs' thinking by changing what they're doing? What are they doing that is so new and different?"

"I'll tell you," said Sam. "During our first meeting, Dennis explained to Sarah and me that one of the problems that a lot of lean consultants have is that they try to get the whole organization going all at once. Just like Lean Mechanics. In Dennis's experience, though, that doesn't work because leaders don't know how to lead in the new way. Dennis suggested that we start working in one of the regions that wasn't progressing as well, with one of its leaders. Dennis went to visit some of our leaders and took a look at their sites, and then we decided that we would start with Maria Diaz, the service leader for the Northeastern Region, since that region seemed to be lagging the farthest behind.

Dennis insisted that Maria go with him to visit the operation's site and explained that they would choose one small part of the operation to work on: the part that was having the most difficulty, and they'd set a challenging goal for this one part to work toward. Dennis explained that he would be teaching Maria a very basic method of improvement and wanted her to personally lead the effort.

At first Maria was hesitant. She complained that she was too busy to personally lead such an effort, especially in such a small area with such a limited payback. Dennis explained that to lead a transformation in leadership she needed to go first and develop her own capabilities. Learn to do before you learn to teach others. Dennis explained that he would be playing the role that he eventually wanted Maria and all her managers to play—coaching Maria to lead improvement toward a challenging goal. Dennis and Maria went to the site at least once every two weeks and, step by step, Maria led the team onsite toward the goal she needed them to achieve. The improvement kata itself is pretty straightforward: set a direction, understand the current condition, set your next short-term target condition and then go crazy experimenting! But following it without skipping a step takes a lot of discipline.

At first, it was hard to get Maria to go, but once they got into a routine and Maria realized that Dennis was going to be right beside her helping her learn how to lead in this new way, things really took off. In fact, she says that she can't remember having so much fun at work in decades. Now she and Dennis are working on a plan for teaching other managers at that site how to coach their teams to improve."

Sam stopped there. He could see from the perplexed look on Mike's face that Mike was confused about something. "Sam," said Mike, "that all seems well and good, and it's great that Maria's behavior really seems to be changing. But doesn't it seem like it's going to take a long time to get all parts of the company going? And that's going to slow down the results. How are you going to get the CEO and shareholders to buy into that?"

Sam nodded. "I know what you mean, Mike," he said. "We struggled with that too. We wanted to go faster, but Dennis convinced us that faster isn't always better. He told us that if we didn't spend the time to build up our leaders' capability to lead improvement, then learn to coach others to do the same, we would resort to quick fixes that are not sustainable. We like to think we can change people's minds by just telling them what to do, but Dennis showed us that the way to change leaders' minds so that they do things differently is by teaching them how to do those things differently, through repeated practice. It is common sense that you can't teach something that you yourself don't understand. Yet we expect our leaders who have no skill in lean thinking to teach others how to be lean leaders.

Now Maria and the site manager of the Northeast service area are working with a couple of other 'slices,' what Dennis calls a process and its associated chain of people, in the Northeast. As those people learn, they'll be able to branch out to other areas in the Northeast. And although it's going a little more slowly, the business results are really improving, and the leaders are raving about how engaging it is to learn this way. Before this, we had trouble getting a lot of them to go to the gemba to see how the work is done, and now we're having trouble getting them to stay away! I wouldn't have believed it myself if I hadn't seen leaders acting in new ways and seen the business results, with my own eyes!"

Mike leaned forward in his chair, gazing intently at Sam. "And let me guess," he said. "I bet that they're actually going to solve the problems each area is having specifically, not just setting up a cookie-cutter set of tools that the areas don't want to use."

"Absolutely right," Sam answered. "Each of our business areas has its own set of challenges and obstacles to overcome. And now that their leaders are going to see how the work is done to get results, they are learning how to help coach and guide people to solve those problems. Things are improving for our people who do the work, our business, and, most importantly, our customers. And best of all, leading this way is becoming just what our leaders do now!"

"Sam," said Mike, excitedly, "it seems like Service 4U is doing things the 'right' way for its customers and leaders. I've been so discouraged that 'lean' didn't work out at NL Services. I was worried it couldn't work anywhere. But what you're doing is totally different—and I believe it's got great potential for positive change for your customers and your people. You don't suppose there'd be a place for me at Service 4U, do you?"

Coaching Tips for Executives (and Others!)

Over the years, Karyn has been able to go beyond finding some common threads that seem to underlie the difficulties of changing leadership behavior. Karyn has found ways of working with and coaching executives and other leaders that have been successful. It's not easy, but with time, patience, and persistence, habits of even senior executives, can—and do—change! Here are some of the tips and tricks that Karyn has learned.

1. Start with a Plan, Then Adapt to Your Learner

In Karyn's experience, there is a fatal flaw in the coaching philosophy of many of the companies she has worked with: letting the executives being coached choose what they want to work on and how they want to be coached. Lean coaches will go to the leaders and ask them to fill out a self-evaluation form and decide which lean tool they would like to focus on learning to use. The problem with this is that without any lean experience, and often without a real commitment to learning, there is no way for the leaders to be able to picture what it is they need to do differently or how to develop the different skills needed as lean leaders.

Think about a coach for a football team. Does the coach ask each player to decide what skill he would like to work on practicing? Or does the coach watch the individual players carefully, as they practice and as they play with the team, to determine where they need to improve? Some players might need to improve the percentage of time they catch passes. Others might need to improve their leverage in blocking the opposing players. Once the coach has determined what each player needs to work on, he tells the player and creates a plan so that the player can practice the needed skills, not the other way around!

If you are the lean coach for an executive (or other leader), you need to think of your role as if you were the coach of a sports team. First you have to spend time with the executive to understand where she is in her thinking and practice. You have to spend the time to clearly grasp the current situation: does she ever go to the gemba to see? If she does, is she really looking and seeing, or is she "checking the box" that she's gone? Once you have determined what her "current condition" is, you need to decide the direction: where does she need to be in the next six months to a year. What's the challenge statement for that particular executive? Then the statement has to be broken down into successive target conditions, and a plan needs to be put in place for what the executive needs to do to reach each successive target condition. This sounds like the improvement kata, but applied to developing a coach. This can and should be done collaboratively with the leader, but the coach must coach!

2. Do Something Differently with the Execs You Are Coaching

And a big part of that plan has to be how to get the executive you are coaching to do things differently. As explained earlier, most executives have deeply entrenched habits from being rewarded for doing things the same top-down, command-and-control way for many years. In order for them to start to develop new, lean leadership habits, it is imperative that you, as their lean coach, get them to *do things differently*—as soon as you possibly can. It's not easy, but the sooner you find a way to get the executive you are coaching to do something differently, the sooner you will see his thinking start to change.

For example, one of the hardest things is simply getting executives to go to see *how* value is created for their customers. Over the years, Karyn has found that the best way to get executives to the gemba is by simply refusing to have coaching sessions in their office—or even in the executive area. Karyn schedules all coaching sessions in the gemba because she knows that if the coaching session takes place in the person's office, where he is comfortable and familiar and old habits are in full force, no new learning is likely to take place. And if an executive refuses to come to the gemba and insists on meeting in his office, Karyn will lean against the door and invite him to go with her to the gemba. Once they are there together, Karyn will question the executive to guide him to grasp the current condition so that he can learn what she has planned for him to learn.

There is an old saying, "Learning hasn't occurred until behavior has changed." If you want your executives to learn—to change their thinking—then you have to get them to change what they are doing first.

3. It's Okay if Your Execs Show Signs of Being Uncomfortable While They Are Learning

Just like any other person, executives feel uncomfortable learning new ways of doing things. Think about it. If someone asks you to do something in a way you aren't used to, let's say speak to someone in a foreign language you are just learning, you're going to feel uncomfortable. You might argue with the person who asked you to practice your new language skills, or you might try to find a way out of speaking to the person. Feeling uncomfortable or scared usually causes us to behave in "fight-or-flight" ways. Because our brain wants us to stay safe, it makes us feel uncomfortable in situations where we might not know what to do. So if we are happy and know what to do, we are comfortable. The problem is, if we're comfortable, we're not learning. All learning takes place outside our comfort zone, past what Mike Rother calls the "threshold of knowledge," in the uncomfortable "learning zone." And since we need the executives to learn, although it might seem counterintuitive, *the best thing we can do for them is make them feel uncomfortable.*

In many of the organizations that Karyn works with, people do not want to make executives uncomfortable in any way. Karyn often hears complaints from lean coaches that a session didn't go well because the executive was negative or grumpy. Karyn has even had executives shout at her when she has asked them to do—or even think about—something that is outside their comfort zone. And although it seems counterintuitive, when Karyn hears frustration or grumpiness in executives' voices or sees that the execs are trying to leave the situation (yes, Karyn has actually chased down executives who are attempting to flee because they are feeling uncomfortable during a coaching session!), she is encouraged. She knows that they have left the comfort zone and are in the learning zone—where they are ready to learn—and exactly where she wants them to be! In Karyn's experience, learning = uncomfortable.

4. Stay with Your Execs While They Are Learning so That You Support Them in the "Uncomfortable Zone"

Now, once you see, by their behavior, that your executives are in the learning zone, the *most* important thing is to stay with them while they are uncomfortable. Again, think about the coach of a sports team. Once the coach has determined what the players need to improve and creates the schedule for them to practice those new skills, does the coach leave the players to struggle through practicing on their own? No, the coach certainly does not. She stays with the players, running right beside them if necessary, encouraging them and supporting them as they learn—every step of the way. This is exactly what needs to happen when coaching an executive. Executives are, first and foremost, people; and like all people, when they do not have confidence—which can be gained only from mastery through doing—they need support.

In Karyn's experience, many lean coaches do not understand this. And since they do not recognize the executives' discomfort as a sign that they are in the learning zone and need support, the lean coaches often do exactly the opposite of what is needed: they leave their executives alone when they are most vulnerable! Again, although it seems counterintuitive, what Karyn has found works best is to stay with the executives once they are in the learning zone. Instead of reducing contact, find ways to increase contact time so that the execs feel supported and cared for while they are learning new ways to behave and think. Spending extra time with the executives, so that they can ask questions and try things out under the watchful eye of their coach—who already has experience and confidence—builds a relationship of trust and caring. And in Karyn's experience, once that relationship is built, the executives will be more willing to try new things in the future because they know they will be safe, under the watchful eye of their coach, while they do!

5. "Whisper in the Leader's Ear . . . "

All of this fits together in a technique that Karyn has used successfully over many years in many service organizations with leaders at all levels. Karyn calls this technique "whispering in someone's ear." Here's how it works. As prework, Karyn spends time in the gemba to learn about the problems that the business area is having and about the leader. Once she has determined a challenging problem to work on that she believes will help the leader learn and progress on his journey and help the business, she will present it to the leader at an opportune moment in casual conversation: "Sandy, I've really enjoyed spending time with you in your Western regional office. Looks to me like they've been having consistent problems with on-time service delivery to customers. And the problem seems to be quite long term. What do you think?" Karyn will then wait for the leader's reaction—in general, some sort of fight-or-flight response:

- **Fight.** Leader (in a raised voice): "What are you talking about? That's not a problem; my managers say that customers aren't complaining and that 75 percent on-time delivery is fine. The industry benchmark is 80 percent, so I'd say that's pretty good!"
- **Flight.** Leader, walking away: "I've got an important conference call in five minutes; we can talk about that later . . ."

Once Karyn sees either of these "uncomfortable" reactions, she knows that she has succeeded in pushing the leader out of the comfort zone and into the learning zone—exactly what she wanted to do and where she wants the leader to be.

After the initial "uncomfortable" conversation, Karyn will then drop the subject and give the leader time to digest the challenge. However, each subsequent time she is with the leader, she will bring up the topic again and insert it into the dialogue. And each time, she will carefully observe the leader's reaction. Eventually—usually within three or four conversations—the leader will be used to the question and conversation . . . and then all of a sudden, the leader will bring up the topic to Karyn as if it is 100 percent her own idea: "Karyn, I've noticed that something seems to be off in the Western Region's on-time delivery. I don't think that this is good for our customers, but I'm not sure how to approach it in the new 'lean' way. What do you think? Could you help me think it through and decide what to do?" Voilà! And as you can imagine, Karyn never mentions that she has been whispering in the leader's ear about this for the past few weeks . . .

The most important thing when using this technique is not to give up after the first time the leader dismisses the idea, and you know he is going to dismiss it. Remember, an uncomfortable reaction means that the exec is ready to learn—and most sales are actually made not on the third or fourth contact but on the twelfth! Keep whispering, and eventually the leaders you are coaching will take your idea and make it their own—and that is *exactly* what you want to happen.

SPREADING BEST PRACTICES OR GROWING LIVING SYSTEMS?

We have criticized the approach of deploying lean tools and argued real lean, the Toyota Way, is about continuous improvement. But if we try something in one area of the company and it works, why not simply mandate it as a best practice? It is simply common sense. Who wants to reinvent the wheel? When someone, someplace in our organization, does something innovative and it has a great result, we should share that practice throughout the company. Anyone in a similar job should implement the best practice. How we do that is always a question: Create a best-practice database so people can look up what they are supposed to do? Use a corporate office to identify best practices, teach them, and then audit to be sure they are followed? So many best practices and so many organizations to spread them to, how can we do it efficiently and so the practices are followed exactly?

McDonald's is one service organization that is obsessive about spreading best practices in the same way everywhere, from having the same potatoes grown in the same way to having equipment and work set up the same all over the world. The McDonald's mission is to "be our customers' favorite place and way to eat & drink . . . and to deliver the quality, service, cleanliness and value our customers have come to expect from the Golden Arches—a symbol that's trusted around the world."

It is a little hard for us to imagine a fast-food restaurant becoming a "favorite place and way to eat & drink." "Trusted" makes more sense. To us the McDonald's brand stands for reliable sameness. Take an international trip to Singapore, Beijing, Frankfurt, Mexico City, or almost any other major city, and if you want a familiar and reliable meal that will guarantee no surprises—McDonald's is there. McDonald's uses a franchise model, which means that the owners in all these locales are different. To guarantee sameness, McDonald's has a strong corporate office and Hamburger University to develop, test, and disseminate best practices.

It works because both the product and the service are based on predictability and reliability for the customer. And deep down it feeds our desire for certainty—you know how to order and what you are getting wherever you are.

Another organization that is based on spreading best practices is Orange Theory Fitness, which makes this promise: "With energetic music, a talented group of fitness coaches and a high-energy studio, you have the recipe for a workout that produces BIG and LASTING results." As a fairly new customer of Orange Theory, I love it. You get into the orange zone where you are at 85 percent of your maximum heart rate and for each minute score splat points—fat cells go splat when you are in the zone. There is a huge screen showing your heart rate, calories burned, and minutes in the splat zone during a one-hour workout. Every Orange Theory has the same bank of treadmills, rowing machines, and floor exercise equipment. There are screens in the floor exercise area that show which exercises you are working on with animated demonstrations and instructions. The fitness coaches have headsets and call out what each group should be doing amid loud, booming music. A room full of about 25 to 30 people work hard and generate bucketloads of money.

All the routines, software, and design of the studios are done at corporate, and you can become a gym member and work out in most major cities in the United States and increasingly around the world. The company expects to double its number of locations each year. It is a great business model and on a fast track of growth. Local managers administer, treat customers nicely, and hire fitness coaches who go through training, but nobody is expected to change the standards. The quality of the many varieties of exercises, equipment, and computer support and the sameness of what the customer experiences serve as the selling point.

McDonald's is a mass goods distributor, and Orange Theory provides a standard experience. Their environments are relatively simple and stable. When the environment, product, and service change very slowly, we can kind of view the organization as a machine with interchangeable parts. This was the situation that Frederick Taylor faced when he developed scientific management. Let the geniuses in the central office do the thinking and the managers do the execution. And it still works under some circumstances. Nonetheless, to the extent that customers will choose to go elsewhere if they do not get good personal service at these establishments—from the front desk, from cashiers, from trainers, from cooks, from fitness coaches—then the management and the local culture that was built will matter. I have experienced a good deal of variation in how I am treated both at McDonald's and at Orange Theory.

When there is variety in the work and a part of our business model is exceptional customer service, we need local managers and team members to innovate and continually improve the work. One great blog warns: "Best practices for professionals is not spread like butter, it's grown like a garden. How can we enable this?"[1]

The blog asks us to think about how to "rehabilitate" the idea of best practices. It then goes on to explain the reasons that we should not simply spread best practices:

1. ***Best is temporary.*** *There may be a current "best way" to do something, but like "world champion" or "world record," it's not going to stay the best for long.*
2. ***Best is therefore a starting point.*** *We are always looking to improve on best, but without knowing the temporary best, we don't know what we have to beat. Like a world record, best is there to be beaten—it's a minimum accepted threshold.*
3. ***Best is contextual.*** *There may be no universal "best way" to do something. The best way to deal with emergency decompression of a Jumbo Jet may not be the best way to deal with emergency decompression of a Harrier jump jet.*
4. ***In a new context, you cannot blindly apply "best" from another context.*** *However you can learn from other "bests"—no context is ever totally alien, and there may be approaches that can inform and advise, that you can build upon.*
5. ***Best practice does not have to be written down.*** *It can live there in the community cloud of tacit knowledge. Usain Bolt's "best way to run a sprint" is probably not even conscious—it's in his muscle memory. However if it can be written down—in a wiki, or a document, or a manual—so much the better, so long as it is immediately updated every time it's superseded and improved.*

Toyota uses the Japanese word "yoketen" for spreading best practices. It provides an image like preparing the soil to transplant a precious tree. The conditions under which it thrives in Japan may not be easy to reproduce in other countries, so we need to experiment to find out how to adapt the tree and the conditions to fit our environment. Toyota certainly has standards such as product engineering specifications, safety standards, equipment standards, and the global improvement process of Toyota Business Practices. And these standards are crucial: when you buy a Camry, you do not want to wonder which "best" version you happen to get—the cars are all expected to be the same. However, there are many more things that can be adapted locally, such as how the equipment is arranged and how work is allocated and how visual management is handled.

The problem limiting local continuous improvement is the world view of command and control from headquarters to transform operations using lean tools and concepts. Even in top-down organizations, the executives will talk about culture all the time. They say they want to change behavior and mindset,

Figure 10.7 Traditional leaders want an improvement mindset, but they focus on results and tools

but what is in their high resolution focus are tools that deliver measurable results (see Figure 10.7).

Since continuous improvement is one of the pillars of the Toyota Way, Toyota encourages kaizen. Don't copy—try to be better through kaizen. Toyota's world view is 180 degrees different from that of most other companies. Toyota works to develop behavior and mindset so that people can use the appropriate tools to strive toward a series of challenges (see Figure 10.8).

Toyota sees the value of living systems of people continually developing themselves and improving the work, within certain clearly defined boundaries. This is central to respect—create an environment to encourage and even force people to think and grow. "Grow like a garden" is a metaphor that is repeated in many ways within Toyota. So, for example, when Toyota opens a new operation, there is a great deal brought in that meets the best technical standards

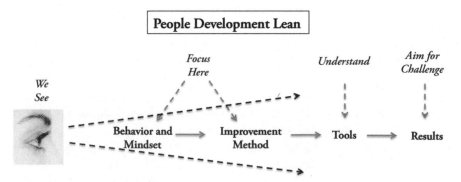

Figure 10.8 Lean leaders want results and customer-centered processes, but they focus on behavior and mindset

known today, but the company very deliberately grows the culture from the ground up. The culture is based on tenets of the Toyota Way and yet is still unique to that location.

Lean as learned from Toyota is intended to be a living system philosophy. If lean is spread wide and thinly, you get the tools without the continuous improvement philosophy. All the learning will be confined to the lean expert group, and we have seen the limitations of that. McDonald's already practices the basics of industrial engineering with well-organized kitchens and restaurants and does not seem to need or want continuous improvement at the work sites. An organization that does believe that people continually improving throughout the enterprise will help achieve the mission needs to take a living system perspective.

> *As a single footstep will not make a pathway on the earth, so a single thought will not make a pathway in the mind. To make a physical path, we walk again and again. To make a deep mental path, we must think over and over the kind of thoughts we wish to dominate our lives.*
>
> —Henry David Thoreau

DEVELOPING LEADERS TO BUILD A DELIBERATE CULTURE

The subtitle of this book is *Lean Transformation in Service Organizations*, and to be honest we have reservations about this title. Are we transforming something that is not lean into something that is lean? We immediately get the impression of a one-time metamorphosis—like a hunk of clay that is transformed into a beautiful statue. This presents the image of lean as a set of tools and methods to eliminate waste, which is all that nasty stuff that increases customer waiting time and cost.

We have emphasized, starting with the Prologue, that lean is a way of thinking centered on the twin pillars of respect for people and continuous improvement. We also emphasized the central role of leadership, but not only in the executive suites. If we want a culture that respects people, starting with customers, and continuously improves, we need leaders at all levels leading this through their actions, which include developing people to truly care about customers and build the skills of improvement. The Toyota Way house gives us a great starting point for what we want to develop in these "lean leaders":

1. Spirit of challenge
2. Scientific approach to improvement

3. Workplace learning
4. Teamwork
5. Respect enough to develop every individual

Of course, getting from here, your starting point, to there, your vision for your customers and organization, is easier said than done. Where should we start? How can we change people to think lean who have decades of successful experience doing the opposite of what we are trying to teach?

It is a journey, and perhaps we should heed the advice of Mark Twain, who said, "the secret to getting ahead is getting started." When we are headed into uncharted territory the only thing we can really plan is the next step.

The world is complex and dynamic, and the future is unknowable. Having some type of vision is critical. Setting a shorter-term direction is powerful. We do not recommend rigidly spreading best practices, nor do we recommend a random walk to eliminate waste, so at least we have set the extreme boundaries.

Let's take stock of what we have recommended in this book and illustrated through many case examples:

1. Lean is a way of thinking focused on the permanent struggle to satisfy each customer.
2. Lean is the evolution of living systems to collaboratively improve toward a common purpose.
3. There are useful lean tools and concepts that can help on the journey to improve how we serve customers a little better every day.
4. It is not enough to "lean out processes," but rather we should use any tools and methods that can help us move in the direction of a clearly defined challenge.
5. Lean is a learning process, learning our way step by step through a series of rapid PDCA loops.
6. Every PDCA loop is a scientific discovery process—Plan for what we will do with a clear expectation, Do, Check what actually happened, and then Act to reflect and learn.
7. Learning to think scientifically requires deep personal change for almost all of us, and it can only be achieved through regular (daily) practice.
8. Practice routines, or kata, can help guide us in developing the mindset and skills we need for continuous improvement.
9. Building a culture of continuous improvement starts with developing the mindset in leaders at all levels who grow into a chain of coaches-learners-coaches-learners throughout the enterprise and even beyond.

With this perspective on lean transformation, one centered on developing people, it seems apparent that lean cannot be rapidly deployed. It requires a patiently built culture, person by person. This is kind of a bummer. We might be asked for a clear plan for lean deployment with a timeline, milestones, measures, and a cost-benefit analysis. The living system view of lean makes that nearly impossible. To some extent doing lean right requires a leap of faith. If we invest in developing our people in the right way with a powerful vision, and if we select and develop leaders to have purpose, passion, and competence, we will better satisfy customers, grow more efficient, and overcome obstacles to each challenge we face. The benefits will not be easy to quantify, but achieving big challenges that have overwhelmed us in the past is a game changer with benefits for years to come far greater than any predetermined cost savings. So start with quantifying what will happen when we meet the challenge.

We honestly cannot advise people that there is any simple way to change the thinking of a mechanistic company that wants to mechanistically deploy lean tools—a mutiny against the board of directors perhaps? It is probably more effective to begin by changing ourselves. Bill George wrote an excellent book on finding our own personal true north to authentic leadership . . . for ourselves.[2] It begins with a passion and a direction and focuses on self-development. Bill George was CEO of Medtronics, a medical device company, when the company went through a major lean transformation. He sees leadership as a journey and warns:

> *There is no such thing as instant leadership. Your journey to authentic leadership will take you through many peaks and valleys as you encounter the world's trials, rewards, and seductions. . . . Maintaining your authenticity along the way may be the greatest challenge you ever face.*

We saw the personal transformation of Joe, who cofounded NTL. His starting-out state was far from that of an exemplary lean leader, and there was every reason to question whether he was capable of becoming an effective leader. Karyn chose to respect and coach him. Through the journey of creating and building NTL, Joe was becoming a different person, and the culture of NTL began to evolve in the direction of service excellence.

In the fictional stories about NL Services and Service 4U, we saw companies with very different cultures moving forward, sideways, and backward. Even at NL Services there were people like Mike who saw the limitations of the company's mechanistic approach and at some point might have the opportunity to build on the company's learning and mishaps and set NL Services on a productive path. Sam blossomed at Service 4U, and who knows, maybe at some point he will be asked back to NL Services and make a huge difference.

The point is that the uncertainty that makes it so difficult to change the course of a large bureaucratic structure also gives us second chances, and third, and fourth . . . Organizations seem to go through phases from lean deployment of tools to management taking responsibility, and some make it all the way to a continuous improvement culture. How this happens varies all over the place, and the journey is seldom steadily upward.

We have argued that true lean must be driven through the line organization—the organization responsible for the work. The goal is a linked chain of managers who are each a learner and a coach. This cannot be shallowly deployed as a quick training program. The ideal model starts at the top and cascades down level by level as Toyota did with the Toyota Way, Toyota Business Practices, and On-the-Job Development.

The factor limiting how broadly and quickly lean can be deployed is the time it takes to develop capable coaches. Every individual must go through the lean leadership learning cycle of awareness, learning to improve through a well-thought-out kata, then learning to coach through a kata. Leaders must be coached through this before they are capable of coaching others. How many capable coaches do you have, internally and externally? Multiply that by the number of people that each coach can handle and the time it takes to coach someone, and you get your capacity. Your understanding of what a coach can handle and how long it takes will grow with experience—PDCA away!

For any individual manager aspiring to be a lean leader, it may be necessary, or at least extremely helpful, to have a personal true north and consider every day another learning opportunity. What do you plan for the day? What do you expect? What happened? What did you learn that can make tomorrow better?

One interesting dilemma is our cognitive bias toward believing if we learn something conceptually, it will translate to actual behavior. As much as we admire Jeff Bezos's enthusiasm about learning from failure, there is clear evidence that more often than not, we do not learn from our mistakes—that is, if we take learning as changing our behavior patterns so we are not susceptible to the same mistake. The *Atlantic* writer Olga Khazan summarizes neuroscience research that shows that as we make mistakes and repeat them, we develop "mistake pathways," a rut our brain gets into that sets us up for future failure.[3] Our brain learns that mistake even if our prefrontal cortex tells it not to. Our hidden brain is a poor listener. Her recommendation: "Instead of dwelling on past mistakes, think about what you want to achieve in the future. If you want to avoid repeating history, it is best *not* to try to learn from it." In other words, it is better to work to achieve a future goal and practice to create new pathways that override the old mistake-ridden ones than to try to talk yourself into changing.

We all have plenty to work on as individuals to become better people and better leaders. Trying to take on responsibility for transforming an entire organization is more often than not beyond our control. But as we learn and grow, we will have a growing influence on others and on the organizations we are part of.

So start with yourself, start small, learn and grow, and get coaching help, and as you do, your sphere of influence will grow. If you have responsibility to transform an organization unit or organization, then also start small in developing learners who become coaches, and your influence will multiply exponentially. Start deep before you go broad. If you cannot follow any of this advice because of the organization's business model and culture, then do the best you can to learn yourself and lie in wait for your opportunities—they will come, or you will create them, just like Joe did.

We wish you well on your journey as we progress on ours. We appreciate your interest in our thoughts and hope that they are helpful to you. Taking the excellent advice of Mark Twain, please get started . . .

Notes

Prologue

1. Jeffrey K. Liker, *The Toyota Way*, New York: McGraw-Hill, 2004.
2. John Toussaint and Roger Gerard, *On the Mend: Revolutionizing Healthcare to Save Lives and Transform the Industry*, Cambridge, MA: Lean Enterprise Institute, 2010.
3. Samuel Smiles, *Self-Help*, London: John Murray Publishing, 1982.
4. James P. Womack, Daniel T. Jones, and Daniel Roos, *The Machine That Changed the World*, New York: Rawson Associates, 1990.
5. James P. Womack and Daniel T. Jones, *Lean Thinking*, 2nd ed., New York: Productivity Press, 2003.
6. K. Anders Ericsson, Michael J. Prietula, and Edward T. Cokely, "The Making of an Expert" (pdf), *Harvard Business Review*, July–August 2007.
7. Mike Rother, *Toyota Kata: Managing People for Improvement, Adaptiveness, and Superior Results*, New York: McGraw-Hill, 2009.

Chapter 1

1. Jeffrey Liker and David Meier, *Toyota Talent: Developing People the Toyota Way*, NY: McGraw Hill, 2007.
2. *Monthly Labor Review*, U.S. Department of Labor, www.bls.gov/opub/mlr/2013/article/industry-employment-and-output-projections-to-2022.htm.
3. http://newsroom.accenture.com/news/us-switching-economy-puts-up-to-1-3-trillion-of-revenue-up-for-grabs-for-companies-offering-superior-customer-experiences-accenture-research-finds.htm.
4. www.forbes.com/sites/micahsolomon/2013/11/17/secret_shopping_four_seasons/.
5. www.theatlantic.com/business/archive/2012/03/the-anti-walmart-the-secret-sauce-of-wegmans-is-people/254994/.
6. We wish to thank David Hanna of the HPO Global Alliance for this section about Dr. Waal's work.

Chapter 2

1. Jeffrey Liker and James Franz, *The Toyota Way to Continuous Improvement*, New York: McGraw-Hill, 2011.
2. Jeffrey Liker and Timothy Ogden, *Toyota Under Fire: Lessons for Turning Crisis into Opportunity*, New York: McGraw-Hill, 2011.
3. Womack, James P., and Daniel T. Jones, *Lean Thinking: Banish Waste and Create Wealth in Your Organization*, 2nd ed., New York: Free Press, 2003.

Chapter 3

1. Dictionary.com.
2. Isadore Sharp, *Four Seasons: The Story of a Business Philosophy*, New York: Penguin Group, 2009.
3. www.heraldrecorder.org/business/like-many-united-fliers-in-recent-years-oscar-munoz-was-recently-on-a-lousy-flight-to-chicago-business-news-oscar-munoz-20154944/.
4. Richard Nisbett, *The Geography of Thought: How Asians and Westerners Think Differently . . . and Why*, New York: Free Press, 2004.
5. Ibid., p. 91.
6. Geert Hofstede, *Culture's Consequences: Comparing Values, Behaviors, Institutions, and Organizations Across Nations*, 2nd ed., Thousand Oaks, CA: Sage Publications, 2001.
7. E. Trist and W. Bamforth, "Some Social and Psychological Consequences of the Long Wall Method of Coal-Getting," *Human Relations*, Vol. 4, 1951, pp. 3–38.
8. David P. Hanna, *Designing Organizations for High Performance* (Prentice Hall Organizational Development Series), 1988.
9. Thomas Johnson, "Lean Dilemna: Choose System Principles or Management Accounting Controls—Not Both," Chapter 1 in Joe Stenzel (editor), *Lean Accounting: Best Practices for Sustainable Integration*, Hoboken, NJ: John Wiley, 2007.
10. www.toyota-global.com/company/vision_philosophy/toyota_global_vision_2020.html.
11. www.youtube.com/watch?v=LJhG3HZ7b4o&ab_channel=FastCompany.
12. www.strategicmanagementinsight.com/mission-statements/general-electric-mission-statement.html.
13. David Hanna, *The Organizational Survival Code*, Mapleton, UT: Hanaoka Pub., 2013.
14. Michael E. Porter, "What Is Strategy," *Harvard Business Review*, November–December 1996, pp. 61–78.
15. www.cbsnews.com/news/something-special-about-southwest-airlines/.

Chapter 5

1. Mike Rother and John Shook, *Learning to See*, Cambridge, MA: Lean Enterprise Institute, 2003.
2. Karen Martin and Mike Osterling, *Value Stream Mapping: How to Visualize Work and Align Leadership for Organizational Transformation*, New York: McGraw-Hill, 2013.
3. www.slideshare.net/mike734/value-stream-mapping-the-improvement-kata.
4. www.zingtrain.com/free_samples/fivestupidways.pdf.
5. www.linkedin.com/pulse/productivity-hacks-want-more-productive -never-touch-things-bradberry?trk=eml-b2_content_ecosystem_digest -recommended_articles-49-null&midToken=AQG5zF5e_mGidw& fromEmail=fromEmail&ut=2wpCxG1Lq1BSY1.
6. www.umich.edu/~bcalab/multitasking.html.
7. Eduardo Lander, "Implementing Toyota-Style Systems in High Variability Environments," doctoral dissertation, University of Michigan, Ann Arbor, 2007.

Chapter 6

1. Paul S. Adler, "Time and Motion Regained," *Harvard Business Review*, January–February 1993, pp. 97–108.
2. Robert E. Cole, "Reflections on Learning in U.S. and Japanese Industry," Chapter 16 in J. K. Liker, M. Fruin, and P. Adler (editors), *Remade in America: Transplanting and Transforming Japanese Production Systems*, New York: Oxford University Press, 1999.
3. For a detailed discussion of this and the standard method for training, see Jeffrey K. Liker and David Meier, *Toyota Talent: Developing People the Toyota Way*, New York: McGraw-Hill, 2007.
4. John Medina, *Brain Rules*, reprint ed., Edmonds, WA: Pear Press, 2009.
5. See a more detailed case study in Richard Zarbo, "Bringing Ford's Ideas Alive at Henry Ford Health System Labs Through PDCA Leadership," Chapter 9 in Jeffrey Liker and James Franz, *The Toyota Way to Continuous Improvement*, New York: McGraw-Hill, 2011.
6. Philip Crosby, *Quality Is Free: The Art of Making Quality Certain*, New York: McGraw-Hill, 1979.
7. Ibid.

Chapter 7

1. Henri Fayol, *Industrial and General Administration*, translated by J. A. Coubrough, London: Sir Isaac Pitman & Sons, 1930.

2. Kiyoshi Suzaki, *Results from the Heart: How Mini-Company Management Captures Everyone's Talents and Helps Them Find Meaning and Purpose at Work*, New York: Free Press, 2002.

3. As we write this, it is too early to know how Toyota's 2016 recent shift to product-focused organizations will turn out. On the surface it appears that Toyota is moving toward something similar to Chrysler's platform organization in R&D, but we suspect there will still be functional organizations within individual units to develop deep technical expertise.

4. Jeffrey Liker and Gary Convis, *The Toyota Way to Lean Leadership*, New York: McGraw-Hill, 2011.

5. Jonathan Escobar, David Hanna, and Jeffrey Liker, "Invest in People, Boost Growth," http://planet-lean.com/the-virtuous-circle-of-sustainable-growth-how-lean-management-practices-at-proctergamble-and-toyota-make-for-an-environment-based-on-customer-focus-and-people-development.

6. http://elisa.com.

7. Michael C. Mankins, Alan Bird, and James Root, "Making Star Teams Out of Star Players," *Harvard Business Review*, January–February 2014.

8. Jeffrey Liker and Thomas Choi, "Building Deep Supplier Relationships," *Harvard Business Review*, December 2004, pp. 104–113.

9. Jeffrey Liker and Timothy Ogden, *Toyota Under Fire: Lessons for Turning Crisis into Opportunity*, New York: McGraw-Hill, 2011.

Chapter 8

1. http://innotiimi-icg.com/fileadmin/user_upload/pdf-Dateien/Publications/3-2014-Gesamtausgabe-sml.pdf (March 2014, p. 10).

2. http://innotiimi-icg.com/fileadmin/user_upload/pdf-Dateien/Publications/3-2014-Gesamtausgabe-sml.pdf.

3. John Medina, *Brain Rules*, 2nd ed., Edmonds, WA: Pear Press, 2014.

4. www-personal.umich.edu/~mrother/Neuroscience.html.

5. www.youtube.com/watch?v=2ynryUjGFt8&ab_channel=Telecom SlayerDOTcom.

6. www.soulsmithing.com.

7. www.sportpsychologytoday.com/sports-psychology-articles/outcome-goals-vs-process-goals/.

8. As described in *The Toyota Way*, Chapter 16.

9. Charles Duhigg, *The Power of Habit*, New York: Random House, 2012.

10. Scott Adams, *How to Fail at Almost Everything and Still Win Big: Kind of the Story of My Life*, New York: Portfolio, 2014.

11. Karl Duncker, "On Problem Solving," *Psychological Monographs* (American Psychological Association) 58, 1945.

12. Michael Ballé and Freddy Ballé, *Lead with Respect*, Cambridge, MA: Lean Enterprise Institute, 2014.

Chapter 9

1. Daniel Kahneman, *Thinking, Fast and Slow*, New York: Farrar, Straus and Giroux, 2011.
2. www.youtube.com/watch?v=Qd8PetCER8E&ab_channel=MikeRother.
3. Robin Wall Kimmerer, *Gathering Moss: A Natural and Cultural History of Mosses*, Corvallis: Oregon State University Press, 2003.
4. Leath Tonino, "Two Ways of Knowing: Robin Wall Kimmerer on Scientific and Native American Views of the Natural World," *The Sun*, Issue 484, April 2016.
5. James Womack and Daniel Jones, *Lean Thinking: Banish Waste and Create Wealth in Your Organization*, 2nd ed., New York: Free Press, 2003.
6. www.youtube.com/watch?v=3f5wxRO7EYM&ab_channel=MikeRother.
7. Durward Sobek and Art Smalley, *Understanding A3 Thinking: A Critical Component of Toyota's PDCA Management System*, New York: Productivity Press, 2008.
8. John Shook, *Managing to Learn: Using the A3 Management Process to Solve Problems, Gain Agreement, Mentor, and Lead*, Cambridge, MA: The Lean Enterprise Institute, 2008.
9. I am grateful to the students and Dunning staff who agreed to participate in the book. The project sponsor was General Manager and Partner John Taylor, and the learner was General Sales Manager Lowell Dunning. The students were Xinhang Li, Mengyuan Sun, Ruqing Ye, and Zhenhuan Yu.
10. http://philosophy.baddalailama.com/2012/11/meta-skills.html.
11. www.slideshare.net/mike734/the-coaching-kata-chain-of-coaching

Chapter 10

1. *Let's Re-habilitate "Best Practice,"* www.nickmilton.com/2015/08/lets-re-habilitate-best-practice.html.
2. Bill George, *Discover Your True North*, 2nd ed., Hoboken, NJ: Wiley, 2015.
3. www.theatlantic.com/video/index/482514/the-cognitive-science-behind-repeating-mistakes/.

For Further Reading

Throughout this book we have referenced various books that you may want to study more in depth. Here are some suggestions for further reading and investigation:

About Kata

Rother, Mike, *Toyota Kata: Managing People for Improvement, Adaptiveness, and Superior Results*, New York: McGraw-Hill, 2009.

Toyota Kata Slideshare site, www.slideshare.net/mike734.

The Toyota Kata website, "How to Develop Scientific Thinking for Everyone by Practicing Kata," www-personal.umich.edu/~mrother/Homepage.html.

Other Toyota Way Series Books

Liker, Jeffrey K., *The Toyota Way*, New York: McGraw-Hill, 2004.

Liker, Jeffrey K., and Gary Convis, *The Toyota Way to Lean Leadership*, New York: McGraw-Hill, 2011.

Liker, Jeffrey K., and James Franz, *The Toyota Way to Continuous Improvement*, New York: McGraw-Hill, 2011.

Liker, Jeffrey K., and Michael Hoseus, *Toyota Culture*, New York: McGraw-Hill, 2008.

Liker, Jeffrey K., and David Meier, *The Toyota Way Fieldbook*, New York: McGraw-Hill, 2006.

Liker, Jeffrey K., and David Meier, *Toyota Talent*, New York: McGraw-Hill, 2008.

Liker, Jeffrey K., and Timothy Ogden, *Toyota Under Fire: Lessons for Turning Crisis into Opportunity*, New York: McGraw-Hill, 2011.

Liker, Jeffrey K., and George Trachilis, *Developing Lean Leaders at All Levels: A Practical Guide*, Winnipeg, MB: Lean Leadership Institute Publications, 2014.

Franz, James, and Jeffrey Liker, *Trenches: A Lean Transformation Novel,* CreateSpace Independent Publishing Platform, 2016.

From the Lean Enterprise Institute

These books are published by the Lean Enterprise Institute in Cambridge, Massachusetts.

Ballé, Freddy, and Michael Ballé, *The Gold Mine: A Novel of Lean Turnaround,* 2005.

Ballé, Michael, and Freddy Ballé, *Lead with Respect,* 2014.

Dennis, Pascal, *Getting the Right Things Done: A Leader's Guide for Planning and Execution,* 2006.

Rother, Mike, and John Shook, *Learning to See: Value-Steam Mapping to Create Value and Eliminate Muda,* 2003.

Shook, John, *Managing to Learn: Using the A3 Management Process to Solve Problems, Gain Agreement, Mentor, and Lead,* 2008.

Toussaint, John, and Roger Gerard, *On the Mend: Revolutionizing Healthcare to Save Lives and Transform the Industry,* 2010.

Ward, Allen, and Durward Sobek, *Lean Product and Process Development,* 2014.

Lean Books from Other Sources

Hoeft, Steven, *The Power of Ideas to Transform Healthcare: Engaging Staff by Building Daily Lean Management Systems,* Productivity Press, 2015.

Ohno, Taiichi, *Toyota Production System: Beyond Large-Production,* New York: Productivity Inc., 1988.

Solomon, Jerrold M., *Who's Counting? A Lean Accounting Business Novel,* Indiana: WCM Associates, 2003.

Spear, Steven, J., *The High-Velocity Edge: How Market Leaders Leverage Operational Excellence to Beat the Competition,* New York: McGraw Hill, 2010.

Suzaki, Kiyoshi, *Results from the Heart: How Mini-Company Management Captures Everyone's Talents and Helps Them Find Meaning and Purpose at Work,* New York: Free Press, 2002.

Taiichi Ohno's Workplace Management, Special 100th Birthday Edition, New York: McGraw-Hill Professional, 2012.

Womack, James P., and Daniel T. Jones, *Lean Thinking: Banish Waste and Create Wealth in Your Organization*, 2nd ed., Free Press, 2003.

Womack, James P., Daniel T. Jones, and Daniel Roos, *The Machine That Changed the World*, New York: Rawson Associates, 1990.

Nonlean Books for Lean Leaders

Adams, Scott, *How to Fail at Almost Everything and Still Win Big: Kind of the Story of My Life*, New York: Portfolio, 2014.

Coyle, Daniel, *The Talent Code*, New York: Bantam Books, 2009.

Deming, W. Edwards, *Out of the Crisis*, Cambridge, MA: MIT Center for Advanced Educational Services, 1986.

Duhigg, Charles, *The Power of Habit*, New York: Random House, 2012.

Greenleaf, Robert, *The Power of Servant Leadership*, San Francisco: Berrett-Koehler, 1998.

Hanna, David, *The Organizational Survival Code*, Mapleton, UT: Hanaoka Pub., 2013.

Johnson, H. Thomas, *Profit Beyond Measure*, New York: Free Press, 2008.

Kahneman, Daniel, *Thinking, Fast and Slow*, New York: Farrar, Straus and Giroux, 2011.

Medina, John, *Brain Rules*, reprint ed., Edmonds, WA: Pear Press, 2009.

Nisbett, Richard, *The Geography of Thought: How Asians and Westerners Think Differently . . . and Why*, New York: Free Press, 2004.

Pink, Daniel, *Drive: The Surprising Truth About What Motivates Us*, New York: Riverhead Books, 2009.

Senge, Peter, *The Fifth Discipline: The Art and Practice of the Learning Organization*, New York: Crown Business, 2006.

Sheridan, Richard, *Joy, Inc.: How We Built a Workplace People Love*, New York: Portfolio Hardcover, 2013.

Wheatley, Margaret J., *Finding Our Way: Leadership for an Uncertain Time*, San Francisco: Berrett-Koehler, 2005.

Index

References to figures are in italics.

3M, 74
4P model, 45–50
  and National Taxi Limo, 360–361
5 why method, 74
5P model, 39–43

A3 coaching
  vs. improvement kata, 339–342
  managing to learn through, 317–321
  managing to teach, 325–327
  in a payroll company, 321–325
accountability, 302–307
Accuri Cytometers, 220–221
Ackoff, Russell, 313
Adams, Scott, 298
Adler, Paul, 187–188, 205
Alice's Adventures in Wonderland
    (Carroll), 275
Amazon.com, 15
andon system, 212–214, 298
automation
  at Henry Ford Health Systems
    Diagnostic Labs, 224–226
  at Toyota machining and forging,
    226–228
automotive recalls, 13–14

Baird, Jen, 256
Bamforth, Ken, 65
basic TPS line, 227
batch processing, *158*
benchmarking best-practice sites, 80–81
best practices, 80–81, 391–395
Bezos, Jeff, 317
Blue Cross Blue Shield of Michigan,
    342–344

Bradberry, Travis, 155
Brain Rules (Medina), 207

cause-and-effect relationships, 299
cells, 157–162
Cho, Fujio, 32, 35, 39
Chrysler, 237–238
CK. *See* coaching kata
clearing the clouds, 90
coaches
  developing leaders as coaches of
    continually developing teams,
    281–296
  developing Toyota leaders as, 30–39
coaching kata, 274, 282–285
  A3 coaching in a payroll company,
    321–325
  managing to learn through true A3
    coaching, 317–321
  managing to teach, 325–327
  role of coaching in improvement,
    344–345
  sales example from Dunning Toyota,
    327–332
coaching tips, 387–391
coercive bureaucracy
  vs. enabling bureaucracy, 187–188
  at the U.S. Post Office, 188–191
Cole, Robert, 192
complacency, 29
Continental Airlines, 57–59
continuous improvement, 29
Convis, Gary, 303, 352–353
Costantino, Bill, 285–288, 290
Crosby, David, 220
CSRs. *See* customer service representatives

ABOUT THE AUTHORS

Dr. Jeffrey K. Liker is Professor of Industrial and Operations Engineering at the University of Michigan and President of Liker Lean Advisors. He is author of the international bestseller *The Toyota Way: 14 Management Principles from the World's Greatest Manufacturer*, and has coauthored eight other books about Toyota including *The Toyota Way to Lean Leadership*. His articles and books have won 12 Shingo Prizes for Research Excellence. In 2012 he was inducted into the Association of Manufacturing Excellence Hall of Fame, and in 2016 he was inducted into the Shingo Academy. Liker lives in Ann Arbor, Michigan, with his wife and children.

    Visit JeffLiker.com

Karyn Ross is a lean consultant and executive coach focused on creating sustainable business culture change in service organizations. She has worked with companies such as Paychex, PrimePay, Zurich Insurance, and National Taxi Limo to help them develop a culture of problem solving and improved business practices. A regular contributor to the Lean Leadership Ways Industry Week Blog, she has also written for *The Lean Management Journal* and *Industrial Engineer* magazine. Ross resides in Naperville, Illinois.

    Visit KarynRossConsulting.com